The War of the Aeronauts

The War of the Aeronauts

Aeronauts

A History of Ballooning
During the Civil War

Charles M. Evans

STACKPOLE
BOOKS

Published by
STACKPOLE BOOKS
5067 Ritter Road
Mechanicsburg, PA 17055
www.stackpolebooks.com

Printed in the United States of America

10 9 8 7 6 5 4 3 2 1

FIRST EDITION

Library of Congress Cataloging-in-Publication Data

Evans, Charles M., 1963–
    War of the aeronauts : the history of ballooning in the Civil War / Charles M. Evans
      p. cm.
    Includes bibliographical references and index.
    ISBN 0-8117-1395-4
    1. United States—History—Civil War, 1861–1865—Aerial operations. 2. Ballooning—United States—History—19th century. 3. United States—History—Civil War, 1861–1865—Technology. 4. Aeronautics, Military—United States—History—19th century. I. Title.

    E492.7 .E93 2002
    973.7'3—dc21
                                     2002020515

In memory of my grandparents,
George Gaudensio Stagi and
Marianna Agostini Stagi

TABLE OF CONTENTS

Acknowledgments ix

CHAPTER ONE   A Yankee Aeronaut Behind
           Confederate Lines. 1

CHAPTER TWO   A Brief History of Early Ballooning 20

CHAPTER THREE   The Great Transatlantic Quest 33

CHAPTER FOUR   Creating an Army in the Air 60

CHAPTER FIVE   Early Operations. 88

CHAPTER SIX   The Union Army Balloon Corps 104

CHAPTER SEVEN   The Battle of Egos 124

CHAPTER EIGHT   Disillusioned Aeronauts 147

CHAPTER NINE   The Balloons Corps and the
           Peninsular Campaign. 165

CHAPTER TEN   The First Confederate Air Force 189

CHAPTER ELEVEN   The Origins of the "Silk Dress Balloon". 203

CHAPTER TWELVE   The Air War over Virginia. 209

CHAPTER THIRTEEN   The Winter of Disappointment 245

CHAPTER FOURTEEN   Thaddeus Lowe's Last Battle. 263

CHAPTER FIFTEEN   The Last Days of the Corps 288

CHAPTER SIXTEEN   After the Balloon Corps 296

Notes 311

Bibliography 338

Index 344

ACKNOWLEDGMENTS

The War of the Aeronauts began as a simple research paper several years ago while I was finishing courses at San Francisco State University. At the time I was the curator of an aircraft museum on the San Francisco peninsula and thought it would be an excellent idea to combine my interest in aviation and ballooning with a graduate course I was taking in the history of the Civil War. Little did I realize the path I was starting on back then would lead me through several years of research into the role that aeronauts played during one of the most devastating episodes in American history.

The story of ballooning during the Civil War took on a life of its own when it came to researching the subject. I became familiar with individuals such as Thaddeus Lowe, John La Mountain, Edward Porter Alexander, James and Ezra Allen, John Randolph Bryan, and many others, and I realized that they had important stories to tell.

However, the stories of aeronauts who served in both the Union and Confederate armies were not to be found in a single book or collection, but scattered through various letters, unpublished memoirs, and documents stored away in archives, or contained within the pages of nineteenth and early twentieth century magazines and newspapers on the back shelves of libraries or on microform. The process of writing this book became as much an exercise in detective work to uncover material that had previously been unknown about the balloons of the Civil War.

As with any work that involved as much research as The War of the Aeronauts, an equal amount of credit goes to the many people and institutions who assisted in its production. My thanks go out to National Air & Space Museum, the National Archives, and the Library of Congress in Washington, D.C., and also to the Virginia Historical Society and Minnesota Historical Society for providing the bulk of the primary research for this book.

I am also indebted to Peter Wilkinson of the South Carolina Historical Society and Kimberly Ball of the Georgia Historical Society for providing invaluable information about the role that Langdon Cheves and Charles Cevor played in the creation of the Confederate "Silk Dress Balloon."

A great deal of appreciation is also extended to Sharon Campbell and Marc Tiar of the Washoe County Library System in Reno, Nevada. Both Sharon and Marc patiently and expertly located all of my numerous—and sometimes difficult to locate—interlibrary loan requests.

I am also extremely grateful to William C. Davis, editor at Stackpole Books in Mechanicsburg, Pennsylavania. As a writer, it is sometimes difficult to find someone who shares your vision when it comes to a story. From the very beginning, William C. Davis provided me with the necessary encouragement to complete this book.

I would also like to thank Leigh Ann Berry, also of Stackpole Books, for graciously enduring my numerous e-mails during the final preparation of the manuscript and for all of her editorial and organizational input. I also need to acknowledge the efforts of Ryan Masteller, also at Stackpole, who shepherded the book toward its final production; and Anthony Hall, whose attention to detail and precision invaluably aided in honing this text in numerous ways.

It is also necessary to mention James P. Kushlan, editor of *Civil War Times Illustrated,* who published my article on Civil War ballooning back in 1996. I am also grateful to one of *CWTI*'s readers, James E. Steckel of Jefferson, Lousiana, who provided a print of Count Ferdinand von Zeppelin originally published in *The Photographic History of the Civil War.*

There are also a number of friends who also contributed significantly to the completion of *The War of the Aeronauts.* The late Samuel W. Taylor of Redwood City, California, who provided me with invaluable insights on writing; and his daughter Sara Weston Taylor, who reviewed an early draft of my manuscript.

I also have to thank one of my mentors, William T. Larkins—author, photographer, and co-founder of the American Aviation Historical Society. William T. Larkins' meticulously researched books on aviation became my example in attempting to do as thorough a job as possible in my own research for *The War of the Aeronauts.*

A debt of thanks also goes to Louise Carli Stagi of Los Altos, California, who generously allowed me to stay at her home during a portion of my research.

And last, but not least, I would also like to thank my mother, Clara Stagi Evans, who volunteered for the arduous task of proofreading *The War of the Aeronauts.* Without her help this book would not have been possible.

CHAPTER ONE

A Yankee Aeronaut Behind Confederate Lines

Rapid thoughts filled Thaddeus Lowe's mind as he and his balloon sailed briskly above the earth. Both the aeronaut and the balloon were swiftly traveling at an altitude of more than 7,000 feet. The temperature was well below the freezing point, but the young aeronaut remained jubilant nevertheless.

"These are the victorious moments which repay all explorers for the hours of disappointment, ridicule, and attacks of all kinds which they are forced to submit to," Lowe later wrote. "Every great invention, every innovation in the history of the world has been laughed at. Columbus was denounced as a faker; Morse was called a crank; Franklin a fool; Charles Darwin ridiculed for years. It seems to be the fate of every man or woman who discovers a new fact, to be made the subject of attacks of the most violent nature, without rhyme or reason."[1]

Lowe was convinced that a natural phenomenon involving air currents flowing from west to east existed in the upper atmosphere. These air currents flowed like great rivers in the sky and harnessing the force they could generate would allow Lowe the opportunity to realize his greatest dream—to journey across the Atlantic Ocean by air.

From years of experience gathered from piloting his balloons Lowe believed that these easterly air currents existed without regard to the direction the wind was blowing at ground level. To prove his point, in early 1861 Lowe announced that he would undertake a journey to test his theory and

vowed to leave Cincinnati, Ohio, at precisely the moment the wind at
ground level was blowing its fiercest in a westerly direction. If his theory was
correct, Lowe calculated that he would land in the Chesapeake Bay region
of Virginia.

Skeptics hounded the young aeronaut for weeks, ridiculing his theory
of an easterly air current as abject foolery. Predictions were made that Lowe
and his balloon would sail to the west and land in the Rocky Mountains, or
at worst, that Lowe would float off and never be heard from again. For his
part, Lowe bore the critics with a stoic resolve that would only be rewarded
if he would be able to prove his theory correct.

Cincinnati was chosen as the departure point for Lowe's great experiment at the suggestion of Joseph Henry. Henry was a renowned physicist
and first secretary of the Smithsonian Institution in Washington, D.C. Lowe
had met with Henry, who supported the theory of a prevailing easterly air
current in the atmosphere and sympathized with the plight of Lowe at the
hands of his detractors.

"I have had some interesting experiences with the public," Henry said
to Lowe in early 1861. "And it is very difficult to get them to take new
devices seriously. Almost every new scientific theory is laughed at."

Henry told Lowe, who at the time was concentrating his Atlantic voyage efforts in the vicinity of Philadelphia with the mammoth balloon *Great
Western*, to conduct his experiment "in some locality in the west" with a
smaller test balloon.

"If you make a success," Henry told him. "Everyone will know about
it."

Henry further counseled not to start his attempt until conditions were
"apparently against" the journey.

"If you sail with an easterly current near the earth and reach the coast,
even tho [sic] you pursue your upper easterly air current, people will say that
you sailed in the lower one. So, make your ascent in the lower westerly
wind."[2]

Lowe took this advice to heart and arrived in Cincinnati in late March
1861 with a balloon aptly named *Enterprise*.

For several days, Thaddeus Lowe was the city's *cause célèbre*, creating
excitement wherever he ventured. With the enthusiastic patronage of Murat
Halstead, the editor of the Cincinnati *Daily Commercial*, Lowe was the subject of banquets and feasts, and gave lectures for several evenings. As Lowe
later recalled, the numerous banquets he attended while in Cincinnati served

to remind him of a saying from Admiral David Farragut, who remarked that the "dinners he was forced to eat on his trip around the world, after the Civil War, had more terrors for him than all his battles."[3]

However, Lowe was forced to endure the banquets and parties forced upon him, as the early spring weather in Cincinnati alternated between rain and snow for several days. The elusive westerly air current had yet to materialize.

On the evening of Saturday, April 19, Lowe was again the guest of honor at yet another sumptuous banquet. The harsh snow and rains had subsided, but up to that point the westerly wind had not presented itself.

Lowe was resplendent in a frock coat and tails and as the evening affair was set to adjourn, the word was passed to him—a strong wind was blowing to the west.

With no time to change into more suitable attire, Lowe grabbed his tall silk hat and dashed to the site of the Commercial Hospital, where the *Enterprise* was kept waiting partially inflated with coal gas provided through a supply valve feeding into the city's infirmary.[4]

Murat Halstead, along with others from the banquet, had also accompanied Lowe to his balloon, where the fifty-five-foot-high ship was now reaching its maximum inflation with over 30,000 cubic feet of lifting gas swelling its silk envelope. Time was of the essence, as far as Lowe was concerned, so not the slightest thought had been given to foraging provisions in preparation for the flight. All manner of foodstuffs and delicacies were scavenged from the banquet and brought to Lowe's balloon.

It was now after midnight, and though Lowe was anxious to embark on his journey a delay was warranted. Halstead, ever the consummate newspaper man, convinced Lowe to delay his departure as he hurriedly composed details of the imminent liftoff and sent the copy back to the *Daily Commercial*'s pressroom for immediate publication.

At 3:30 A.M. Halstead, along with two pressmen, laboring under the burden of a sheaf of newspapers, returned to the Commercial Hospital. The men dumped their bundles of the *Daily Commercial*, still damp with wet ink, into the basket of the *Enterprise*, as Halstead pressed a carafe filled with coffee into Lowe's hands. The time for departure had come. Lowe leapt into the basket and gave word to the two men holding the balloon's mooring lines to cast off.

With an air of solemnity, Lowe doffed his silk hat to the crowd below. As Halstead wrote in the edition of the *Daily Commercial* that Lowe carried aboard the *Enterprise*, "The sky is almost cloudless, moon shining, . . . A prosperous voyage to you, Professor Lowe."[5]

One thing that Lowe had remembered to stow away in the *Enterprise* was a satchel packed with measuring instruments of his own invention and specification. Included in the kit were several thermometers; a mercury barometer, which served as an altimeter measuring his ascent; a marine compass; a pair of field glasses; a driftmeter that calculated his speed; as well as a few other essential items that Lowe deemed necessary for the journey.[6]

Rising steadily, the balloon initially drifted with the westerly wind, but as the ascent reached 7,000 feet Lowe's faith in the great eastern air current was vindicated. The *Enterprise* now began traveling rapidly toward the east, the jet stream pushing Lowe's ship at a rate of more than 80 miles per hour.

As the balloon gained altitude the ambient temperature aboard the *Enterprise* dropped to zero degrees Fahrenheit, producing a curious reaction within the balloon's silk envelope. During the inflation process in Cincinnati a significant amount of water condensation had been formed as the coal gas filled the envelope. Now, as the temperature dropped below the freezing point, the condensation turned to ice, forming droplets of "fine, glassy, bead-like hail."

"In the absolute stillness I could distinctly hear [the hail] falling upon the silk and rolling down the neck of the balloon," Lowe recalled. "Being night, it was impossible for me to see it, but under similar circumstances in the day time, I have seen a miniature snowstorm going on inside the balloon when I have left a warm [current] for a cold current of air."[7]

Lowe opened the inflation valve at the bottom of the balloon's neck, releasing a "bushel" of hail into the basket. The net effect caused the balloon to ascend even higher. Lowe took a reading with the mercury barometer. Given the pitch-black conditions of the early morning darkness the instrument was difficult to read. Although he realized the mercury barometer was not a precise measure of altitude due to variable factors such as weather conditions, pressure differential, and water-vapor content from clouds, the instrument provided a relative figure of accuracy that could be counted on. To his own astonishment Lowe was able to determine that the balloon was now at an elevation of more than three miles above the earth's surface.

Soon dawn approached on the eastern terminator.

"The streak of light rapidly running around the horizon resembled bands of molten gold," Lowe later recalled. "When the sun itself appeared I was never more astonished and surprised. It was entirely different from our

A photo of Thaddeus Sobieski Constantine Lowe taken in 1859. Lowe's quest was to become the first person to cross the Atlantic Ocean by balloon and in April, 1861 he undertook a test flight in preparation for the crossing. The result of the flight significantly altered his plans forever.

NATIONAL AIR & SPACE MUSEUM

everyday luminary. There was a total absence of its usual dazzling appearance. It resembled a disk of burnished copper, as such a disk would appear when not in the bright rays of any powerful light."[8]

The sun's warming rays quickly thawed the morning chill, raising the ambient temperature significantly in a matter of minutes. This too had an effect on the *Enterprise* as the gas contained within the envelope now began to expand, causing the balloon to rise to an even greater altitude. Lowe quickly checked his mercury barometer.

"In a few moments I ascended to a height of four and one-half miles, probably 5,000 feet higher than the balloon could have gone by its own lifting power."[9]

The sensation was spellbinding. Suspended above the clouds, the balloon was moving rapidly eastward, but an eerie calm prevailed within the control basket. As Lowe described it, "I could have carried a lighted candle without protection, and I left loose sheets of papers about without fear of their being disturbed. I was floating with, as well as within, the undisturbed atmosphere. Consequently, there was not the slightest sense of motion whatever."

Still, Lowe felt it wise to take some precaution and began to vent off gas from the control valve, causing the balloon to descend about a mile very rapidly.

Time acted as if it were in suspension as the *Enterprise* sailed ever onward over the surface of the earth. Below, a rich tableau of scattered farmhouses and cultivated fields presented itself to the lone aeronaut. Hours had passed since Lowe left Cincinnati and he began to wonder about his location. With his field glasses he caught a glimpse of what he believed to be the western slopes of the Alleghenies looming on the horizon. At this point he decided to descend from the jet stream to a lower altitude.

Soon, Lowe caught sight of two men working in a field below him. Now within 200 feet of the ground, the aeronaut hailed the two men from above.

"WHAT STATE IS THIS!?" Lowe shouted to the men. The two men looked in every direction except upward.

Lowe shouted again. The men, still wondering from where the voice emanated, called back.

"VIRGINIA!"

With that Lowe shouted "thank you" in return and proceeded to pour out sand from the ballast bags he carried aboard. As the sand hit the ground, the two farmhands realized that the voice that had hailed them came from above. The shock of the curious apparition hovering in the sky sent them fleeing into the nearby woods for safety.

Back aloft and once again in the jet stream, the world was a smaller place to Lowe. The Alleghenies loomed ahead. Rising only to peaks of 4,000 feet or so, they were not a truly formidable mountain range. But from Lowe's perspective the mountains now looked even more insignificant, stretched out like a caterpillar grinding its way along the earth.

Once again a peaceful calm prevailed, created by the jet stream that surrounded the balloon, cradling it in a vacuum of silence. Far above the world was an infinite tapestry of blue sky and cumulus formations, wondrous streams of gossamer vapor. To Lowe it felt as if he were touching the veil of heaven itself.

As Lowe ventured onward a distinct and ominous rumbling was heard from somewhere down below, far into the distance.

"I heard the cannonading with which the Virginians were celebrating their secession," Lowe later recalled.[10]

By now the balloonist had crossed over the Alleghenies, when a new phenomenon presented itself. The airstream, which had been flowing rapidly to the east, began to change course as the balloon approached the

Blue Ridge Mountains. Although still maintaining an easterly draft, the air current was now drawn into a stream that began forcing Lowe and his balloon into a southeasterly direction.

Lowe had ascertained the change of direction with a quick glimpse of his compass and was initially pleased with the new attitude his ship was taking.

"I found myself near the coast and decided I had better return a little inland and find a better landing place than on the rice fields I saw coming into view."

However, Lowe little realized the area of potential danger he was about to enter as he ventured over the border of the Carolinas.

Going as far as necessary to clear the marshy fields of rice, Lowe presently came upon a plantation where several white and black workers were laboring in the fields. Releasing gas from the envelope the *Enterprise* descended near ground level.

Several of the black field workers apprehensively approached the balloon as Lowe requested assistance in mooring his craft to earth, but the white planters ordered them to stay back.

"The planters kept warning me that they would not be responsible for the consequences if I persisted in staying," Lowe recalled. The planters backed up their threat with muskets ready in hand.

Being more afraid of damage to the *Enterprise* by a stray shot than for his own person, Lowe hastily cut loose a sandbag and began to ascend once more. As he sailed off one of the planters shouted from behind, "Hello, mister! I reckon you've dropped your baggage!"[11]

Without the burden of the now lost "baggage," Lowe's balloon rose to an altitude of some two miles and once again he was swept along the current of the eastern jet stream. From the ground Lowe occasionally thought he heard shots being fired, as "people below thought I was only a short distance from them, and having never seen such an object before, kept up a firing, thinking to 'bring the quarry down.'"

Presently Lowe arrived near Pea Ridge, South Carolina, appropriately named by reason that nothing would grow there except peas and pitch pine. Once again, Lowe began his descent, hoping that the area would yield a reasonably safe place to land.

Lowe reportedly encountered a tribe of Native Americans who believed that the balloon was an incarnation of the "great hawk," and immediately fled to shelter believing they were in great danger.

Lowe continued to sail on hoping to encounter someone on the ground who would assist in safely tethering the *Enterprise* before it made landfall. Soon he approached a group of sharecropper huts on the outskirts of yet another plantation. Lowe landed in the midst of the crude shelters, where he encountered a number of "negroes and ignorant whites" who watched his movements with intense interest.

With some effort Lowe secured the *Enterprise* by means of a heavy land anchor that he managed to trap around a "heavy rail fence." Still in need of assistance to moor his ship properly, Lowe looked in vain toward the cowering villagers who remained timidly locked away in their homes.

A woman presently emerged, however, to offer assistance to the balloonist. Lowe described her as a "white woman, possibly 18 or 20 years, standing fully six feet high and well proportioned." Lowe explained to her that he needed someone to steady the control basket until he could release enough gas from the balloon to allow it to remain firmly on the ground.

Lowe found an apt assistant in the young woman as she immediately took hold of the mooring line. As the *Enterprise* was made secure the villagers were overcome with curiosity and emerged to where Lowe was tending to the craft's deflation. Overjoyed with the triumph of establishing that his theory of an eastern jet stream was indeed correct, Lowe basked in the accomplishment of having traveled more than 650 miles in the nine hours since he left Cincinnati.[12] Yet he was unaware of the dangers that were about to confront him.

At this point, it must be said that the time and place Lowe had chosen to conduct his test flight were not exactly propitious.

The United States was in turmoil and war clouds were gathering. Ever since the November presidential election that brought Abraham Lincoln to office, Southern states had begun formal acts of secession from the Union over the issue of states' rights and slavery, forming the Confederate States of America. Conditions of open rebellion existed throughout the Southern states. The week before Lowe's flight, the Confederate general P. G. T. Beauregard had laid ruin to the Union army's garrison at Fort Sumter in South Carolina. Two days prior to Lowe's departure the Confederates had seized the federal arsenal at Harpers Ferry in Virginia. And on the very day Lowe prepared for his flight, April 19, 1861, President Abraham Lincoln had ordered the blockade of Southern ports.

For Thaddeus Sobieski Constantine Lowe, civilian balloonist, self-proclaimed professor and scholar, and New England–born Yankee, the situation

Thaddeus Lowe's route from Cincinnati, Ohio, to Union(ville), South Carolina. Lowe's balloon, Enterprise, *traveled approximately 650 miles in nine hours on April 20, 1861.*

that was developing at the time and place of his landing in South Carolina was rapidly becoming very dangerous.

In the meantime, Lowe continued the process of securing the *Enterprise*. The curious now emerged from all directions, some on horseback or drawn by wagons, most by foot. Alarmingly, many in the crowd also shouldered shotguns and muskets as they drew near. Although Lowe continued to tend to his business, these developments scarcely went unnoticed.

At this point, Lowe decided to pull the release cord connected to the *Enterprise's* inflation valve, which caused the balloon envelope to rapidly vent its gas. The result forced the onlookers to immediately clench their noses, as the foul, sulfurous odor of the gas permeated the air. Lowe advised the crowd to "keep to windward" to avoid contact with the noxious fumes. Suspicions began to circulate among those present that the strange visitor, still garbed in his elaborate frock coat and silk hat from the previous evening, was possibly the living incarnation of the devil himself. The presence of vile sulfur in the air only fueled the rampant speculation.

Aware of his growing predicament, Lowe attempted to appease the crowd. Going to the control basket of the now nearly deflated *Enterprise*, Lowe withdrew some of the food from the banquet that had been hastily stowed away. The food was varied, consisting of several cakes, crackers, bread and butter rolls, cold meats, chicken, and various fruits. Lowe himself sampled the food to demonstrate that it was perfectly safe and then started to pass the bounty around.

Lowe also passed around several rubber bottles filled with water that had frozen in the upper elevations of his journey in order to demonstrate exactly how cold the upper regions of the atmosphere had been. He even took a knife and cut one of the bottles open to reveal the ice contained inside.

"This was the worst thing I could have done," Lowe said later. "For immediately one man asked how could anyone but the devil put so large a piece of ice through so small a place as the nozzle."

Compounding this was the fact that some of the food that had been exposed to the elements also froze along the journey. Some of the apples and oranges that had been under blankets were perfectly good, while others that had not were frozen as hard as rocks.

"Instead of impressing them that I was an ordinary human being, [I] gave them more cause for alarm than ever."[13]

As the *Enterprise* now lay fully deflated, some in the crowd summoned up the nerve to challenge the stranger in their midst. An elderly man now spoke up, declaring that a Yankee capable of doing all of the things Lowe presented was too dangerous an individual to allow in their community. According to Lowe, the man summed up his opinion by stating that the stranger should be "shot on the spot where he dropped from the skies."

Unfortunately for Lowe, a number of others in the crowd shared the same sentiment.

At this point the tall, young woman, who had aided Lowe in securing the *Enterprise* on landing, approached the aeronaut.

"Most of these men are cowards," she told him. "All the brave men of the neighborhood have gone off to war."[14]

Debate continued among the crowd, however. The more brazen approached the basket and attempted to decipher the purpose of Lowe's scientific equipment. Lowe made the decision to bring an end to the uninvited intrusion and reached into his satchel and pulled out a Colt revolver he had packed along with his instruments for just such a contingency.

Lowe made it abundantly clear to the crowd that the first man to make a hostile move toward him "would go into eternity," as he brandished the revolver aggressively. The demonstration proved to be effective and the crowd immediately drew back in fear that the stranger would make good upon his threat. Sensing that the crowd at least had his undivided attention for the moment, Lowe suggested that a committee be appointed to escort the balloonist and his equipment to the nearest county seat and allow the authorities there to determine his fate.

After some debate it was decided that Lowe would be taken to Unionville,[15] the nearest county seat, which was about twenty miles from Pea Ridge. As Lowe finished folding the delicate fabric of the balloon envelope into the *Enterprise's* control basket, arrangements were made to fetch a suitable team and wagon to transport the balloonist and his equipment.

As he waited for the team to arrive, Lowe was invited by the young woman who had befriended him to join her family for some refreshment. Although Lowe kept his eyes "alertly upon the belligerents" who still seemed intent upon causing him injury, Lowe graciously accepted the invitation.

Gradually as Lowe became more aware of his surroundings, the poverty that marked the area became abundantly clear to him. He learned from his hosts that the white people who inhabited this particular region of South Carolina were known as "clay-eaters" because of "their often repulsive and disgusting dietetic habits." And the outward appearance of the clay-eaters also apparently matched their name. Lowe described most of the men he saw as "ferocious brigands, with long, dirty unkempt hair, and long beards, mostly sandy red in color, reaching to their short rotund stomachs, wearing slouch hats with unclean hands and faces, and ragged and tattered clothing."[16]

Lowe also observed that the black slaves and poor whites lived in nearly identical quarters.

"A casual glance over the place would not enable you to discern which huts were occupied by the one class and which were occupied by the other," he later recalled.[17]

Inside the woman's cabin, Lowe learned that she lived with her father and brother. It was about three o'clock in the afternoon and it was decided to prepare food quickly in order for the men to set out on their journey to Unionville. Food was scarce for the inhabitants of Pea Ridge, and the meal offered to Lowe consisted mostly of corndodgers and a jug of "Louisiana molasses."[18]

Reacting to the meager bounty, Lowe recalled, "I still had a satchel full of sweet and dainty delicacies. So, desiring to return in some measure the cordial, though rough hospitality of the friendly woman . . . I distributed its contents freely. I ate their corn dodgers and then praised the former highly, to the evident delight of my hostess who made them."

Following the meal, Lowe ventured outside the cabin when he heard the wagon and team pull up outside. He was astonished to see that a team of six mules pulling a heavy wooden lumber wagon was to be his transport.

"My whole outfit only weighed a little over 200 pounds," Lowe recalled. "So, I asked them why they had brought so many mules. The driver replied that when he started he thought he had to load in that great, monstrous balloon, so he put on two extra animals."[19]

The ride to Unionville was conducted with an ersatz guard made up of a number of clay-eaters, each carrying a shotgun as they rode their "shaggy" horses beside the wagon bearing Lowe and his balloon. Having gone without sleep for nearly twenty-four hours, the exhausted aeronaut catnapped during the monotonous ride, which finally ended in Unionville at ten o'clock that evening.

As the wagon entered town its first stop was the Unionville jailhouse. Rousing the jailer from his sleep, the men escorting Lowe talked at great lengths about the mysterious stranger. The men talked in low tones so that Lowe was not able to clearly understand exactly what was being said.

Finally, the jailer spoke up. Essentially he told the men that if what they said of the stranger was correct, then it would be no use to place him in jail. It was already filled with a large number of Yankee abolitionists. He suggested that it would be better to take Lowe to the nearby inn and keep him under guard until morning.

When the party arrived at the inn a curious thing occurred. After waking up the innkeeper, a Mr. Black, Lowe was escorted into the inn's vestibule. On seeing the balloonist the hotelkeeper immediately rushed up to meet him, addressing him by his honorary title, "Professor Lowe."

It turned out that Mr. Black had met Lowe when the balloonist was in Charleston, South Carolina, the year before, performing meteorological tests with one of his balloons. Black was one of the privileged few who had been allowed to venture skyward with Lowe on a tethered excursion.

Black told the Pea Ridge men that the balloonist was a distinguished scientist and scholar. Apparently Black's word carried weight in the community around Unionville and the confused clay-eaters began to offer their sincerest apologies to Lowe for their suspicions of him. The balloonist good-naturedly accepted their apologies, adding that they rendered a "real service" by helping to transport him and his balloon to a city with rail connections. He asked Black if it would be possible to rouse his kitchen servants, as late in the evening as it was, and prepare a fine meal for his "guards."

Following the meal, Black told the clay-eaters that he would vouch for Lowe's character and assume responsibility for the balloonist. Lowe, who felt some debt toward the men for transporting him to Unionville, paid them for their services. This set off another series of apologies and regrets for their previous behavior.[20]

Afterwards Lowe retired to the best room that Black had available, where the balloonist immediately fell into a deep sleep.

At seven o'clock in the morning, a rapping on the door from Mr. Black disturbed Lowe's sleep. Lowe replied that he was still very tired and "did not care to rise before noon." The innkeeper told Lowe that an "ugly crowd of people" had gathered around the inn. Apparently news of the mysterious visitor staying at Black's Inn had spread throughout the area, and a throng of some 3,000 people had congregated wishing to capture a glimpse of him.[21]

Lowe quickly dressed and rushed downstairs where he was met by the county sheriff, the editor of the Unionville newspaper, and a Mr. Thompson, a member of the South Carolina legislature.

Many in the mob gathered outside had witnessed Lowe floating over the area the previous day, and the same suspicions of devil association and Yankee trickery that had sprung up in Pea Ridge were now also rampant outside Black's Inn. Despite Black's assurances that Lowe was "all right," the suspicions that surrounded the balloonist's intentions remained high. However, the first order of business was determined to be that the crowd must be dispersed around Black's Inn before something violent occurred. It was suggested that Lowe be presented to the city by means of a carriage ride around town.

With the sheriff driving, Lowe, accompanied by Black and Thompson, took to the streets of Unionville. For nearly three hours the balloonist waved and bowed and generally did his utmost to prove, at the very least, he did not emanate from the infernal reaches of the netherworld.

Yet when Lowe told his newly found benefactors that he had set out from Cincinnati the previous morning and had traveled nearly 700 miles in nine hours, he could sense doubt. At first Lowe suggested that he could send a telegram to Cincinnati to verify his claim. However, the telegraph service to the North was now suspended because of the war. Lowe then suggested that perhaps a more tangible proof could be produced.

Although he had some misgivings about showing the sheriff and the legislator the copies of an "abolitionist newspaper," the distribution of which he knew potentially carried the penalty of death in South Carolina, Lowe's sense of pride and accomplishment overcame this fear. When the party finished their tour of the city, Lowe went to the control basket of the *Enterprise* and brought back the copies of the Cincinnati *Daily Commercial* that had been brought to Lowe's balloon just prior to takeoff.

After reading the article written by Murat Halstead in the special edition of the *Daily Commercial*, it was declared that "nothing further was necessary" to prove the balloonist's claim of aeronautic achievement.

"From this time on I was of increasing interest to them, and they all desired me to visit them at their homes," Lowe recalled afterwards.[22]

One of the homes that Lowe visited while in Unionville was that of Legislator Thompson. There, as he toured the greenhouse with Thompson's wife, Lowe was told that the family's eldest son had formed a regiment and was on his way to Manassas Junction, Virginia. As the woman spoke and displayed the great pride she took in her greenhouse garden, she mentioned that she would be sending her son, "eggs, chickens, fresh butter, etc., until the Southern army could reach Washington."

"Poor lady," Lowe later said. "Like many other mothers she had great confidence—unfounded in this, as in many other cases—in her son's ability to go wherever he pleased."[23]

For the remainder of the day Lowe visited a number of other homes and places in Unionville, including the town's newspaper office. There he obtained a certificate attesting to the time, date, and place of his landing, signed by Unionville's most prominent citizens. The following day Lowe packed up his belongings and had the *Enterprise* transported to the rail depot, where he took leave of Unionville and went on to Columbia, South Carolina.

Lowe noted the large number of Confederate troops aboard the train that was northward bound. The trip was relatively uneventful until the train pulled into the junction at Columbia.

As Lowe made arrangements to board a train going to Washington, D.C., a gruff voice was heard from behind.

"There he goes. That's the fellow with that gun on his back and infernal machines in his satchel."

The "gun" was actually Lowe's long mercury barometer in its leather case that the balloonist had slung over his shoulder.

A man with a long beard, carrying a revolver stopped Lowe from going any farther. He had only two words to say to the balloonist as he motioned toward him with his pistol.

"To jail."

Apparently Lowe's exploits had preceded his arrival in Columbia, for yet another crowd with hostile intentions had gathered. As the bearded man led Lowe away, shouts of "Tar and feather the damned Yankee," and "That's too good for him. Better hang him," followed.[24]

Lowe once again sensed his imminent demise if swift action wasn't taken. Instead of walking to the jail, where he would be followed by the agitated mob, he suggested to his bearded captor that it was advisable to make use of a taxi carriage, which was loitering near the depot. His captor agreed once Lowe offered to pay for the ride himself, and they were soon off to the jailhouse.

Once there, Lowe was met by a very sullen sheriff who informed him that news of his appearance in Pea Ridge and Unionville had quickly circulated throughout the area and that his arrest had been ordered by the civil and military authorities. Lowe protested that he had been thoroughly questioned in Unionville and that authorities there were completely satisfied as to the merit and purpose of his presence in South Carolina. Nonetheless, the sheriff ordered that Lowe be held in the county jail pending further investigation.

Lowe's incarceration, however, lasted all of fifteen minutes, as his case was "uppermost . . . in the minds of officials." Soon, he was brought to a room where he was met by several people, including the mayor of Columbia, W. H. Boatwright.

Lowe told Boatwright of his purpose for being in South Carolina and presented the *Daily Commercial* and the certificate signed by the people of Unionville as evidence. The mayor considered the balloonist's case and then asked if Lowe was acquainted with any of the officers or faculty of South Carolina College in Columbia.

"I was not," Lowe recalled. "But . . . I had heard Professor Joseph Henry speak of the president of the college, and that as Professor Henry was my friend and co-worker, I presumed that if they would send for the president of their college they would be able to gain more information of me and my work from him."

Shortly thereafter the president and members of the South Carolina College faculty arrived at the jailhouse. All were aware of Lowe's work and spoke in glowing terms of the balloonist's accomplishments. Even the formidable front of the taciturn sheriff crumbled as Lowe's achievements in aeronautics were recounted. As Lowe later reported, "They then took a vote as to giving me my liberty, and it was unanimous in my favor."

Mayor Boatwright then took it upon himself to draft what was essentially to serve as Lowe's "passport" for travel in the Confederate States:

Columbia, South Carolina, April 22, 1861

THIS IS TO CERTIFY, that Professor T.S.C. Lowe, now accidentally in our midst, is a gentleman of integrity and high scientific
attainments, and I bespeak for him the courtesies of all with whom
he may come across in contact, and trust that this letter, to which I
have affixed the seal of the City of Columbia, South Carolina, will
answer as a passport for him through the Confederate States of
North America.

(Signed) W. H. Boatwright, Mayor[25]

Although Lowe was again declared a free man, a dilemma once again presented itself with the enormous crowd that had gathered outside the jail-house.

"The mayor feared trouble from the people who did not under-stand the situation," said Lowe. "He suggested . . . that we take a walk through the streets of the city and visit the college and other interesting portions of the town.

"Taking his arm, we left the jail—to meet another astonishing and disappointed crowd. The mayor and the officials of the college were being extremely popular, the people made way, and no attempts were made to crowd upon us . . . It was soon noised about that my presence was perfectly satisfactory and the crowd dispersed."

During his tour around the city, Lowe learned that the last train to Washington D.C., had departed that morning. All other trains were blockaded from entering the North at Manassas Junction. Lowe was forced to opt for a much longer rail journey out of the Confederacy that would take him back to Cincinnati, Ohio, through Louisville, Kentucky, which at this time still had a Southern rail service. Since the train to Louisville was not scheduled to leave Columbia until later that afternoon, Lowe parted company with Mayor Boatwright and the college faculty members, and retired to a hotel room near the railyard.

Again the exhausted aeronaut reported another brush with an untimely demise.

"My guests had just departed when a knock came at the door. On opening it, two rough looking individuals confronted me, and demonstrated by their belligerent appearance that my examination might have been eminently satisfactory to the authorities, but was far from being so with them.

"I saw they were there for the purpose of making a disturbance, and that any weakening on my part would be dangerous. So, looking them squarely in the eye, I ordered them to leave my apartment immediately, and not dare to approach me in any way. They evidently thought discretion the better part of valor and they quickly disappeared."[26]

It quickly dawned upon Lowe that, despite his ability to make a favorable impression upon the elite members of Columbia's population, his continued presence in the South posed a serious risk to his personal well-being. Following the threatening visit Lowe decided it was time to leave, and made arrangements with a local drayage company to haul the *Enterprise* to the depot, where he patiently waited for the next northward bound train to arrive.

The train that pulled into Columbia's depot was unusually long, made up of extra cars to accommodate passengers making an exodus to the North. Lowe took note that the train was crowded with "people of unusually fine appearance and intelligence" who were anxious to return to their

homes and businesses. Although the journey eventually took more than
four days to complete, the atmosphere aboard was decidedly solemn and
serious, with a "marked absence of all the jollity or freedom in conversation
one meets with on a train filled with passengers."[27]

Thaddeus Lowe passed the next several days making a number of observations that would deeply influence his thoughts in the days and months to
come. It was difficult not to notice the mass concentration of Confederate
troops at the various train stops, all making their way northward.

"At all the stations along the way tents were pitched, and what seemed
to be recruiting posts were established," Lowe recalled. "Occasionally at the
larger towns a brass band would salute the train with its martial music, but
there was a marked lack of that ardent patriotism so generally felt when a
band is playing [a] popular aire. . . . "The Girl I Left Behind," was about the
only tune we heard, and that the bands played everywhere."[28]

The overt military presence was also felt on board the train. At one
point a Confederate colonel named Todd, along with two uniformed soldiers, went from car to car attempting to convince passengers that "their
duty was to the Confederate states."

"He seemed little to dream that his words were falling on unwilling ears
and unresponsive hearts," Lowe later said of Colonel Todd. "I never heard a
single response given by any one on the train to any of his speeches."

Not only did Colonel Todd address passengers on the train, but at
every stop along the way he would also repeat the same speech to crowds
gathered at depots, where his "harangue would bring forth the wild southern yell of the backwoodsmen and others who were assembled."

On April 26, the train carrying Lowe and his fellow Northern passengers made its final stop in Louisville, Kentucky. The somber mood of the
passengers still persisted as they boarded a ferryboat that would eventually
take them up the Ohio River to Cincinnati.

"Even here the large ferry boat, which had heretofore always floated
the Stars and Stripes, was without a color of any kind. This looked ominous
and added to feeling of depression all on board experienced."[29]

Although the ferryboat provided reasonably smooth sailing, Lowe
noticed that river traffic, which was ordinarily brisk, had come to a standstill because of the threat of war.

When the vessel finally reached the shores of the Ohio border, a sight
greeted Lowe and his fellow passengers that instantly provoked a unanimous
reaction.

"A tall flag staff came into sight," Lowe recalled. "From the head of which a beautiful new Union flag floated. In a moment the passengers seemed to rise as one man, their depression disappeared, and with a will and force that were startling in their intensity, they gave cheer after cheer for the old flag."[30]

When Lowe finally reached Cincinnati he discovered the entire city embroiled with news concerning the war. While Lowe's sponsor, the *Daily Commercial*, accorded the aeronaut's accomplishment with front-page coverage, particularly noting that the feat marked the "first time in history of the daily press that [a newspaper] has been distributed at 1,200 miles distance from the place of publication on the same day,"[31] developing news of the Southern rebellion took center stage.

Although Thaddeus Lowe had completed a most remarkable journey, the true test of his aeronautical ability was yet to come.

CHAPTER TWO

A Brief History of
Early Ballooning

As Thaddeus Lowe made his way back to Cincinnati to consider the possibility of offering his services to the Union cause, the advancement of aeronautics stood at the point of what would be tremendous change during the course of the war. Prior to the 1860s the art of ballooning was still considered by many a curious frivolity. Feats of aerial daring and short tethered and untethered flights were the stock and trade of many assorted balloonists in the prewar period. Often referred to as aerialists, aeronauts, and professors, these men—and even a few women—astounded crowds at county fairs, exhibitions, and military celebrations throughout the country. However, by the time war broke out between the North and South, the science of ballooning could actually trace its origins back nearly eighty years.

Although man's wish to emulate the flight of birds is nearly as old as recorded history, with the mythical tale of Daedulus and his magnificent wings of feather and wax dating back to the time of ancient Greece, the invention of the balloon was unique. Unlike the invention of the airplane in the twentieth century—which, in many ways copied the example of winged creatures to achieve flight—the application of the principles of lighter-than-air flight does not exist in nature. In 1783 two brothers, Etienne and Joseph Montgolfier from the village of Annonay, France, idly watched a fire of burning leaves and became fascinated as wispy embers floated in the air. The more they watched the more fascinated they became with the densely heated air and its properties. Paper manufacturers by trade, the brothers wondered what would happen if they constructed a large paper bag and placed it over a fire to capture the heated air that rose upward.

On June 15, 1783, the brothers tested their idea with a bag that was nearly 33 feet in diameter, the opening of which was held over a fire fueled by sheep's wool. When the bag was sufficiently filled with hot air, it was released and rose to a height of over 1,000 feet. The age of the balloon had arrived.

The news of the Montgolfiers' flight set off a sensation in France, but they were not the only individuals working on lighter-than-air flight in France at that time. Shortly after the Montgolfier flight Jacques Alexander Cesar Charles, a Parisian physicist, began work on his own craft. Charles's lighter-than-air creation was to utilize a design approach significantly different from that of the Montgolfiers. Instead of filling a balloon envelope with hot air, Charles opted to use "inflammable air," the gas also known as hydrogen.

Knowledge of hydrogen dated back as far as the sixteenth century, when a Swiss alchemist by the name of Theophrastus Paracelcus discovered the chemical reaction that occurred when metal such as iron was dissolved by sulfuric acid. The result produced an odorless, colorless, and tasteless gas that proved to be highly flammable if ignited, hence its early popular name, "inflammable air."

In the eighteenth century some of the earliest scientific experiments were performed on hydrogen. These experiments served to provide a better explanation of the gas and its properties. In 1766, Henry Cavendish, an English physicist, demonstrated that "inflammable air" was distinct from other combustible gases, and also learned that the gas was seven times lighter than atmospheric air. It was also discovered that water was created when the gas was burned, which prompted Cavendish to name the gas hydrogen, which is Greek for "maker of water."

Jacques Charles avidly followed the work of Cavendish from his laboratory in Paris and also initiated a number of experiments involving hydrogen gas. However, up to this time, no practical use for it had been discovered. When news of the Montgolfier balloons reached Charles it sparked a flash of inspiration. The superior lifting capability that hydrogen gas displayed over heated air would serve as a more efficient means of constructing a lighter-than-air craft, he reasoned. So, with the assistance of two Parisian manufacturers, Jean and Noel Robert, Jacques Charles set out to build a better balloon.

The Robert brothers proved to be extremely innovative in their construction of the balloon envelope. Instead of utilizing heavy linen paper, as the Montgolfiers had, the Roberts developed a process by which silk fabric could be coated with a natural rubber gum suspended in linseed oil, which they referred to as "lutestring."[1] Also, because the silken envelope that the Roberts created was more globular than that of the Montgolfiers, the apparatus was dubbed the *Globe*. However, this name was eventually ignored when it debuted before the public, which took to the more colorful description, *balloon*, which translated from the French into "ball" or "large sphere."

On August 23, 1783, Jacques Charles began inflating the *Globe* with hydrogen for its public debut at Champ de Mars in Paris. He used a crude hydrogen generator that consisted of a large wooden barrel containing iron filings that had a pipe connected to the envelope's inflation valve. Hinged doors were fashioned into the top of the barrel, which allowed Charles to pour sulfuric acid over the filings inside, causing the chemical reaction that produced hydrogen.

The inflation process was arduous, taking over four days to complete. More than 200 pints of acid and a ton of iron filings were consumed in the production of the gas. The inflation was hampered by the tremendous heat created by the chemical process that, in turn, caused leaks to appear in the *Globe*'s envelope. When the balloon was finally inflated it was transported by torchlight—a dangerous proposition considering the envelope contained over 22,000 cubic feet of hydrogen—to Champ de Mars field on the morning of August 27, 1783.[2]

Throughout most of the day crowds gathered, restlessly waiting in anticipation of the balloon's liftoff in the afternoon. Despite a tremendous cloudburst that erupted late in the day, the *Globe* was launched—unmanned—shortly after five o'clock. According to one eyewitness the *Globe* "rose majestically in a shower of rain."[3] Within two minutes it had risen to more than 2,000 feet and then vanished into a dark cloud.

The *Globe* landed in the village of Gonesse the following morning, fifteen miles away from Champ de Mars. Terrified villagers there, convinced that the *Globe* was a contrivance of the devil, completely destroyed the balloon shortly thereafter. However, the *Globe* proved that hydrogen was a suitable lifting agent for lighter-than-air flight, and opened the door to more experiments.

More than 4,000 people were in attendance to witness the ascension of the *Globe* from Champ de Mars that day. Among those present was the American statesman and inventor Benjamin Franklin, who was in Paris along with John Adams and John Jay to negotiate the peace treaty officially ending the Revolutionary War between Britain and the United States. One jaded spectator casually remarked to Franklin after the *Globe*'s ascension, "Of what use is it?" Franklin reportedly replied, "Of what use is a newborn baby?"[4]

Franklin, of course, realized that Jacques Charles's experiment held great promise. Although a human being had yet to ascend in a balloon, the time for such an event was near.

Etienne Montgolfier had also seen the flight of the *Globe* and not wishing to be trumped by the advent of gas-filled balloons, soon made plans for a new demonstration of a montgolfier-type hot-air balloon[5] that would carry its first passengers. However, instead of carrying human cargo, the new montgolfier was to carry a sheep, a rooster, and a duck aloft to prove whether the upper atmosphere was safe for sentient beings.

At the Palace of Versailles on September 19, 1783, before a crowd that included King Louis XVI and Marie Antoinette, the barnyard aeronauts were launched in a wicker cage[6] attached by an intricate netting system to a linen paper montgolfier that was kept inflated by an onboard furnace. After a brief flight all three creatures returned to earth, little worse for wear, save for a touch of air sickness.[7] The experiment was deemed a success.

Among the first to arrive at the spot where the montgolfier landed was Jean-Francois Pilatre de Rozier, a young physicist from Metz, who was fascinated with the new invention. De Rozier begged the Montgolfier brothers for the honor of becoming the first human aerialist in history. The following month his wish was granted when he made his first flight in a tethered montgolfier balloon.

After his first flight de Rozier made several more tethered voyages, eventually carrying passengers with him. In Paris on November 21, 1783, de Rozier, accompanied by the Marquis d'Arlandes, a French infantry major, accomplished the first untethered freeflight in a balloon. Although the aeronauts later reported that they "ascended calmly and majestically into the atmosphere,"[8] at least one ground observer had a different perspective.

"The Gallery [control basket carrying de Rozier and the Marquis] hitched among the top boughs [of a tree]," wrote Benjamin Franklin, who observed the flight with great interest. " . . . the body of the balloon lean'd beyond and seemed likely to overset. I was then in great pain for the men, thinking them in danger of being thrown out, or burnt for I expected that the balloon being not upright the flame would have laid hold of the inside that laid over it."[9]

Franklin was nonetheless impressed with the flight, especially when de Rozier and the marquis landed safely some five miles away from their starting point. The inventive American immediately began to conjure up various uses for the new form of transportation. Although Franklin tempered his enthusiasm by noting that the balloon would "hardly become a common carriage" in his lifetime,[10] he firmly believed there existed some rather prophetic possibilities. As he wrote in 1784:

> [The balloon] is a discovery of great importance. Convincing sovereigns of the folly of war may perhaps be one effect of it, since it will be impossible for the most potent of them to guard his dominions. Five thousand balloons, capable of raising two men each, could not cost more than five ships of the line, and where is there a prince who could afford to cover his country with troops for its defense as that ten thousand men descending from the clouds might not in many places do an infinite amount of damage before a force could be brought together to repel them.[11]

As for de Rozier, the plucky young Frenchman continued his balloon ascents, as all of Europe became caught up in "balloon fever." However, in June, 1785 de Rozier made an ill-fated attempt to cross the English Channel with a dangerously hybrid balloonship consisting of both hydrogen and hot-air balloon envelopes. As de Rozier made history in becoming the first man to take flight, he marked his place in the record books a second time when he became world's first air fatality as he and a passenger were killed just off the coast of France near Boulogne. The hydrogen portion of his balloon ignited 3,000 feet above ground.

Yet, the tragedy that took de Rozier's life hardly dampened the enthusiasm that embraced ballooning as a whole. Civilian flight continued in France with more than seventy-six lighter-than-air ascents recorded from 1783 to 1790.[12] Only the aftermath of the French Revolution in 1793 managed to severely curtail civilian flights.

As civilian ballooning waned in France, however, the French armed forces began to take a keen interest in what ballooning had to offer in its military application. Working from a proposal written by an amateur military strategist by the name of Thomas Martyn, the French military was sufficiently convinced to begin adopting tethered hydrogen-filled balloons for use as reconnaissance platforms in 1793.[13] *Les Aérostatiers,* as the French military balloon service was known, lasted until 1802 before being disbanded by Napoleon Bonaparte. The French service actually consisted of a number of balloons during the course of its existence with *Le Entrepenant*, or "Enterprise," being the first commissioned. Over the years *Les Aérostatiers* proved to be instrumental, particularly during the national crisis following the revolution when the new French Republic found itself under attack from Holland, Austria, and Great Britain. In 1793 *Le Entrepenant* was used to observe Dutch and Austrian troop movements during the siege of Mauberge, tethered to heavy cables near the front line. Later, the balloon was transported to Belgium, where it took part in the siege of Charleroi and Fleurus.

As far as its success as a weapon of war was concerned, the French military balloon service garnered a mixed review. Communication from officers aloft to men stationed on the ground was often hampered by poor visibility of signal flares and flags. Moreover, messages sent to the ground by means of ballasted sandbags occasionally fell into enemy hands. One thing was certain, the balloon represented a new element on the battlefield and had the psychological effect of draining morale from enemy forces.

The Americans, as indeed the world, took particular note of French aeronautical developments in the last decade of the eighteenth century. In a letter from George Washington to Louis Le Béque du Porotail in April 1784, Washington wrote:

> I have only newspaper accounts of air-balloons, to which I do not know what credence to give. I suspect that our friends at Paris in a little time will come flying through the air, instead of ploughing the ocean, to get to America.[14]

Although it would be quite some time before the French, or anyone else for that matter, would come to America "flying through the air," one thing was certain. The invention of the balloon itself was ready to make the great migration to the New World.

In late 1784, John Jeffries, an American doctor living in London, and Jean-Pierre Francois Blanchard, a French balloon enthusiast and inveterate dreamer, collaborated to build the first balloon to cross the English Channel. On January 5, 1785, Blanchard and Jeffries left the White Cliffs of Dover and sailed east to the coast of France. A new milestone had been passed—the uninterrupted flight between two nations separated by a large body of water.

In America the balloon's debut was tenuously coming to fruition. News of the Channel flight of Blanchard and Jefferies had reached the United States and there ensued a rush to build the first American aerostat capable of carrying a person into the air. In Philadelphia public subscription to raise funds for the construction of a balloon began in 1784. The effort attracted a wide stratum of Philadelphia society, including Philadelphia mayor Matthew Clarkson, naval architect Joshua Humphries, and artist Charles Wilson Peale. However, this initial effort to construct America's first balloon was to be upstaged by a Maryland tavern owner by the name of Peter Carnes.

Like many Americans, Carnes had learned of the early French balloon experiments through newspaper accounts, which proved to be his only construction guide. Unlike his European counterparts who looked on the balloon as a means of a scientific advancement or military one-upmanship, Carnes's motivation was strictly economic. When his balloon was finished, Carnes took out a number of newspaper advertisements announcing a public demonstration of his creation, which was to be held at Blandesburg, Maryland. The admission price for the demonstration was $2.00.

Carnes's first demonstration consisted of tethered hot-air balloons. With throngs of paying attendees clamoring for even more aerial curiosities, the enterprising tavern owner soon learned that public interest in balloons was eminently exploitable. Several more exhibitions occurred with a 35-foot diameter balloon.

On June 24, 1784, Carnes was demonstrating his balloon in Baltimore when a thirteen-year-old boy named Edward Warren stepped from among the crowd and told Carnes that he would be willing to take to the air. As a Baltimore newspaper account described the moment:

". . . [Warren] bravely embarked as a volunteer . . . and behaved with the steady fortitude of any old voyager. The 'gazing multitude below' wafted to him their loud applause, the receipt of which, as he was soaring aloof, he politely acknowledged by a significant wave of his hat. When he returned . . . he met with a reward, from some of the spectators, with a *solid*, instead of *airy*, foundation, and of a species which is ever acceptable of this *lower world*."[15]

Although Carnes retired from ballooning after an accident that nearly took his life, American interest in lighter-than-air flight continued unabated. Exhibitions continued throughout Europe, with some of the continent's premier showmen touring in the United States. In 1793, Jean-Pierre Francois Blanchard, the veteran of the first English Channel crossing, made a public flight in Philadelphia with President George Washington in attendance. Even the formal study of aeronautics was recognized with the formation of a "Balloon Club" at the College of William and Mary in 1785, that was started at the behest of inventor/statesman Thomas Jefferson, who was an avid balloon afficionado.

At the beginning of the nineteenth century the world witnessed an even greater fascination with the power of manned flight, and in America the sentiment was equally ardent. As with the flights of Peter Carnes in 1784, most aeronauts who plied their trade in America saw ballooning strictly as a means of generating income. Although early balloonists, such as the French-born Eugene Roberston, and the first female aerialist in the United States, Mademoiselle Johnson, enthralled early nineteenth-century spectators at large venues, they did little to further the study of aeronautics or to even improve upon the basic balloon designs laid out by the Montogolfiers and Jacques Charles. The advancement of ballooning would come with individuals who combined both the talent for showmanship and a sincere pursuit of scientific knowledge in order to bring a degree of understanding to flight.

The first important advancements in the science of ballooning came with developments that aided in freeflight navigation and control. Freeflight navigation, in particular, was often looked upon by early balloonists as something best left in the hands of God. Balloons, for the most part, behaved at the whim of air currents at any given moment. However, in 1836 Charles Green, an English aeronaut, pioneered the first major advancement in balloon navigation—the guide rope.

Green's guide rope was simplicity at its best. It consisted of 1,000 feet of coiled rope controlled by a winch installed at the side of the control basket. When extended to its full length during a flight altitude of less than a thousand feet, the rope could trail along the ground, which allowed the friction it generated to act as ballast for the balloon, as well as a partial brake and a means of directing the balloon before it landed. The latter benefit was considered the guide rope's chief asset as the majority of ballooning accidents occurred during landing after a freeflight.[16]

Green employed this system to good effect in November 1836, when he made the journey from London, England, to Nassau, Holland, a distance of 373 miles, in 18 hours. When news of Green's incredible journey circulated around the world, conquering new distance records would become the obsession of nineteenth-century aeronauts.

Portrait of John Wise from the 1840s. Wise was one of the first American balloonists to study aeronautics from a scientific perspective.

FROM AN ENGRAVING IN

JOHN WISE, A SYSTEM OF AERONAUTICS

In the United States a new generation of aerialists emerged, prepared to challenge the aeronautical prowess of the Europeans. One of the most important aeronauts of this era was John Wise.

Born to a German immigrant family in Lancaster, Pennsylvania, on February 24, 1808, Wise is generally credited with being the first American aeronaut to make significant contributions to the science of ballooning through his meticulous study of atmospheric conditions and innovations in balloon construction.

As a young boy Wise was apprenticed as a cabinetmaker to a Philadelphia piano manufacturer. At the age of fourteen, Wise came upon an account of a balloon voyage in a German language newspaper, which prompted him to make a momentous decision in his life.

"When I first conceived the idea of making a balloon, I had never seen an ascension in with one, nor had I any practical knowledge of its construction," Wise said, many years later.[17]

However, Wise approached ballooning in a fashion quite unlike that of many of his contemporaries. He intended to take to the air for his own pleasure in the pursuit of aeronautical knowledge and generally eschewed the raucous carnival spectacle that surround ballooning at the time.

Without much of a budget to work with, Wise constructed his first balloon from cotton muslin sheets, instead of the lighter and more desirable silk used in most balloons at the time. Wise couldn't afford the costly varnish found on most balloon envelopes, so he concocted his own sealing compound from birdlime suspended in linseed oil. The finished balloon was 28 feet in diameter, had a gas capacity of 13,000 cubic feet, and weighed 186 pounds. The wicker control basket underneath the balloon measured only two and a half feet in diameter and the bottom was less than four feet deep.[18] Wise also devised his own portable hydrogen generator, which consisted of the usual iron filings in a barrel that produced gas when decomposed by acid.

Although John Wise generally looked down on balloonists who made their ascensions purely for the profits derived from paid admissions, he was nonetheless forced to sell tickets to defray the costs of construction. Wise took to the air on May 2, 1835, from the area of Ninth and Green Streets in Philadelphia. His first flight that day was a short, but harrowing ride, during which the newly baptized aeronaut struggled to maintain control of his balloon as it bounced off buildings and rooftop chimneys in the surrounding neighborhood. Wise landed some 400 yards from his departure point after only a few moments.

But the young aeronaut was undaunted. Handing his coat, boots, and instruments to a bystander, Wise was off once again. This time he began to master his new ship and the disturbing lack of control he experienced on his first attempt soon vanished. When Wise eventually landed he found himself in Haddonfield, New Jersey, nine miles north of Philadelphia.[19]

Wise's early balloon experiments were fraught with frustration and danger. When he attempted his second balloon ascent on May 18 he found that the gas envelope had been sabotaged when someone had spilled sulfuric acid over it. On another occasion in July, 1835, Wise was aloft near Womelsdorf, Pennsylvania, when the balloon's control valve, which allowed for inflation of the lifting gas for ascent and venting of gas for descent, became tangled in the balloon's netting. The problem was compounded when Wise discovered that heat from the sun was rapidly expanding the gas inside the balloon's envelope almost to the point of bursting. When the envelope did burst it fortunately produced only a mild puncture, allowing the balloon to descend safely. An accident one year later, however, almost ended the balloonist's career altogether.

In 1836, Wise constructed a new twenty-four-foot-diameter balloon made of silk, which he called the *Meteor*. On May 7, 1836, he was giving a demonstration of the *Meteor* before a group of people in his hometown of Lancaster. The weather was unsettled, with a number of lingering showers in the area that had hampered Wise throughout the day. It was evening by the time he had finished his ascents and commenced deflating the *Meteor*.

As the hydrogen gas vented, a curious bystander stepped forward from the crowd carrying a storm lantern. The flame from the lantern came in contact with the hydrogen permeating the air and a tremendous explosion took place, hurling Wise over ten feet in the air and causing severe burns to him and all others in the immediate vicinity.

"[The explosion made] a report like a park of artillery, throwing me violently back . . ." Wise later recounted. "[It] set fire to the clothes of some . . . severely scorching the faces and hands of others.

"In a few moments I was aroused from my fixed position by an agonizing pain through my whole body, which soon concentrated itself in my hands and face. I felt as though the very heart's blood was oozing through the skin."[20]

Blinded and in severe pain, Wise spent several days in a hospital and many weeks convalescing. Although his eyesight eventually did recover, the accident left him with second thoughts about his aeronautical career.

"Pecuniarily bankrupt in the business," Wise later wrote. "And almost so in reputation as an aeronaut."[21]

For the next year or so after the accident Wise retired from ballooning and eked out a living as a scientific instrument maker in Philadelphia.[22]

As John Wise temporarily left the world of aeronautics there were other American aeronauts who were destined to make their contributions to the field. William Paullin, who also hailed from Pennsylvania, was chief among them. Born in 1812, Paullin actually predated Wise in flight when he first demonstrated a balloon of his own design in Philadelphia in August, 1833.

Paullin was more of a showman than the scientific-minded Wise. On one noteworthy ascent in 1834, he strapped a parachute to a dog and dropped the animal to the ground from an altitude of more than 1,000 feet.

Paullin also experimented with varying the type of lifting gas used in balloons. Most aeronauts manufactured their own hydrogen gas at a considerable risk. By the 1830s many eastern cities had developed gas manufacturing plants that supplied heat and illumination to residents. Most of these plants used gas derived from heated coal, which was considered to be less volatile than pure hydrogen. Coal gas was also somewhat heavier than hydrogen, which meant that for a balloonist it lacked the lifting power that hydrogen produced in equal amounts.

Paullin believed that a larger balloon envelope could compensate for the lack of lift inherent in coal gas, and put this theory to work on July 27,

1837, when he flew a balloon from the Philadelphia Gas Works near the Schuylkill River. Although the flight that day was not particularly remarkable, it did prove that a more readily available and safer substitute for hydrogen could be utilized. Paullin's experiment would prove to be significant during the next two decades to come, when balloonists would set their sites on bigger ships with grander purposes in mind.

In the meantime, John Wise began to grow tired of a ground-bound life in Philadelphia. In 1837 he resumed his ascents with a twenty-five-foot-diameter balloon he dubbed the *Experiment*. The balloon was a holdover from the period prior to his hydrogen accident with the *Meteor* in 1836 and was not up to the rigors of numerous flights. Wise began construction of a new balloon in 1838, using cambric muslin fabric, coated with a boiled linseed oil varnish. The balloon was also innovative in other ways.

Wise was aware that some of the most dangerous maneuvers with a balloon occurred during landing. Even though a balloonist would ordinarily vent gas upon descent from the envelope's gas valve, the envelope still remained virtually filled once landfall had been made. Serious accidents often occurred on the ground when partially filled balloon envelopes would suddenly be seized by violent wind gusts that would drag them uncontrollably along. Experienced balloonists often compensated for the wind by selecting landing areas near forests, which would act as a windbreak until the balloon eventually deflated, but this method was hardly foolproof and not always possible.

Wise devised a novel and simple way to reduce these hazards. His solution became known as the "rip panel." The rip-panel was a large section sewn into the top half of the balloon envelope that was attached to a rope hanging over the control basket. This "rip-cord" was painted bright red to distinguish it from the control valve cord. When the balloon landed, the aeronaut simply yanked the rip-cord, exposing a large hole at the top of the envelope that quickly vented the gas to the atmosphere. This simple innovation made landings safer and more predictable and is still used by modern balloonists.[23]

With two balloonists actively practicing their craft in Pennsylvania, it was inevitable that John Wise and William Paullin would eventually perform together. Although the exhibition staged at the Pennsylvania Farmer's Hotel in Philadelphia on July 4, 1840, was billed as an "aerial duel," there was no bitter rivalry between these two men, as would be the case with other aeronauts.

Wise, who had never used anything but hydrogen before in an ascent, learned that the coal gas made available from the Philadelphia Gas Works did not deliver the lifting capability he was ordinarily used to. To perform that day he discarded the wicker control basket and precariously stood on a board attached to the balloon's netting.[24]

By the mid–1840s the goals and aspirations of many aerialists had changed. Perhaps spurred by reports of long-distance balloon travel in Europe, or even the expansionist surge in the United States associated with the mantra of Manifest Destiny, John Wise was one individual who firmly believed in the far-reaching possibilities that balloon travel had to offer. Having performed over fifty ascents, Wise was arguably America's most experienced aeronaut. His flights had allowed him to reach considerable altitudes and he noticed the atmospheric changes that seemed to regularly occur.

"Like the sea," Wise wrote. "The atmosphere is filled with a system of tides and currents as regular and periodic as the blood in its courses through the venous and arterial system of the human body."[25]

There was no question in Wise's mind that these atmospheric currents could be harnessed. With his experience and background to support him, John Wise began to explore the possibility of taking on a greater challenge.

The Atlantic Ocean.

CHAPTER THREE

The Great
Transatlantic Quest

The art of ballooning in the United States reached a zenith in the years just prior to the Civil War. It would be a golden age in American ballooning, one that would not be surpassed for several decades. It was a period when American aeronauts challenged the sky with greater feats of daring and did so with balloons that were markedly advanced over the aerostats flown of an earlier generation. Although crudely made hot-air montgolfiers and gas-filled charliers still existed and were used by numerous amateur balloonists performing at county fairs and exhibitions throughout America, the concept of the professional aeronaut began to emerge during the late 1840s and 1850s.

Following the aerial duel in Philadelphia between John Wise and William Paullin in 1840, Paullin accepted an offer to tour the nations of South America with his balloons. This left Wise as the foremost authority on aeronautics in the United States, a reputation that the aeronaut took very seriously especially as the public and the press conferred the honorary title of "Professor" upon him. Although he continued to give public exhibitions of his flying skills, Wise harbored a grander ambition.

During the winter of 1842 John Wise began to explore the possibility of traveling to Europe from the United States in a gas-filled balloon. He discussed his theory of upper air currents with a number of scientific minds in Philadelphia.

"I endeavored to demonstrate the existence of a steady easterly current in the upper atmosphere," Wise later wrote, "I proved, as clearly as could be done by theory, that such a voyage was perfectly practicable and likely to succeed under fair conditions . . . I claimed that an achievement of my purpose would do something more than to supply safe and rapid passage to Europe . . . that it would give to men a more intimate acquaintance with the laws which govern the vast ethereal sea which surrounds the earth."[1]

The portion of the "vast ethereal sea" that most interested Wise was what is now known as the jet stream. The jet stream is a high-speed westerly wind that occurs at altitudes from 10,000 to 40,000 feet. Wind speeds of over 100 miles per hour exist in this upper stratum, although at the time Wise proposed his theory the full extent of the jet stream's force was not fully realized.

Wise noticed this aerial phenomenon several years before his formal declaration of a transatlantic flight. On one ascent in 1834, he told friends in Lancaster that he would visit them in the course of a flight that would begin in Carlisle, some fifty miles to the west.

"I will be carried to Lancaster via the atmospherical currents that always blows from west to east in the higher regions of air," Wise stated.[2] From then on Wise was always certain to make careful note of atmospheric conditions during his ascents.

By 1843 Wise was convinced that the idea of a transatlantic voyage was within his grasp. On paper Wise had designed a balloonship that he believed would be capable of crossing the Atlantic. All that he lacked was the necessary funding to begin construction.

In December, 1843, Wise petitioned the United States Congress to fund his aeronautical project. The reception that Wise was accorded was less than he expected.

"This petition," Wise said. "Was received, read, and referred to the Committee on Naval Affairs where it slept."[3]

In spite of this, Wise continued with his transatlantic dream. In order to continue with his aeronautical explorations, he began manufacturing balloons for other aeronauts. During the 1840s and early 1850s, Wise also toured the country with Kinney's Mammoth Pavilion, a traveling circus act based in Columbus, Ohio. Although Wise generally disdained the idea of commercializing aeronautics, he justified his activities by investing the money he received toward the Atlantic flight.

The notion of a transatlantic flight got an unexpected boost in April, 1844, when the New York *Sun* printed a long article telling of a balloon flight originating in England that landed, with its aeronauts, on the shores of South Carolina. The story described the voyage in great detail and even named some of England's most well known balloonists as the flight's participants. The story was soon revealed to be a hoax, however, perpetuated by a then unknown writer by the name of Edgar Allen Poe. Still, the fact that Poe's hoax was widely believed and deemed plausible only seemed to add to the conviction that Wise had when it came to a transatlantic crossing.

In 1850 Wise published his theory on atmospheric air currents in a book entitled *A System of Aeronautics*. Wise used the opportunity to petition Congress again in 1851 to provide $20,000 to be used in the construction of a one-hundred-foot-diameter balloon capable of lifting over sixteen tons.

In this second petition to Congress, Wise prophetically pointed out that pioneering the first long distance transatlantic air voyage carried far reaching possibilities for the development of balloon transport. The balloons of the day would be similar to:

> . . . the puny vessels of eight and one hundred tons burden with which Columbus discovered the New World as compared to the monster leviathan three decker of three thousand and four thousand tons which now move with such speed and safety upon the mighty deep.[4]

Wise's petition was presented by Illinois Senator Stephen Douglas, the same individual who would later run an unsuccessful bid for president of the United States against Abraham Lincoln in 1860.

In his presentation to the Senate, Douglas highly praised Wise's past achievements and the merit of the proposed project.

"I think this subject should be treated seriously," Douglas said. "[Wise] is undoubtedly a gentleman of high character and of scientific attainments, and I hope his petition will go to one of the regular committees."[5]

When the petition was passed on to committee, however, it went straight back to Naval Affairs, as it had in 1843. As Wise summed up his experience with Congress, "The Committee on Naval Affairs never made a report, and I . . . very speedily gave up all hope of obtaining assistance from Congress."[6]

Although Wise failed in his attempts to secure public funding for his Atlantic voyage, the lure of transoceanic travel by air was by no means over. As John Wise's book *A System of Aeronautics* circulated throughout the United States and Europe, a new generation of aeronauts were fascinated enough with Wise's vision to take up the challenge. The decade of the 1850s would mark the return of William Paullin following his extensive tour of Latin America, and also witness the ascendancy of new names to the field.

John Steiner was among those who actually emigrated from Europe to America with the hope of being the first to cross the Atlantic by air. Born in Germany, Steiner came to the United States in 1853. He was an experienced balloonist in Europe and had accomplished more than forty ascents prior to his arrival in the United States.

In 1858, Steiner publicly declared his intention to build a balloon with a diameter of one hundred feet. In a widely circulated letter printed with his name, the aeronaut was quoted as saying:

> I am satisfied in my own mind that with such an apparatus I could cross the Atlantic in seventy-five hours and the whole cost would not be more than $20,000. The balloon, net-work, and valve would weigh about two thousand pounds, and the boat and rigging three tons and a half. This will leave about eight tons ascending power, for provisions, passengers, and ballast.
>
> It would require three good navigators, and one astronomer, besides myself. I would suggest New York as the starting point and am certain I would strike within two hundred miles of any given distance in Europe. I would suggest May as the time for making the experiment, and would make the attempt in 1859 if I could get the Government or others to assist me.[7]

While John Steiner was sincere in his desire to be the first to cross the Atlantic, his grandiose plans never took flight. However, by the late 1850s a more formidable contender emerged to accept the transatlantic challenge. His name was Thaddeus Sobieski Constantine Lowe.

Lowe was born in Jefferson Mills, New Hampshire, on August 20, 1832. His rather elongated name is believed to come from the fictional character Thaddeus Sobieski Constantine, portrayed in *Thaddeus of Warsaw*, a popular novel from around the time of Lowe's birth. In later years, Lowe chose to shorthand his first three names with the initials T. S. C.[8]

As a young boy Lowe developed a keen sense of observation that eventually led to his aeronautical interests.

"I was intently interested in scientific investigation," Lowe later said. "In botany, geology, and especially mechanics and chemistry, and my mind was centered on the possibility of an airship or machine at an early age."

Lowe was allowed to pursue his interests when at the age of eleven he joined his brother as an apprentice at the shoe-making firm of Nash, French & Company in Hingham Centre, Massachusetts, near Boston. According to Lowe, the firm's proprietor encouraged him and his brother and often allowed them time off from their work to pursue their studies.

Lowe's earliest experiments with flight centered on the construction of kites. At first the kites were built as a diversion. However, when Lowe was sixteen he built a kite that carried a lantern aloft as a demonstration of its lifting ability. From there, Lowe's kites grew even larger.

"I built a . . . monster kite," Lowe recalled. "And arranged with a boy for the use of his dog to be honored with the first skyward ride, thinking that if he came down safely I would build one large enough for myself."[9]

At the last moment, though, Lowe's friend had second thoughts about volunteering his dog for the experiment, and hid him away. This left Lowe to seek out another candidate to go aloft.

"I knew where I could get a cat," said Lowe. "Being trusted with the keys of the store, . . . I went in and borrowed the big black Tom Cat and put him into an old wire cage. I then borrowed the watchman's large clear glass lantern and pasted thin red tissues over half of the lantern."

Lowe then attached the lantern to the cage holding the cat and went to the launch site. There he attached the cage and the lantern toward the end of the kite's tail and ordered his assistants to "Let go," sending the kite, the cat, and the lantern into the air.

The wind caught hold of the kite, soon sending it nearly 1,000 feet high, at which point the boys tied the attaching line to a hitching post. From the ground the lantern appeared to be spinning, alternately showing red and white light as it hovered above.

"We [then] visited different parts of the village to see the effect and hear what the wonder-stricken people had to say," Lowe said. He also added "the next morning Hingham newspapers announced an unusual changeable light in the heavens."

After "voting the cat's aerial ride a success," the boys decided to reel in the kite. Lowe noted that when the kite finally touched down, the lantern was still glowing brightly as were "the eyes of the cat."

"Thinking to soothe [the cat] by kindly strokes I opened the cage and instantly there went forth a black streak into the still greater darkness of night and we never saw him afterwards. . . . He trusted me for the last time."

Although Lowe repeated his experiments with kites carrying lanterns, he vowed never to frighten an animal in such a way again.[10]

At age eighteen, Thaddeus Lowe had the opportunity to attend a scientific lecture given by a Professor Dinkelhoff in Boston.[11] While performing some experiments on stage the professor called for a volunteer to assist him. Lowe jumped at the chance.

Lowe demonstrated remarkable aptitude and the professor eventually offered the young man a chance to tour with him for the remainder of his lecture dates.

"This . . . not only gave me a chance to continue with my studies," said Lowe. "But a chance to travel as well."

For the next two years Lowe served as Dinkelhoff's assistant. During his apprenticeship he managed to save up enough money to afford a portable scientific laboratory. By 1852 Lowe felt that he had gained sufficient knowledge to begin giving science lectures on his own.[12]

Lowe's lecture career was successful by most accounts. Standing six feet tall, broad in proportions, and quite mature looking with his trademark handlebar mustache, Lowe presented his lectures and demonstrations with a depth of knowledge that belied his young age. He used the lecture podium to further his own study of aeronautics and began collecting any written material he could find on the subject. One demonstration that Lowe performed involved duplicating the hydrogen experiments of the eighteenth-century Italian physicist Tiberius Cavallo.

> One [lecture] was given on soap bubbles. I explained all about them . . . and impressed upon my audience that they were heavier than air . . . Then I told them that on the following evening I would still lecture on soap bubbles, but I would reverse the situation. I would illustrate the lecture by soap bubbles which would ascent, instead of fall . . . my first bubbles were filled with air and fell. The second were charged with hydrogen and ascended like balloons.[13]

During the course of one lecture in New York, Lowe managed to capture the particular attention of a young French girl in his audience. She was nineteen-year-old Leontine Augustine Gauchon. Gauchon's father had been a member of King Louis Phillipe's royal guard, but was forced to flee from France with his family following the revolution of 1848.

Lowe characterized the encounter with Leontine Gauchon as "the greatest and best thing that ever happened" to him. They married on Valentine's Day, 1855.

Married life did not deter Lowe from his ambition to take to the air. By 1856 he had saved enough money to purchase a balloon capable of carrying him aloft. However, Lowe's first taste of true aeronautics soon left him wanting more.

"No sooner did I begin to operate my balloon," Lowe later wrote. "Than I saw that I must have a larger one to accomplish my purpose."

Lowe also intended to cross the Atlantic by balloon.

Although he had most likely read John Wise's *A System of Aeronautics by* this time, he later stated that his inspiration for a transatlantic voyage came to him many years before:

> I was confident that there was an upper eastern current. I remem-
> bered as a boy lying on my back under the trees, I had often seen
> through the leaves overhead, the clouds moving in different direc-
> tions, the higher ones going east and the lower ones west, and it
> occurred to me that once in this upper current, I could sail across
> the Atlantic and land on the continent of Europe.[14]

Lowe actually claimed during his lecture tour to have tested the theory of prevailing eastern currents in the upper atmosphere as early as 1853. He experimented with small, hydrogen balloons that he constructed and "released to find out the exact direction of air currents."[15] The results convinced him that a voyage to Europe was possible, though a balloonship large enough for the task was required first.

He began giving public exhibitions and charging fees for excursions— one dollar for short trips and five dollars for longer ones. Leontine also contributed to the endeavor by staging marionette shows for children.[16] With the money earned from this Lowe was able to begin construction of a larger balloon.

Meanwhile, John Wise was also actively seeking funds for his own transatlantic scheme. As early as 1843, Wise had described the kind of craft he believed would be necessary to make the crossing:

The balloon is to be 100 feet in diameter, which will give it a net ascending power of 25,000 pounds. . . . A sea-worthy boat is to be used for the [control] car, which is to be depended on in case the balloon should fail to accomplish the voyage. . . . The crew is to consist of three people: an aeronaut, a sea navigator, and a scientific landsman.[17]

As Wise learned however, convincing enough people that the idea of the voyage was practicable was fraught with disappointment. The U.S. Congress turned down his petition for a funding grant twice by 1853, and there were even many journalists who questioned the merits of the plan.

"How can a man be so arrogant," one newspaper editorial wrote in 1853. "As to say he knows which course the wind will take?"

Another wrote, "We have discussed Professor Wise's plans for his aerostat with several experts. The consensus is that if the aeronaut succeeds it will be more through fortune than good planning."[18]

Despite the sometimes negative reaction to his plans, Wise forged ahead. He continued to build balloons for other aeronauts and temporarily relocated to Troy, New York, where he first met a former merchant marine by the name of John La Mountain.

Not much is known about La Mountain prior to his involvement with John Wise. He was twenty-nine years old, and described as "thin and ascetic, [with] a pair of clear, penetrating eyes, and a strong chin masked by an unruly spade beard [that] dominated his features."[19]

He was, however, an apt pupil in the art of ballooning and under Wise's tutelage La Mountain eventually developed skills ranging from envelope construction to freeflight navigation.

In October, 1858, John Wise took out an advertisement in the Troy *Whig* announcing that he was seeking investors willing to finance the construction of a balloon capable of flying across the ocean. Wise's cost estimates had obviously risen considerably from the time he made his appeals to Congress, for he claimed he needed $30,000 to realize his goal. Although the ad elicited few takers at first, an interested party did eventually step forward.

Oscar A. Gager of Bennington, Vermont, wrote to Wise and agreed to discuss the possibility of underwriting the voyage. Wise excitedly wrote back to Gager that he would send his apprentice, John La Mountain, to Vermont with a balloon to give the financier a demonstration flight. La Mountain

John La Mountain was a merchant marine before he joined John Wise in his quest to cross the Atlantic Ocean by balloon. La Mountain quickly earned a reputation as a skilled aeronaut in his own right. LIBRARY OF CONGRESS

apparently had very little trouble convincing Gager as to the merits of a long-distance balloon flight, as Wise later reported that Gager, "being better supplied with worldly goods, agreed to supply the necessary money . . ." [20]

With Wise as the "aeronaut," La Mountain as the "sea navigator," and Gager signed on as the "scientific landsman," the trio set forth to prepare for their transatlantic attempt. Wise began preparations for the flight by delegating to La Mountain the task of constructing the balloon's envelope. At a rented shop located on the county fairgrounds in Lansingburg, New York, La Mountain worked for twelve days supervising a group of local seamstresses during the construction process.

Enormous amounts of material were used in the aerostat's construction. Over 2,200 yards of Chinese silk were employed, while an estimated 6 miles of cordage was used in the balloon's intricate web of suspension ropes. [21]

Slung beneath the balloon envelope was an oblong wicker basket, barely long enough to accommodate the crew of aeronauts and their provisions. However, there was extra room for passengers inside the lifeboat suspended below the control basket that was connected by a network of rigging and a rope ladder.

The lifeboat, which was deemed to be a necessity for an ocean crossing, was built by a New York shipwright. If the accounts of the day can be believed, the lifeboat was truly a remarkable engineering achievement in its own right. It was sixteen feet long and four and a half feet wide and said to be capable of housing up to six men on a 500 mile ocean voyage if necessary. It was complete with oars, oarlocks, and hand-operated paddle wheels. The paddle wheels also had a dual purpose, serving as an auxiliary air propulsion unit in case the jet stream failed to move the ballonship once over the ocean. Amazingly, the lifeboat reportedly weighed only 118 pounds.[22]

After six months of painstaking labor the balloon, appropriately dubbed the *Atlantic*, was completed in the spring of 1859. It was a giant among aerostats, standing over 100 feet high when fully inflated and capable of lifting a total weight of 25,000 pounds. However, there were indications that the construction period had not gone very smoothly. In a public statement made to a newspaper in 1859 Oscar Gager was particularly generous in his praise of the "practical seaman" John La Mountain, but scarcely mentioned Wise at all:

> The balloon *Atlantic* is altogether the work of Mr. La Mountain, who bought the materials and built the balloon without advice or instructions from anyone . . . the plan was his and whatever credit attaches to the original scheme is his. The balloon boat, also with its peculiar fanlike apparatus for propelling it through the air, is the invention and property of Mr. La Mountain.[23]

Indeed, in some newspaper accounts it was reported that ownership of the balloon had passed to La Mountain, although Wise was to serve as "director-in-chief" for the voyage.

As news of the giant balloonship spread throughout the country, the skeptics still voiced dour predictions of failure. These predictions undoubtedly also had their effect on the crew of the *Atlantic*. With a vast expanse of ocean to traverse there was hardly any margin for error, despite the safety devices installed on the vessel. In May, 1858 officials from the city of St. Louis extended an offer to Wise, La Mountain, and Gager to bring the *Atlantic* to Missouri for a trial excursion. The city even offered to provide free gas in order to entice the aeronauts to begin their flight from St. Louis. Although Wise was confident that the jet stream could safely carry the *Atlantic* to Europe, the suggestion of a long-distance test flight proved to be a sound idea, and the offer was accepted.

The *Atlantic* and its entourage arrived in St. Louis in late June. The city fathers had hoped that the liftoff of the test flight could coincide with the upcoming Fourth of July celebration. On July 1, however, John Wise ordered that the balloon be connected to the city's gas main located near Washington Square in downtown St. Louis. As one newspaper reported:

> The crowds commenced gathering within the enclosure at one o'clock in the afternoon, but the usual heat of the day deterred the majority of spectators from reaching the grounds until four or five o'clock. The enclosure contained from six to eight hundred people, and the streets, open lots, board piles, and house tops were filled for squares around.[24]

The *Atlantic* was not the only balloon present that day in Washington Square. Local balloonist Silas Brooks also took the opportunity to inflate his much smaller, one-man balloon, *Comet*, which he intended to use as a pilot ship on the initial leg of the *Atlantic*'s eastward journey.

During the inflation of the balloons a bystander couldn't resist helping himself to the sumptuous provisions that had already been stowed away in the *Atlantic*'s control car. A scuffle broke out when the individual began drinking some of the wine and had to be forcibly subdued and hauled away. By 5:30 in the afternoon the *Atlantic* and *Comet* were ready for launch.

Prior to liftoff, John Wise addressed himself to the crowd, stating that he was, "not certain of success, as the ascension depends as much upon the friends around us as upon the aeronauts themselves." He then ordered the ground handlers surrounding the *Atlantic* to "follow orders" exactly, which they all agreed to do. Shortly thereafter the lifeboat was slung beneath the wicker control car and the journey was ready to begin.

Besides Wise, La Mountain, and Gager, the *Atlantic* was to take on one more passenger, a reporter by the name of William Hyde from the St. Louis *Republican*. Although Hyde was a novice to balloon flight, he eagerly approached the journey despite the possible dangers that lay ahead.

"The aeronauts had very kindly allowed me to accompany them," Hyde wrote. "On condition that if at any time my weight should prove an obstacle to the success of the voyage, I was to be landed—not thrown off as ballast, of course, but brought safely to the ground and exchanged for substance of lesser gravitation—while the others were to go on."[25]

It was late in the afternoon when Wise gave the word to the ground handlers clinging to the *Atlantic*'s lifeboat to "cast off." With the crowd cheering, the *Atlantic* majestically rose into the air. Silas Brooks began his ascent with the *Comet* and soon the two aerostats towered over the St. Louis cityscape as spectators gazed with awe from down below.

Although the *Atlantic*'s gas envelope was capable of containing 100,000 cubic feet of gas, Wise had ordered the inflation to cease when the St. Louis city gas meters reached only half that amount. Experience had taught Wise that as the balloon rose higher into the atmosphere the gas enclosed in the envelope expanded commensurably. At an altitude of over three miles gas expands to twice its volume and at six miles gas can expand more than three times. As the *Atlantic* broke the two mile mark its huge silken envelope swelled to full capacity.

"I do not think I ever before experienced such an exhilaration of spirit," wrote William Hyde, totally enraptured by the first moments of his first aerial experience. "Such real joy. Our motion was perfectly steady. There was no rocking of the boat or car, no rustling of the silk, nothing indeed, but the receding forests and fields beneath us to tell us we were not posed between earth and sky in a dead tomb . . . My feeling was that ballooning, besides being most pleasant and swift, was the safest mode of travel known."[26]

As nightfall approached all was well aboard the *Atlantic*. For the first leg of the journey the aeronauts availed themselves of the view afforded them from the *Atlantic*'s lifeboat. Below, the prairies of Illinois spread invitingly before them, bathed in an ethereal twilight glow. Beyond that was the mighty Mississippi, already cloaked in evening darkness. At a little past 7:30 P.M. Brooks landed the *Comet*, leaving the *Atlantic* to continue onward with its solo journey.

With the last rays of the sun receding below the western horizon, the temperature quickly dropped, causing the balloon to lose altitude as the gas trapped in the envelope contracted in the cold. Wise made the decision to drop ballast and the balloon soon rose again, allowing for a rather unexpected phenomenon.

"We enjoyed the rather unusual occurrence of beholding the sun rise in the west," Hyde noted. "Apparently rise, I should say. For the glorious luminary had only disappeared as our craft sank and came again in sight as the mysterious influence of the sandbag increased the distance between us and the earth."

Wise and La Mountain were both satisfied that the eastward journey was proceeding well enough. The *Atlantic* was being propelled by the force of the lower jet stream and was traveling at a speed of 80 to 100 miles per hour. The compass showed a slight northeasterly direction, and to confirm their bearing, La Mountain also relied on his sextant to track the balloon with celestial bodies in the sky.

The full day's work that John Wise had put into preparing the *Atlantic*'s launch had obviously taken its toll on the fifty-one-year-old aeronaut. Wise took a last note of the slight northward drift of the balloon and advised La Mountain, "to do as he deemed best and report his reckoning in the morning." The exhausted Wise then wished his fellow aeronauts "good night and Godspeed" and clambered up the handrails of the rope ladder from the lifeboat to the control basket and proceeded to curl himself up in a corner of the control basket for a well deserved rest.

Wise's rest almost proved to be eternal. He had unknowingly placed himself in an area of the control basket that was downdraft of the balloon's inflation valve. A significant amount of gas seeped from the valve and slowly began to suffocate him.

Fortunately for Wise, Oscar Gager called to him from below in the lifeboat sometime after 9 P.M. Receiving no answer, Gager climbed up into the basket where he found Wise comatose and nearly dead. Gager pulled Wise away from the gas to fresh air, and frantically shook the veteran aeronaut until he began to regain consciousness. As William Hyde recounted: "The proficient balloonist . . . had been taught a valuable lesson and took good care thereafter to keep the lower end of the gas bag out of the way of his smeller [sic]."[27]

Wise soon regained his spirits and in an attempt to keep the crew's mind off the numbing cold, led them all in a chorus of "Hail, Columbia."[28]

The rest of the night's journey was relatively calm. Early in the morning, however, a new phenomenon awed and bedazzled the travelers. As William Hyde wrote:

We were floating in a sort of transparent vapor which . . . seemed to be made up of luminous particles. . . . It gave the balloon a phosphorent appearance, as though it was charged with fire. So powerful was this, that every line of the netting, every fold of the silk, every cord and wrinkle, was as plainly visible as if illuminated

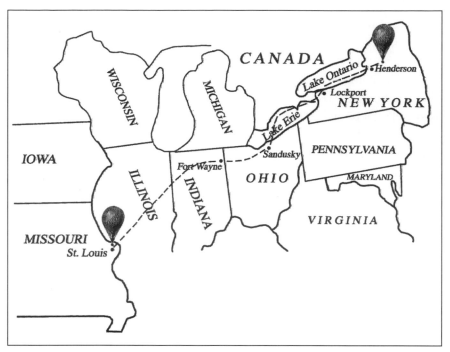

The route of the Atlantic *from St. Louis, Missouri, to Henderson, New York. The 804-mile journey set an air travel distance record for its time.*

by torches. . . . The phenomenon became more striking as we increased our altitude.[29]

The *Atlantic* and its crew had experienced a discharge of atmospheric static electricity, otherwise known as St. Elmo's fire. With more than 50,000 cubic feet of flammable gas aboard, it was fortunate that the *Atlantic*'s gasbag didn't ignite and burst into flames.

Sunrise for the crew of the *Atlantic* came at 4:15 A.M. on the morning of July 2. As the balloon sailed over a large town, John La Mountain declared that it was Fort Wayne, Indiana. The *Atlantic* had traveled nearly 500 miles since leaving St. Louis. From their altitude of nearly three miles high, Wise, La Mountain, Gager, and Hyde now caught their first glimpse of the *Atlantic*'s next major challenge looming before them on the eastern horizon.

Lake Erie.

At 7 A.M. the *Atlantic* sailed over the town of Sandusky, Ohio, situated on the lake's bank. La Mountain released gas from the *Atlantic*'s envelope, allowing the balloon to descend to about 500 feet above ground level. A strong wind was blowing from the west. La Mountain was confident that the *Atlantic* could continue onward to Buffalo, New York, "by sailing a few hundred feet above the surface."[30]

La Mountain's decision turned out to be judicious, as the easterly-blowing gale swiftly propelled the aeronauts over the lake. During its journey the *Atlantic* passed several steamboats as it flew near the Canadian shore. Just before 10:30 A.M., Hyde noted that the balloon had traversed the entire length of Lake Erie, a distance of 250 miles, in only three hours.

By 11 A.M. the *Atlantic* had crossed the Welland Canal in Canada and was within twenty miles of Buffalo. La Mountain cut ballast and the *Atlantic* rose to a height of nearly one mile. La Mountain intended to use the eastern jet stream to propel the *Atlantic* directly into Buffalo, but he mistimed the release of ballast, causing the balloon to drift eastward.

Just before noon, the *Atlantic* was sighted over Niagara Falls on a course for Lockport, New York, and from there it was on to Lake Ontario. Here, a series of misjudgments occurred that nearly took the lives of all on board.

A wild storm raged around Lake Ontario, drawing the *Atlantic* into its clutches as it neared the southern shores. As the storm grew worse, it was agreed the balloon would descend to the ground depositing Gager and Hyde near Lockport, so Wise and La Mountain could attempt to continue the journey all the way to the eastern seaboard. However, as the balloon neared the ground it was caught in the tremendous force of the storm, overshooting Lockport altogether. Soon, the occupants of the uncontrollable balloon found themselves teetering between the craggy New York shoreline and the turbulent waters of Lake Ontario.

In a desperate attempt to gain altitude and rise above the storm, all of the balloon's ballast was cut away and any nonessential gear was thrown overboard. La Mountain hung precariously below the wicker control basket and—with axe in hand—hacked away at any unnecessary fixtures attached to the lifeboat. First the ironwork comprising the hand-operated paddle wheels were cut away, and next the oarlocks and oars. The boat itself had begun to take on water as it dipped into the icy lake below, which caused it to act as an anchor that threatened to tow the *Atlantic* under the raging surf. La Mountain was sorely tempted to separate the cords attaching the boat from the control basket and send it adrift as well. However, the shoreline remained several miles away and the lifeboat represented the crew's only chance for survival if they were forced to abandon the balloon.

With all unnecessary weight jettisoned, the *Atlantic* managed to gain some altitude. The balloon was skimming above the water at about thirty feet. The storm was now blowing the *Atlantic* toward a densely forested area that skirted the lake. Although the sight of land was welcomed by the aeronauts, John La Mountain realized the greatest danger now lay ahead.

"The perils of land are even more terrible than those of the water," La Mountain ruefully noted to his comrades. "It would be easier to meet death by drowning than to have our bodies mangled by dashing against rocks and trees."[31]

The *Atlantic* crossed the shore at speed and was hurled through the treetops. La Mountain attempted to bleed off gas in order to keep the balloon envelope from acting as a sail, as Oscar Gager dropped the land anchor. The force of the collision with the trees almost knocked the four aeronauts out of the control basket altogether. The balloon's silk envelope was punctured by the branches of the thick forest canopy, and the still-underslung lifeboat was reduced to splinters as it crashed into the trunks of several stout trees.

Finally, after what seemed an eternity, the *Atlantic* came to rest, tangled in the fork of an elm tree. Miraculously, the only injuries sustained by the aeronauts were slight contusions. However, the tree branches had reduced the *Atlantic*'s balloon envelope to shreds.

It was soon discovered that the balloon had landed near Sacket's Harbor in the township of Henderson, New York. After climbing down from the *Atlantic*'s control basket, La Mountain observed the time—2:20 P.M. It was the first time in almost twenty hours the aeronauts had felt the ground beneath them.

More significant, however, was the fact that the *Atlantic* had traveled nearly 809 miles, a distance record that no aeronaut had ever accomplished before.

Despite the near tragic conclusion to the voyage of the *Atlantic*, the journey was hailed as an astounding success. When Hyde's account of the trip was published it served to fuel the hope that a transatlantic aerial voyage would be imminent. However, shortly after the flight a war of words erupted between John Wise and John La Mountain that created a bitter acrimony between the two men.

It all started when a reporter for the Troy *Times* by the name of George Demers sat down with La Mountain to get his account of the trip. In the article La Mountain harshly criticized Wise for incompetent and unprofes-

The voyage of John Wise's balloon, Atlantic, nearly ended in disaster after traveling over 800 miles from St. Louis, Missouri, to Henderson, New York. Wise, and fellow traveling companions John La Mountain, Oscar Gager, and William Hyde, miraculously survived the balloon's harrowing crash. LIBRARY OF CONGRESS

sional actions. He accused Wise of falling asleep while grasping the taut cord connected to the gas valve, allowing 5,000 cubic feet of gas to escape and then afterwards, repeatedly failing to correctly assess the course heading the balloon was on.

"From first to last, I have been robbed of just credit . . . and placed in a false position by this man," La Mountain was quoted as saying of Wise. "He has conveyed everywhere the idea that I was a fellow of some pluck, but having no scientific knowledge of ballooning, and that his wisdom barely compensated for my blunders."[32]

In conclusion, La Mountain vowed to recover the *Atlantic* and rebuild the remains for a transoceanic voyage under his own direction.

It is not exactly known whether the words and sentiments attributed to La Mountain in the article were entirely his own or the concoction of

Demers, the Troy *Times* reporter. Whatever the source, John Wise responded in a letter to *Harper's Weekly* that he bore "no ill feelings" against La Mountain.

"I verily believe that no trouble would have arisen with him had he not placed himself in the hands of an indiscreet relation connected to the Troy *Times*." Wise further went on to state, "This person [Demers] is attempting to build up a reputation for Mr. La Mountain by destroying mine, which I have been more than 20 years in acquiring."

As bitter and protracted as the postflight squabbling of the *Atlantic's* crew was, it did not cast a permanent shadow over the transatlantic quest. Observing from the sidelines was Thaddeus Lowe.

Lowe had placed his own transatlantic aspirations on hold for several months and noted the efforts of Wise, La Mountain, and Gager with great interest. When it seemed that the general effort had ground to a halt following the St. Louis to Henderson flight, Lowe forged ahead with his own plans of Atlantic conquest. As it turned out, Lowe's ambitions were to be even greater than those of any previous Atlantic challenger.

Lowe began construction of his balloonship on July 15, 1859, in Hoboken, New Jersey, with financial backing from a number of local investors. Lowe correctly reasoned that any balloon would gradually lose its buoyant gas through normal leakage during a 3,000 mile voyage across the ocean. The more gas a balloon contained, the longer a voyage could be sustained. Bearing this in mind Lowe set out to build the largest balloon the world had ever seen up to that time.

Work on the balloon was conducted in utmost secrecy, with as many as sixty seamstresses employed in sewing together the huge silk envelope. By September, 1859, the work was completed.

The proportions of Lowe's aerostat dwarfed the dimensions of the *Atlantic* in almost every respect. The envelope was more than 130 feet long and had a capacity of 726,000 cubic feet—more that seven times the capacity of the *Atlantic*. Lowe's vessel was also designed to support a massive control car and an equally large lifeboat. The basket, made of rattan, was twenty feet in diameter and featured wraparound seating and a trapdoor in the bottom floor, which led to the lifeboat slung beneath it.

The lifeboat was also unique. It was thirty feet in length and equipped with a paddle wheel driven by a four horsepower steam engine provided by John Ericsson, the acclaimed naval architect who would be best remembered in history as the designer of the U.S. Navy's first ironclad, the

Thaddeus Lowe's City of New York *was indeed a grand creation. Its envelope measured over 130 feet long, and 104 feet across. Additionally, a steam-powered lifeboat hung suspended under the control basket in the event that the giant balloon was forced to land in the Atlantic Ocean during its journey.* HARPER'S WEEKLY

USS *Monitor*, during the Civil War. The lifeboat also housed an eight-foot-diameter propeller wheel, which was to "act on the atmosphere in raising or depressing the course of the balloon."[33]

When fully assembled and inflated the entire balloon reached over 200 feet in height and was reported to have cost nearly $22,000.[34] From Lowe's own calculations the mammoth balloon would have a lifting power of 22 1/2 tons if filled with hydrogen and 16 tons if filled with less buoyant coal gas. When Lowe's balloon was ready for its unveiling to the public he had settled on a name for his gargantuan creation. It was to be called *The City of New York*.

The City of New York was scheduled to launch from the Crystal Palace at 42nd Street and Sixth Avenue in New York City in October, 1859. Although Lowe received mostly favorable press coverage for his Atlantic crossing, there were, again, those critics who predicted that nothing but disaster would come of the project.

"Professor Lowe's rally seems to be more distinguished by a rash and daring recklessness than anything else," read one New York editorial. "He had been encouraged . . . with funds or the promise of funds, and has built himself a balloon as high and large as the Tower of Babel. . . . If this is a specimen of his wisdom and forethought, we cannot but fear he will be disappointed . . . We wish him success, and perhaps someday, someone will succeed in reaching the other side of the Atlantic. Lowe does as well to mouth the forlorn hope as anyone, but many will have to fall . . . before one succeeds."[35]

In a public statement to New York newspapers, Lowe defended the merits of a transatlantic voyage in terms of its greater importance. That it was much more than just the self-aggrandizing ambition of one individual.

"It is time," Lowe said. "That one should make a bold push . . . and endeavor to effect some practical demonstration which shall revive the spirit of inquiry and investigation. If nothing is done but to talk and theorize . . . the aeronautical art will remain where it is."[36]

Interest in Lowe's monster balloon was intense. Public notices were widely distributed throughout the city and throngs gathered at the Crystal Palace, paying 25 cents a head to witness the inflation. New York newspapers posted daily accounts of the inflation process, which was painstakingly slow. Lowe was told by the superintendent of the city gas company that 500,000 cubic feet of coal gas could be supplied in a 24 hour period. But as Lowe soon found out, only 50,000 cubic feet of gas per day could actually be supplied.

"That would have required at least ten days," Lowe later said. "In ten days a very considerable amount of gas would escape, as at that time there was no balloon silk that was perfectly tight. It did not require much of a calculation to see that at this rate there would be a continuous inflation and no ascent."[37]

Lowe did manage to ascend from Crystal Palace with a much smaller balloon in order to test out various items of measuring equipment he planned to take with him in *The City of New York*. With the balloon never more than one-third inflated, however, Lowe called off his plans for the voyage at the end of October.

Immediately, he was accused of perpetuating a "humbug" on the people of New York. A poem lampooning Lowe and the fees he collected from the public during the inflation of *The City of New York* typified some of the derisive sentiment hurled at the aeronaut:

> I've seen your Gas Bag, Mister Lowe,
> And paid a quarter for the show.
> I haven't had so grand a treat
> Since Blondin come his circus-feat.[38]

> But when will you inflatuate?
> The season, Lowe, is getting late—
> You said you would, some time ago,
> Yet you continue for to show!

> You stay and stay, and feather your nest,
> While Vic(toria) and Nap(olean), and all the rest,
> Are waiting for your flying visit;
> It ain't a dodge, nor nothin', is it?

> I've heard it whispered, Mister Lowe—
> I re'ly hope it isn't so—
> I'm sure I don't pretend to know:
> They say—you never meant to go.

> A man is lucky that's got brass—
> A man is lucky that's got gas:
> With brass and gas, and backers, too
> A smart man ought to wiggle through![39]

Even John Wise, still smarting from his own treatment in the press in the aftermath of the St. Louis to Henderson flight, could not resist in adding his own fuel to the fire.

"Mr. Lowe is an aeronaut of 17 months and of no scientific attainments," Wise wrote in an editorial to the New York *Express*. "He had not made ten reputable ascensions. By profession he is a 'Magician'. . . by practice in balloon progress an unscrupulous plagiarist.

"He has appropriated to himself the credit of inventions and improvements in balloon making and sailing that justly belong to me, having been published in my book issued eight years ago. . . . Mr. Lowe has unscrupulously attempted to pirate my hard earned and weatherbeaten thunder in balloon progress to his own glory, or shame, as the case may yet be . . ."[40]

At the depths of this derision, Lowe himself admitted that he, "was on the horns of a dilemma." Yet, salvation for the transatlantic project presented itself with a host of new financial backers led by John C. Cresson. Cresson was the president of the Franklin Institute in Philadelphia, and equally important, the president of the board of directors for the Philadelphia Gas Works. Cresson learned of Lowe's unfortunate experience with the New York gas company, and invited the aeronaut to bring his balloon to Philadelphia, where a sufficient gas supply would be provided free of cost.

Packing the entire balloon and its equipment took two full freight cars. Lowe arrived in Philadelphia by mid-November to begin re-testing the craft for an Atlantic flight.

Thaddeus Lowe was not the only aeronaut making headlines in the autumn of 1859. John La Mountain, who had thoroughly distanced himself from his former partners John Wise and Oscar Gager, had recovered the remains of the *Atlantic* and reconfigured the balloon into a vessel roughly one-third the size of the original. With Lowe's *City of New York* being readied for launch in Philadelphia, La Mountain saw himself in a race for the prize of completing the first Atlantic Ocean crossing.

"Mary, I have been thinking . . . the matter over," La Mountain said in a letter to his wife in September. "I'm going across the ocean with my small balloon. They have secretly built a big balloon in New York, to head me off the Atlantic voyage, but I am going to show the people of this country a trick that they don't dream of now. Lowe shan't have the credit for my discoveries. If, after my one ascension, you shouldn't hear from me, make up your mind that I've landed in Europe."[41]

La Mountain had found a new financial backer for the project in John A. Haddock, editor of the Watertown *Reformer* in New York. On September 22, 1859, La Mountain and Haddock embarked on a trial ascent with the rebuilt and slimmed-down *Atlantic*. More than a week would pass before the outside world heard from the pair again.

After the pair's departure from Watertown, the excursion courted disaster almost from the start. Haddock, unaccustomed to the frigid cold that accompanied travel at high altitude, immediately became severely ill. As the journey progressed into the night the balloon held a northeasterly course, heading far away from civilization. By the next morning the aeronauts found themselves above a dense forest of spruce trees, which suggested to La Mountain that the balloon had drifted into the vast and unpopulated Canadian wilderness.

Compounding the aeronauts' dilemma, a morning rainstorm prevented the sun from warming the *Atlantic*'s gas envelope. With its limited capacity, the lifting power of the gas contained in the bag was not enough to sustain the balloon in flight. La Mountain and Haddock were forced to land and abandon the *Atlantic*.

After packing whatever supplies they could carry with them, the next several weeks were a grueling test of survival. After exhausting their food supply the men were forced to eat anything in the forest they could find.

"We found two tiny white frogs," Haddock later recalled. "Which we ate raw. Not hind-quarters alone; we were not dainty; fore-quarters, heads, bones and all. I never tasted a sweeter morsel in all my life."[42]

After trekking for days in the Canadian wilderness, La Mountain and Haddock came upon the encampment of Angus Cameron and a party of Indian and French Canadian lumbermen. They were saved.

Before leaving the wilderness, La Mountain managed to salvage as much of the remains of the *Atlantic* as he could, once again. The trip back to Watertown for Haddock and La Mountain was a triumphant series of heroes' welcomes. Most news accounts had given the aeronauts up for dead, so it was a pleasant shock when they finally emerged out of the Canadian forest.

After La Mountain and Haddock were reunited with their families there was a great demand for their accounts of the journey on the New York lecture circuit. However, in the aftermath one thing was plainly obvious. Any hopes of crossing the Atlantic for John La Mountain were now at an end.

Thaddeus Lowe, on the other hand, continued to pursue the Atlantic quest from his new base of operations in Philadelphia. But as winter approached, Lowe decided to delay and wait until the spring to make another attempt with *The City of New York*.

"Even my enthusiasm did not rise to the point of attempting to buffet the Atlantic storms of winter," Lowe said. "Such an experiment required the most favorable conditions, and though it was a great disappointment for me . . . I reluctantly stored the great airship in winter quarters."[43] For the rest of the year and into early 1860, Lowe and his wife journeyed to Charleston, South Carolina, where he "spent the winter ascending and studying the various air currents" in a smaller balloon.

Upon returning to Philadelphia in the spring, Lowe was anxious to embark on his voyage across the ocean. According to Lowe, the project's Philadelphia backers insisted that more tests of the upper air currents be conducted before allowing him to depart. However, his balloons were actually to serve a different purpose that was more in the realm of public relations for the city.

In May, 1860 the city of Philadelphia hosted a delegation from Japan that was in the United States to commemorate the tenth anniversary of Commodore Perry's historic visit to that nation. The major components of Lowe's massive balloonship, which was now renamed *The Great Western*, were prominently on display, along with a smaller ship. Lowe dazzled the Japanese visitors, who had never seen a passenger-carrying balloon before, by taking several of them on their first ascent in his smaller balloon.

"All of this, of course, was excellent publicity," Lowe said. "The greater the interest of the public, the greater my hope of realizing the means necessary for my cherished plan, for I found the project more costly than I had first anticipated, and the long delay of winter had eaten into my capital."[44]

As a consequence, Lowe was compelled to "keep up the interest . . . of the public" in order to obtain additional subscriptions for the project.

During the summer of 1860 Lowe made his first trial experiments with *The Great Western*. True to the promise made by John Cresson, Philadelphia Gas Works was able to supply sufficient quantities to inflate the balloon's massive envelope. On June 28, Lowe took to the air with *The Great Western*. Garrick Mallory, an associate editor for the Philadelphia *Inquirer* was on board to capture the historic occasion:

"When Mr. Lowe was over the city . . . he burst out from the hoop above into the involuntary exclamation, 'Here at last is *The Great Western* afloat, after all the prophesies against her, and a half million witnesses to the fact!' Well might he rejoice. After years of labor and hardship he had triumphed over every obstacle."[45]

While the large balloon proved to be more difficult to control, Lowe managed to maintain absolute mastery of it while in the air. Within very little time *The Great Western* rose to an altitude of over two and a half miles, where it was carried eastward toward Atlantic City, New Jersey. When Lowe valved off gas for descent, *The Great Western* was swept in a lower westward current that landed the ship only eighteen miles from where it had started.

Although Lowe declared that he and *The Great Western* were ready, his investors in the scheme still urged caution. It is possible that the investors were reluctant to invest the amount of money that was required to prepare for the voyage, when Lowe's balloons served their own commercial purpose whenever they were publicly exhibited in Philadelphia. For instance, the standard admission fee to watch the inflation of *The Great Western* was twenty-five cents, just as it had been in New York. Additionally, concerns also arose over the actual airworthiness of *The Great Western*.

William Paullin was among those who witnessed the maiden flight of *The Great Western*. The veteran Philadelphia aeronist had apparently voiced grave reservations about Lowe's chances of successfully crossing the Atlantic to his old friend John Wise, which prompted Wise to write the following letter to Lowe on September 9:

> Since yesterday your present position was presented to me in such a light that it put me really under a slight conviction that you had come serious intentions to make the attempt in good faith. Now if I am right, permit one to say that your plan and machinery is too incongruous—and the odds therefore are decidedly against you, both as to making a fair start, as well as in the successful termination of the trip if you should ever get started. These were the reasons for my refusal of your invitation to accompany you when you had prepared the outfit [the balloon] for last fall in New York.
>
> From a conversation with Mr. Paullin two weeks ago I learned that your balloon was somewhat dilapidated. He represented to me it was entirely unfit to be used with some of the ponderous contrivances in the detail of the machinery. I wish you to understand that it was not Mr. Paullin who [said] these things. He gave me no

opinion about the matter. He only gave me a description of the condition of the balloon and the result of the trial trip.[46]

With Lowe pressing his backers for action, it was finally decided that higher counsel was required to intervene in the matter. John Cresson suggested that Joseph Henry, the highly regarded physicist and first secretary of the Smithsonian Institution in Washington, D.C., should be consulted. Cresson drafted a letter to Henry in December, 1860:

> The undersigned citizens of Philadelphia, have taken a deep interest in the attempt of T.S.C. Lowe to cross the Atlantic by aeronautic machinery, and have confidence that his extensive preparations to effect that object will add greatly to scientific knowledge.
>
> Mr. Lowe has individually spent much time and money in the enterprise, and, in addition, the citizens of Philadelphia have contributed several thousand dollars to further his efforts in demonstrating the feasibility of trans-Atlantic air navigation.
>
> With reliance upon Mr. Lowe and his plans, we cheerfully recommend him to the favorable consideration of the Smithsonian Institution, and trust much aid and advise will be furnished by that distinguished body as may assist of the attempt in which we take a deep interest.[47]

The letter was signed by a veritable who's who of the Philadelphia scientific community, according to Lowe.

Joseph Henry was an appropriate choice to guide the aeronaut along in his journey. In his long career Henry was credited with perfecting the electromagnetic telegraph and laying down several principles involved in the study of electrical transmission. He continued to broaden his scientific interests while at the Smithsonian Institution, where he maintained standardized records of meteorology. Accordingly, he took an avid interest in the prospect of a transatlantic flight.

"I do not hesitate to say," Henry wrote back to Lowe. "That provided a balloon can be constructed of sufficient size, and of sufficient impermeability to gas, in order that it may maintain a high elevation for a sufficient length of time, it would be wafted across the Atlantic. I would not, however, advise that the first experiment of this character be made across the ocean, but that the feasibility of the project be thoroughly tested, and experience accumulated by a voyage over the interior of our continent."[48]

Although he was disappointed, Lowe accepted Henry's opinion. In January, 1861, Lowe met Henry in person, during which the respected scientist further outlined his opinion on Lowe's quest.

"You must start your trial voyage in some locality in the west," Henry told Lowe. "If you make a success everyone will know about it."

The words reverberated in Thaddeus Lowe's mind. Time, however, was running short. With the election of Abraham Lincoln in November's election, the nation stood on the brink of dissolution. Lowe would journey to Cincinnati and embark on one of the most harrowing balloon voyages of his career. It was to be a journey that would culminate in South Carolina and prove that the theory of an easterly prevailing air current did exist.

Unfortunately, the tenor of the country had changed. For the next several years an ambition as grand and expansive as taking a vehicle of the air and attempting to bridge one of the most formidable barriers on earth would be replaced by the necessities of survival in a world of war and destruction. There would be no more flights of scientific pursuit or pleasure. After Lowe returned to Cincinnati in May, 1861 from his flight to the South the hopes and dreams of the great Atlantic quest, at least for the time being, had also come to an end.[49]

CHAPTER FOUR

Creating an Army
in the Air

War fever had swept the land by the time Thaddeus Lowe returned to Cincinnati from his balloon trip to South Carolina in April, 1861. The fervent ardor that compelled men to enlist for military service was as much inspired by a strong sense of adventure as it was by any feelings of enraged patriotism. Nevertheless, having seen firsthand the deadly serious preparations the South was making along the railheads that lead back to Kentucky, Lowe realized that the inevitable conflict was to exact a costly toll.

"From what I had seen," Lowe later wrote. "I was fully confident that the country was facing a severe struggle, and [with] patriotism getting the better of my desire to attempt a crossing of the Atlantic, I decided to offer my services to the Government."

Lowe saw the potential in introducing aeronautics as a legitimate branch of the military. He was of course aware of the use of tethered observation balloons by the French army during the 1790s. Yet, even with this precedent Lowe acknowledged the difficulty he was to encounter in introducing a new element to the art of warfare.

At this period, ballooning was looked upon by the public at large simply as an expression of the showman's art and indeed, with rare exception, balloonists themselves looked no higher.

So, it was extremely difficult to impress even those in power that ballooning belonged to the realm of science and to be of any benefit, must be handled scientifically. This was the only claim I could lay to superiority but it seemed almost impossible to get a hearing.[1]

Probably unknown to Lowe, however, was that there had been attempts to introduce aeronautics to military use in the United States prior to the Civil War. During the Seminole Wars in Florida in the 1830s and 1840s, Col. John H. Sherburne wrote to Secretary of War Joel Poinsett, suggesting that balloons might be assigned for service with government forces in Florida. Although not an aeronaut himself, Sherburne made the suggestion with a solid degree of understanding of the situation in Florida. He had been involved in military operations there since 1837.

In many ways, Sherburne's proposal foreshadowed the methods that would be used by aeronauts in the Civil War. He believed that tethered ascents should be made in the evening, so they wouldn't be spotted by the enemy, and that fixed positions could be ascertained by observing campfires in the distance.

Sherburne had gone as far as contacting Charles Ferson Durant, an early pioneer balloonist, who had agreed to put together a balloon outfit for the cost of $900. Poinsett referred Sherburne's proposal to Gen. W. K. Armistead, commander of military forces in Florida. Armistead refused to give any consideration to the idea and further discussions of the plan came to an end.[2]

The second serious proposal to use balloons in conjunction with the U.S. military came about during the Mexican War of 1846–48. One of the most important military objectives of the war was the battle for Veracruz, which was heavily protected by fortifications at the castle San Juan de Ulúa. Planning went on for months to discuss ways of taking the castle and capturing the city.

When word leaked out about the difficulty the military was experiencing planning this expedition, none other than John Wise voiced an opinion. In a widely published newspaper article entitled, "Easy Method of Capturing the Castle of Vera Cruz," Wise outlined how a tethered balloon could be maneuvered over San Juan de Ulúa out of range of Mexican artillery, and then commence to bombard the fortress with percussion torpedoes and shells.[3] Although the plan generated a fair amount of publicity

for Wise, it was not considered very seriously by the military, who successfully took the city in March 1847 by traditional ground assault.

By 1861, Thaddeus Lowe was to find that fifteen years had done little
to change official attitudes to military aeronautics.

After collecting his belongings in Cincinnati, Thaddeus and Leontine
returned to their Philadelphia home in May. Not long afterwards, Lowe
received a letter from Murat Halstead, who, in the aeronaut's words, "had
not been idle in my interests." Halstead had written on Lowe's behalf to
Salmon P. Chase, the former Ohio senator who had recently been
appointed as treasury secretary in Lincoln's cabinet. Chase's response was
very encouraging toward Lowe's proposal:

> My dear Halstead,
>
> I think very well indeed of your ideas about Prof. Lowe and
> have spoken of them to the Secretary of War and to distinguished
> officials. They are well received, but there is some difference of
> opinion as to the balloonists to be employed. I shall urge your
> man.[4]

In his accompanying letter to Lowe, Halstead apologized for Chase's
use of the phrase "your man," adding that he addressed Chase "so warmly
on the subject as to become [Lowe's] champion in the matter."[5] Halstead
concluded his letter by urging Lowe to travel to Washington and meet with
Chase as soon as possible to demonstrate in person that he was, "a man of
science and a gentlemen and therefore not a showman."[6]

Lowe followed Halstead's advice "to the letter," and brought with him
the *Enterprise*, the balloon with which he had made the voyage from
Cincinnati to South Carolina. He arrived in the nation's capital in early
June.

Lowe, however, was not the first balloonist to arrive in Washington to
offer his services. That distinction went to a Rhode Island aeronaut named
James Allen.

Allen was born in Barrington, Rhode Island, on September 11, 1824.
As a young boy he was forced to find employment in a variety of jobs ranging from farm labor to working in cotton mills. After returning from a three
year stint in the merchant marines in 1841, Allen settled on the printing

trade for a period of time in Providence, Rhode Island. His ambitions changed in 1846, when he witnessed his first balloon ascent in Wilmington, Delaware. The experience inspired him to seek out other aeronauts and devote his life to learning the art of ballooning as a trade.

In 1857, Allen made an acquaintance with Samuel King, an exhibition balloonist from Philadelphia. King found the young Allen possessed an aptitude for aeronautics and allowed him to join him as an assistant. The pair went on to perform numerous public ascents all over New England in the years leading up to the Civil War. In early 1861, King and Allen ended their partnership, and James Allen returned to Providence where he briefly resumed the printing trade.

Following Abraham Lincoln's declaration of an "insurrection" in the Southern states on April 15, 1861, a call went out to raise 75,000 troops to quell the Southern rebellion. James Allen immediately responded to the call and volunteered his services and aeronautic equipment directly to Rhode Island governor William Sprague. He was immediately assigned to the state's 1st Regiment, Detached Militia, which was under the command of Gen. Ambrose Burnside.

Echoing the patriotic fervor of the times, the *Providence Post* gave the gallant aeronaut a suitably eloquent send off. "Allen, our New England Aeronaut," it read. "Has promptly volunteered his services, with balloons for reconnoitering purposes, and leaves us tonight for the seat of operations. He possesses the qualities that a man needs in the profession; good temper, courage, quickness of perception, and that order of mind, which enables him to act in an emergency. Success to Allen."[7]

Success, however, would not come easily for Allen. In May, 1861, Allen enthusiastically loaded up two balloon outfits, a portable hydrogen gas generator, and 1,500 feet of tether rope on a railcar bound for Philadelphia. He was under orders from Governor Sprague to join up with the 1st Rhode Island Regiment. However, the governor failed to provide the aeronaut with written orders and he was subsequently detained in Philadelphia. Swept up in the chaos and confusion that was so prevalent in the early days of the war, Allen found himself by early May stuck in Philadelphia with his equipment, unable to reach Washington by rail due to sabotage inflicted on bridges leading to the capital by Confederate sympathizers. He finally arrived in Washington at the end of May, although he did not attempt any formal demonstrations of his balloons until June.

Portrait of James Allen in his later years. The Rhode Island aeronaut was among the first balloonists to volunteer his services to the Union army.

LIBRARY OF CONGRESS

On June 9, 1861, Allen prepared the larger of his two balloons for inflation under the supervision of Maj. Albert Myer, the Union army's chief signal officer. Although he brought his own gas-generating equipment, the aeronaut opted to tap into the city's gas main at Massachusetts Avenue and Third Street. The balloon was constructed of oilcloth linen, and measured out to be thirty-five feet in diameter, standing over fifty feet tall. When the inflation was completed volunteers walked the balloon to the 1st Rhode Island Regiment's camp at Caton's Farm, which was about a mile north of Washington near Glenwood, Maryland. Here, the balloon was attached to its portable windlass and with Allen on board was sent aloft to the full extent of its 1,500 foot tether for a trial ascent. Satisfied that the balloon had performed as promised, aeronaut and balloon were hauled in. The next day the 1st Rhode Island Regiment broke camp and were ordered to Chambersburg, Pennsylvania, where they would join a column commanded by Maj. Gen. Robert Patterson that was moving to secure the Federal arsenal and armory at Harpers Ferry, Virginia.

Securing the armory was crucial for the Union army. Over 17,000 muskets were stored at Harpers Ferry, along with the production equipment to manufacture the Model 1841 rifle, otherwise known as the "Mississippi Rifle." The battle for the arsenal was shaping up to be a formidable one and the accompanying journalists had already caught wind of the aeronautical experiment that had been conducted on June 9. One correspondent wrote that James Allen and his balloon were to be used, "To reconoitre the position and force of Confederate troops at Harpers Ferry."[8]

Unfortunately, the opportunity to prove his balloons as a means of intelligence gathering was denied to James Allen during this campaign. Far removed from city gas mains, Allen was forced to rely upon his own portable gas-generating equipment to supply his balloon. To Allen's disappointment, he was not able to obtain a sizable enough supply of zinc (as an alternative to iron) with which to generate the necessary amount of gas.

As for the armory at Harpers Ferry, Confederate troops overwhelmed Union forces, who were forced to abandon the position on June 18, 1861. The captured manufacturing machinery was dismantled and sent to new facilities in Richmond, Virginia, and Fayetteville, North Carolina, where they became the core of the Confederacy's ordnance supply.

Following the defeat at Harpers Ferry, James Allen along with the rest of the 1st Rhode Island Regiment were ordered to return to Washington on June 19, where makeshift headquarters known as Camp Sprague— named in honor of the Rhode Island governor—were established. For nearly a month Allen patiently waited for an opportunity to once again prove the value of his balloons on the frontline.

On July 5 Brig. Gen. Irvin McDowell, commander of the Union troops south of the Potomac River, was preparing the offensive that was to be mounted against Confederate forces at Manassas Junction in Virginia. James Allen was ordered to bring his balloons directly to McDowell's headquarters at Camp McDowell, on the right bank of the Potomac near one of the Union army's advanced positions at Falls Church. There, Allen and his balloons were placed under the supervision of Lt. Henry L. Abbot, an engineer and officer on General McDowell's staff.

Abbot first encountered James Allen and his balloons on July 8. Allen was struggling with his equipment, which prompted the young lieutenant to express serious doubts as to the usefulness of Allen's aeronautical experiment:

> I went to their location and found that one of [Allen's balloons] was an old cotton affair which had long been in use, while the other was made of silk and was in good condition. They were accompanied by a crude apparatus for generating hydrogen by the action of

dilute sulphuric acid upon iron turnings, but in spite of all their
efforts the operators had only succeeded in about half filling the silk
one. By working all day and night we succeeded in accumulating
sufficient gas.[9]

When Allen's balloon was finally ready for launch Abbot accompanied
him on the ascent. A fierce wind played havoc, preventing the balloon from
rising any more than 500 feet. Abbot later recalled that because of the strong
wind Allen, "dared not to pay out more rope and let us rise higher."[10]

The short flight did allow Abbot to evaluate the balloon's potential as
an observation platform, but his review was decidedly mixed:

> I at once began observations and found the results rather disap-
> pointing. The view commanded a wide range of country undulat-
> ing in character, with much wooded land and interspersed open
> fields, but the motion of the balloon caused by the wind was so
> great that it was impossible to keep my field telescope directed
> upon a single object long enough to study its character, and even
> with my smaller binocular I doubted whether it would be possible
> to count the guns in a battery at any considerable range. Further-
> more, the trees so masked the fields behind them that no close esti-
> mate of the number of troops present could well be made.[11]

Abbot reported his dismal evaluation to General McDowell, adding
that the balloon's gas-generating equipment could not be depended upon
in field service.

"I am satisfied that the balloon must be filled to be advantageously
used," Abbot wrote to a commanding officer. "I am making every effort to
generate the necessary gas with our defective tanks, and still more defective
system of labor." [12]

In an attempt to salvage the situation, Abbot recommended that Allen's
balloons could still be effectively used if they were transported to Alexandria, Virginia, and inflated with the city's supply reservoir of coal gas and
then towed back to the front by a detachment of ground handlers.
McDowell approved of the plan and Allen was ordered to transport his balloons by rail to Alexandria.

Arriving in Alexandria on July 13, Allen began the inflation process early the next morning with hopes that the wind would not be as fierce as it had been on the 8th.

"The old cotton balloon was filled first," Abbot said. "But no sooner was it conducted to one site than a loud puff was heard and its fragments fell to the ground."

The balloon's collapse led a quartermaster observing the inflation to ruefully remark to Abbot, "I didn't join the Army to be a bird."

With the cotton balloon irreparably ruined, all remaining hopes were pinned on Allen's silk aerostat. The inflation of the 35,000-cubic-foot balloon consumed more than a few hours, but was successful. All that was left was to tow the balloon back to Falls Church.

Although James Allen preferred that members of the 1st Rhode Island Regiment be used in the delicate task of ground handling his balloon, they were not available. In their stead, Abbot rounded up sixty volunteers from Elmer Elsworth's New York Zouave Regiment.

The New York Zouaves were rather an appropriate choice to take on the job of towing Allen's balloon, if only for the sake of their extravagant appearance. Patterned after the French colonial armies of the period, the Zouaves were renowned for their elaborate drill exercises and even more so for their gaudy uniforms. Bright colors combined with baggy trousers, gaiters, brilliant sashes, and short, open jackets, with a fez topping off their headgear, was *de rigeur* dress of the day for the Zouaves. If their purpose as a force for warfare had not been established, they could have easily been mistaken for circus performers.

Although the Zouaves may have looked perfect for their role as balloon handlers, their effectiveness in the actual execution of the task was an altogether different matter. Trouble began almost as soon as the sixty-man detail began to maneuver the balloon down the Washington Pike.

"The wind began to rise," Abbot recalled. "And the men in their brilliant uniforms executed vigorous calisthenics as the gusts came. We worried along nearly to the point where our branch road [to Falls Church] diverged when suddenly a furious gust occurred."

The Zouaves struggled with the balloon. Caught in the heavy gusts, the balloon packed a fierce power, almost as if it were determined to wrench itself free. Eventually, the balloon overcame its handlers when it impaled itself on one of the telegraph poles that lined the Washington Pike. With a puff of gas from the ruptured envelope, James Allen's aerostat would again fail to live up to its promise. However, not everyone was disappointed by the accidental damage to the balloon.

"I rode back to Arlington, not sorry to be rid of what I had become convinced was destined to be certain failure," Abbot said afterwards. "General McDowell remarked that he was glad to be relieved from an experiment for which the means provided were so inadequate."[13]

Following the events that led to the destruction of his balloons, James Allen opted to return to Providence following the end of his ninety-day service agreement with the 1st Rhode Island. Although Allen concluded that "balloons could not be introduced into U.S. service without an entire different arrangement,"[14] the Union army's association with aeronautics was far from over.

Thaddeus and Leontine Lowe arrived in Washington on June 5, 1861, where they took up residence at the National Hotel. Despite the fact that James Allen was already at work in Washington with his balloons, this did little to discourage Lowe. On the contrary, as Allen was haphazardly pressing his balloons and equipment into action without adequate preparation, Lowe was methodically establishing a protocol and operational regimen for aeronautics that would yield better results.

Upon his arrival Lowe immediately called upon his old friend Joseph Henry at the Smithsonian and presented his plan to introduce his balloon for aerial reconnaissance. Although Lowe planned to incorporate all of the principles he had learned in his time as an aeronaut, including his recent experience with navigating the jet stream in freeflight, there was an additional element he planned to add to aerial reconnaissance in a tethered balloon that no other aeronaut had ever attempted. The telegraph.

Lowe outlined his plan to carry aloft a battery-powered telegraph key that was to be connected to the ground by a wire running along one of the tethers anchoring the balloon to the ground. The plan struck a responsive chord with Henry, as the physicist had played a prominent role in the invention of the electron magnets and relay junctions introduced into modern telegraph systems decades before.

"[Henry's] clear decisive mind grasped the idea at once," Lowe concluded. "He assured me of his cordial support and went into the work as a patriotic duty."[15]

Lowe then called upon Salmon P. Chase at the Department of the Treasury. The meeting was brief, but productive. Chase assured Lowe that he still maintained great interest in the plan and that he would take up the matter with the president personally.

Meanwhile, Professor Henry approached Secretary of War Simon Cameron on Lowe's behalf. Cameron was cautious about putting Lowe into service, especially as James Allen was still attempting to prove his mettle under General McDowell's command. Cameron requested that Henry and Lowe conduct trials and prepare a full report of the results.

Lowe grew impatient at the indifference displayed by the Washington bureaucrats. "Discouragement and difficulty attended every effort to secure attention."[16] However, through Professor Henry's perseverance, permission was given to fund limited experiments of Lowe's balloon *Enterprise* on the grounds of the Smithsonian Institution. Among those who assisted Lowe was Joseph Henry's assistant, William Jones Rhees, chief clerk at the Smithsonian.

"Lowe accordingly brought his balloon to the Smithsonian Park," Rhees later recalled. "And had connections made with the gas-mains near the Columbian [*sic*] Armory. He made repeated ascensions with a captive balloon to the height of a thousand feet between the 10th and 21st of June."[17]

After securing additional ground crew, Lowe also had the inflated balloon transported to various locations in the city to simulate the various conditions it would be subjected to in the field. During these exercises particular emphasis was placed on perfecting the means of transmitting telegraphic messages from the balloon's control car to the ground, a project that utilized Professor Henry's immense expertise.

The most crucial part of Lowe's experiment came on June 17, 1861, when the *Enterprise* was towed, fully inflated, to Pennsylvania Avenue directly across from the White House. From there Lowe prepared to ascend as a large crowd gathered to look on. Accompanying Lowe was George McDowell of the American Telegraph Company and Herbert C. Robinson, a local telegrapher. On board the *Enterprise* was a telegraph key with a wire that ran down one of the balloon's tether cables that connected directly to the telegraph relay office in Alexandria, Virginia, the War Department, and the White House.

When Lowe gave the signal, the three windlasses attached to the balloon were slowly let out and soon the *Enterprise* was more than 1,000 feet over the city. From this lofty perch Lowe dictated the following message to the president:

The telegraph message sent to Abraham Lincoln by Thaddeus Lowe from the balloon Enterprise *marked the first time in history that an electronic transmission was sent from an aerial platform to earth.* LIBRARY OF CONGRESS

Balloon *Enterprise*
In the Air
June 17, 1861

To His Excellency Abraham Lincoln, President of the United States.

Dear Sir:

From this point of observation we command an extent of country nearly fifty miles in diameter. The city, with its girdle of encampments, presents a superb scene. I have the pleasure of sending you this first telegram ever dispatched from an aerial station and acknowledging indebtedness to your encouragement for the opportunity of demonstrating the availability of the science of aeronautics in the service of the country. I am your Excellency's obedient servant.

T.S.C. Lowe[18]

Lowe's demonstration was nothing short of a masterstroke of ingenuity that was not lost on the commander in chief. After Lowe returned to earth, Lincoln, who witnessed the demonstration from the second floor of the executive mansion, invited Lowe to stay overnight at the White House. As for the *Enterprise*, it was brought to the White House grounds, where it remained prominently moored on the front lawn throughout the rest of the day and evening.

With the opportunity of a lifetime at hand, Lowe discussed with Lincoln the vast potential that aeronautics could yield to the Union war effort. Lincoln listened intently as Lowe outlined his plan for an Aeronautical Corps that not only could survey battlefields and enemy troop positions, but also, with the use of the telegraph, could even direct ground artillery to targets that gunners could not see.

"We talked till late into the night," Lowe said of the meeting. "We then retired—he wearied with the cares of State, and I almost too excited to sleep, so enthused was I at the prospect of being directed to form a new branch of the military service."[19]

The following morning Lowe had breakfast with the president. Afterwards, Lincoln called in his secretary and dictated a letter of introduction on Lowe's behalf to Lt. Gen. Winfield Scott, the general in chief of the Union army. With the endorsement of the president behind him, Lowe was certain that aeronautics had finally come of age.

Abraham Lincoln was an early proponent in using balloons to gather reconnaissance information after witnessing Thaddeus Lowe's demonstration in Washington, D.C. PHOTOGRAPHIC HISTORY OF THE CIVIL WAR

Lowe's confidence was reinforced over the next few days as reports of his success with the aerial telegraph was widely reported in a number of Northern newspapers.

"Doubtless with the aid of powerful telescopes, the use of this balloon will enable the commander of a force to inspect thoroughly the interior of works opposed to him," read one article in the Washington *Evening Star.* "To know instantly any movements of the enemy; and that, too, without the slightest danger to those making the observations."[20]

The New York *Herald* reported, "With this telegraph apparatus and the means of making an aerial reconnaissance, a general may be accurately informed of everything that may be going on within a long day's march of his position in any direction."[21]

On June 21 Joseph Henry made his report to Secretary of War Simon Cameron concerning the results of Lowe's balloon experiments. Henry's conclusions were extremely favorable toward Lowe's efforts:

Smithsonian Institution
June 21, 1861

To the Hon. Simon Cameron,
Dear Sir:
In accordance with your request made to me orally on the morning of the 5th of June, I have examined the apparatus and witnessed

the balloon experiments of Mr. Lowe, and have come to the following conclusions:

1st. The balloon prepared by Mr. Lowe, inflated with ordinary street gas [coal gas], will retain its charge for several days.

2nd. In an inflated condition it can be towed by a few men along an ordinary road, over fields in ordinarily calm weather, from the places where it is filled, to another 20 or more miles distant.

3rd. It can be let up into the air by means of a rope, on a calm day, to a height sufficient to observe the country for 20 miles around or more, according to the degree of clearness of the atmosphere. The ascent may also be made at night and the camp lights of the enemy observed.

4th. From experiments made here by Professor Lowe, for the first time in history, it is conclusively proved that telegrams can be sent with ease and certainty between the balloon and the quarters of the commanding officer.

5th. I feel assured, although I have not witnessed the experiment, that when the surface wind is from the east, as it was for several days last week, an observer in the balloon can be made to float nearly to the enemy's camp (as it is now situated to the west of us) or even float over it and then return eastward by rising to a higher elevation.

This assumption is based on the fact that the upper strata of wind in this latitude is always flowing eastward. Mr. Lowe informs me, and I do not doubt his statement, that he will, on any day which is favorable, make an excursion of the kind mentioned above.

6th. From all the facts I have observed, and the information I have gathered, I am sure that important information can be obtained in regard to the topography of the country, and to the position and movement of the enemy, by means of the balloon, and that Mr. Lowe is well qualified to render service in this way by the balloon now in his possession.

7th. The balloon which Mr. Lowe now has in Washington can only be inflated in a city where street gas is to be obtained. If an exploration is required at a point distant from the transportation of the inflated balloon, an additional apparatus for the generation of hydrogen gas will be required. The necessity of generating the gas renders the use of the balloon more expensive, but this, where important results are required, is of comparatively small importance.

From these preliminary experiments, as you may recollect, a sum not to exceed two hundred or two hundred and fifty dollars was to be appropriated, and in accordance with this, Mr. Lowe has presented me the enclosed statement of items, which I think are reasonable, since nothing is charged for labor and time of the aeronaut.

I have the honor to remain,

Very respectfully, Your Obedient Servant,

Joseph Henry,

Secretary, Smithsonian Institution.[22]

Even though Lowe had secured the endorsement of Washington's highest civilian authorities, convincing the military of the practicality of using balloons as a part of frontline reconnaissance was a challenge in its own right. By the time Lowe met with Lincoln, James Allen's balloons had already failed to make any contribution to military intelligence at the battle of Harpers Ferry and reports of the aeronaut's ongoing equipment problems were widely known. The arrival of yet another unproven aeronaut, who would potentially divert men and resources from the war effort, met with some resistance.

"It is almost impossible to realize to what extent ignorance sometimes finds lodgement in high places," Lowe said. "Doubtless every inventor, every man who has a new idea, is destined to make a desperate fight for the life of his special ambition."

However, on June 21, the day Joseph Henry sent his report to Secretary of War Cameron, Lowe received a telegram from Capt. Amiel Whipple of the Union Army Bureau of Topographical Engineers. Whipple was Lt. Henry Abbot's supervising officer during the experiments with James Allen's balloons. Captain Whipple directed Lowe to bring his balloon and the aerial telegraph apparatus to Arlington, Virginia.

The *Enterprise* required reinflation, but a delay caused by the Washington Gas Company kept Lowe from complying with the directive until the following afternoon. After it was inflated the balloon was taken by a small detachment across the Long Bridge to Arlington House, where Lowe and the balloon remained until the following morning. At 4 A.M. on June 22, Lowe was ordered to proceed to Falls Church.

At the junction of the Alexandria & Loudoun Railroad, the *Enterprise* was carefully tethered to a flat car. The rail route to Falls Church passed through a dense forest. Lowe asked the depot guards if there was any known Confederate activity ahead. The guards answered there was not, but Lowe decided to make a tethered ascent to determine if it was safe to proceed. Once satisfied the route was clear, the balloon was reeled back in and the train began its journey.

After traveling two miles the train stopped briefly at Bailey's Cross-Roads. There, Lowe was informed by residents that a Rebel scouting party was in the area, but left when they saw the balloon. Despite the fact that the detachment assigned to Lowe numbered less than twenty men, the Confederates assumed that the balloon would be accompanied by a "large force."[23]

At Falls Church Lowe reported that the *Enterprise* "was kept in constant use for two days." Captain Whipple made several ascents during this period, and Maj. Ledyard Colburn of the 2nd Connecticut Volunteers was also sent aloft and "sketched a fine map of the surrounding country and observed the movements of the enemy."[24] When the map was shown to some Union volunteers, "who were familiar with the vicinity of the Fairfax Court House, [they] at once recognized it, and the roads, lanes, stream, and dwellings." Just as important was the discovery of Rebels encamped at the Fairfax Court House.[25]

Although Lowe knew that his field demonstration was successful, he did not realize the full extent of the impression he made upon some commanders in the field. Major Colburn's commanding officer, Brig. Gen. Daniel Tyler, was a skeptic of balloon reconnaissance until he received the map made during the ascent on June 23.

"I have not been much of a convert to ballooning in military operations," Tyler said in his report to General McDowell. "But the last ascent made by Major Colburn . . . and map of the country, rough as it is . . . convince me that a balloon may at times greatly assist military movements."[26]

Lowe returned to Washington on June 25. The following day he was informed by Captain Whipple that the Bureau of Topographical Engineers was prepared to adopt the balloon for reconnaissance purposes. Whipple also requested that Lowe "furnish a full account of the method of operating the balloons in the field, and to make estimates for their construction, etc."[27] Lowe complied, but the next day when Lowe called upon Whipple he was informed that it had been decided to give the contract to build the balloons to another aeronaut who had submitted an estimate to build balloons for $100 to $200 less than Lowe.

The rival aeronaut was John Wise.

It was not Wise's original intention to offer his services to the Union army as an aeronaut or balloon builder. At the outbreak of hostilities in April, 1861, Wise was busy in his hometown of Lancaster, Pennsylvania, drilling a company of volunteers for the war effort. In May, 1861, Wise wrote to Secretary of War Cameron, "I am forming a company here of picked men now nearly full and well drilled in the rifle manual. These men would serve for three or five years . . . Would such a company be acceptable?"[28]

Cameron's response came a month later and was not quite what Wise expected. As Wise later recalled, "When the war . . . broke out, Cameron . . . wanted me to make a trial of the balloon as a means of reconnaissance."[29] Wise's reputation as the nation's foremost aeronaut obviously influenced Cameron's decision to engage Wise's expertise in the matter of aeronautics—especially with James Allen and Thaddeus Lowe already in Washington.

It is also probable that Wise's treatise on the aerial bombardment of Veracruz written during the Mexican War had resurfaced and was given serious consideration. At any rate, Cameron directed Maj. Hartman Bache, the acting chief of the Union Army Bureau of Topographical Engineers, to get in contact with Wise.

Major Bache was an appropriate choice to investigate the possibility of incorporating aeronautics within the Topographical Bureau, as he was also a grandson of the same Benjamin Franklin who had foreseen the use of balloons in warfare eighty years before. Bache sent a telegram to Wise on June 12 asking for the estimated cost of a balloon with 500 pounds of lift and the amount of pay Wise would expect to operate it. Wise immediately replied that a balloon fitting Bache's description would cost $300. As for operating the balloon, Wise declared his services would be provided "gratis, in the cause of the Union."[30]

Nearly two weeks passed before Bache was in contact with Wise again. Following Thaddeus Lowe's demonstration in Washington and limited field service at Falls Church, Bache turned to Captain Whipple for his assessment. After witnessing Lowe's trials, Whipple believed that Bache's minimum requirement for a balloon capable of 500 pounds of lifting power was not large enough. On June 26, Bache telegraphed Wise requesting a cost estimate for a 20,000 cubic foot balloon capable of carrying over 1,200 pounds aloft. Wise sent his reply the same day, stating that such a balloon would cost $850 and take two weeks to construct. Wise added that the cost of building the balloon was based entirely on the cost of the materials alone, and that he had no "desire to make profit on a war balloon, but earnestly wished to introduce a mean of Topographical and Hydrographical Engineering into governmental use that is not appreciated, even if known, to the engineering world." [31]

It was with this information that Captain Whipple told Thaddeus Lowe on June 26 that his services as a balloon builder would not be required. Whipple, however, was still impressed with Lowe's organizational skills and expertise in handling balloons in the field. He reportedly told the young aeronaut, "that it was possible [he] might be employed to operate the balloon after it was made."[32]

Lowe responded to Whipple's suggestion with great indignation. "To the latter part of his remarks I replied that I would not be willing to expose my life and reputation by using so delicate a machine, where the utmost care in construction is required, which should be made by a person in whom I had no confidence. I assured him that I had greater experience in this business than any other aeronaut, and that I would guarantee the success of the enterprise if entrusted entirely to my directions."[33]

Although Lowe felt that the decision to go with Wise's balloon was a setback to his cause, he did not feel it was an absolute defeat. "Feeling confident of the ultimate results, and not being willing to abandon my cherished plans for the benefit of the Government after so much expenditure of time and my own means, I instituted a series of experiments, on my own account, in the Smithsonian grounds, which brought together many officers and scientific men, who strongly recommended the adoption of my system of aeronautics."[34]

The bitter seeds sown during the intense rivalry between the aeronauts during the earlier transatlantic attempts were now resurfacing and developing into a full-scale feud. While Lowe acknowledged that Wise, "had won considerable distinction in his profession," he ultimately concluded that the only "argument advanced in favor of Mr. Wise was that being much older than I, he must know more."[35] And while James Allen would soon be eliminated from the competition to direct the course of the nascent aeronautical corps, another aerialist soon entered the picture.

John La Mountain, Wise's erstwhile partner in the failed *Atlantic* venture, also petitioned war secretary Cameron for an appointment as an offi-

cial aeronaut. La Mountain was no less confident in his abilities to serve the
Union when he wrote:

> The undersigned begs leave to present to your attention the subject
> of employing in connection with the military movements, a com-
> petent aeronaut, and to offer his services in that direction.[36]

In his letter La Mountain also maintained that ballooning "demonstrated
. . . perfect practicality . . . when conducted in accordance with the principles of science."[37] La Mountain was also certain to back up his claim as a
"skillful balloonist" by including a petition signed by a number of prominent
citizens of Troy, New York, who hailed the aeronaut, "as one of the most
scientific balloonists in the country . . . and . . . a gentleman of thorough
practical information, upright, honest, and indefatigable, and one who may
be relied on to perform all promises, when performance is possible."[38]

La Mountain also acknowledged the disadvantage that balloons had
when in service far from city gas works, but offered his own solution:

> I have a portable apparatus of my own invention and used solely by
> myself, with which I can manufacture gas for inflation from the
> decomposition of water, at a barely nominal rate of expense. This,
> with balloons and appurtenance necessary could be carried in a sin-
> gle wagon with the train of the army and gas could be generated
> and the balloons filled at a few hours notice whenever there was
> coke or charcoal and water.
>
> This is the only apparatus of the kind in the world. No other
> aeronaut can fill his globe [envelope] except where gas works are
> located, without carrying an immense and cumbersome quantity of
> material as to interfere with the celerity of conveyance, and there-
> fore render his services impracticable.[39]

Unlike Lowe and Wise, La Mountain didn't receive a response from
Cameron. A month later, however, La Mountain received a letter from
Gen. Benjamin Butler, commander of Union forces headquartered at
Fortress Monroe in Virginia. Butler was desperate for reliable intelligence
reports. He had underestimated the strength of Confederate forces during
an engagement at Big Bethel, Virginia, and was grasping for any straw that
would salvage his tarnished command. When he learned of La Mountain's

offer of service to Cameron he quickly seized on the opportunity to press the balloonist into action.

Playing to La Mountain's ego Butler wrote that he believed that the aeronaut's contributions would be, "of the greatest importance" and, "cannot fail to prove of much benefit."[40] Moreover, Butler even promised to use his influence at the War Department to secure La Mountain a commission should the experiments prove to be successful. The aeronaut was quick to submit his reply:

> Your letter of the 5th is received. I accept with pleasure your kind proposal. I will have my balloons and apparatus in readiness to start for your headquarters by the first of next week. I will bring with me two balloons together with my complete apparatus.[41]

While La Mountain neglected to mention it in his letter to Butler, he also decided to bring along two assistants with him from Troy.

Meanwhile, Thaddeus Lowe was still snarled in his attempts to make headway with his efforts in Washington. In addition to this, the news that John La Mountain was on his way to Virginia had reached Lowe by late June and it was not well received.

"Mr. La Mountain was simply a balloonist," Lowe said of his rival. "[He] had neither the least idea of the requirements of military ballooning or the gift of invention."[42]

Rivalries among balloonists aside, the Union army faced greater challenges in July, 1861. When hostilities broke out in April the great enlistment drives that drew thousands of young volunteers to the ranks of the various state regiments that served alongside the Regular army were limited to service terms of only three months. By late July and early August, many of these original enlistees would be discharged from military service. The possibility of thousands of soldiers going back home and depleting the ranks forced military leaders in Washington to face the imminent emasculation of the Union army.

Of equal concern was a vocal public sentiment in the North pushing for a swift campaign that would crush the Rebels in a sweeping blow. Union newspapers and politicians took up the battle cry: "Onward To Richmond!" with a fervor that pressured for decisive military action. While there were protests within senior army ranks that most of the officers and men were still too green to enter into a major offensive, the decision was made to strike the Confederacy a crippling blow at the rail junction of Manassas, Virginia.

General McDowell planned to lead an attack force of 30,600 men in an assault against the Confederate general Pierre Gustave Toutant Beauregard and his 20,000 men that were occupying a defensive line along the Bull Run creek, five miles to the north of Manassas. Beauregard was one of the first bona fide heroes of the South, having pulverized the Union army's defenses at Fort Sumter with the opening bombardment of the war.

McDowell realized that he was ill-prepared to engage the Confederates in battle. Not only saddled with an inexperienced force, McDowell was also compromised by poor logistical support. When given his assignment, the general didn't even have up-to-date maps of Virginia.

Reconnaissance became a crucial element in the attack. Although scouts and spies on the ground had already determined the size and general location of Beauregard's forces, an aerial view would pinpoint the precise locations and strengths of the opposing force. There was hope that the first actual test of a military balloon in action would bring McDowell's army an added dimension in intelligence gathering.

John Wise had actually completed work on his balloon on July 16. On July 17 he received a telegram from Captain Whipple inquiring how soon he could be in Washington with his equipment. McDowell's troops were already beginning their advance on Centreville, near Beauregard's forces at Bull Run, and the aeronaut's services were desperately required.

Wise left for Washington on July 17 with his son Charles and arrived the following day. Wise found the situation somewhat chaotic. Whipple had already left with McDowell's army and left no immediate instruction for the aeronaut. "I found it impossible to see the Secretary [of War], but the matter was referred to General [Winfield] Scott," Wise said. "He in turn referred me to the Bureau of Topographical Engineers."[43]

On July 19, Wise received a telegram from Whipple at Centreville. "I received an order to inflate the balloon from the Washington gas works, and when filled proceed to Centreville."[44]

Wise's balloon was brought to the gas main near the Columbia Armory, where it was discovered that Thaddeus Lowe was already at work inflating the *Enterprise*. Whipple in fact had played both sides of the fence when it came to the two aeronauts. When it was uncertain whether John Wise would arrive in Washington in time to meet up with McDowell's troops, Whipple had contacted Lowe as a standby.

"I was suddenly required by Captain Whipple to fill my balloon and transport it to the interior of Virginia," Lowe said. "I . . . set about making the proper preparations for the voyage . . . and I was ready to start [but] I was unable, on account of the absence of Captain Whipple, to procure the men and means for the inflation and transportation."[45]

Although Lowe lacked authorization, he had proceeded to inflate his balloon believing that he would be able to round up enough volunteer ground handlers to transport it to McDowell's headquarters. However, when Wise appeared, Lowe was reluctantly forced to abandon his plans.

"To my disappointment, I was informed by the director of the gas company that another balloon had arrived and was to be used instead of mine," Lowe said. "On receipt of this information I removed my balloon from the inflating pipes, to give place to the other balloon, and ceased all other efforts."[46]

With Lowe forced to cede his place, Wise and his son quickly set to work. They carefully unfolded the new balloon and connected it to the armory's gas main. The balloon's envelope was made up of 450 yards of raw Indian silk, twice the normal thickness of most balloon silk since it was intended for military service. The balloon's netting and cordage were of fine linen fashioned from Italian flax thread, while the hoops that suspended the rigging for the control basket were made of hickory wrapped with linen cord and sealed with fish glue. For the control basket, traditional willow and cane construction was used with sheet armor plating added to the floor to protect the occupants from ground fire.

Wise also devised measures to keep the balloon from falling into enemy hands. As part of the balloon's ballast there were a number of percussion grenades and bombs. If Confederate forces were to overrun the position where the balloon was moored, Wise could rain down a barrage of explosives and then sever the tethering cables and float off with the hope that a favorable wind would carry the balloon to Union lines.[47]

With his balloon completely inflated, Wise was ready to proceed to Centreville. However, orders were delayed in providing Wise with an army detail to transport the balloon and it wasn't until after midnight on July 20 that an escort of twenty-two men and a wagon arrived under the direction of Maj. Albert J. Myer to begin the twenty-five mile journey.

"The progress of towing the balloon over canal, telegraph wires, through woods and over creeks made it a tedious business," Wise later recalled. "By noon of the day of the battle we had not got halfway."[48]

After crossing the Potomac and coming to Fairfax Road, the balloon detachment could hear the sounds of battle growing louder as they approached. By this time the balloon was fastened to the horsedrawn wagon, which was ballasted with supplies.

"The rattling of infantry and thundering of artillery greeted our train," said Wise. "It created so much excitement and animation in our command as to hurry onward the balloon."[49]

Indeed, as the party neared its objective Major Myer became impatient to reach the scene of the battle. Against Wise's better judgment, Myer ordered the wagon master to whip the mules into a trot. Almost immediately the balloon became snagged in the upper branches of some roadside trees. When Myer ordered his men to try to force it free, larger holes were torn in the bag.[50]

"The balloon swaying to and fro as it was hurled along brought it heavily against the branches of a tree, which so damaged it as to render it useless by the time we could reach the headquarters of General McDowell," said Wise.[51]

Myer ordered that the balloon return to Washington for repairs.

Thaddeus Lowe learned about the fate of Wise's balloon on Sunday, July 21. By this time, the battle at Centreville was in its full fury. More troops were thrown into the fray from both sides. Beauregard's troops were joined by reinforcements from Gen. Joseph E. Johnston, and the combined army was successful in repulsing McDowell's initial advances. Not long after, additional Confederate troops under the command of Thomas "Stonewall" Jackson appeared. Reports of the beleaguered Union army were rapidly filtering into Washington.

"Urged by several patriotic individuals, and still hoping to render some service to the Army at Centreville or Manassas, I commenced on Sunday morning to make preparations for inflating and transporting my balloon," Lowe said. By evening, Lowe was on his way, assisted by a detachment of some twenty men, some of whom had aided in John Wise's ill-fated attempt to reach the front.

"Unfortunately, when we arrived at Falls Church I was informed of the retreat of the Army," Lowe noted. In fact, the Union army was completely routed and in disarray as remnants of McDowell's forces, mixed in with civilian sightseers from Washington who had ventured out to witness what they hoped would be the spectacle of a Confederate defeat, were now clogging the roads leading back to the capital. In all of the confusion swirling around him, Lowe elected to remain in Arlington with his inflated balloon, hoping that he would be able to gain information regarding the approach of the enemy.

A severe rainstorm erupted that Sunday evening, adding to the disorderly retreat. Lowe remained at Falls Church until the following afternoon. Despite a tremendous wind that buffeted the *Enterprise*, Lowe managed to safely maneuver the balloon overland until he and his escort reached Fort Corcorran, twenty miles north of Falls Church. Despite the lengthy journey under the most severe conditions, Lowe's balloon remained remarkably intact and still charged with the gas he obtained in Washington two days before.

On Wednesday morning the weather cleared, allowing Lowe to ascend from inside the fort. Although the gas in the balloon's envelope had depleted to the point where it could carry no more than 500 pounds aloft, it was more than enough for Lowe.

"I obtained an altitude of about three and one-half miles," Lowe later reported. "[I] had a distinct view of the encampments of the enemy, and observed them in motion between Manassas Junction and Fairfax."

Lowe was only able to accomplish the one ascent, as there were no gas facilities at Fort Corcorran that could recharge the *Enterprise*. Yet, the flight proved, at least in Lowe's mind, that a properly managed balloon could render useful service in adverse situations.

On his return to Washington, Lowe became increasingly impatient over the lack of military recognition for his achievements. He felt that his experimental ascent around Washington and the field demonstrations at Falls Church and Fort Corcorran vindicated his belief that he should be appointed superintendent of the army's aeronautical corps.

"I have accomplished all I have undertaken without a single failure," Lowe wrote to Hartman Bache, at the Topographical Bureau. "With very imperfect means and with scarcely any aid from the Government . . . I can truly say that I have not, . . . been governed by a desire for pecuniary gain, but I have been actuated by a wish to increase my reputation and advance the art to which I have devoted my life, by demonstrating the importance [of balloon observation] to the country in its present critical condition."[52]

Lowe's impatience spilled over into suspicions that government officials were still playing favorites with other aeronauts who had not measured up to the task as he had. He held John Wise and John La Mountain in particular contempt.

"Both of [these] aeronauts had backing of one kind or another and both assiduously courted the attention of whatever officer of the Topographical Engineers happened for the time being to be in charge. . . .

"Without a doubt there were influences of some kind holding back the decision [to appoint an official aeronaut]," Lowe said. "These delays were maddening. Inquiry was made every hour and I was chafing to get into action."[53]

Lowe had made the rounds at the War Department and Gen. Winfield Scott's headquarters to no avail. Despite having a letter of introduction from Lincoln, the chief of the army refused to even meet with the aeronaut. Finally, Joseph Henry again interceded with the president on Lowe's behalf. On July 25, Lowe received a message from Lincoln to spend the evening at the White House.

Through Joseph Henry, Lincoln was aware of the difficulties that were confronting Lowe and his upward struggles with military bureaucracy.

"He had hoped that the letter of introduction . . . to General Scott would have so clearly indicated to the General the president's desire in the matter," Lowe said. "But Lincoln was not willing to leave any stone unturned that might aid in crushing the rebellion."

Seated at an old table in the Oval Office, Lincoln became pensive the more he spoke with Lowe. The defeat at the battle of Bull Run, as the press was now calling it, had exacted a heavy toll on Union forces. Four hundred and eighteen Union soldiers had lost their lives, and the wounded and the missing numbered 2,000 more. Morale had been shattered and the capital itself was in peril of falling into Confederate hands.

According to Lowe, Lincoln "expressed the thought that had General McDowell had the information that only observations from a balloon could give, the result might have been different."[54]

Looking up at Lowe, the president said, "Professor, I wish you would confer with General Scott again at once."[55] Then, taking up a pen and a sheet of paper he scrawled the following note:

Will Lieut Genl. Scott please see Professor Lowe once more about his balloon?

> [Signed] A. Lincoln
> July 25, 1861[56]

Again, Lowe swelled with renewed confidence.

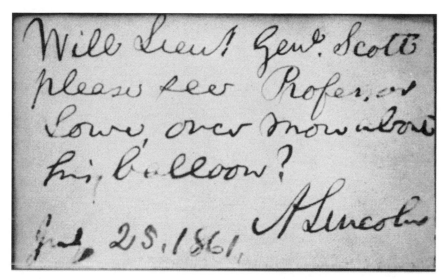

Lincoln's note to Gen. Winfield Scott. NATIONAL AIR & SPACE MUSEUM

"The first time I called on General Scott it was at the behest of the president that I might lay my plans before him for his consideration," Lowe thought to himself. "But there was no mistaking the intent of the message I now carried though clothed in the gentle language so characteristic of Lincoln."[57]

Thaddeus Lowe's long journey through the ranks of indifference, however, was not quite over yet. The next morning, Lowe went to Scott's headquarters in the War Department Building, where he met the general's orderly and presented his note from the president. The soldier looked Lowe over carefully and told him that Scott was in a meeting and could not be interrupted. Lowe was told to come back in two hours.

Two hours later Lowe returned and was met by the same orderly. This time the soldier left Lowe waiting for a few moments. He then returned to report that the general was still in a meeting and could Lowe return later. Lowe reluctantly complied.

Lowe again arrived at Scott's headquarters and was met by Scott's orderly for a third time. This time Lowe was told that Scott was now having lunch and could not be disturbed. Again, Lowe was told to leave and to come back later.

The routine began to grow very old by the time Lowe arrived back at the general's headquarters for the fourth time. Once again, Lowe was met

Gen. Winfield Scott was among those in the Union army who felt that aeronautics had no place in the military. The 75-year-old general reluctantly agreed to give Lowe and his balloons a trial only after Abraham Lincoln reportedly intervened on the aeronaut's behalf.

PHOTOGRAPHIC HISTORY OF THE CIVIL WAR

by the orderly who now informed Lowe that General Scott was taking a nap, and could not be disturbed for any reason. Would Lowe return the next day?

Lowe decided that enough was enough and that he couldn't wait any longer. Lowe returned to the White House.

"All this time the president was awaiting the results of my conference with General Scott," Lowe said. "With some heat, possibly, I reported that General Scott could not be seen on official business even at the president's suggestion, he looked at me for a moment, laughed, arose and seizing his tall silk hat bade me 'come on.' He proposed to find out what was the matter with Scott."[58]

According to Lowe, Lincoln called for a carriage and moments later the president and the aeronaut were on their way to the War Department Building. As soon as they reached the general's office, the sentry at the door called out "The President of the United States." The same orderly, who had rebuffed Lowe before, quickly emerged from the office.

Upon entering, Lincoln and Lowe discovered that the old general seemed rather startled by the unexpected visit.

"General," Lincoln began. "This is my friend Professor Lowe, who is organizing an Aeronautics Corps for the Army, and is to be its Chief. I wish you would facilitate his work in every way, and give him a letter to Admiral Dahlgram [*sic*], Commandant of the Navy Yard, and one to Captain Meigs, with instructions for them to give him all the necessary things to equip his branch of the service on land and water."[59]

Lowe noted the sudden change in atmosphere as General Scott directed his orderly to comply with the president's directive. With official letters in hand, Lowe returned to the White House with Lincoln, secure in the knowledge that he was now the "Chief of the Corps of Aeronautics of the United States Army."[60]

However, as Lowe was to point out in later years, "My troubles had barely begun, so cumbersome was the official machinery, so interwoven the bands of *red tape*."[61]

CHAPTER FIVE

Early Operations

Thaddeus Lowe worked quickly to consolidate his role as chief aeronaut of the Union army following his meeting with Lincoln and General Scott in late July. However, the president did not go so far as to grant official military status to the Union army Aeronautical Corps, as Lowe named the new service, nor did Lowe receive a military commission. The "Corps"—which would be redubbed the "Balloon Corps" by the press—was a civilian unit attached to the Union Army Bureau of Topographical Engineers and was subject to the favor and whim of anyone who had authority over the Aeronautical Corps's services at any given time.

In the early months of the war Lowe managed to capture the imagination of the public and, more importantly, prominent Washington officials. The plucky young aeronaut was able to push his role as chief aeronaut as far as the title would allow. Circumstances also played in Lowe's favor during this time. The city of Washington was gripped in panic following the rout of the Union army at Bull Run. Rumors were rampant that the Confederates planned to storm the capital at any time. Reliable intelligence was necessary to calm these fears and Lowe's services were urgently needed. With renewed zeal, Lowe threw himself into a new round of balloon observations.

One flight made during the final week of July, 1861, was fraught with high drama. Lowe decided that he would attempt a freeflight voyage starting from Arlington House[1] in Virginia and continuing over Confederate positions.

"I started soon after sunrise while the atmosphere was clear," said Lowe. "And sailed directly over the country occupied by the enemy as the lower current was blowing toward from the west. Having seen what I desired I rose to the upper current and commenced moving toward the east again, until over the Potomac, when I commenced to descend, thinking that the under-current would take me back far enough to land near Arlington House."[2]

As Lowe's balloon settled near the earth, gunfire erupted from the ground. Union troops who were not aware of the aeronaut's mission, or his allegiance, opened fire on the *Enterprise*.

"I descended near enough to hear the whistling of the bullets and the shouts of the soldiers to 'show my colors.'" Unfortunately, Lowe had neglected to take a Union flag along with him.

"Knowing that if I attempted to effect a landing there, my balloon and very likely myself would be riddled, I concluded to sail on and to risk descending outside of our lines."

Lowe realized the jeopardy he was placing himself in. If captured the Rebels would be well within their rights to execute him as a spy. Yet, Lowe reasoned he was faced with few choices as he sailed deeper into Confederate territory. He had dropped his remaining ballast, which ruled out another ascent into the easterly air current that could have brought him back to safety. Up ahead he spotted a wooded glen that would at least provide some degree of camouflage. Over the densest portion of the woods, he valved off the balloon's remaining gas.

Below, the tall trees tore into the silk envelope, preventing the basket from touching the ground. Lowe leapt from the basket, landing hard and spraining his ankle in the process. In tremendous pain he furiously pulled at the entwined material and was eventually able to stow the remnants of the balloon in the control basket.

Although well concealed in the dense woods, Lowe's situation was not enviable. He was 5 1/2 miles from Alexandria and more than 2 miles from the Union's frontline. His injured ankle, which made it painful to attempt to walk even a few steps, compounded his woes. Faced with no better alternative, Lowe remained quiet as he awaited the coming evening.

Fortunately for Lowe, his wife, Leontine, had accompanied him to Arlington House. She had watched his progress throughout the morning through the lens of a powerful telescope and witnessed his landing several miles beyond Union pickets. Despite her fears that the worst was in store for her husband, Leontine maintained a level composure and began to put together a plan of rescue.

Volunteers from the 31st New York Regiment offered to assist Leontine, and scouts went on ahead behind enemy lines to locate the aeronaut. When the scouts returned they told Leontine that Lowe was in a dense thicket on the edge of Mason's Plantation. It would be impossible to direct a detail of men to the location and affect a rescue without coming into conflict with the Rebels.

Undaunted, Leontine made the decision to go it alone. She disguised herself as a farm woman and requested a horse and wagon with instructions on how to get to Mason's Plantation. Under the cover of darkness she left on her mission.

Against tremendous odds, Leontine succeeded in finding Lowe. They both managed to load the damaged balloon in the back of the wagon, where Lowe also remained concealed. As Lowe later recalled:

Mrs. Lowe led the horse and wagon out from the woods as nonchalantly as she had entered. As she reached the roadway, she clearly discerned the outlines of several figures and was conscious that curious eyes were watching her.

Fortunately the descent of the balloon had been hidden from the eyes of the enemy's pickets by the woods so Mrs. Lowe was not accosted and reached the Union Lines without molestation.[3]

Despite his harrowing experience, Thaddeus Lowe did not earn much respite when he returned to Washington. He angrily sent a statement to the War Department declaring that the Confederates did not possess balloons and that Federal troops in the field should be so notified. "Air vessels seen thus far, and probably all that will be seen hereafter, are for Union purposes," Lowe stated bluntly.[4]

On July 29, a telegram was delivered to Lowe at the National Hotel. It was from Captain Whipple, who was still in Arlington:

If you will at once repair your balloon, and will superintend its transportation to this side of the Potomac, the U.S. will employ you temporarily as follows:

The U.S. will pay for the gas used for the inflation; will furnish twenty men to manage the balloon; will pay thirty dollars per day each day the balloon is in use for reconnaissance on the Virginia side of the Potomac. The balloon [is] to be ready for use within twenty-four hours.[5]

Whipple's note was not met with great enthusiasm by Lowe, particularly after his brush with near disaster. First of all, Whipple's offer of remuneration was unsatisfactory, given the fact that it was to be paid only when the balloon was actually used. Although Lowe was adamant that he did not want to profit ungainly for his services, he also felt that his time was valuable and that a regular schedule of compensation was more in order. Lowe informed Whipple that he would be willing to work for, "ten dollars a day"—the equivalent salary of a fully commissioned Union colonel—and that he "would guarantee entire success."[6]

Furthermore, the *Enterprise* was severely damaged and required extensive repair. The balloon was never designed for rigorous military service and, as John Wise had pointed out earlier, Lowe suggested to Whipple that a new balloon be constructed specifically for the purpose of reconnaissance in the field.

In the meantime, however, Lowe carried out repairs to the *Enterprise* in an attempt to comply with Whipple's directive to have the balloon ready for service. Working under duress, the repairs were hastily completed and the envelope inflated. Lowe then rounded up yet another "inexperienced" detail to transport his balloon to Arlington.

Once on the road to Arlington a heavy storm blew in. The detail struggled to control the balloon as it was gripped in the fierce wind. Lowe was no doubt aware that James Allen had lost one of his balloons on the same road just a few weeks earlier under similar conditions. Not wishing to see his repair efforts come to naught, Lowe decided to abort the mission, release the gas from the *Enterprise*, and return to Washington.

"This was an unlooked for calamity," Lowe said afterwards. "But a situation over which I had no control, and one which gave the enemies of the Aeronautic Corps an opening wedge . . . Captain Whipple went so far as to say that the operations with war balloons would be given up."[7]

Indeed, Captain Whipple wrote to the Bureau of Topographical Engineers that, "Lowe's balloon filled at our expense has burst. I wish nothing more to do with it."[8] Although Whipple did not have authority to make a final decision to suspend Lowe's activity, as field supervisor of balloon operations his opinion carried a lot of weight. Less than a week after Lowe was given permission to forge ahead with his Aeronautical Corps by Abraham Lincoln himself, the entire scheme of military ballooning was in real danger of being scrapped.

In Whipple's defense, his frustration with military ballooning was completely understandable given its recent history. After the Bureau of

Topographical Engineers's experiences with both James Allen and John Wise, Whipple felt certain that Lowe would complete a trio of failures. However, Whipple underestimated Lowe's resolve in proving his ability to overcome adversity.

Lowe once again enlisted the aid of Joseph Henry at the Smithsonian. On August 2, Henry drafted a letter to Whipple with the hopes that Lowe would be given permission to carry on:

> I regret very much to learn from Mr. Lowe that you think of giving up the balloon operations, and I write to express the hope that you will make further attempts. A single successful observation will fully repay all that you have yet expended.
>
> The experiment of Wednesday was rendered abortive by the accidental occurrence of a thunder-storm which could not be foreseen. At this season of the year thunder-storms occur generally in the after part of the day or night, and I would therefore advise that the balloon be filled immediately after the clearing off of the sky, and then used as soon as possible after daylight the next day.
>
> Mr. Lowe came to this city with the implied understanding that, if the experiments he exhibited to me were successful, he would be employed. He has labored under great disadvantages, and has been obliged to do all that he has done, after the first experiments, without money. From the first he has said that the balloon he now has was not sufficiently strong to bear the pressure of a hard wind, although it might be used with success in favorable situations and in perfectly calm weather.
>
> I hope that you will not yet give up the experiments, and that you will be enabled with even this balloon to do enough to prove the importance of this method of observation, and to warrant the construction of a balloon better adapted to the purpose.
>
> I remain, very truly, your obedient servant,
> Joseph Henry[9]

Henry's letter evidently succeeded in greasing the right wheels. Lowe was granted an appointment with Maj. Hartman Bache at the Bureau of Topographical Engineers's headquarters. Although Bache was sympathetic to Lowe's cause, the aeronaut sensed that a passive attitude would not bring results. Lowe brought with him a list of his observations in the field and his accomplishments over the past two months since arriving in Washington, and reminded the Bureau Chief that he performed all of these services, "without recompense."

Lowe explained in his report that additional balloons were necessary to sustain the number of ascents required to make aerial observations useful.

"It is very probable that balloons will be wanted for some time to come in the vicinity of Washington and Alexandria to watch the movements of the enemy and prevent a surprise," Lowe wrote. "While the army is making preparation for another movement a lighter balloon . . . can be constructed in time to move with the troops, and be ready before and during an engagement to furnish the means of observations of the greatest importance."

To make field use of balloons more practical, especially when military operations were located far away from city gas supplies, Lowe pounded in the message that portable gas generators were a vital key to any successful results that aeronautics might yield. Lowe wasn't the only aeronaut to bring up the subject of gas generators in the field. James Allen brought equipment with him from Rhode Island, which unfortunately proved a dismal failure, while John Wise had been asked by Major Bache earlier for an estimate on procuring such an apparatus. However, when Wise brought back an estimate from Morris & Company in Philadelphia of "about seven thousand dollars," plans for the device were quickly abandoned on the grounds, "that it cost too much."[10]

Lowe, on the other hand, had been working on a portable gas generator of his own design since his arrival in Washington.

"Having made the necessary inquiries, I find that the apparatus can be constructed by mechanics now in the Government employ in Washington," Lowe told Bache. "The whole weight of the material to inflate the balloon for several days' use will not exceed four tons, and can be carried in two or three wagons . . . The whole expense for inflating will not exceed $300, including transportation."[11]

The major was duly impressed with Lowe's presentation. Although the controversy that surrounded the introduction of ballooning to military operations was far from over, Bache made the decision to allow Lowe to continue. Bache drafted a letter for Lowe to pass on to Whipple, directing the captain to authorize Lowe to build a balloon for military use. Lowe promptly received the following letter from Captain Whipple:

> You are hereby employed to construct a balloon for military purposes capable of containing at least 25,000 cubic feet of gas, to be made of the best India silk, . . . with the best linen network, and

three guys of manila cordage from 1,200 to 1,500 feet in length. The materials you will purchase immediately, the best the markets afford and at prices not exceeding ordinary rates.[12]

Whipple directed that the balloon was to be made in Philadelphia and that Lowe would be paid five dollars per day during the process of collecting the various materials and the balloon's construction. In addition to this, Whipple informed Lowe that on completion of the balloon and its successful inflation in Washington Lowe was to be paid ten dollars per day, "as long as the Government may require your services."[13]

The terms of the directive were acceptable to Lowe, and he and Leontine made preparations to leave Washington for Philadelphia the next day.

"From this time until the 28th of August was consumed in the construction of the first substantial war balloon ever built," Lowe wrote in triumph.

While Thaddeus Lowe would not return to action for nearly a month, there was one aeronaut still active in his duty to the Union. John La Mountain remained in the service of Gen. Benjamin Butler at Fortress Monroe[14] in Virginia. Although La Mountain underestimated the difficulties and expense involved in transporting his equipment to the remote outpost at Old Point Comfort on the mouth of the James River, he and two assistants who volunteered to accompany him from Troy managed to arrive at the fort on July 23.

Located deep in Confederate territory, Fortress Monroe was one of the few forts in the South that remained under Union control following the outbreak of hostilities. Less than sixty miles away from the Confederate capital at Richmond, the fort was also one of the most formidable obstacles to complete Rebel dominance of the area. Fortress Monroe was originally built in 1819 as a coastal defense against a foreign invasion from the sea and for the protection of the Gosport Naval Shipyards, which were now in Confederate hands. Constructed at a cost of 2½ million dollars, its substance matched its massive scale with 35-foot granite walls ringing all seven sides of the structure, which was set on an island of more than 70 acres. On the side facing the sea there was a water battery of forty-two gun embrasures.

From the sea, the only access to the fort was through the waterway known as Hampton Roads, which was the convergence of the James, Elizabeth, and Nanoset Rivers. By land, Fortress Monroe was equally isolated. The land approach was exceedingly difficult with a beach that was roughly

"Balloon view" of Fortress Monroe in Virginia. Although this aerial portrait of the Union fort was not rendered with the assistance of John La Mountain, or any other aeronaut, it was a popular trend among publishers to associate innovation with the new, aerial additions to the Union army. HARPER'S HISTORY OF THE GREAT REBELLION

600 feet in width on the west side of the fort, and a narrow access bridge connected to the road that lead to the village of Hampton on the east.[15]

To say that Fortress Monroe lacked the supplies and amenities of outposts located nearer to Washington, D.C., would be more than just understatement. Although it is not known what John La Mountain expected to encounter at Fortress Monroe, what he did discover on his arrival was an extremely grim situation. Butler's forces had dwindled to only 2,000 troops following the debacle that claimed 76 lives at the battle of Big Bethel on June 10. Estimates of Confederate strengths in the area numbered more than 10,000 at Norfolk and 8,000 at nearby Yorktown.

Although Lincoln had ordered a naval blockade of Southern ports in April, the poor shape of the Union navy, compounded by the loss of the Norfolk shipyards, left little protection for Fortress Monroe. Additionally, many of Butler's volunteers from state militias were nearing the end of their three month enlistment term and the general feared losing control of the area from a lack of manpower.[16]

The Confederates were not that much better prepared to launch a major offensive. Before abandoning the Norfolk shipyards in April, the retreating Union forces saw to it that nearly all of the ships that remained behind were scuttled, and the repair facilities set ablaze. Time would be needed to rebuild the fleet and without a combined land and sea assault any attempt to capture the heavily fortified stone bastion would be difficult.

Sickness had also ravaged Rebel troops. As Confederate general John Bankhead Magruder reported to his headquarters in early August, "The sickness among the troops in the Peninsula is grave, . . . all diseases taking more or less a typhoid character. Some idea of its effect can be formed when I say that the Fifth North Carolina Regiment, composed over 1,000 strong, has now less than 400 for duty."[17]

Yet, the extent of the Confederates' strengths, as well as their weaknesses, was not known by Union forces defending Fortress Monroe. Rumors were still rampant that Rebels would overrun the fort.

La Mountain labored under severe weather conditions during his first week at Monroe. His portable gas-generating equipment was cumbersome and the necessary supplies—enormous quantities of sulphuric acid and scrap iron shavings—were difficult to come by. While records of La Mountain's gas-generating equipment are sketchy, it can be assumed that it was constructed along the lines described by John Wise in his book, *A System Of Aeronautics*. As such, 144 pounds of sulphuric acid added to 125 pounds of iron shavings would optimally produce 600 cubic feet of hydrogen gas in one hour.[18]

La Mountain at first underestimated the supplies necessary to produce sufficient gas. Records indicate that he initially purchased sixty carboys—large glass containers—of sulfuric acid. This combined with scrap metal salvaged at the fort only produced enough gas for a few ascents. La Mountain eventually requisitioned an order of 5 tons of sulfuric acid and 5,000 pounds of metal shavings as his operations developed.

As was the case with Thaddeus Lowe, La Mountain was still a civilian and had agreed to perform his ascents without compensation until he could prove the military value of reconnaissance ballooning. Working without any pay was a hardship the aeronaut endured for several months.

But the greatest challenge facing La Mountain was the fact that he was still relying on the latest incarnation and remnants of the *Atlantic*.

Salvaged from the voyage that almost claimed his and John Haddock's lives in the Canadian wild, the *Atlantic* was a mere shadow of its former self. Whereas the original *Atlantic* was more than 100,000 cubic feet in capacity,

John La Mountain
sketched this map of
the Confederate Army's
position at Sewall's
Point, Virginia, on
August 10, 1861.

the now much diminished balloon was scarcely more than 5,000 cubic feet, barely capable of carrying one man aloft along with the necessary ground tethers. In spite of this, La Mountain displayed a perseverance in his work in Virginia that would compel him to overcome adversity for lack of better equipment.

La Mountain's first balloon ascent of any significance at Fortress Monroe came on August 10, 1861. His report provided the first definitive account of the actual strength of Confederate forces in the vicinity:

Maj. Gen. Benj. F. Butler,

Sir: I have the honor to report that on the 10th of August I made two ascensions, in which I attained an altitude of 3,500 feet and made observations as follows:

About 5 or 6 miles northwest of Hampton I discovered an encampment of the enemy, but owing to the misty state of the atmosphere, caused by the recent rain, I was unable to form a correct idea of their numerical force, but should judge from 4,000 to 5,000.

There were no vessels or encampments of any kinds either at York or Back Rivers or at New Market Bridge. On a branch of the James River, about 5 miles from Newport News, is a large encampment of the enemy, from 150 to 200 tents, also an encampment in the rear of the Pig Point batteries of from 40 to 50 tents.

At Norfolk two large ships of war are lying at anchor in the
stream, one of which appeared all ready for sea, with sails bent, etc.
No operations at Tanner's Creek. I illustrate what I saw by the
accompanying hasty diagram. The guns which I discovered in a
previous ascension proved to be only heavy field pieces mounted
on carriages. Along the coast below Sewell's Point no batteries or
enemy were visible.

> With respect,
> John La Mountain, Aeronaut[19]

The possibility of a large concentration of troops near Hampton was of
particular interest to Butler. Hampton was under the nominal control of
Butler's troops from Fortress Monroe, but the general had touched off a
firestorm when he agreed to return a fugitive slave to a Confederate colonel
on the condition that the colonel swear an oath of allegiance to the United
States. Rumors began to circulate that Butler planned to use the village of
Hampton as a sanctuary for runaway slaves, and the Confederates were
determined to subvert such a plan at any cost.

In reality the rumors had substance. By the beginning of August, 1861,
more than 800 runaway slaves had appeared at Fortress Monroe seeking
food and sanctuary.[20] They were generally given some provisions before
being sent on to Hampton.

On August 7, Confederate forces led by General Magruder swept
down on Hampton and burned the town to the ground. Butler called the
raid, "a wanton act of destruction,"[21] but Magruder justified his actions. He
rationalized that the town, "was the harbor of runaway slaves and traitors,
and being under the guns of Fort Monroe, it couldn't be held if taken . . .
the town itself would lend great strength to whatever fortifications they
might erect around it, [so] I determined to burn it at once."[22]

Butler was not aware of the apprehension Magruder had for the
artillery in place at Fortress Monroe. On Butler's orders, John La Mountain
began making daily ascents from the fort, looking for signs of Rebel activity. The weather had cleared by this time, making it easier for La Mountain
to observe the surrounding countryside.

Not all of La Mountain's ascents during this period were from the confines of Fortress Monroe. On August 3, the aeronaut tethered one of his
balloons to a steam propelled gunboat, the USS Fanny. The combination of
an aerial platform attached to a sea-going vessel was a concept that had
never been tried before, and in essence this was the first military application

of the idea that would evolve into the aircraft carrier of the twentieth century.

For La Mountain, however, being on the cutting edge of military innovation was probably the furthest thing from his mind. The *Fanny* could maneuver closer to the shores of the Rebel-controlled riverbanks along Hampton Roads, which would have been impossible for La Mountain to accomplish without risking a freeflight ascent. Out in the middle of the Elizabeth River, La Mountain ordered the windlass securing his balloon to the deck of the *Fanny* to begin unwinding the tether. As La Mountain ascended to 2,000 feet, the *Fanny* "proceeded slowly down toward Sewall's Point, drawing the balloon while up in the air."

La Mountain's reconnaissance continued on to Pig Point and Craney Island, where the aeronaut signaled to his ground crew to reel him in. Once back at Fortress Monroe, La Mountain reported that behind the trees at Sewall's Point he could see the Rebels constructing earthworks and fortifications, with artillery squarely aimed at the fortress and the shipping in the channel.[23]

Over the next few days La Mountain continued his observations, both from Fortress Monroe and from the gunboat. His intelligence reports revealed that the Confederates had shifted their priorities. Magruder's raiders were no longer in the vicinity of Hampton, but a large encampment of Confederates was discovered about three miles beyond New Market Bridge. A considerable force was also camped on the east side of the James River, some eight miles above Newport News. However, at Sewall's Point, "there were now more than one thousand rebel troops."[24]

In spite of the buildup at Sewall's Point, La Mountain's reports brought welcome news to the beleaguered commander at Fortress Monroe. As Benjamin Butler reported to Winfield Scott on August 11:

> I . . . inclose herewith a copy of a report of reconnaissance of the position of the enemy made from a balloon, . . . The enemy has retired a large part of their forces to Bethel, without making any further attack on Newport News.[25]

From La Mountain's work it was clear that Fortress Monroe was not in imminent danger of being assaulted anytime soon.

The same could not be said for Benjamin Butler's own position. In light of the poor performance of his troops mustered at Big Bethel and his inability to prevent the siege on Hampton, Butler was relieved as commander of the Union forces in Virginia in August, 1861. His successor was Maj. Gen. John Ellis Wool.

Butler was none too pleased at receiving the news relieving him of his command, as he related in a letter to his close friend Montgomery Blair, the U.S. postmaster general:

> What does it mean? Why this? I supposed when I saw the president one week since that I had his confidence. Now I am superseded and no duty assigned to me. . . . I have witnessed the disgusting scene of a burning village when I had only 2000 men against 5000 and could not oppose it, the enemy coming down because they knew I had no troops.
>
> Is this because General Scott has got over his quarrel with General Wool, or is it a move on the part of the president, or is it because my views on the Negro question are not acceptable to the government? I suppose the last. Meanwhile, I am in the dark.[26]

Before Butler's departure for Washington, La Mountain approached the general to discuss another use for his balloons apart from reconnaissance. Borrowing a page from John Wise's Mexican War proposal, La Mountain suggested that he could arm his balloon with grenades and bombs and conduct an aerial raid on Rebel positions.

Butler apparently gave serious thought to the idea. Just prior to leaving Fortress Monroe, Butler submitted the following letter to Thomas Scott, the assistant secretary of war, regarding La Mountain's plan:

> I enclose herewith a communication from John La Mountain, a balloonist, who has been very successfully employed in making reconnaissance in this neighborhood. Situated as we are, surrounded by enemies at many points, the knowledge of the disposition of their forces thus acquired is of great advantage. La Mountain is a daring and apparently reliable man and thus far I have taken the liberty to encourage his efforts.
>
> I take leave to call your attention to that portion of his communication in which he proposes to use the balloon for war-like purposes. Is it not worth the experiment? The proposition is new and daring, but with the explanations he has given me I think it might have an element of feasibility in it; at any rate the cost is not large in comparison with the results so far.

Please advise me whether I shall go farther with him, either in reconnaissance or otherwise. He suggests one difficulty, the absence of silk to repair the balloon, and enough might be found in Philadelphia.[27]

At the same time Butler also submitted a list of La Mountain's expenses that the aeronaut had borne out of pocket:

MATERIAL AND FIXTURES FOR
AERONAUTICAL RECONNAISSANCE:

60 carboys of Vitrol @ $1.50 ea.	$ 90.00
9712 lbs. oil of Vitrol [acid]	$ 242.80
Freight on above to Fortress Monroe from Philadelphia	$ 60.00
3 Tanks, 3000 Gallons	$ 150.00
5000 lbs. of iron turnings @ $15 per ton	$ 32.50
Packages and Carting on above	$ 10.00
2 Copper Pipes, Rubber Flanches, etc, bolts and hose	$ 86.50
Transportation of Balloon Equipment to Fortress Monroe	$ 77.19
Balloon *Atlantic*, Net and Car	$ 350.00
160 lbs. of Linen Rope @ 30¢	$ 48.00
22 days board for three persons @ $1 per day	$ 66.00
Total	$1212.99[28]

The summary of expenses also included the aging balloon *Atlantic*. It would seem that La Mountain may have reasoned that by including the *Atlantic* as one of his costs he intended to use the proceeds to partially compensate himself for his work at the fort. The balloon was now in a fragile condition and La Mountain planned to discontinue its use and return to Troy to retrieve a new balloon for service.[29] In spite of its numerous repairs and subsequent downsizings the *Atlantic* was deemed suitable enough by General Butler to be acquired by the government for military use.

As for Benjamin Butler, after his removal from Virginia it turned out that his military career was far from over. In May, 1862, Butler commanded the force that occupied New Orleans and was made military governor of the region. His harsh and somewhat draconian rule ultimately earned him the dubious sobriquet, "Beast Butler."

John La Mountain returned to Fortress Monroe toward the end of August, 1861, with a new balloon that he christened *Saratoga*. The *Saratoga* was larger than the *Atlantic* and was capable of achieving higher altitudes. However, La Mountain found that the situation at Fortress Monroe after Butler's departure had substantially altered.

Butler's successor at first appeared to be the perfect ally in furthering the aeronaut's endeavors. John Wool was also from Troy, New York, and had raised a company of volunteers at the beginning of the war. He was also an acknowledged hero and veteran of both the War of 1812 and the Mexican War.

Wool was also seventy-two years old at the time of his appointment to the Department of Virginia. With nearly fifty years of military service Wool suffered from the inflexibility of age and tradition that Thaddeus Lowe characterized in an older generation of officers who were, "centered on the make-up of an army as it was always known with no interest for innovations."[30]

While Butler made sure that La Mountain's expenses were remitted to the government, the aeronaut soon learned that this was all the general had dealt with prior to his departure. La Mountain's arrangement with Butler was strictly as a civilian balloonist under personal contract, and as such he had no military standing. Furthermore, Butler left no word to the incoming commander regarding the balloonist's activities. Shortly after Wool arrived at Monroe, La Mountain took the opportunity to introduce himself, which only prompted confusion from the general.

"I have not received any instructions regarding a balloonist," Wool wrote to Secretary of War Cameron. "And find no instructions here at Fortress Monroe on the subject."[31]

While John La Mountain's ascents suffered from the privations of being so far in advance of frontline operations in Virginia, Thaddeus Lowe was quickly readying his new balloon for service in the area of the Potomac. The recognition that Lowe received from his appointment as chief aeronaut was not limited to public and military officials in the vicinity of Washington. Lowe had also managed to capture the attention of the national press, which turned out to be of critical importance at a time when morale among the Northern populace was extremely low.

Frank Leslie, whose illustrated newspaper was one of the most widely read journals in the country, wrote to Lowe shortly after his appointment as chief aeronaut. Leslie hoped that Lowe would permit one of his artists to accompany the aeronaut during his balloon operations. Leslie assured Lowe that military security would be strictly observed, "so that the publicity given to [Lowe's exploits] could not prejudice government plans."[32]

Still a showman at heart, Lowe was delighted at the prospect of having a unit publicist assigned to accompany his ascents.

"I consented to Mr. Leslie's request," Lowe said. "And he sent Mr. Arthur Lumley who proved not only an artist of splendid ability, but a most companionable addition to the Corps. His presence enabled me to secure many fine illustrations of our work and life. His quick mind caught the dramatic moments in action . . . and his facile pencil perfectly portrayed them."[33]

Frank Leslie's Illustrated News was not the only journal publicizing Lowe's exploits. Other publications were equally enamored with the aeronaut, with the Washington *Star* going so far as to write the first of what would be many tall tales that would be associated with the lore of the Aeronautical Corps:

A late rumor seriously believed by some individuals is that General Scott went up in Professor Lowe's balloon and discovered Jeff Davis, Lee, and Beauregard at breakfast together at Manassas Junction, with a mere sprinkling of 80,000 men in the tented fields surrounding that locality.[34]

The Professor, however, was not immune to the various lampoons that also cropped up as a result of his newfound celebrity. The Cincinnati *Commercial*, which had supported all of Lowe's endeavors to-date, published the following poem that poked fun at the aeronaut's ambitions:

> *Professor Lowe would fain get high*
> *At Government expense;*
> *With big balloon he'd scale the moon*
> *To spy Virginia fence;*
> *To spot the camps of rebel scamps*
> *With telegraph and glass—*
> *You ask me, friend, how will this end?*
> *And I reply—in gas![35]*

If Lowe paid attention to these barbs, he didn't mention it in his recollection of this period. It was a golden time for Lowe, in which the prospect of opportunity and even greater accomplishment lay ahead.

The time for trials was over.

CHAPTER SIX

The Union Army
Balloon Corps

D uring most of August, 1861, Thaddeus Lowe busily worked away in Philadelphia overseeing the construction of the newly requisitioned war balloon. The Northern press was among those who enthusiastically supported the new military project.

"Professor Lowe [is] . . . to build a mammoth balloon for the army," reported the Philadelphia *Inquirer.* "His balloons are the only ones of all that the Government have tried that have proved successful. A balloon reconnaissance of the late Bull Run disaster would no doubt have saved us our retreat."[1]

Lowe's progress on the aerostat was remarkable. Within a week the envelope for the 25,000 cubic foot balloon was completed and Lowe was busy assembling the rigging when Captain Whipple paid him a visit at the Philadelphia Assembly Buildings. True to the intent of his letter that originally commissioned the balloon, Whipple was there to inspect the new craft and its materials. Apparently all was in order. Following his return to Washington, Whipple gave his authorization to compensate Lowe for his time and the materials used on the project.

Lowe named the new balloon *Union* in honor of it being the first balloon to assume active duty in the Northern army. His limited experience in the field with the *Enterprise* gave Lowe a number of insights that he duly incorporated in the improved design. Lowe also labored fastidiously to ensure that the *Union*'s gas envelope was sealed as tightly as possible, applying two coats of balloon varnish that was composed of a "secret formula" known only to him. In his later years, Lowe confided the formula to a twentieth-century aviation pioneer by the name of Ray Knabenshue, where it was revealed that the varnish was a variation of John Wise's original varnishing formula consisting of boiled linseed oil, benzine, and japan drier, the latter being used to speed up the curing process.

Even with the addition of japan drier the varnishing process took over two days to complete. After the outer shell of the balloon was sealed, the envelope was turned inside out and coated with neat's-foot oil, a lubricant produced from boiled cattle feet, in order to keep the silk fabric pliable.[2]

One of the most important features of the *Union* was the incorporation of bright red, white, and blue bunting attached to some of the balloon's rigging, and a large stars and stripes pennant festooning its control basket. Lowe was mindful of how Union troops had fired on him under the mistaken belief the unadorned *Enterprise* was a Confederate balloon during his freeflight ascent from Arlington, and he was determined not to repeat the same mistake again.

By the end of August, Thaddeus and Leontine Lowe were once again in Washington. Lowe requested from the Topographical Corps that a trained and dedicated ground crew be used in handling the balloon, particularly in its transportation to the front lines, where damage was mostly likely to occur. Although the necessity of a regular ground crew was ingrained on certain officers such as Lt. Henry Abbot, who had witnessed the destruction of James Allen's balloon in June from mishandling, the request nonetheless set off a round of bureaucratic inertia.

Once again Amiel Whipple served as the reluctant middleman in the negotiations. Although it would be logical to assume that a detail from the Bureau of Topographical Engineers would be assigned to work with Lowe's balloons, since the Balloon Corps was nominally assigned to this branch, there were no enlisted men available in the bureau at this time. Whipple approached General McDowell for a detachment, and McDowell in turn suggested that a crew could be procured from one of the volunteer militias.

However, when Whipple placed his formal request with McDowell's chief of staff, Gen. James Barnett Fry, the transfer of the men was refused. There was to be no assignment of men from McDowell's I Corps for duty as frivolous as tending to a balloon.

The decision touched off a flurry of telegrams between McDowell's headquarters and the Bureau of Topographical Engineers. Whipple relayed

Gen. George McClellan proved to be a major ally to the Balloon Corps during his tenure as commander-in-chief of the Army of the Potomac. Always eager to seize upon new military technology, McClellan used the Corps during a number of major campaigns.

PHOTOGRAPHIC HISTORY OF THE CIVIL WAR

his frustration to the bureau's chief, Maj. Hartman Bache, in no uncertain terms.

"Unless men are made available for this assignment," Whipple wrote. "It is doubtful that substantial benefit from aerial ascensions will be secured."[3]

Whipple then proceeded on his own authority to enlist the help of any company commander that would spare the necessary men for balloon duty. His efforts paid off when Capt. Richard Butt of the 14th New York Regiment agreed to Whipple's request. Whipple was even able to secure permission from Butt's regimental commander, Brig. Gen. Erasmus Keyes, for the transfer.

Whipple believed that he had the situation finally resolved. Although Keyes' brigade was attached to McDowell's I Corps, Whipple assumed there would be no problem in having the transfer approved. Once again Whipple submitted his request to McDowell's headquarters, but this time it was completely ignored.

Whipple was at his wit's end. He loudly complained to his superiors that Lowe was in Washington with a balloon that the Bureau of Topographical Engineers had funded along with a $10 a day salary that was being paid to the aeronaut whether he was actively in service for the army or not. Finally, Whipple wrote to Maj. Israel Woodruff, also of the Bureau of Topographical Engineers, that the only way to resolve the matter would be to appeal directly to the recently appointed commander of the Army of the Potomac, Maj. Gen. George Brinton McClellan.

Following the losses of the national armory at Harpers Ferry, the naval shipyards in Norfolk, and the nearly disastrous battle at Bull Run in July, the eastern operations of the Union army were completely reorganized. On August 15, 1861, General McClellan was named commander of this new unit of the Union army that became known as the Army of the Potomac.

Unlike other Northern commanders, McClellan had a true appreciation for combining the latest developments in technology with his military strategy. He was among the first Union officers in the 1850s to recognize the value of rifled infantry weapons and their tactical use in entrenched warfare as opposed to bloody, full frontal assaults. As a vice-president for the Illinois Central Railroad before the war, McClellan was also quick to seize upon combining the rapid mobility of the railroad with troop deployment. And McClellan was the first commander to use the telegraph for strategic communications, which he effectively demonstrated during his brief tenure as a commander of the western theater, where in July he effectively prevented a force of 10,000 Confederates from invading Ohio at the battle of Rich Mountain.[4]

When word of Whipple's difficulty in securing men to handle Lowe's balloon reached McClellan, the general proved to be extremely supportive. On August 28, Lowe received the following telegram from Major Woodruff:

Sir:
Get the silk balloon in readiness for inflation immediately. A detail of thirty men will repair to the Columbian [sic] Armory to aid you in the inflation and transportation of the balloon.[5]

Although the problem of a regular ground crew had been resolved for the time being, Lowe was faced with the prospect of providing a crash course in the fundamentals of proper balloon handling to his newly acquired detail. The routines that Lowe practiced with the men were basic, but crucial to any success that would be achieved. The men quickly learned how to lay the balloon envelope out on the ground with a soft barrier of underlay between it and the earth prior to inflation to prevent any chafing of the delicate silk material. Lowe impressed upon them the importance of how unwieldy a balloon could become in a strong wind during transportation, and stressed on them to heed his instructions to the letter when on the road to the frontlines.

The continued inconvenience of inflating the balloon in Washington from the city gas works was particularly frustrating to Lowe. He explained to Captain Whipple during their meeting in Philadelphia that he had devised a portable apparatus for generating hydrogen and only required a small additional grant in funding to construct it. Whipple, however, put off Lowe's request as he was still cautious in his belief of the balloon's ability to serve in the field, and did not care to risk further expenditures until the results of field operations could be fully ascertained.

On the day after his new detail arrived at the Columbia Armory, Lowe received a telegram from Whipple instructing him to bring the *Union* to Fort Corcoran to make observations. General McClellan wanted the aeronaut to arrive before daybreak, "and ascend as soon as it may be light enough to watch for movements of any bodies of men."[6]

On the evening of August 28, the *Union* was carefully guided by tethers through the streets of Washington and on to the road leading to the fort. Upon his arrival Lowe ascended, discovering that the Confederates had entrenched themselves behind earthworks dug into nearby Clark's and Munson's Hills. The news was not particularly encouraging. Later that day, Lowe moved his balloon to Ball's Crossroads. The crossroads proved to be an extremely dangerous location for an observation as it was located more than a mile from the relative safety of the Union forts that ringed the Washington area.

"There, the enemy opened their batteries on the balloon," Lowe said. "Several shots passed by it and struck the ground beyond. These shots were the nearest to the U.S. capital that had been fired by the enemy during the war."[7]

Following his initial observations in the field, Lowe reported that he and the balloon were kept in constant use for the next several days. Although the *Union* still required to be frequently returned to Washington to replenish its gas supply, the balloon was proving to be reliable and effective in frontline use.

"Confidence in this new means of observation soon began to be manifested," Lowe recalled with pride. "Many officers made ascensions."[8]

On September 7, Lowe was accompanied on an ascent from Fort Corcoran by the Army of the Potomac's commander. From an altitude of 1,800 feet, McClellan gained a full appraisal of the enemy's position opposing the capital. It marked the first time in history that a commanding general had observed an opposing force from the air.

With the obstacles that Lowe had overcome in proving the value of aeronautics in warfare, the importance of the moment was not lost on Lowe. Although McClellan would later fall to criticism for being too conservative in taking decisive military action against the South, Lowe had only admiration for McClellan's command abilities.

"The task of McClellan was enough for a superhuman," said Lowe. "He was determined not to sacrifice his men, and for this reason . . . he would not move until his army was complete and perfectly organized as a fighting machine. McClellan also resisted the importunities of politicians, statesman and people to march at once, and this required strength of character of no ordinary kind."[9]

Lowe proved to be of great assistance to McClellan, as the general was in need of good intelligence, allowing him time to organize his army into an effective fighting force. Reports of the enemy's movement constantly flowed into McClellan's headquarters. The general was determined not to waste his men and resources on minor skirmishes.

"Many alarms were given," said Lowe of this tense period in the war. "And in every instance after an examination had been made by means of balloon the troops were sent back to their quarters and allowed to rest without danger of being surprised."[10]

Lowe also attracted notice from other officers on McClellan's staff. Brig. Gen. Fitz-John Porter became a firm supporter of balloon reconnaissance after accompanying Lowe on an ascent in early September. From that point on, Lowe was repeatedly asked by Porter to reconnoiter enemy positions. On September 7, Lowe made the following report to Porter following one of his ascents:

Brig. Gen. Porter,
I have just concluded another ascension and had a distinct view of Falls Church. In answer to your inquiry I can say that there is no appearance of the Enemy in or about Falls Church other than has been reported before.
Very Respectfully,
Your Obt. Servt,
T.S.C. Lowe[11]

Lowe continued working under Porter, who had just been given command of his own division within the Army of the Potomac. In typical fashion, Lowe followed up his reconnaissance on the 7th with more ascents the following day:

> According to your request I made two ascensions this morning. The first a little after 4 o'clock. At that time, no lights were visible. At 5 o'clock one light to the right of Munson's Hill & one at Taylor Corner appeared, nothing more could be seen.
>
> I ascended again at 6 o'clock & had a clear view of the works on Munson's Hill, but observed nothing unusual. The strong wind prevented me from attaining an altitude to observe with distinction anything beyond these points. I will ascend during the day and report to you.
>
> Very Respectfully,
Your Obt. Servt,
T.S.C. Lowe[12]

Lowe's steadfast devotion to his duty did not go unnoticed by Fitz-John Porter, who was completely in awe of the aeronaut's work and praised Lowe in glowing terms.

"I am desirous to see you prosper, and I think you are now on the road," Porter told Lowe in a telegram. "I have recommended an increase of two balloons and moveable inflating apparatus, and as soon as the utility of the science is made apparent (which will depend on your energy) I have no doubt of success.

"Strike while the iron is hot," Porter concluded. "If I can aid you in any manner don't hesitate to call."[13]

Porter then directed Lowe to bring the *Union* to Chain Bridge, which was located three miles to the north of Georgetown and was a vitally important position to hold. This was not only because it was one of the main access points for an invasion of Washington, D.C., but also because it maintained the receiving reservoir that supplied most of the water to Georgetown and the capital.[14] Lowe was to assist Brig. Gen. William "Baldy" Smith and his assessment of the enemy's position near Chain Bridge. Although Lowe reported no further Confederate activity in the area, Smith must have been impressed enough with Lowe's performance to relay his praise of the aeronaut to his superiors. On September 11, Lowe received another telegram from Fitz-John Porter, which he characterized as most "gratifying."

"I have nothing special [to express]," Porter said. "As your balloon is near Chain Bridge, I suggest you ask General Smith if he has anything. I presume if you can rise in the morning he would like it. *You are now of value* [Lowe's emphasis]."[15]

The official support that Lowe had pushed for for so long had finally materialized. Requests for ascents at various points from the frontline near Arlington were beginning to overwhelm Lowe's resources. Feeling that the opportunity was at hand to finish outfitting the Aeronautical Corps, Lowe drafted a detailed letter to General Porter outlining his needs.

"An addition of two balloons would be required with capacities as follows," Lowe wrote in his proposal. "One of 30,000 cubic feet, and one of 20,000 feet built of the best India silk and linen cordage, with all of my late improvements and appliances. The cost of these air vessels, complete, for the largest, fifteen hundred dollars; the smaller balloon would be twelve hundred dollars."[16]

The routine of having to remove a balloon from service once the gas inside the envelope was expended and being forced to return to Washington for reinflation also began to be a nuisance. Lowe used the opportunity to make his case for a portable hydrogen generator.

"A portable inflating apparatus would be required for the purpose of inflating a balloon at any point where common gas cannot be obtained," Lowe wrote. "A portable gas generator is also necessary for the purpose of replenishing the balloons when the gas is partially expended. This would save the expense of an entire reinflation and also keep the balloon ready for observation at all times. Besides, the hydrogen being more buoyant than coal gas, a greater altitude can be obtained."[17]

Lowe estimated that the cost of the gas generator would "not exceed five-hundred dollars," and suggested that ship carpenters and coppersmiths already in government service could build the apparatus according to his specifications in Washington without much effort. Lowe was also confident that if his proposal was approved, both the balloons and the hydrogen generator could be in service within two weeks, providing that "the weather prove fine, while coating the [balloon's] material."[18]

While Lowe lobbied for two new balloons to be pressed into service, he made no mention of working with any additional aeronauts to pilot them. Although John La Mountain was still laboring with his own increasingly brittle equipment at Fortress Monroe, Lowe stated, "I feel confident of being able to keep the Government constantly informed of the movements and position of the enemy." He further discouraged the prospect of hiring additional new pilots by adding that the new balloons could also be left unmanned on their tethers and, "be used for letting up various colored signal lights" to relay instructions to Union troops in the surrounding vicinity."[19]

As Lowe waited for a reply he continued his daily ascents and once again proved his "value" to the service. Meanwhile, other Union officers began to take notice of Lowe's work and wished to employ the aeronaut on their behalf. General Smith wrote an appeal directly to McClellan stating that he deemed "it of much importance that a Balloon be permanently attached" to his division.[20] Although Lowe's status was to remain as "aeronaut on demand," he received a telegram on September 23 to report directly to Smith's division at Fort Corcoran.

"At about 8:30 to-morrow morning I wish to fire from here at Falls Church," read Smith's orders. "Will you please send the balloon up from Fort Corcoran?"[21]

Smith had a plan that had never been tried before in the history of warfare. The gun batteries at Fort Corcoran were to be used to harass the Confederates entrenched in earthworks at Munson's Hill and Falls Church. Fort Corcoran was one of the smaller fortifications in the Washington area and its limited armament consisted of only two smoothbore howitzers and three rifle-barreled Parrott guns.[22] When it came to a barrage attack on the Rebel positions, Fort Corcoran's gunners had precious little firepower to waste.

Smith was fully aware of the limited resources that were on hand but was determined to stretch them to their limits. As September 24 dawned, Lowe was prepared to ascend over the fort with the *Union*. In addition to Lowe's ground crew, two officers from General Smith's staff were also present for Lowe's pre-launch briefing. One of the officers gave Lowe a telegram outlining the plan devised by the general's staff:

Two mounted orderlies will be sent you, so that you can . . . report and send to these headquarters during the time of fire. It is very important to know how much the shot or shell fall short, if any at all.[23]

The instructions were clarified by a telegram that followed:

If we fire to the right of Falls Church, let a white flag be raised in the balloon; if to the left, let it be lowered; if over, let it be shown stationary; if under, let it be waved occasionally.[24]

Although the records of September 24 do not reveal the reason why the aerial wire telegraph that Lowe had demonstrated in Washington several months before wasn't used, Lowe quickly assimilated the simple instructions and prepared to cast off. Soon the aeronaut had ascended to more than 1,000 feet and the signal was given to commence firing.

As Lowe signaled from the air to the mounted orderlies sent by Smith who, in turn, relayed trajectory instructions to the gun batteries, it marked the first time in warfare that an accurate artillery barrage was conducted at an enemy that could not be seen by the gunners on the ground.

"The battery marksmen, without seeing who or what he was firing at . . . made such an accurate fire that the enemy was demoralized," Lowe later said.[25]

The demoralizing effects of Lowe's ascents on the Confederate psyche could not be underestimated. Without a comparable countermeasure to the Union's balloon, or the ability to destroy the craft with ground fire, Rebel generals began to issue orders to field commanders to camouflage earthworks. As one order from General Beauregard's headquarters read:

The General commanding this Army Corps wishes every precaution taken to prevent the enemy from discovering from balloon or other means the numbers of our advanced commands or outposts. No lights should be kept at night except where absolutely necessary, and then under such screens as may conceal the lights from observation. Further, tents, if used, ought to be pitched under cover of woods and sheltered in all cases as far as possible from accurate computation.[26]

The threat posed by aerial observation also prompted creative methods on the part of the Confederates to try to deceive Lowe. It wasn't at all unusual for a division commander to order men to create "dummy artillery" from fallen logs, and to place them in abandoned Confederate positions in order to give the appearance that the location was still active and fully manned. The dummy artillery pieces, which were often referred to as "Quaker guns" in mock deference to the pacifist religious sect, were rarely convincing enough to fool a balloon observer. More often than not, aeronauts could discern even the most minute details, as Lowe related in an incident that—if his interpretation of the events are accurate—could have brought a swift ending to the war during the Peninsular Campaign in May, 1862.

During the course of directing ground fire on an unseen enemy position, a target far off in the distance was selected. According to Lowe, the observing balloon was at a "height of one to two thousand feet and could very well discern a distinguished group of officials in a field beyond the tall timber."[27] Although it was not known just who the "distinguished group of officials" were, the order was given to fire in the general direction of the meeting, with the balloonist adjusting range and trajectory of the shots.[28]

Years after the incident, Thaddeus Lowe came across the recollections of Confederate general James Longstreet on the events of that day:

> While the order to open was going around to the batteries, President Davis and General Lee, with their staff and followers, were with me in a little open field near the rear of my right. We were in pleasant conversation, anticipating fruitful results from the fight, when our batteries opened. Instantly the Federal batteries responded most spitefully. It was impossible for the enemy to see us as we sat on our horses in the little field, surrounded by tall, heavy timber and thick undergrowth; yet a battery by chance had our range and exact distance, and poured upon us a terrific fire. The second or third shell burst in the midst of us, killing two or three horses and wounding one or two of our men. Our little party speedily retired to safer quarters. The Federals doubtless had no idea that the Confederate President, commanding general, and division commanders were receiving point-blank shot from their batteries.[29]

From Longstreet's retelling of this incident, Thaddeus Lowe was convinced that the havoc rained down upon the Confederacy's high command that afternoon was a direct result of balloon-directed artillery fire. On reflection, however, the aeronaut concluded that it was, "strange that the Confederacy's most prominent citizens should not have connected the direct fire with the balloon."[30]

Sketch of the balloon Union *at Gen. Irvin McDowell's camp, September, 1861.*
HARPER'S WEEKLY

When word of Lowe's latest exploits at Munson's Hill and Falls Church made the rounds at McClellan's headquarters, there were many who became convinced that aeronautics was the magic key to the Union's success in suppressing the rebellion. On September 25, Lowe received a message from Montgomery C. Meigs, quartermaster general of the Union army. Not only was Lowe's request for two more balloons and portable hydrogen-generating equipment approved, but Meigs reported that, "upon the recommendation of General McClellan" two additional balloons were also to be constructed.[31]

The news was far beyond Lowe's wildest expectations. McClellan's order meant that a total of five balloons would be brought into service. And the addition of the gas generators finally meant that the need for city gas mains, which had hamstrung field operations, could be done away with. Lowe now had his orders in hand and immediately contacted Capt. John Adolph Bernard Dahlgren at the Washington naval shipyards to set aside the men and materials needed to build the generators to his specification before his leaving for Philadelphia to supervise the construction of the new balloons.

Prior to leaving the Washington area Lowe made one more ascent with the *Union* at Upton's Hill, Virginia, on September 30. Along with Gen. Irvin McDowell, Lowe took up his first foreign observer, the Count de Paris. The count was the grandson of the former French monarch Louis Phillipe and was well acquainted with the aeronaut's work from his fellow expatriate, Leontine Lowe. Serving as an aide-de-camp at McClellan's headquarters, the aristocrat was duly impressed with the vista presented from Lowe's balloon.

"I received many complimentary remarks during the day from the officers," said Lowe, "who were satisfied of the value of the balloon for reconnaissance."[32]

With the expansion of the balloon service now assured, Lowe could no longer deny the need to expand the pool of pilots beyond himself. The records indicate that Lowe did hire another aeronaut, John R. Dickinson of Delaware, who served as an assistant and was left in charge of the *Union* while Lowe was in Philadelphia. But professional rivalry—or as others would say, professional jealousy—immediately disqualified such able candidates as John Wise and John La Mountain from joining his Aeronautical Corps. However, Lowe's prewar aeronautical career had brought him into contact with numerous other balloonists who did not ruffle his ego to the same extent.

When Lowe arrived in Philadelphia one of the first people he contacted was veteran aeronaut William Paullin. Paullin eagerly accepted Lowe's offer of employment and in many ways proved to be a logical choice. He had accumulated more than twenty-five years as an aeronaut—a record that was eclipsed only by John Wise in terms of experience in the field. Additionally, Paullin's stint as a performer in Latin America during the early 1850s also suggested that he was adaptable to working under various and changing conditions such as he would experience in service with the Union army. And unlike his open disdain for John Wise's craftsmanship in the art of balloon building, Lowe was sufficiently satisfied with Paullin's ability to place him in charge of overseeing much of the work on the new balloons. Relieved from having to remain in Philadelphia for the duration of their construction, Lowe returned to Washington on October 11.

The very next day Lowe was back in the air, once again reporting to General Smith, who was directing operations at Johnson's Hill. The portable gas-generating equipment was not ready for field service, so Lowe had the *Union* inflated at the Columbia Armory and prepared for another arduous night journey.

"Our progress was slow, the night being very dark," Lowe said. "We were constantly apprehensive of running the balloon against trees or other obstacles. After passing through Washington and Georgetown, crossing numerous flag ropes and telegraph wires stretched across the streets, we reached the road to Chain Bridge."[33]

The wind picked up as Lowe's crew started down the road and the fully inflated balloon became difficult to control. A number of trees that impeded their progress had to be cut down and on several occasions the ground handlers had to pull the balloon across open fields in order to proceed.

The balloon crew finally reached Chain Bridge at around 3 A.M. on the morning of October 13. There they found the bridge clogged with artillery and cavalry on their way to Virginia, where preparations were being made by McClellan to engage the Rebels at Ball's Bluff. Chain Bridge was constructed of iron and woodwork trestles that covered its roadbed, making it impossible to tow the balloon over the bridge in a conventional manner. With Johnson's Hill on the other side of the Potomac, Lowe was posed with a seemingly impossible dilemma:

> In order to take the balloon over my men were obliged to mount the trestle-work and walk over the stringers, only eighteen inches wide and nearly 100 feet above the bed of the river. Thus, with the balloon over their heads, myself in the car directing the management of the ropes, the men getting on and off the trestle-work, with a column of artillery moving below, and 100 feet still lower, the deep and strong current rushing over the rocks, while the sky was dark above, the scene was novel, exciting, and not a little dangerous.[34]

At daybreak Lowe's exhausted party made it as far as Lewinsville, where they rested with the balloon tethered to several trees. But the wind—which had mercifully subsided at Chain Bridge—now returned with a vengeance and was whipping itself into a full gale "tearing up trees by the roots where the balloon was anchored." The double strength silk used in the construction of the *Union's* envelope was able to withstand the force of the wind, but the cords used in the balloon's netting suddenly gave way and the envelope escaped.

Powerless to retrieve it, Lowe and his men watched helplessly as it ascended toward the heavens.

"In less than an hour it landed to the eastward on the coast of Delaware, a distance of over 100 miles," Lowe later recalled.

Amazingly, the *Union* survived its solo journey. It landed in the village of Seaford in Sussex County, on the farm of an individual who was said to have "secession tendencies."[35] Despite the sentiment of some of the more superstitious individuals of Seaford who wished to burn the foreign object, the "secessionist" farmer held the balloon in safekeeping, hoping to collect a reward from its owner.

Lowe quickly learned of the balloon's whereabouts and dispatched an associate to Sussex County, who not only had to deal with the farmer, but also a local sheriff who had received a telegram from the Bureau of Topographical Engineers to retrieve the balloon as lost government property. Lowe's associate apparently possessed ample credentials to lay claim to the remains of the *Union* and subsequently returned the errant balloon back to Lowe. The farmer, incidentally, ended up $25 richer for his troubles.[36]

Shortly afterwards, the *Union* was shipped via the Delaware Railroad on to Philadelphia, where Lowe had gone in order to oversee the completion of the four new balloons and hydrogen generators. He would not return to frontline duty with the Balloon Corps until November 10.

In actuality, Lowe split his time between Washington and Philadelphia. At the Washington naval shipyards, work was nearing completion on the hydrogen gas generators. The generators proved to be a unique creation on Lowe's part. Whereas other gas generators, primarily those used by James Allen and John La Mountain, were either ineffective in the field or too cumbersome to make transport practical, Lowe's design was remarkably efficient and maneuverable.

The construction of Lowe's first gas generators started with a pair of standard issue army wagons. On each of the wagons a large wooden tank about eleven feet long by five feet high was constructed. Inside each of the wooden tanks there was a copper liner. Although copper was not entirely resistant to the corrosive elements of the sulfuric acid with which it would come in contact, it proved to be adequate enough to seal the interior of the tank sufficiently in the field. Additionally, the wooden tanks were built with extra strength to withstand the tremendous bursting pressures that developed inside during the chemical reaction that formed the hydrogen.

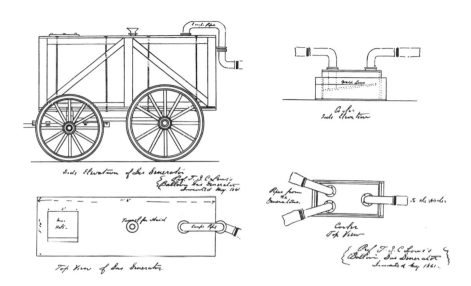

Profile drawings of Lowe's portable hydrogen gas generator. Lowe submitted his invention to the U.S. Patent Office but his patent for the device was denied. Nevertheless, Lowe's gas generators proved to be extremely effective in providing hydrogen to Union military balloons on the battlefield. NATIONAL AIR & SPACE MUSEUM

On the top of the tank there was a hinged metal plate that allowed the metal filings to be deposited inside. Also on the top, located near the middle, was a funnel-shaped copper pipe where the undiluted sulfuric acid was poured. On the end opposite the filler plate there was a copper "escape" pipe that allowed the hydrogen to flow into a large rubber hose. The rubber parts for the generators were supplied by Goodyear's Rubber, Belting, and Packing Company of Philadelphia.

The rubber hose lead to a gas purifier, another wooden box with copper hose fittings that contained a solution of lime and water. The purifier served a dual purpose. It was effective in filtering out inert elements in the gas, such as carbonic acid, and also cooled the gas significantly as it escaped the volatile environment inside the generator.[37] Generally, two purifiers were connected one after another between the generator and the envelope. After passing through the second purifier the gas was, "delivered, barely warm, into the balloon."[38]

When the inflation process was started the hose from the second purifier was inserted directly into the valve of the stretched balloon enve-

Sketch of Lowe's hydrogen gas generators at work in the battlefield. The small boxes between the generators and the balloons acted as gas purifiers that also cooled the hydrogen as it passed through the hoses. Lowe claimed that a typical balloon could be inflated in just a little over 3 hours using one generator.

ASTRA CASTRA, EXPERIMENTS AND ADVENTURES IN THE ATMOSPHERE

lope after "a clear stream of hydrogen" was obtained.[39] A balloon could be inflated in about three hours and fifteen minutes from a single generator. But Lowe discovered that the inflation time could be cut in half when two generators were used to inflate one balloon.

Supplies for the generators were carried in separate wagons. Four barrels of iron filings each weighing over 800 pounds and 10 glass carboys containing a total of about 40 gallons of sulfuric acid were the primary ingredients for a single inflation. The supply wagons also carried spare rubber hoses, copper pipes, and assorted hardware to maintain the generators in the field. Because of the weight involved, a team of four horses was required to draw each hydrogen generator and supply wagon to an inflation site. The carboys of acid were stowed in a separate wagon drawn by two horses.[40]

Lowe also prescribed a strict method of mixing the metal and acid together. The iron was shoveled through the metal plate on the top of the generator and the acid was poured into a copper funnel. With the tank about one-third filled with iron, five carboys of acid were first poured into the generator. This was followed by a brief waiting period that allowed the gases to expand in the tank and then three more carboys of acid were poured in. According to Lowe, the careful combination of these two elements reduced the possibility of rupturing the wooden tank from the pressure of the rapidly expanding gas.[41]

Following an inflation, hinged doors were opened at the side of the generator and the decomposed contents of metal acid were raked out onto the ground wherever operations were taking place. Little thought was given to the toxic residue left behind from the generators, giving the Balloon Corps the dubious distinction of being an early contributor to the long-standing problem of military pollution.

Nonetheless, Lowe was justifiably proud of his accomplishment. He even went as far as to engage a draftsman to render his idea on paper for a formal patent application. Lowe eventually contracted to have twelve generators constructed for the Balloon Corps during the war. Though his patent for the process was never approved, Lowe made certain that the origin of his invention was never in question. The words "Lowe's Balloon Gas Generator" were boldly stenciled on each of the devices constructed for the Balloon Corps.[42]

Meanwhile, the new balloons were quickly taking shape in Philadelphia. They were similarly outfitted along the lines of the *Union*, with the addition of stronger cord netting that was now capable of withstanding a strain of twenty-five tons. Lowe was determined not to allow the same set of circumstances that caused the *Union's* envelope to rip away from its netting to occur again.

As had been the case with the *Union*, each of the new balloons was given a staunchly nationalistic or dramatic name. As per Lowe's instructions, the new balloons were christened *Intrepid*, *Constitution*, *United States*, *Washington*, *Eagle*, and *Excelsior*.

Curiously, as the balloons neared completion Lowe gave serious attention to their appearance. The *Enterprise*[43] and the *Union* were relatively drab balloons with their envelopes colored a vague shade of brown resulting from the staining absorbed during the varnishing process. Although Lowe had decorated the *Union* with various red, white, and blue bunting and furls in order not to be fired on by Union troops, the aeronaut decided to give the new balloons a full-blown treatment in patriotic decoration.

The *Constitution* and the *Washington*, for example, were each colorfully finished with a huge portrait of George Washington on their envelopes.

Even the restored *Union* received its share of patriotic embellishment. As it underwent repairs to its envelope in Philadelphia, the *Union* was finished with a huge American eagle spreading its wings on the one side, with a plethora of stars and stripes and "other devices of the Professor's fertile fancy."[44]

The wicker control baskets varied in appearance, some painted bright blue and dotted with several white stars while others were adorned with red and white vertical stripes in addition to the white stars and blue field. The names of the new balloons were also boldly emblazoned in large block letters on each of the envelopes.

The sizes of the new balloons also varied considerably. The rebuilt *Union* and a sister ship named *Intrepid* represented the largest of the new balloons. Each balloon had a 32,000 cubic foot capacity and was capable of carrying five men aloft while tethered to four ground cables.

Next in size were the *Constitution* and the *United States*. These balloons had a total capacity of only 25,000 cubic feet but were capable of lifting three men while remaining tethered to four ground cables. The *Washington* was somewhat smaller coming in at 20,000 cubic feet of capacity, but capable of carrying two men.

When concerns arose that Lowe's gas generators might not be able to produce enough hydrogen gas to inflate the larger balloons quickly enough in the field, an order was placed for two smaller balloons. The *Eagle* and *Excelsior* were constructed in December, 1861, and were only 15,000 cubic feet in capacity. At less than half the size of *Intrepid* and *Union*, the *Eagle* and *Excelsior* could carry only one man when they were secured by four ground cables, or nominally two men if one of the ground cables was removed. However, the *Eagle* and *Excelsior* could be inflated in much less time than their larger counterparts and could be placed into service more readily.

With authorization to outfit each of the balloons as completely as possible, Thaddeus Lowe saw to it that his balloons would be completely repairable in the field. The list of sundries included with each balloon was extensive. Spare parts such as extra inflation valves, valve springs, stay hoops, and sandbags were a few of the major components that each individual balloon carried, but extras such as linen balloon cord, sailmaker's twine, mesh sticks for knitting the balloon network, and plenty of extra silk and reinforced muslin to repair tears were also necessary. The diversity and singular purpose of most of the supplies furnished with each balloon were extraordinary in the sense that most of the items requisitioned had never been used for military purposes. This, in turn, presented a considerable amount of confusion when the materiel came into the pervue of army quartermasters. Nevertheless, the Balloon Corps was rarely deprived of its necessary supplies in the early stages of the war.

Lowe was also meticulous in devising procedures for the inflation of each balloon, and expected ground crews to follow his instructions to the letter. Heavy brooms were standard equipment, used to thoroughly sweep inflation sites of all ground debris. Additionally, large sheets of canvas, appropriated from worn-out or captured tents, were laid out afterwards so that the delicate silk envelopes would have a protective barrier between them and the ground. Lowe was so particular on this subject that he even donated the remains of his giant balloonship, the *Great Western*, as an inflation pad. Regrettably, the *Great Western* had deteriorated to the point where it was no longer air-worthy since Lowe mothballed his Atlantic quest for the war effort.[45]

During the period in which Lowe's new balloons were being constructed in Philadelphia, back in Washington, D.C., Capt. Amiel Whipple of the Bureau of Topographical Engineers was relieved of his duties supervising the Balloon Corps. Whipple, who was promoted to brigadier general in September, 1861, and later mortally wounded at Chancellorsville in 1863, was replaced by Col. John N. Macomb.

As with Whipple, Macomb was also assigned to the Bureau of Topographical Engineers. As such, Macomb came to his new duties with some familiarity of the particular requirements of Lowe and his Balloon Corps. In August, when Whipple was desperately trying to detach a permanent crew for the Corps, Macomb also lent his assistance in the endeavor.[46]

Macomb would prove to be a staunch ally of Lowe's cause during his tenure overseeing Balloon Corps operations. However, his initial encounter with the unusual requirements of the Corps left him to remark that, "ballooning for the army is a very expensive business."[47]

Expense would be just one element of the Balloon Corps's legacy. While Lowe's new balloons were now ready for action, little did anyone realize that some of the most spectacular engagements involving the Balloon Corps would not come on the battlefield, but would result from the clashes of immutable and uncompromising egos from within the Corps itself.

CHAPTER SEVEN

The Battle of Egos

A s Thaddeus Lowe's new balloons were being readied to enter into service with the Union army in November, 1861, John La Mountain's fortunes at Fortress Monroe were in serious decline.

Benjamin Butler's replacement as commander at Fortress Monroe, Gen. John Wool, continued to use La Mountain's reports of enemy activity, but was not altogether willing to secure additional funding for the aeronaut's further endeavors. By August, 1861, La Mountain's sole reliance on the dilapidated *Atlantic* forced the aeronaut to return to Troy, New York, to retrieve additional supplies and finish work on a new balloon.

In New York, La Mountain encountered a number of problems that impeded his return to Fortress Monroe, as he explained in a letter to Wool:

> I have been unavoidedly detained here longer than I expected when I left the Fortress, and for two reasons—1st, I was obliged to purchase and connect to my gas apparatus a larger engine & boiler. 2nd, in conducting my final experiments, previous to my departure for the Fort, I received several severe burns in my face from a jet of gas which accidentally caught fire and haveing [sic] caught cold in the wounds from my experiments my Physician advises me to delay my departure for a few days.[1]

Several days after Wool received this letter from La Mountain, the aeronaut unintentionally raised a number of questions when he sent one of his assistants to collect funds that were owed under arrangements made with Wool's predecessor, Benjamin Butler. Francis Raveneth was a longtime associate of La Mountain, having also grown up in the aeronaut's home-town of Lansingsburg, New York. However, Raveneth's loyalty to the Union became a subject of intense scrutiny when members of a so-called "Citizens' Committee" addressed a letter to the commander at Fortress Monroe accusing him of being a Confederate spy and a traitor. The basis for the condemnation stemmed from public remarks Raveneth reportedly made, "expressing his desire for the thorough defeat of the Union." The letter went on to state that Raveneth was "deemed here by all Union men to be a dangerous man at this juncture of national troubles."[2]

Interestingly, the committee's letter took great pains not to portray La Mountain in any seditious light. Indeed, it described "Professor La Moun-tain" as a man of great integrity, "as we know him to be a strong Union man and a patriot."[3]

While the letter did level grave charges against La Mountain's assistant, the matter was apparently resolved to the aeronaut's personal satisfaction as Raveneth continued to work as La Mountain's chief assistant and was after-wards entrusted with the collection of accounts due from the army. As La Mountain stated in a letter to General Wool:

Dear Sir,

This [letter] will introduce to you my Partner Mr. Francis Raveneth. Will you please cause to be paid to him the amount of my Bill rendered to Gen Butler. . . . I need this money at the pres-ent time as I have new purchases to make and old bills to pay and as yet have received nothing from Government.

I will report myself at your headquarters as soon after the return of my Partner as possible. As I have sufficiently recovered from my accident by that time and shall need the funds due me to make immediate despatch.[4]

The letter, however, had little effect on Wool regardless of the question of national loyalty that surrounded Raveneth. When Butler was relieved of his command at Fortress Monroe he had left absolutely no instructions regarding La Mountain's activities. When La Mountain returned to the fort ten days later with the new balloon, *Saratoga*, and his portable gas genera-tor, the welcome he received from Wool was that of abject perplexity. Since

La Mountain was employed only through a personal contract that existed between the aeronaut and General Butler, Wool opted to leave the decision to continue balloon reconnaissance from Fortress Monroe in the hands of the secretary of war.

In a letter dated September 18, 1861, Wool requested clarification from the War Department and handed the letter over to La Mountain to deliver personally in Washington. The general rationalized this action by concluding that since there would be no more ascents from the fort until the matter was officially settled, the aeronaut might as well be put to use as a messenger.

La Mountain's journey to Washington proved to be the beginning of a controversy that would pit La Mountain against his rival Thaddeus Lowe, and threaten to bring an early end to aeronautics in the Union army.

Upon his arrival in the capital La Mountain quickly learned that Lowe had been placed in charge of organizing an aeronautical corps for the Army of the Potomac, and was nominally designated "chief of aeronautics." The news was not well received by La Mountain, who also learned that Lowe would soon be given permission to construct several new balloons for aerial reconnaissance.

In spite of this, La Mountain found that he was not entirely without support among military officials in Washington. Lowe's early demonstrations with the *Union* had made a favorable impression on a number of generals. On the day after La Mountain arrived in Washington, Gen. William "Baldy" Smith addressed a formal request to McClellan's assistant adjutant general.

"I deem it of much importance that a balloon be permanently attached to this division," Smith wrote. "Not only for the present, but to move with it, and owing to the distance from the gas works in Washington, I request that an inflating apparatus be purchased to accompany the balloon. I have to ask that the Major General [Commanding] will order one to be sent."[5]

La Mountain, with his own balloon and hydrogen-generating equipment, discovered that his services were in great demand by various field commanders willing to seize on the novelty of aerial reconnaissance. But with Lowe in charge of the Balloon Corps, La Mountain was effectively prevented from accepting any offer to freelance.

Although the record is not clear on La Mountain's precise reaction to his rival having control of aeronautical activities within the Army of the Potomac, heated emotion and raised voices were undoubtedly rampant.

General McClellan ordered Fitz-John Porter to hold a meeting between the two aeronauts in order to try to resolve their differences. The result of the meeting was summarized in a letter written by Porter to McClellan's inspector general, Col. Robert Barnes Marcy who was also, incidentally, McClellan's father in law:

> In compliance with the instruction of the Commanding General I called Professor Lowe and Mr. La Mountaine [*sic*] to my quarters on the 20th instant and conducted the interview in a manner to ascertain the feelings of each party in relation to the contemplated employment of both in the United States Service as aeronauts and according to the wishes of the commanding General.
>
> Each party is aware that at present and in all probability then will be in the future, ample field for the employment of both, and that operations may for the present, not require united actions, or observations from the same locality. If, however, they should be thrown together I am assured by both of them that all shall work for the interests of the Service.[6]

Porter went on to attempt to designate the duties for each man, though in the case of La Mountain, his future with the Army of the Potomac seemed somewhat nebulous:

> Mr. La Mountaine seemed to be aware that Professor Lowe had been engaged in this vicinity and regarded the field here as his specialty unless more than one was required. When there was no necessity for more than one he would retire. This point was broached by Mr. La Mountaine and voluntarily the offer was made by him.[7]

General Porter was quick to pick up the passion that each man held for his chosen profession, and the desire each had for his own individual success. However, as the general noted, each man presented his agenda in respect to his personal motivation:

> I think the Commanding General can rely upon the cordial co-operation of both to forward his view and in working for the Service. Both are zealous—Mr. La Mountaine has a powerful incli-

*Gen. Fitz-John Porter. Porter was
given the unenviable task of acting as
arbitrator between Thaddeus Lowe
and John La Mountain.*

PHOTOGRAPHIC HISTORY OF THE CIVIL WAR

nation to action, the desire to obtain a subsistence,' and no doubt
will work to the best of his ability—of which I know nothing.

Professor Lowe is also actuated by powerful motives—not the
least of which is, as stated by him, to form the science of the aeronaut and to perfect utility to the purpose to which applied.[8]

Porter's remark that La Mountain was solely motivated by monetary
gain was not entirely fair. The aeronaut had not been paid in several months
and owed his assistants and several suppliers a considerable amount. Still,
Porter was able to see the advantage that a second aeronaut could bring to
the army, particularly one who could supply his own equipment:

Mr. La Mountaine, I found on inquiry, claims the ownership of
two balloons, one large and one small, the former for one man, the
latter for two—but which he says [of the latter] he must enlarge.
He also claims an inflating machine which can carry at any time to
the point desired. I would respectfully suggest that he be tested and
a report of his ability be made wherever he may be located.[9]

In making this note in his report, Porter was unaware that one of La
Mountain's balloons, the *Atlantic*, was barely serviceable and would not hold

up to the rigors of extended use. Nevertheless, the fact that La Mountain had two balloons and his own inflation equipment—regardless of their overall condition—would be a key reason for Porter's recommendation that Thaddeus Lowe be similarly outfitted:

> I would also suggest that Professor Lowe be provided with means of taking observations and of inflating, and a similar report be made of his operations and their utility.
>
> Professor Lowe seems desirous of making ascensions passing over the Enemy's locations and availing himself of the Eastly current to bring him to the point of departure again. I would recommend the experiment if balloons can be procured and the benefit to the Service will compensate for the risk of its falling in the hands of the Enemy.[10]

Although Lowe was an acknowledged master in ascertaining the shifting wind currents between the earth's surface and the jet stream, conducting freeflight ascents under wartime conditions was extremely dangerous, a fact that General Porter would himself eventually learn firsthand. In addition to the danger, reporting shifting battlefield developments required swift communication to field commanders. The time involved in floating above battle lines and then finding a desirable wind current to carry an aeronaut back to safety would more than likely render any intelligence gathered useless by the time it was received.

Lowe was probably made aware of these deficiencies in freeflight reconnaissance after his meeting with Porter. Later, when John La Mountain actually performed his own freeflights over enemy lines, his most rabid critic was none other than Thaddeus Lowe.

Following his meeting with Lowe and La Mountain it was probable that Fitz-John Porter may have felt that the battle between the two aeronauts was finally laid to rest. But as it was shortly revealed, the bitter rivalry was far from over.

La Mountain returned to Fortress Monroe to collect his equipment for his new assignment. He was now officially classified as a "free lance balloonist" with his salary established at $10 a day. Although Gen. William "Baldy" Smith had requested a full-time aeronaut assigned to his division, La Mountain's first assignment was under the command of Brig. Gen. William B. Franklin.

Franklin's division was stationed at Cloud's Triadelphia Mill, 3 1/2 miles west of Alexandria along Holmes Run and the Little River Turnpike.

In comparison to the early stages of the war, by early October, 1861, action from both sides had ground to a virtual standstill as Union and Confederate leaders contemplated their next major moves in the field. During this lull La Mountain decided to preempt Thaddeus Lowe's plan to perform freeflights over Confederate positions. La Mountain explained his rationale for attempting the risk of freeflight reconnaissance in the following way:

> Typical ascensions, with balloons attached to the earth by cords, do not allow the attainment of an altitude sufficient to expose a considerable view. There is no other method by which a satisfactory observation of large forces, their approximate strength and positions, more especially in thoroughly patrolled and strongly fortified districts, can possibly be secured.
>
> To the eye of the aeronaut—who can, by the knowledge his art affords him of the direction and depth of different strata of the atmosphere, sail directly over points impenetrable by pickets or scouts—secrets of the most important character are clearly revealed. The country lies spread before him like a well-made map, with all its varieties of hill and valley, river and defile, distinctly defined, and with every fort, encampment, or rifle-pit within a range of many miles, manifest to observation.
>
> It would be impossible to concentrate large bodies of men, or make important defences [sic], of which no knowledge could be procured by such a reconnaissance.[11]

On October 1, La Mountain inflated the *Saratoga* from the city gas works at Alexandria, Virginia, and proceeded on to the area of Cloud's Mill. There, he waited several days for the right atmospheric conditions to occur. Finally, on October 4, La Mountain made his freeflight ascent.

The flight was reasonably uneventful. The *Saratoga* rose to a reported altitude of 8,000 feet, where it entered into an easterly current that carried it in view of Washington, D.C. La Mountain proved that he was Lowe's equal in the mastery of upper air currents when he landed safely near Beltsville, Maryland, several hours later.[12]

For his next ascent with Franklin's division, La Mountain reverted back to a tethered flight. At Camp Williams, La Mountain ascended on October

14, just before daylight, where he observed numerous campfires in proximity to the railhead near Springfield. Although the size of the Confederate force—estimated at some 8,000 men—was probably somewhat exaggerated, the sighting confirmed that a considerable Rebel contingent was to be reckoned with along the picket lines to the west and northwest of Union positions.[13]

Later that same day La Mountain performed another freeflight over enemy territory, inspecting the Confederate camp directly opposite Camp Williams. Although the results of La Mountain's ascent aren't known, his successful flight began to grab attention from other area commanders, particularly Irvin McDowell, the ill-fated commander of the Union forces at Manassas who had originally downplayed the strategic use of aeronautics. Now commanding only a division, McDowell requested a balloon and gas generator for his use.[14]

General Franklin, however, chose to keep La Mountain and the service of his balloon close to his own lines. On October 18, La Mountain was ordered to go aloft from Cloud's Mill and again the aeronaut chose to venture upward untethered. His observation that day turned out to be significant. As he maintained an altitude of about 1,400 feet over Confederate territory he observed a heavy artillery battery not far from Franklin's position, consisting of six to ten heavy field pieces. A half mile from this position La Mountain reported that he discovered an encampment of approximately 1,200 Rebels. All along Aquia Creek, La Mountain claimed to have discovered evidence of the beginnings of reinforced earthworks. In addition to this, the aeronaut also observed that the once substantial force stationed near the Fairfax Station railyard had diminished quite significantly.

Yet, when La Mountain returned to earth and made his report to Franklin, the general was not impressed.

"It is physically impossible to see Aquia Creek from Cloud's Mill," said Franklin in a letter to McClellan. Aquia Creek was some thirty miles away from Franklin's base of operations and the general could not visually grasp the vantage point that La Mountain enjoyed poised as he was 1,400 feet over the field. "It is likely Mr. La Mountain observed Occoquan Creek, only 14 miles from our position."[15]

The truth of the matter was that La Mountain had indeed accurately spied Confederate activity near Aquia Creek. During a conference with his generals held at the Fairfax Court House on October 1, Confederate president Jefferson Davis ordered that an artillery works be placed near the entrance to Aquia Creek, which overlooked a narrow stretch of the Potomac. This eventually allowed Rebel guns to unleash artillery barrages against Union ships.[16]

Unfortunately, the skeptical General Franklin declined to take any action based on La Mountain's intelligence gathering.

La Mountain's freeflights were not without their own share of danger. On one mission, as the aeronaut was returning back toward his own lines, he descended toward the Union camp of Gen. Louis Blenker's German brigade.

"The adventurous La Mountain came very near to being shot," reported a correspondent with *Scientific American*, not long after the incident occurred. "The German regiment, mistaking him for a secession buzzard, blazed away at the aeronaut for several minutes."[17]

Having already exhausted his ballast in order to capture the upper air current, La Mountain had little choice but to bear the brunt of the assault.

"One bullet passed rather unpleasantly close to my head," La Mountain wrote in his report to General Franklin. When the balloon settled to earth his ordeal grew even worse.

"An infuriated crowd of officers and men . . . were intent upon destroying the balloon and myself," La Mountain wrote afterwards. "My netting was cut by their knives, they refused me the privilege of alighting, dragging me by the ropes over the rough ground, causing much danger and some damage, although I showed them my passes and otherwise explained my position.

"The officers seemed to be more unreasonable than the men, and paid no attention to my explanations."[18]

La Mountain was eventually able to convince the men of the German brigade that they were fighting on the same side. Later, when he met with General Blenker, La Mountain reported that he "was received with courtesy." Nevertheless, the experience was extremely disturbing and La Mountain strongly requested that Franklin inform division commanders in the area of his operations in order to prevent a repeat occurrence of the ordeal.[19]

In spite of the troubles he experienced with Blenker's brigade, La Mountain's reconnaissance work was progressing well and his services were in steady demand, particularly in light of the fact that Thaddeus Lowe was still preoccupied with the construction of new aeronautical equipment in Philadelphia and Washington. Accordingly, La Mountain was assigned a detail of forty men, along with his own assistants who had accompanied him from upstate New York. La Mountain also negotiated something of a financial coup with the Union army's Quartermaster Office, when he agreed to sell both the *Atlantic* and *Saratoga*, and their attendant equipment, to the government for a sum total of $3,338.14.[20]

La Mountain's exploits even began to garner notice in the press. One such article, written in a decidedly humorous vein, promoted some of the mythology that circulated around balloons and aeronauts:

> LaMountain has been sent up in his balloon, and went so high that he could see all the way to the Gulf of Mexico, and observe what they had for dinner at Fort Pickens (Florida). He made discoveries of an important character, my boy, and says that the rebels have concentrated several troops at Manassas.
>
> A reporter . . . asked him if he could see any negro insurrections, and he said that he did see some black spots moving around near South Carolina, but found out afterward that they were some ants which had got into his telescope.[21]

Other journalists were more taken with the actual application of La Mountain's efforts on the battlefield. A war correspondent with the Boston *Journal* spent considerable time with La Mountain at his base of operations and provided remarkable insights into the aeronaut's work:

> Being at La Mountain's headquarters, he kindly invited me to accompany him on a reconnaissance. Having faith with him in that everpresent upper current towards the east, I did not hesitate, though I knew that the lower currents toward the west would in a very few minutes carry us far over inside the enemy's lines. Stepping into the car with him, he cut loose, and in a moment, as it were our great army lay beneath us, a sight well worth a soul to see—brown earth fortifications, white tented encampments, and black lines and squares of solid soldiery in every direction. So enchanted was I with the scene that I well nigh forgot that we were drifting enemyward, until Fairfax Court house lay beneath us, and I had my first sight of the enemy, in the roaming squads of rebel cavalry visible in that vicinity.
>
> Soon Centreville and Manassas came in full sight, and there in their bough huts lay the great army of the South. All along they

stretched out southeasterly toward the Potomac, on whose banks their batteries were distinctly visible. So plain were they below, their numbers could be noted so carefully that not a regiment could escape the count.

I do not have time at present to give you as full description as I would like of that great scene, a scene that would furnish material for a long letter; enough to say that it was superlatively grand and interesting.

The Professor, satisfied with his reconnaissance, as well he might be, after noting down the strength of the forces and their position, discharged ballast and started for that higher current to bring him back. Now I acknowledge I looked anxiously and (I am sure I was excusable) nervously for a backward movement, conscious that to come down where we were was death, or at least the horrors of a Richmond tobacco prison.

Up, up we went, but still bearing west and south. I looked at the Professor's face. It was calm and confident, so I felt assured that all was right. The assurance became a settled thing, when in a few moments we commenced passing gently back to the east.

We had struck the Professor's current!

Back, back we went, as though a magnet drew us, until our own glorious stars and stripes floated beneath us, and we came down, gradually and smoothly into the encampments of General Franklin's division, where we were surrounded by enthusiastic soldiers who had been excitedly watching the trip.[22]

Unknown at the time of his flight, the Boston *Journal*'s correspondent had borne witness to one of La Mountain's final wartime exploits in the air with the *Saratoga*. On November 16, 1861, the balloon *Saratoga* escaped from its anchors at Cloud's Mill and was lost forever.

La Mountain pointed the finger of blame for the incident on a poorly trained enlisted man who had been in charge of securing the balloon to its base. But no matter where the responsibility actually lay, La Mountain was now left with only the extremely decayed remains of the *Atlantic* as his sole means of conducting aerial reconnaissance for Franklin's division. La Mountain continued to perform ascents with the *Atlantic*, but each flight grew more hazardous with the severely deteriorated balloon. It was hardly a secret that Thaddeus Lowe was in the midst of constructing several new war balloons at this time and La Mountain was undoubtedly aware of this fact.

Realizing that the days of his service as an aeronaut for the Union would soon come to an end if he continued to use the *Atlantic*, La Mountain began a campaign to create a more workable alternative to his situation. He took his case directly to General Franklin.

"Permit me to call your attention to an important point in connection with the reconnoitering service of your division," La Mountain began, in a rather lengthy letter to the general. "I allude to the indispensable necessity, in order that any services may be efficiently performed, for the provision of additional balloons."[23]

La Mountain went on to point out that his services in the field of aerial reconnaissance had already yielded significant results and his own daring freeflight ascents, in his opinion, went further in providing valuable information on the enemy than Thaddeus Lowe's more conservative tethered observations.

"Balloons attached to the earth by cords do not allow the attainment of an altitude sufficient to expose a considerable view," La Mountain said. "There is no other method by which a satisfactory observation of large forces, their approximate strengths and positions, more especially in thoroughly patrolled and strongly fortified districts can possibly be secured."[24]

La Mountain attempted to make Franklin understand the adverse conditions he was forced to work under as a result of losing the *Saratoga*.

"When I came in this department I had two balloons," La Mountain stated. "One of these, the *Saratoga*, possessed a capacity of 25,000 cubic feet, and was in passably good condition—The other, the *Atlantic*, has a capacity of but 12,000 [cubic] feet. It is an old balloon, and having been in use during the summer at and about Fortress Monroe, and subject while inflated to the intense heat of that section, has become extremely tender and friable."

La Mountain hoped that Franklin would endorse a solution to his problem similar to the arrangement that had been made with Thaddeus Lowe.

"I think . . . that you see the necessity for the application I now make that an order may be issued to furnish me with material for two balloons," La Mountain said. "It would be essential to have cloth manufactured for the purpose, and I will inform the proper parties where it can be cheaply procured.

"I should desire to make balloons and manufacture the twine for the netting myself, as there is no person in the country who could do the work to my satisfaction, and very few who can do it at all. . . . All the necessary labor could be performed here, with great saving to Government, and without interrupting my regular operations."[25]

Despite the fact that La Mountain knew that Thaddeus Lowe had built several balloons for the military and that they were now ready for use in the field, his desire to construct his own balloons was not without its merit. Balloon construction was a highly individualized process. Most experienced balloonists during this period were more comfortable with trusting their lives to a craft made by their own hands than a balloon made by another. General Franklin initially agreed with La Mountain's position on the matter.

"The balloon that La Mountain has is worthless, or nearly so," Franklin wrote in a dispatch to Colonel Macomb of the Topographical Bureau. "If he is to be retained in the service of the U.S. he ought to have at least one new one, and I think that his proposition as to its manufacture is a good one."[26]

However, the wheels of military bureaucracy undoubtedly ground the requisition for the materials La Mountain needed into dust. La Mountain received no immediate reply to his request and his reconnaissance work in Franklin's division came to a complete standstill in December, 1861.

Meanwhile, away from the front lines, Thaddeus Lowe was completely absorbed with the organization and operations of the Union army's Balloon Corps. In spite of the meeting that took place between himself, La Mountain, and Fitz-John Porter in September, Lowe had little intention of cooperating with his rival, and proceeded to organize the Corps into a unit that would function solely under his own control.

Although Lowe managed to convince military officials of the need to construct six military balloons, he was experiencing difficulty in locating aeronauts who were experienced enough as pilots and, as equally important, possessed of personalities that would not clash with his own ego.

"I was exceedingly busy," Lowe later wrote of this period. "Not only was I personally supervising the making of balloons . . . but I was hiring and training assistants, men who I knew were thoroughly reliable and competent."[27]

By means of a search that was no doubt extremely painstaking for Lowe, he was able to enlist a number of qualified balloonists, some with very familiar names.

William Paullin, the acclaimed Philadelphia aeronaut who was only surpassed in his number of years' experience in the art of ballooning by the venerable John Wise, joined up with Lowe in October, 1861, while Lowe was completing construction of the new military balloons. John Steiner, the German balloonist who had once harbored plans of a transatlantic crossing and was nearly drowned in Lake Erie as the result of a balloon flight in 1857, was also added to the Balloon Corps's roster. And finally, John B. Starkweather, a balloonist from Boston, Massachussetts, was also brought on board. Rounding out this small clique of civilian specialists was Clovis Lowe, Thaddeus Lowe's own father, who, while not an aeronaut, was proficiently trained by his son in the maintenance and handling of aerostats. Lowe senior proved himself to be invaluable in training the ever-changing complement of enlisted men assigned as the Corps's ground support crew.

By early December, 1861, there were three other qualified balloon pilots in Lowe's Balloon Corps, in addition to Lowe himself. The pilots and balloons were deployed at various locations along Union army lines.

"The balloon *Constitution* is at Budd's Ferry—General Hooker's division," Lowe wrote in a dispatch to Lt. Col. A. V. Colburn, McClellan's assistant adjutant general, on December 3, 1861. "The *Washington* with gas generating apparatus and materials, is *en route* for Port Royal, South Carolina. The *Intrepid*, of larger dimensions, is at General Porter's division, Hall's Hill. The *Union*, same size, is intended for Poolesville, and is now ready, but has been delayed at the navy-yard for work on gas-generating apparatus that was promised me three weeks ago."[28]

The *Union* and *Washington* in fact remained at the Columbia Armory in Washington, D.C., under the supervision of Clovis Lowe. With winter fast approaching, Thaddeus Lowe began to express his doubts on how well the four large balloons he had already constructed would perform in adverse weather conditions. Freezing rain, ice, and snow were all detrimental to balloon operations, and the large balloons would be subject to weather that could render them essentially useless. In addition to this, General McClellan was also preparing his strategy for the invasion of the South through Virginia and South Carolina, and he definitely sought to incorporate the use of his newly formed Balloon Corps into his plans.

Lowe could foresee that his balloons and pilots would be forced to perform under the most primitive and adverse conditions imaginable, and probably far away from Union supply lines. In his dispatch to Colonel Colburn, Lowe explained the necessity of adding the small balloons to the Balloon

Corps's inventory, while maintaining his reasons for keeping the two larger balloons (*Union* and *Washington*) in reserve:

> The interests of this branch of service require the immediate construction of two small balloons, for the following . . . reasons . . . :
>
> These two small hydrogen balloons, as compared with the larger ones, will be particularly serviceable at the present time, as they require one wagon less each for moving [hydrogen] generators, while the diminished amount of material required will also tax our transportation facilities to a much less extent.
>
> [Additionally] the most important advantage gained will be that a light balloon, of small dimensions, well filled with hydrogen, presents so much less surface to the wind, and can consequently be used in heavier weather.
>
> . . . [I am] Hoping the general will allow me to construct the two smaller balloons, while the larger ones are held in reserve as future contingencies may determine.[29]

Lowe's insistence that the *Union* and *Washington* be kept in reserve immediately brought him into controversy again with John La Mountain. La Mountain's request for materials to construct new balloons met with no results. Consequently, La Mountain continued to perform ascents under General Franklin's command with the decrepit *Atlantic*, although each flight grew more hazardous until he was forced to abandon its use in mid-December, 1861.

La Mountain was well aware of the balloons that were being kept in reserve in Washington, and he incessantly lobbied Franklin to override Lowe's control over them. When Franklin proved to be of no use in the matter, La Mountain turned to Colonel Macomb to settle the matter.

La Mountain informed the colonel in no uncertain terms that his work as an aeronaut was completely useless unless he was provided with means to continue his reconnaissance work. In December, La Mountain came to Washington, beginning a series of desperate attempts to wrest away one of the unused balloons at the Columbia Armory by any means necessary.

In an emergency dispatch, Clovis Lowe frantically informed his son that La Mountain was planning to take one of the reserve balloons that were under his charge. La Mountain's initial efforts paid off almost immediately.

"Colonel Macomb has taken the balloon *Union* to General McDowell & put La Mountain in charge," the elder Lowe wrote in December, 1861.[30]

It was difficult to get a message to Lowe. He was working to coordinate John Starkweather's pending departure for Port Royal, South Carolina, and was finalizing the various transportation details. A few days later, Clovis Lowe followed up with another urgent note to his son.

It is necessary I should see you on balloon business immediately. Col. Macomb has taken the balloon *Union* and given the charge of it to La Mountain. Will you come up or shall I come down. Despatch without delay.[31]

La Mountain already filed a formal requisition for the balloon, stating that "the necessity for efficient aerial reconnaissance in Gen. Franklin's division" was absolutely requisite for his continued service. The smaller balloon *Washington* was also requested in La Mountain's requisition.[32]

When word of La Mountain's action in Washington eventually reached Thaddeus Lowe, the chief aeronaut's reaction was immediate and unyielding. Under no circumstances would La Mountain be allowed to take possession of the two balloons.

Before the balloons could be taken from the Columbia Armory and transferred over to McDowell, Lowe was able to convene a meeting with General McClellan. Lowe told the commander that the balloons being held in reserve were necessary for the planned Southern assault. He reminded McClellan that he was already preparing his aeronauts for expeditions in Port Royal, South Carolina, and Cairo, Illinois, in addition to service around the nation's capital and northern Virginia. Lowe clearly expected the resources of the Balloon Corps to be stretched to its limits in the following months.

Lowe also did little to disguise his utter contempt for La Mountain, going as far as to state that his rival's use of freeflight reconnaissance missions yielded few tangible results and were nothing more than rabid attempts at garnering publicity in the Northern press. Lowe also alleged that the government was paying La Mountain and his assistants much more than their efforts warranted.

La Mountain's attempt to take away the balloons Lowe had built was the final straw in his grudging peace with the aeronaut. Despite his pledge of cooperation to Fitz-John Porter in September, Lowe now steadfastly refused to work with La Mountain in any capacity.

In view of Lowe's formal protest to McClellan, La Mountain's requisition for the balloons was suspended. However, the battle for control over the aerostats, and ultimately control of the fledgling Balloon Corps, had only just begun in earnest.

When La Mountain learned of McClellan's decision to bar him from taking the balloons, he immediately retaliated by accusing Lowe of keeping the unused balloons for purposes other than the war effort. According to the story La Mountain was spreading around, Lowe was intent on resuming his professional ballooning career after the war, and intended to use the military balloons for commercial exhibition. La Mountain also publicly scoffed at Lowe's use of the aerial telegraph, and stated that the only true way to gather aerial intelligence was by actually sailing over enemy positions in untethered freeflight, as he had done in General Franklin's service.

Lowe immediately refuted the charges and mounted a verbal offensive of his own. The attack that Lowe chose to make upon La Mountain revealed more about Lowe's own seemingly fragile ego and single-minded protectionist attitudes toward the Balloon Corps than it did of his rival's inadequacies in the field of aerial reconnaissance. Lowe seized upon the various published accounts of La Mountain's freeflight ascents, particularly the accounts that lampooned the use of balloons in warfare. In his statements, both private and recorded, Lowe ridiculed La Mountain's efforts to-date, claiming that they had yielded no effective results.

"When my name and reputation as an aeronaut becomes mixed up with such extravagant statements, it places me in a very unpleasant light before the public," wrote Lowe in a letter of protest to General McClellan. "If you should desire to create two separate branches of aeronautics in order to appease the situation that has arisen, these organizations should be as far apart from each other as possible."[33]

Loathe to even mention La Mountain by name, Lowe was adamant that any ballooning activity that resulted in failure or national disgrace would permanently scar the effort that he had put into the Balloon Corps thus far.

"My efforts to further the interests of ballooning may be rendered nugatory," Lowe said. "Or become identified with experimental efforts of those whose theories are widely different from mine. Besides, if such exaggerated statements as the enclosed [articles regarding La Mountain's activity] obtain publicity, the use of balloons for war purposes will soon be treated with ridicule and soon become very unpopular."[34]

With his ire raised, Lowe was not reasonably disposed to stop his war of words. In another letter, this time addressed to McClellan's assistant adjutant general, Colonel Colburn, Lowe continued to vent his anger.

"These outside efforts have . . . interfered with my management, and identified my movements with those of whom I have had no knowledge," he complained, once again veiling any direct reference to La Mountain. "I do not wish to find fault with any aeronauts [McClellan] desires to employ, but I think the movements independently conducted, without head or direction, confuse and retard the general business, leading to a complication of the aeronautic department.

"The men under my direction, as well as myself, are perfectly willing to perform any duty, however hazardous, in the prosecution of the aeronautic service, but would rather prefer to see a unity of action, and have this branch of the service placed under an acknowledged head, who should control all balloon movements under . . . [McClellan's] direction, and do not have the whole Corps responsible for the experiments of those who are not acting in concert with them."[35]

The control that Lowe wished to retain over all balloon operations was apparent. Those who were involved with military planning, however, had little patience for the bursts of unbridled egotism and jealousy between individuals who were still considered only as civilian adjuncts to the war effort. With the upcoming Peninsular Campaign in its early planning stages, and the maneuvering of Union troops under the commands of Henry Halleck in St. Louis and Don Carlos Buell in Louisville, Kentucky, there was no great sense of importance in settling a dispute between two civilian balloonists at McClellan's level, or so it was thought. Colonel Macomb was given the unceremonious task of becoming the Balloon Corps's peacekeeper.

Taking into account General Franklin's endorsement of La Mountain's performance in the field thus far, Macomb was inclined to keep the aeronaut in service with the Union army. Macomb looked past the flurry of allegations and counter-allegations that had cropped up between the two aeronauts and in a letter to Lowe attempted to settle the matter decisively:

> You will please turn over to Mr. J. La Mountain, Aeronaut in the employment in the United States and on duty with the Army of the Potomac, one of the large sized balloons now in your hands here, together with its netting, valve, hoops & car, and take from him duplicate receipts for the same to enable you to account for the property to me.[36]

Lowe received Macomb's letter, but it didn't have the desired effect.

"Mr. La Mountain . . . returned to me and reported that Mr. Lowe refused to comply with the request," Macomb said. "Whereupon I wrote the annexed order for the property to be delivered at once to Mr. La Mountain."[37]

Macomb's order to Lowe was rather more insistent this time:

You will at once deliver to Mr. J. La Mountain the balloon and other articles called for by my letter to you, of the 15th instant, and see that everything which I have directed to be turned over is in good order. . . . This matter admits of no further delay.[38]

Once again La Mountain approached the Columbia Armory with Macomb's directive in hand, but was met with even more obstinate refusal by Lowe and his assistants.

"Mr. La Mountain returned to me this morning & reported that Mr. Lowe refused to recognize my authority and would not obey the order," Macomb later reported.[39]

When Macomb demanded explanations from Lowe as to why he refused to obey a directive to relinquish his control over the balloons, the aeronaut simply claimed that events La Mountain claimed to have transpired were a gross and deliberate misrepresentation. By this time, Macomb was no longer able to accept Lowe's evasiveness as reasonable conduct. When he accused Lowe of acting in a duplicitous manner, Lowe went over Macomb's head and stated his case directly to Colonel Colburn.

With the war between the aeronauts escalating, the entire future of the Balloon Corps hung in the balance. The ongoing squabble was attracting considerable attention, and even staunch supporters of aerial reconnaissance began to tire of the ongoing feud. Lowe surely realized that his position as chief aeronaut was tenuous, as he steadfastly refused to obey military authority.

Even in the field, Lowe's assistants were acutely aware of the chief aeronaut's position. John Steiner, who was assigned to Union army operations in the upper Potomac in February, 1862, wrote to Lowe:

"I saw by the papers that John La Mountain was going to take your place. If so let me know. I will quit . . . I will not serve around J. La Mountain."[40]

Although his situation was dire, Lowe also knew that he held a distinct advantage by refusing to bow down. After all, he had the support of several influential generals, the secretary of the Smithsonian, and even the president of the United States himself. Lowe gambled that his personal reputation and connections would see him through the internal conflict.

Yet, as more pressure was placed on Lowe to release control of the balloon, he reached deeper into the depths by conjuring up unfounded allegations and even more excuses as to why the balloon could not be handed over. In a particularly volatile letter to the adjutant general, Gen. Seth Williams, in February, 1862, Lowe went off on an entirely new tangent to protect his position within the Balloon Corps.

"This machinery is entirely new," Lowe said in his letter, referring to the balloons and the portable hydrogen gas generators he was still hoping to patent. "And the designs are original with me. I have taken pains to instruct all the aeronauts in the service employed by me, in its use, and without such instruction, I am unwilling to risk this machinery in their hands knowing that they are honest men and skillful in their profession. I feel more confidence in their use of it than I can in a person who has no reputation in his profession in the minds of scientific men."[41]

However, Lowe was unwilling to admit that it was his proprietary interests in the Balloon Corps that prevented him from cooperating with La Mountain. Finally removing all veiled references, in the same letter to Williams, Lowe pulled out all the stops as he attempted to grind his rival's reputation into the ground:

[La Mountain is] a man who is known to be unscrupulous, and prompted by jealousy or some other motive, has assailed me without cause through the press and otherwise for several years. . . . He has tampered with my men, tending to a demoralization of them, and in short, has stopped at nothing to injure me.

This man La Mountain has told my men that he is my superior and is considered so by the Commanding General . . . He says that he is paid by Lieutenant Colonel Macomb two hundred dollars more per month than I am paid. . . .

I do not think that I should serve this man by giving to him possession of my improved balloons and portable gas generator for his examination. . . .

Without the improvements that I have made in the manufacture and management of balloons, they could be of little service to
the Government; add to that my invention of the portable gas generator, which I am using for the benefit of the Government Service, I submit that I should not be interfered with in the
management of this matter, at least until I have instructed men in
the use of my invention.[42]

No matter what Lowe personally thought of La Mountain's ability or
reputation, there is absolutely no evidence to corroborate Lowe's claim that
La Mountain misrepresented his standing or salary within the Union army.
It was well known to both the press and field commanders who encountered La Mountain that his status was that of a freelance balloonist. La
Mountain was paid exactly the same amount as Lowe for his services—$10
a day.

Regardless of their validity, Lowe's charges meant that more explanations were required to justify the continued existence of the civilian Balloon
Corps. In a letter to General Williams, Macomb, clearly exasperated over
the entire situation, was once again forced to detail the costs:

The sum of $500 a month is the total amount paid for the services
of Mr. La Mountain & his two assistants. The statement that [La
Mountain's] own pay is of that amount for a month is therefore
untrue.

The pay of Mr. Lowe for himself & two of his assistants of the
lowest grade comes to $525 a month.

His own [Lowe's] pay is $10 a day & Mr. La Mountain's is
nearly as much.[43]

In the meantime, as Lowe managed to create considerable controversy
while managing to remain master of the military balloons, John La Mountain and his assistants remained idle in Washington, D.C. For La Mountain,
it was an intolerable situation. In what was to be a futile effort, he tried to
persuade General Franklin to intervene on his behalf. In a letter to the general, La Mountain once again summed up his personal frustration along
with his own litany of charges:

There are stored in the Armory in Washington, new balloons
which cost the government $1500 each, and which are under

charge of Prof. Lowe, who I understand wishes to keep them (as he
has done all winter) from being used by me, and to buy them for a
trifle after the War is ended, thus depriving you of the information
I might obtain if I had a good balloon, and all through motives of
professional jealousy at my superior Reputation as an Aeronaut.

In view of this, if you could see General Marcy personally, and
state to him these facts I have no doubt your influence would procure an order from him at once, for a Balloon with which I could
be of immediate service. Hoping this may strike you favorably and
that you will give the matter an early attention, I remain,

Very respectfully your obedient servant,
John La Mountain,
Aeronaut[44]

Not long after La Mountain's letter was received, the general obliged
the aeronaut by writing on his behalf. Franklin's words, however, oddly
lacked the conviction that would bring about swift action:

Mr. La Mountain is of no use to the Army without a large balloon.
If, as he says, there are three balloons in store in Washington, I
respectfully recommend that he be allowed to take one of them.

I think that his qualities as an aeronaut are as good as those of
others, but I acknowledge that I have had few opportunities of
judging of them.[45]

Despite Franklin's somewhat ambiguous letter, another requisition was
made to Union Army Headquarters to place one of the military balloons
into La Mountain's charge. But the effort would come to nothing. Lowe's
political connections and successful character attacks on La Mountain
resulted in a decision to dismiss La Mountain from any further service
within the military.

The final word on the matter was made public shortly thereafter. As the
Philadelphia *Inquirer* reported on March 19, 1862:

Notwithstanding attempts of interested parties to create a contrary
impression, we learn from the best authority that Professor Lowe is
head of the Aeronautics Department of the entire army.

Professor La Mountain, who once had a position of some sort,
is no longer connected with the army.[46]

It was an unceremonious announcement that did nothing to credit or highlight La Mountain's efforts, which always seemed to be affected by the most severe deprivation. But as capable an aerialist as he was, John La Mountain was not a match for the driving ambition and eminence of Thaddeus Lowe. With a clash of egos as immense as the one that erupted between these two men, there was no room for more than one person to take charge. From this time onward, the responsibility for the successes and failures of the Union army's Balloon Corps would rest on the shoulders of just one man.

CHAPTER EIGHT

Disillusioned Aeronauts

The controversy that embroiled Thaddeus Lowe and John La Mountain may have been a distraction, but it was not really an impediment as far as the deployment of the Balloon Corps to field service. With considerable press attention devoted to the Union army's establishment of an aeronautics program and a substantial amount of money already invested in what had become the world's first extensive use of aeronautics in military action, Union leaders were anxious to have their faith and confidence in the Balloon Corps actually pay off.

By the end of 1861, Lowe had supervised the construction of a number of balloons and hydrogen generators and had received several aeronauts who could work compatibly under his direction. However, there was one element of the Balloon Corps yet to be unveiled.

It was known as the *George Washington Parke-Custis*, a 122 foot barge built in 1853 that was originally used to haul grain, coal, and other goods on the Potomac between Washington and Mount Vernon prior to the war.[1] The U.S. Navy purchased the ship in 1861 for $150 and it was residing at the naval shipyard in Washington, D.C., at the time Lowe was constructing his hydrogen generators.

Lowe immediately seized upon the potential of using the barge as a means to expand the operations of the Balloon Corps. It is not known whether Lowe was inspired by reports of John La Mountain's balloon being towed by a steam tug near Fortress Monroe, but he intended to use the barge in a similar manner and obtain useful intelligence of Confederate activity along the Potomac and other waterways.

The George Washington Parke-Custis *was arguably the world's first aircraft carrier. Although it originally began its life as a barge, Thaddeus Lowe ordered the craft to be outfitted to accommodate his balloons and support equipment.*

Lowe was initially refused permission to use the barge by Captain Dahlgren, superintendent of the Washington shipyards. Its usefulness as a coal tender was deemed vital to naval operations. Dahlgren, however, relented after Lowe took his case directly to Secretary of the Navy Gideon Welles, who was intrigued with the prospect of combining aerial capabilities with naval vessels.

Work on the *George Washington Parke-Custis* began in October, 1861, and progressed quickly. Its long, flat, wide deck lended itself to Lowe's plans. A small deckhouse was erected at the boat's stern, which was to serve as a ready room for the aeronaut when the vessel was under way. At the stern were also two of Lowe's hydrogen generators. The hold of the barge had only a depth of 5 1/2 feet, but that was more than adequate to contain all the supplies that went along with balloon operations, including the large quantities of metal filings and sulfuric acid required to feed the hydrogen generators.

When the conversion work was finally completed in early November, the *George Washington Parke-Custis* was fully equipped to support Lowe's balloons. Although it lacked its own mode of propulsion and had to be towed from location to location, it nevertheless represented the first water vessel purposely designed to be used in support of an aerial apparatus and could be arguably identified as the direct forerunner to the twentieth-century aircraft carrier.

A steam tug, the *Coeur de Lion*, was used to move the balloon barge at various points along the Potomac. By November 10, 1861, Lowe was ready to get under way. The barge was towed to the mouth of Mattowoman Creek in Maryland, near Marbury, under orders from General McClellan. John Starkweather and John Steiner, the Balloon Corps's newly appointed assistant aeronauts, were also along for the maiden voyage, which also marked the first use of Lowe's recently completed hydrogen generators.

Thaddeus Lowe was obviously pleased with the result of the barge's first outing when he wrote to Colonel Colburn two days later:

> I have the pleasure of reporting the complete success of the first balloon expedition by water ever attempted. I left the Navy ship-yard early Sunday morning . . . having on board competent Ass't Aeronauts, together with my new Gas Generating Apparatus which, tho' used for the first time, worked admirably.[2]

Lowe spent his time on the barge constructively. Aside from drilling Starkweather and Steiner on how to conduct inflation and tether procedures on board ship, actual observations were also conducted. On November 11, Lowe was joined by Gen. Daniel Sickles, a commander under General Hooker, along with several others for a reconnaissance.

"We had a fine view of the Enemy's camp fires during the evening," Lowe later wrote. "[We] saw the Rebels constructing new batteries at Freestone Point [Virginia]."[3]

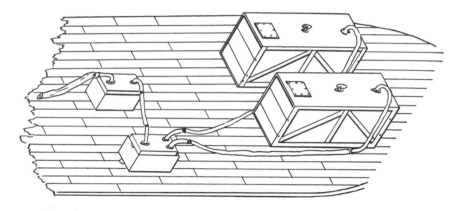

The aft deck of the George Washington Parke-Custis *was outfitted with two portable hydrogen gas generators, allowing the balloons to be operated far away from city gas supplies.* NATIONAL AIR & SPACE MUSEUM

When the balloon barge returned to Washington it didn't remain idle for very long. On November 16, the aeronaut received word from Colonel Colburn that McClellan wished to have a balloon and aeronaut ready to accompany Gen. Thomas W. Sherman's expedition to Port Royal, South Carolina. Colburn was unclear as to exactly when the balloon and aeronaut would be needed, but promised, "three or four days' notice" before the required departure date. With Port Royal deep inside Confederate territory the mission would prove to be the most demanding test for the Balloon Corps yet.

By the time Lowe was contacted about the South Carolina expedition, the invasion of Port Royal had already begun. A week earlier, on November 7, Union admiral Samuel Dupont, with an armada of 75 warships and 12,000 troops, succeeded in overwhelming poorly trained Southern artillerymen manning the heavy guns at Fort Walker and Fort Beauregard.

With Hilton Head and Bay Point under Federal control, the way was open for the use of ground troops through Port Royal Sound.

"The balloon for the South is all ready," Lowe reported to Colburn on November 21. "Can you tell me from what place I shall ship the materials for making gas? If from here I must have them sent from Philadelphia to this city (Washington, D.C.), that they may be ready."[4]

When all was in readiness, Lowe and Starkweather prepared to leave Washington. During Lowe's absence, John Steiner was left in charge of the *Intrepid*, and operated the balloon in the vicinity of the upper Potomac until February, 1862.[5]

"General McClellan desires that you send a balloon to Fort Monroe this evening at latest by to-morrow evening's boat to go to Port Royal," Colburn wrote in a dispatch to Lowe. "The transports will leave Fort Monroe day after to-morrow."[6]

In addition to transporting a balloon and aeronaut for use in the Port Royal invasion, Lowe was also instructed to make a reconnaissance for Brig. Gen. Joseph Hooker's division stationed near Budd's Ferry, Maryland, at Posey House. A complete balloon outfit comprising of the *Washington* and necessary supplies had already been shipped to Hooker's headquarters. In a dispatch, Lowe informed the general that he and Starkweather, along with Lowe's other assistant, William Paullin, would be ready to depart Washington, D.C., by November 24 with the *George Washington Parke-Custis* in tow behind the steamer *Coeur de Lion*.

Not far from Washington, the hamlet surrounding Budd's Ferry was considered an important strategic point. Directly across the Potomac from Budd's Ferry were the shores of western Virginia. As Lowe and his crew aboard the *George Washington Parke-Custis* came into view of Budd's Ferry there was noticeable apprehension over just how far they would be from Rebel artillery fire. Fortunately for Lowe it was a military correspondent for the New York *Herald* attached to Hooker's division who was among the first to witness the balloon barge's arrival:

This afternoon, about four o'clock, a steamer was seen coming down the river towing a nondescript sort of craft. As they came near the steamer was found to be the *Coeur de Lion*, and the craft in tow the balloon vessel of Professor Lowe. . . .

On going aboard the *Coeur de Lion* I saw Professor Lowe, with who I had a previous acquaintance, and he promised me an ascent.

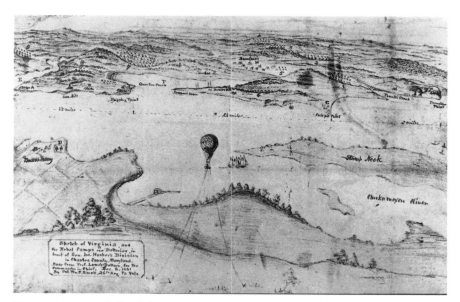

Panoramic map of Confederate positions around the lower Potomac sketched by Col. William F. Small on December 8, 1861, from Lowe's balloon tethered at Budd's Ferry. NATIONAL ARCHIVES

A consultation was held and it was determined that the *Coeur de Lion* should anchor in the shelter of Mattowoman Creek for the night, and that a special messenger should be sent to appraise General Hooker of the arrival of Professor Lowe.[7]

A sergeant from the 4th Michigan Regiment was ordered to deliver the news to Hooker and the *Herald* reporter volunteered to act as a "guide," having already gone to Hooker's headquarters at Posey House before:

> We had traveled three miles through a dense forest, with mud half-knee deep in some places, and had gone half mile out of our way in addition. When we reached our destination the Sergeant delivered his dispatches, which were immediately acted upon, and we started on our cheerless way back, arriving on board the *Coeur de Lion* at eleven o'clock, having tramped through the mud since half-past six o'clock.[8]

Hooker's orders were intended to waste little time the following morning.

"The safest and most convenient place for anchoring your steamer will be about one mile below your former anchorage," Hooker wrote back. "The balloon is now near Posey House, and it is from that point I desire to make the ascensions, if agreeable to yourself."[9]

Lowe complied with Hooker's directive. He and William Paullin prepared the balloon for launch, and General Hooker personally accompanied the aeronauts on a reconnaissance of the Virginia shoreline.

The observations taken that day proved to be the first of many over the next few weeks. They revealed numerous Confederate encampments along a two mile stretch that included a particularly heavy concentration at Quantico. On December 8, Hooker ordered Col. William F. Small, of the Topographical Engineers, to render an exact panoramic map of the area opposite Budd's Ferry from Lowe's balloon.

Afterwards, William Paullin was left in charge of balloon operations on the upper Potomac under Hooker's command. Paullin was adept at impressing the officers with whom he worked, and even earned a note of favorable review from Colonel Small in a field report.[10] Unfortunately, Paullin's career with the corps would end abruptly only weeks later. Lowe discovered that Paullin was supplementing his income as an aeronaut by engaging in the manufacture and sale of ambrotype photographs to the soldiers. Lowe viewed this as a dereliction of duty to the Balloon Corps and dismissed Paullin in January, 1862.[11]

Following the balloon barge's brief stopover at Budd's Ferry, Lowe and his party proceeded on to Fortress Monroe, arriving two days later on November 27. Once there, Lowe made a formal presentation of the balloon *Washington* and its personnel to General Sherman, although the balloon barge itself was to return with Lowe to the capital.

"By direction of Genl. McClellan, I send to your command a balloon and aeronautic apparatus, in charge of Mr. J. B. Starkweather, Aeronaut," wrote Lowe. "Mr. Starkweather will require thirty men and a good officer. Should it be necessary to take observations at various points there will be required two ordinary Army wagons, to convey the gas generators and materials. Anything further that will be required will be made known by the Aeronaut."[12]

Starkweather's presence with Sherman's Port Royal expeditionary force was yet another milestone in the brief history of the Balloon Corps. Although John La Mountain had operated from Fortress Monroe the previous summer, Starkweather's duty with Sherman's division would mean that the balloon would be used deep inside Confederate territory, far from the safe harbor and supply channels of a heavy fortification, even one as remote as Fortress Monroe. However, one of the more challenging aspects of the Port Royal operation, as far as Starkweather was concerned, would be the seeming indifference of the expedition's commander, Thomas W. Sherman.

Sherman was a career soldier and a decorated veteran of the Seminole Wars and the Mexican War. A stern and unyielding taskmaster from Rhode Island, Sherman was described as an, "officer of unquestioned ability, but . . . in some ways unfitted to handling volunteers not inured to iron discipline."[13] And just as many old guard officers of the Union army were resistant to new developments in military technology, Sherman also had absolutely no desire for a balloonist to accompany his expeditionary force.

Starkweather's arrival at Fortress Monroe was greeted somewhat half-heartedly. Living up to his reputation for cautiousness, General McClellan had ordered a thorough balloon reconnaissance of the South Carolina coast. However, Sherman chose to ignore the directive completely and staged the Port Royal invasion relying on reports from ground scouts instead. While troop transports left Fortress Monroe on an almost daily basis, Starkweather remained behind, unable to secure passage.

Finally, in early January, 1862, five weeks after his arrival at Monroe, Starkweather managed to board the transport ship *Empire*. Arriving at Hilton Head on January 3, the aeronaut was fully prepared to be placed into service in some capacity. Starkweather was in for bitter disappointment, as Sherman had no intention of utilizing any form of aerial observation. As the military operation proceeded, months literally passed by as Starkweather remained impatiently idle.

"I have not had a chance to operate with the balloon," Starkweather bitterly complained in a letter to Lowe. "I have not had any orders from the General . . . The balloon is all in good order and ready for use at any moment, if I should be called upon. You say that you are anxious that every member of the Aeronautic Department should render all the valuable service possible. I am anxious to do the same . . . All I want is the chance.[14]

Lowe attempted to intervene on behalf of his assistant, but Sherman was obstinate in his opposition to using the balloon under his command. Selective obedience to certain orders was something of a character trait with Sherman. Later in the war, when he was in charge of the 6th Division in Tennessee, he neglected to order his troops into battle near Vicksburg while under General Halleck's command. He suffered dire consequences for his negligence when he belatedly and haphazardly entered the battlefield and suffered a wound that necessitated the amputation of his leg.

As Starkweather's cloud of frustration mounted, a silver lining did manage to present itself. By March, 1862, the success of the Port Royal invasion caused the War Department to form a new theater of war, known as the Department of the South. Brig. Gen. Henry Washington Benham replaced Sherman at Port Royal. Benham was also a veteran of the Mexican War, but his pre–Civil War military career had focused on overseeing the construction of harbors and coastal defenses. An engineer by trade, Benham proved to have a more open-minded approach to employing the balloonist under his command.

Although the new commander was initially preoccupied with planning the capture of Fort Pulaski and James Island, he eventually met with Starkweather. Plans were soon put into action to have the aeronaut scout the area beyond his position on the island of Hilton Head.

Starkweather was quick to discover, however, that the coastal winds that constantly blew over the island in the early spring weather made ascents extremely difficult.

In a letter to Thaddeus Lowe, Starkweather recounted his problems.

"The balloon could not be used to any advantage on this island," he reported. "It was too near the seacoast and the wind has been blowing from the sea and shore."[15]

In addition to adverse weather, other problems cropped up that hampered Starkweather's operations. Among the aeronautic supplies that had been delivered to Fortress Monroe back in December, there were only "thirteen barrels of iron filings and eight carboys of sulfuric acid."[16] From these initial supplies no more than two inflations of the *Washington* could be made. Although the lack of supplies had not really posed a problem during Starkweather's period of inactivity with General Sherman, with his services now in demand from General Benham the shortages became critical.

On one occasion, following the capture of Fort Pulaski, Georgia, in April, 1862, Starkweather was ordered to move his balloon from the fort to aid Gen. Isaac Stevens' forces in the capture of nearby James Island. Starkweather, who had already had the *Washington* fully inflated for observation duty at Fort Pulaski, requested that the balloon be towed to James Island, suspecting that he lacked a sufficient supply of acid to produce hydrogen at the more remote location. When Benham informed Starkweather that time was of the essence, and that the delay involved in securing a transport could not be afforded, the aeronaut reluctantly deflated the balloon. However, when Starkweather arrived on James Island his suspicions were proven correct when he discovered that he indeed lacked sufficient supplies.[17]

To make matters worse, when Starkweather wrote to Lowe about his supply problems, Lowe attempted to remedy the situation by arranging to have a supply ship sent south. But the ship never made it to Hilton Head, as a result of being wrecked in one of the numerous storms that frequently ravaged the southeastern coast.

Supplies eventually did reach Starkweather and he did manage to perform some service for the Union. From Fort Pulaski, Starkweather was ordered to take observations of nearby Savannah, Georgia. On April 19, the *Washington* was inflated and placed on the steamer *Mayflower*, where Starkweather and Lt. P. H. O'Rorke were able to note the number of Confederate gunboats positioned along the Savannah River. A few days later Starkweather again took to the sky, this time observing Confederate fortifications under construction on the southeastern side of Savannah and a nearly completed Confederate ironclad moored in the town's harbor.[18]

But this period of activity was relatively short-lived. In June, Starkweather was ordered to take the *Washington* from Fort Pulaski to James Island—thirty-five miles away—for observations. Once again, the balloon was inflated and the *Mayflower* was to be used to tow the balloon. Unfortunately, the coastal winds which had hampered Starkweather earlier, now returned with a vengeance. The *Mayflower* became unwieldy in the choppy waters of Port Royal Sound. Despite the best efforts of the *Mayflower*'s crew, the stormy weather proved to be too much and the steamer ran aground. The *Washington*, which was firmly tethered to the deck of the steamer, tore loose from the impact and was thrown up against the ship's bridge. The delicate silk of the envelope was caught up in part of the bridge's superstructure, causing considerable damage to the fabric.

When Starkweather assessed the damage inflicted on the *Washington*, it was determined that the tears sustained were far too serious to be repaired in the field. Reluctantly, Starkweather was forced to ship the remnants of his balloon back to Washington, D.C., essentially ending the Balloon Corps's operations in the deep South.

As for Starkweather himself, after Port Royal he appeared only to serve as an assistant directly working with Lowe, and for the remainder of his career within the Corps, he did not operate a balloon far removed from the area of northern Virgina.

John Starkweather's experience working with inflexible generals in the field was in sharp contrast with the early work of John Steiner. Steiner was assigned to patrol the upper Potomac with the balloon *Intrepid*, where he enjoyed a reasonably good working relationship with Union generals. Steiner reported primarily to Gen. Charles Stone, commander of Stone's brigade at Edward's Ferry. Stone proved to be fairly progressive in accepting the new technology of aerial reconnaissance, and Steiner was kept in almost constant employment during his period of service with the general.

Observations along the upper Potomac were not without their dangers, though. On one occasion in January, 1862, Steiner and a mapping party were ordered by Stone to ascend on a dawn patrol. Apparently, a group of Confederate snipers had maneuvered themselves close to the launching site overnight, and as the balloon rose, the Rebels opened fire. A volley of minié balls filled the air and the cap of one of the officers was shot clear off, though miraculously no one on board *Intrepid* sustained injury. Afterwards, Steiner wrote to Lowe of the incident and requested that he be issued a revolver so that next time he could return the enemy's fire.[19]

Despite the dangers, Steiner reveled in the constant activity under Stone's command. The work was varied and even the prospect of cheating death had a certain exhilaration to it. Steiner was ready for greater challenges in early 1862. So when word began to filter through various channels that General McClellan had ordered an invasion of the Confederacy through Illinois, Steiner immediately volunteered his services.

In light of his enthusiasm to embark on operations in a new theater of war, Steiner would soon discover many of the same frustrations and deprivations that had demoralized John Starkweather in South Carolina.

On February 17, Colonel Macomb relayed orders from McClellan to Lowe to "send a balloon with the inflating apparatus to Cairo, Illinois."

On February 21, 1862, Steiner received orders from Thaddeus Lowe to prepare himself and the balloon *Eagle* for transport. Cairo—located on the banks of the Mississippi—was the Union army's assembly point for its intended invasion of the western frontier of the Confederacy. At Cairo the aeronaut was to report to Brig. Gen. George Washington Cullum, acting chief of staff to Gen. Henry Halleck, commander in the Department of the Mississippi.

At the time of Steiner's appointment, nearly 100,000 Union soldiers served in the Department of the Mississippi; however, the organization of the army there was seriously lacking. It was said that when Halleck originally arrived to take command of his army he had to send an aide to buy maps from a St. Louis bookstore in order to have even a rudimentary understanding of the area's geography.[20] On the whole, it looked like the perfect opportunity for an ambitious aeronaut to prove his worth.

Yet Steiner encountered difficulties with Halleck's army from almost the start. When he arrived in Cairo, Steiner immediately sought out General Cullum and presented his papers. The general met the aeronaut with a cold air of indifference, informing him that no one at departmental headquarters was even aware that a balloon had been assigned and that his arrival must be some sort of mistake. Steiner's difficulties were also compounded by his heavy, German-accented English that made communication even more difficult.

"I can not git eny ascistence here," wrote Steiner to Lowe. "Thay say that know nothing about my balloon business thay even laugh ad me. Let me hear from you as soon as possible and give me a paper from headquarters to theas blockheads hoo I am. All the officers hear are as dum as a set of asses."[21]

Lowe attempted to intervene on Steiner's behalf and a letter was drafted by Gen. Lorenzo Thomas, McClellan's adjutant general. The missive, which ended with the phrase, "By order of the Secretary of War," went to great lengths to convey the general in chief's desire to integrate aerial reconnaissance with the movements of the Union army in the West.

"Respectfully referred to Major General Halleck, . . ., in order that the aeronaut sent to Cairo may be paid & receive necessary assistance. He is available for service wherever he may be required in the Department of the Mississippi."[22]

Despite the letter from Thomas, very little in the way of formal recognition was forthcoming to Steiner. Halleck's staff refused to put Steiner and his balloon into service, claiming that the orders drafted in Washington were never received.

While Halleck's officers continued to turn a blind eye to the potential benefits of aerial reconnaissance, Steiner and his balloon were not completely ignored. As the Union army was massing in Cairo, the Rebels prepared to be attacked. About six miles south of their positions at New

Madrid, Missouri, the Confederates constructed a gun battery on a large sandbar known as Island No. 10. The location of Island No. 10 was ideally suited for defense, being situated on a crescent-shaped bend in the Mississippi River. Additionally, the batteries on shore at New Madrid and on Island No. 10 were defended by over 7,000 Confederates. Confederate leaders realized the importance of blocking navigation of the Mississippi to the Yankees, and were determined to defend their fortifications.

The Union attack on New Madrid and Island No. 10 was to be a joint effort by both the Union army and navy. Adm. Andrew H. Foote was in command of a flotilla of six gunboats and eleven mortar boats, which also included several "Pook Turtles," the Union's new ironclad gunboats.

During strategy planning sessions in Cairo, Foote learned of Steiner and his reconnaissance balloon. Although Halleck and his staff probably in all likelihood portrayed Steiner's presence as someone's idea of a poor carnival act that the Department of the Mississippi was saddled with, Foote took exception. He sought out Steiner and requested that the aeronaut prepare his equipment.

Foote intended to use Steiner and the *Eagle* to reconnoiter the enemy's position on Island No. 10 from the deck of one of the admiral's flatboats. Steiner was also to observe the accuracy of the fire from Foote's mortar boats onto the Rebel fortifications.

News quickly spread of the use of the balloon with Foote's command. A correspondent with the St. Louis–based *Daily Missouri Democrat* was particularly enthused with the decision to put Steiner into action:

> The enemy's forts can be closely inspected, the number of guns and their range obtained. It can be learned whether or not they have an infantry force in the rear, which for some time has been a matter of speculation. The attempt to evacuate can be immediately discovered, and the effect of our own shooting can be learned and corrected if in any respect at fault.[23]

On March 23, Steiner inflated the *Eagle* and prepared for an onboard launch from an anchorage not far from Foote's own flagship, the *Benton*. High winds and a raging torrent of rain that day and for the next two days prevented Steiner and his balloon from being used. The miserable weather conditions also had its affect on the advancing Union army as floods caused water to rise to a depth of four feet in some areas.[24] However, by March 26 the winds finally subsided and allowed the aeronaut to make a successful launch.

Accompanied by Col. N. B. Buford and Capt. H. E. Maynadier, Steiner was able to demonstrate the unique ability of his aerial observation post. From a vantage point of over 1,200 feet, the results of Foote's bombardment of Island No. 10 could be fully assessed. While it was obvious that the Rebel positions had taken a pounding from the gunboats, it was observed that a number of shells had overreached their targets and not been effective.[25]

On returning to earth, Buford and Maynadier communicated slight corrections in the trajectory of the shells fired from Foote's mortar boats. With the mortars now able to achieve pinpoint accuracy, it was the finishing blow to the Confederates on Island No. 10. On April 7, 1862, ground forces led by Gen. John Pope were successful in capturing the position. Over 3,500 Confederates along with numerous arms and artillery pieces were captured. It was an important victory for the Union. The Mississippi was now open to Northern navigation all the way south to Fort Pillow, Tennessee.

Despite his successful contribution to Admiral Foote's naval bombardment of Island No. 10, Steiner found that he was still unable to line up employment with the army. Although he continued to lobby Halleck's staff for an assignment, none was forthcoming. Fed up with his constant presence at departmental headquarters, Steiner was eventually told that perhaps he would be put into service if he joined up with the army headquarters in St. Louis. Steiner reluctantly left Cairo and arrived in Missouri in April, 1862.

"I came here but I finde no such papers arrivid here," he wrote to Lowe. "I told the Gen. here how I was situateed and ounder wot sircumstands I had bid send out here. He loock ad me a momment and then sed I can doo nothing for you and walk off, and such has bin my treedment every ware."[26]

Although Lowe had attempted to channel all of his resources and connections within the army to come to the aid of his assistant, the remote location of Steiner's assignment made favorable intervention on his behalf difficult if not altogether impossible. Once again, generals rigidly schooled in the traditional methods of nineteenth-century warfare were not flexible or farsighted enough to see the value of an airborne scout.

Meanwhile, the Union army in the west was involved in a number of bloody battles as Steiner and his balloon remained idle. In late March, Halleck ordered troops under the commands of Don Carlos Buell and Ulysses S. Grant to mount an offensive against the Confederate stronghold at Corinth. The combined forces of Buell and Grant totalled over 75,000 men.

The Rebels, led by Albert Sydney Johnston, were at a numerical disadvantage with only 44,000 troops concentrated in and around Corinth. But Johnston had no fear of the approaching Yanks.

"I would fight them if they were a million," he defiantly told his corps commanders. Johnston's words, however, would come at a high price.

On the morning of April 6, the fury between the two opposing forces erupted. Confederate forces fought a protracted and stubborn battle with Union troops near a small log church named Shiloh, just north of Corinth. The battle soon became a tangled bloodbath with waves and waves of men from both sides sent against one another. At the heart of the slaughter was a zone so hazardous to human life that it was aptly named the "Hornet's Nest" by those fortunate enough to have survived.

Late in the afternoon of April 6, General Johnston became a casualty on the Confederate side when he was shot in the leg and bled to death. His successor, Pierre Gustave Toutant Beauregard, ordered the remaining Rebel troops to withdraw from Shiloh and return to Corinth by the end of the day on April 7.

The final toll at Shiloh was devasting. The Union suffered a loss of over 13,000 men—1,754 killed, 8,408 wounded, and 2,885 captured or missing. The losses for the smaller Confedearte force were equally horrific—1,723 killed, 8,012 wounded, and 959 missing or wounded. With a combined casuality count of nearly 24,000 men, the grim reality of the war was clearly brought home to both the North and South.

While one of the most important campaigns of the Civil War played out, John Steiner could do little more than be an observer from the sidelines.

"I could have bin of grade servis at Corince [Corinth]," Steiner wrote to Lowe in June. "[I] explained it to General Halleck at Pittsburgh Landing, but he told me stay ad Cairo ontill he wold sende for me."[27]

Steiner regretfully concluded that he, "was satisfied that General Halleck [was] no friend to the Aeronatics Core."

The stubborn official will that prevented Steiner from taking to the air remained. While Steiner vented his displeasure in a number of letters to Lowe, reports of the aeronaut's treatment were leaked to the Northern press. Some newspapers began to openly question the circumstances that forced Steiner to remain grounded.

"Captain Steiner is now at Cairo . . . with all necessary appurtenances for making [aerial] observations," wrote one reporter in the Philadelphia *Inquirer.* "Very strangely he has had no orders to proceed with his labors . . . [Steiner] should be afforded an opportunity to inform us whether the enemy are in certain positions, as stated, or not."[28]

The Philadelphia correspondent was particularly harsh in his assessment of military leadership that failed to take advantage of the new technology they were offered.

". . . What can be expected when the matter is left to the discrimination of one or two fossils who have no time for anything else but to prepare official dispatches wherein 'I' largely figures."[29]

Condemnation by the press, however, did little to further Steiner's cause. By June, the aeronaut had spent four months of virtual inactivity with the Union army in the West and his situation offered few prospects of an improvement in the future. To make matters worse, the salary that was to be paid to Steiner—$5.25 per day, with the aeronaut paying for his own food rations—was being withheld. Steiner was still a civilian, and since the headquarters for the Department of the Mississippi claimed not to have received any orders regarding his official status, he was not subject to any remuneration.

In desperate straits, Steiner once again took his case to a high-ranking Union commander. This time it was Gen. John Pope, commander of the Army of the Mississippi.

Perhaps aware that his appallingly poor command of the English language was something of a detriment in making his position clear, Steiner enlisted an individual with somewhat greater—though still not perfect— fluency to assist him in drafting a letter to the general. Steiner was also certain to enclose all copies of correspondence he had had with Lowe and members of General Halleck's staff up to this time.

Sir,

Enclosed you will find several papers to which I wish to call your atention [*sic*]. I was ordered to report—on my origanal [*sic*] orders—to Commanding Officer at Cairo, Ill. by Major General Halleck on the 21st of April, 1862, which I have done but received no further orders up to this time.

I cannot see why I am kept out of active service so long. I am anxious to be placed in proper relation with your Command if agreeable to you.

Please return inclosed papers with your reply and oblige your obedient servant,

J.H. Steiner,
Aeronaut—U.S.A.[30]

Unfortunately for Steiner, Pope was reassigned to a new command in Virginia and proved to be of no help whatsoever. Now down to the last penny of his own financial resources, Steiner was ready to throw in the towel and said as much to Lowe in letters.

"I am here like a dog wisout a tail and I dond know ware I will be ebel to draw my pay for no one seams to know eny thing abought this thing."[31]

Another letter to Lowe reflected much of the same emotion from the neglect imposed upon him.

"I am treeded wis contempt," wrote Steiner. "If I had the means to return to Washington I wold start today. I can git no pay out here."[32]

The salary woes continued to dog Steiner. Finally in June, some money was paid out to Steiner after Lowe wrote several letters to the Army Paymaster's headquarters in Washington. However, paymasters with the Army of the Mississippi grudgingly paid only half of what was actually owed to the aeronaut. The question over the remainder of Steiner's salary would not be resolved for several months to come.

On June 28, 1862, John Steiner wrote to Lowe requesting transport for himself and his balloon equipment back to Washington. Steiner would remain with the Balloon Corps, although the aeronaut's initial enthusiasm would never burn as bright again.

In many ways the early efforts of the Balloon Corps were disappointing, though not through lack of effort on the part of Lowe and his assistants. Within the Union army there were those who saw the activities of Lowe and his aeronauts as some sort of extension of a carnival act and resisted the imposition of having to be saddled with a balloon. They viewed the use of balloons as a heinous waste of men and materiel.

In retrospect, it would be simple to say that many of the Union's field commanders simply lacked the vision to employ aerial reconnaissance to its fullest advantage. The rigid views that many of the old school generals held were hard to dispel. Their training and experience were on the battlefield of wars and skirmishes fought decades before. The concept of a "soldier in the air" was completely alien to them.

Yet support for Lowe and his grand experiment was still strong among the upper echelons of the army and government, including McClellan himself. And more importantly, the Balloon Corps's efforts were beginning to exact a toll on the morale of Confederate forces that encountered the sight of the huge globes in the sky. For Lowe, however, the most important mission for the Balloon Corps was yet to come.

CHAPTER NINE

The Balloon Corps and the Peninsular Campaign

T he beginning of 1862 proved to be a difficult time for Thaddeus Lowe, as the aeronaut tenaciously stuck to his position as chief aeronaut. This was in spite of the fact that many Union field commanders still regarded his efforts with suspicion.

However, as rumors circulated that the army was planning a major offensive against the South, Lowe discovered that the army's general in chief—George B. McClellan—remained a key supporter of his work.

Still, the difficulty in maintaining the fleet of balloons was proving a daunting task for Lowe, and with the departure of two of his aeronauts, he was forced to seek out competent replacements.

Yet the potential for great things still lay ahead for the Balloon Corps as McClellan began to finalize his strategy for the long-delayed Peninsular Campaign. Prodded by Lincoln and other Northern political leaders to take decisive action against the South, McClellan's plan was to plunge the Army of the Potomac into a full assault in Virginia. Always weighing in on the side of cautiousness, McClellan planned to make intelligence gathered by aerial observation an integral part of his invasion.

Meanwhile, as plans for the Virginia assault continued to evolve, Thaddeus Lowe was looking for new and different ways that his balloons could be of use to the Union cause.

Lowe's early demonstration of the aerial telegraph was part of the reason that he had been allowed to form the Balloon Corps in the first place, and the aeronaut was successful in convincing McClellan on the need to expand its range. A special "telegraph train," consisting of a horse-drawn wagon that carried a telegraph key, a heavy 150 volt lead-acid electrical storage battery, and a large, stretcher-like spool containing over five miles of insulated wire, was added to the corps' inventory. If it was deemed necessary that observations from a balloon needed to be directly transmitted to a field commander, this could be accomplished by connecting the wire running from the balloon to the nearest telegraph pole.

As Lowe recounted, "[The telegraph train] enabled me to make reports directly from the car of the balloon while viewing the enemy's position. The line [was] otherwise useful for transmitting other messages not connected with my department."[1]

Along with the telegraph train, Lowe also gained the invaluable services of Parker Spring, a Western Union telegrapher whose work would later prove invaluable to the Balloon Corps at the battle of Fair Oaks.

Lowe was also among the first to employ the use of artificial light on the battlefield. With the gas generators used to inflate his balloons, Lowe had an almost constant supply of hydrogen at his disposal which he used to construct an "oxyhydrogen" arc lamp that was capable of providing tremendous illumination. Lowe originally used the lamps to supervise the inflation of his balloons at night but soon discovered that the powerful light source could also be used to illuminate other tasks, such as "felling timber, building bridges [and] wharves, crossing streams, building earthworks, etc."[2]

"One of these lights would be sufficient for at least two thousand persons to work by, with as much convenience as by day-light," Lowe claimed. "With this apparatus, light can be thrown two miles distant sufficiently powerful to work by. The cost is trifling."[3]

Lowe also experimented with other types of signaling devices. He developed airborne flares that burned in red, white, blue, or green smoke that could be used to signal troops in mass movements. In a similar vein, Lowe used some of his rare free time to create an intricate system of signal flags that visually transmitted aerial observations and trajectory corrections to gun batteries in the event the airborne telegraph failed or was otherwise unusable.

The subject of aerial photography was also touched on during Lowe's tenure as chief aeronaut of the Balloon Corps. While Lowe could not lay claim to being the first American to actually photograph landscape from the air—that distinction going to Samuel King of Philadelphia in 1859—the aeronaut definitely envisioned its application to the field of battle. In December, 1861, Lowe was in correspondence with William G. Fullerton, a professional photographer from Philadelphia. Lowe was intrigued with the idea of exploring this new dimension to aerial observation.

"As soon as other matters connected with the balloons are accomplished, I shall give the photographic matter a thorough and practical test."[4]

Unfortunately, the bulky nature of glass plate photography equipment precluded its use during the war and no aerial photography is known to exist. But Lowe could be excused for not pursuing this particular innovation. Spare time to pursue experiments was at a premium as supervision of the Balloon Corps dominated every aspect of Lowe's life.

"I was principally occupied in visiting different balloon stations and keeping everything in order," Lowe said.

During this period the aeronaut's father, Clovis Lowe, proved to be of inestimable assistance to his son. Severe winter weather took its toll on several of the balloons placed in service in early 1862. Evidence of the type of damage the aerostats suffered comes in a dispatch sent to Lowe in January, 1862.

"The balloon *Intrepid* got an inch of ice on it last night and is reported much injured," wrote Brig. Gen. Charles Pomeroy Stone from Pooleville. "[It] has suffered in its varnish from the excessively bad weather."[5]

The weather was particularly troublesome, as Lowe noted himself.

"Usually the coming of Spring thrills with the joy of awakening nature," he said. "But there were no thrills that Spring of 1862. It was a season of terrible storms and incredible rains, and never before nor since have I known a worse one."[6]

However, the troubles experienced by Lowe were minor when compared to the tasks facing General McClellan. In the months that had passed since the Union's humiliating and costly defeat at Manassas Junction, McClellan had rigorously transformed a conglomeration of ragtag volunteer regiments into a cohesive fighting force. A meticulous planner, McClellan refused to jeopardize the formation of his army by mounting any significant engagements with Confederate forces in the East during the latter part of 1861 and early 1862.

By March, 1862, however, McClellan was ready to launch an invasion of the South with the objective of capturing the Confederate capital at Richmond, Virginia. But reaching this objective was not going to be an easy task. Although a land-based attack on Virginia was originally contemplated, it was ruled out, partly on information gathered through Lowe during one of his ascents.

"On the 7th [of March, 1862,] General Berry, of General Heintzelman's command, ascended several times and discovered the evacuation of Occoquan, which was reported," Lowe said. "This was the first indication of the retirement of the enemy from Manassas."[7]

Later that same day, a young journalist by the name of George Alfred Townsend accompanied Lowe on one of his ascents. Lowe's balloons were always an attraction for news reporters, who invariably wrote glowing stories of the newfangled military technology. Townsend's account for the Philadelphia *Inquirer* spared little in the way of ebullient detail:

Say the Professor, 'Will you make an ascension with me to-night?'

'Where?' I answered, greatly astonished as to the meaning of the Professor's inquiry, 'to the moon?'

'Hardly, tonight,' was the reply; 'but if you will go up with me, to-night, in the balloon, here is an opportunity.'

. . . Soon with my coat, and gloves, and hat, I went to the balloon camp. The moon, then, was shining brilliantly, and the grove in which the balloon was harbored was splendidly illuminated by the light on high. [I] Had made an ascension with the Professor on several occasions before, but always during the day time. A night ascension was something decidedly novel, and I looked forward to it with great pleasure.

There she lifted herself—the balloon, with her beautiful round sides and shining silk—eagerly struggling, it seemed, to free herself from the cords that bound her below. Speedily the Professor's corps of men were assembled, and the work of disengaging the balloon from the bags of sand to which the netting was attached was commenced. Then the basket was adjusted at the bottom, and the balance of the balloon regulated to the weight to be lifted. All this was done with the greatest speed and precision.

'Now boys, all at the ropes,' commands the Professor, 'and we shall try how she lifts.' The balloon is raised a few feet, and all is pronounced 'O.K.'

'Now in with you,' remarks the Professor, 'and see how the ballast is.'

. . . the 'guy ropes' are manned, and at a given signal the men in the middle loose their hold from the ropes and withdraw to the sides—

Now we slowly ascend, the men at the 'guys' slowly and regularly 'paying out' the rope. Up we go, with that gently oscillating movement which is characteristic of a balloon's motion when the weather is calm. Upward we rise—four, five, six hundred feet. There is little wind here, and the cold becomes more sensible. The balloon is being wafted off towards the East, and we can look directly down the chimney of the house at which we supped. Beneath, the camp-fires of the soldiers appear like as but a handful of glowing embers.

The reflection of the moon on the earth beneath gives to it the appearance of a vast extended sea, where the waves are tossing and sparkling in the rich moonlight. Higher and still higher we ascend, until it appears but an easy task to pluck with our hands a star from the firmament above. Gazing into the mysteries of the heavens, the stars multiply by thousands and tens of thousands, until, dazzled and dimmed by the sight, I was obliged to cast my eyes downward for fear of that becoming dizzy I should, by losing my balance, be precipitated from the balloon.

The wind is getting a little stiffer, and the basket commences to swing. The resistance to the wind, caused by the men below, who prevent, as far as possible, the balloon from following the direction of the current, causes the netting to grate against the side of the balloon, and the collapsing and expansion of the silk to produce a flapping noise, highly suggestive of a break somewhere. Still, the grandeur of the scene compensates for any momentary fear that may exist, and after a few repetitions, the aeronaut becomes used to the sound.

Now the order is given to draw down slowly, and in a few minutes we are again on terra firma. The balloon is made fast for the night, and the guards, who sleep in close proximity to the balloon, is consigned its safe keeping.[8]

With the main body of the Confederate army in Virginia withdrawn from Manassas Junction it was surmised that they had fallen back to organize a massive defense of Richmond. There was a justifiable concern that a repeat of the Manassas debacle would occur if an invasion by land took place. For the most part, McClellan was determined not to waste his men and resources in a bloody head-on battle with the Confederate army defending its capital.

Therefore, in order to reach Richmond as many as 150,000 men were to be transported by more than 400 steam transports from the area surrounding Washington, D.C., to the Union stronghold at Fortress Monroe, 200 miles to the south at Hampton Roads. It was to be one of the greatest feats in military logistics ever attempted.

For his part, Thaddeus Lowe was an ardent supporter of McClellan's strategy.

"The magnificently trained, disciplined, and equipped Army of the Potomac was ready to march to the cry of 'On to Richmond,'" Lowe recalled.

The Peninsular Campaign, as McClellan's plan became known, was not without major drawbacks. By transporting more than 150,000 men of the Army of the Potomac to Virginia, Washington, D.C., would be left with only a modest defense force to ward off a likely Confederate attack if the Union offensive proved to be a failure. The concerns of a poorly defended capital were compounded by rumors of Confederate forces ready to strike while the Army of the Potomac was engaged to the south.

"[There was] information that Gen. 'Stonewall' Jackson was approaching the Upper Potomac by way of the Shenandoah Valley and fear gripped Washington," said Lowe. "The Government was fearful to the point of panic whenever a Confederate force marched northward, though Washington was well fortified to resist any attack a hostile force might make."[9]

Under orders from Lincoln, McClellan reluctantly detached over 40,000 men under the command of Gen. Irvin McDowell. McDowell's force was to remain behind in defense of the capital, where they became the backbone of the newly created Department of the Rappahannock. The effect was that McClellan's invasion force was reduced by approximately 25 percent.

Regardless of the reduced manpower available, plans for the invasion carried on. Lowe received his first notice of the army's new battle plans via telegram from General Porter.

"Have your balloon out to Fairfax Court house at as early an hour tomorrow as possible," wrote Porter. "Major Stone will give all the facilities you desire. Show this to him."[10]

At Fairfax the following day, Lowe was met by Stone and was presented with orders detailing the Balloon Corps' new mission.

"You will make arrangements, without delay, to send to Fortress Monroe, Virginia, a balloon with all the requisite apparatus and material for inflating," Lowe was informed by Lt. Col. Macomb. Macomb's orders had come directly from General McClellan.

Lowe himself was not able to go to Fortress Monroe. By this time he had employed other aeronauts to take on the additional duties heaped on the Balloon Corps. Among these new aeronauts was Ebenezer Seaver.

Very little is known of Seaver's prewar life. It is not even known whether or not he had any experience in ballooning. Lowe actually hired Seaver in November, 1861, where he began to work with Clovis Lowe, assisting in the maintenance of the balloons and their equipment. However, with the departures of Starkweather and Paullin, and the temporary sidelining of Steiner over the issue of back pay, Seaver was soon promoted to the position of full-fledged aeronaut early in 1862.

Keeping with the somewhat eccentric nature of the Balloon Corps, Ebenezer Seaver took it upon himself to design a uniform to distinguish the corps' personnel in a unique fashion. Although the Balloon Corps was a civilian adjunct, the honorary rank of "captain" was often bestowed on Lowe's assistants, and Seaver felt that a suitable uniform should exist to dignify the title. Clovis Lowe described Seaver's fanciful creation in vivid detail:

> I met [Seaver] with a great deal of cordiality and introduced him to a large number of officers. General Sickles could not have put on so many things or so many shoulder straps as he did.[11]
>
> In the course of the evening you would hear one officer inquire of another 'What do all those stripes on one shoulder mean?' Finally, one more bold than the rest inquired of Mr. Seaver what the 'A.D.' on his straps meant, and he answered 'Aeronautics Department.'
>
> [Seaver] was then told that they were not aware that there was any such department. Before they got through with him, he wished he had the money he had spent for his uniform.[12]

As an aside, it is also interesting to note that Seaver chose to state that he was affiliated with the "Aeronautics Department." Even though Lowe formalized balloon operations, the civilian unit never actually had an official

*Union army Balloon Corps aeronauts Ebenezer Seaver (left) and
John B. Starkweather (right).* LIBRARY OF CONGRESS

name. Lowe often referred to his unit as the "Aeronautics Corps," although the army and most press correspondents eventually popularized the term "Balloon Corps." Eventually a simple brass cap insignia fashioned in the shape of a balloon and topped by the letters "B C" signifying Balloon Corps, was adopted by the Union's aeronautical personnel.[13]

Manner of appearance notwithstanding, Seaver's first assignment as an aeronaut was to replace William Paullin at Budd's Ferry, Maryland, following Paullin's dismissal for dereliction. When McClellan was preparing his invasion of the Virginia peninsula, however, Seaver's services in gathering advance intelligence at Fortress Monroe were deemed to be of greater importance.

There was a certain amount of adventure in preparing Seaver for his journey to Monroe. Seaver was still detailed to operations with General Hooker's division at Budd's Ferry when orders were received by Lowe to send an acronaut to Virginia. Making the trip from the capital aboard the balloon barge *George Washington Parke-Custis*, Lowe personally supervised Seaver's preparations.

"I proceeded from Washington . . . to Budd's Ferry [in order to ship] the balloon and apparatus . . . for Fort Monroe, Virginia," Lowe later explained. "The dispatch I had sent to Mr. Seaver to get the apparatus in his charge ready to move had not been received and I found the balloon on the Virginia side of the river inflated where it had been in use."

Lowe spent most of the evening of March 13 deflating the balloon and "getting the things together" for shipping the next morning. But the crew of the *George Washington Parke-Custis*, which was in tow behind a steamer tug, had difficulty maneuvering away from the makeshift wharf on the shore.

"On examination it was found impossible to turn the balloon barge until some repairs have been made to her rudder post," stated Lowe in his report to Colonel Macomb. He went on to explain that the barge had been damaged in a recent storm and that to get the equipment moving he would unload the hydrogen generator, put it on wheels, and ship it to Fortress Monroe with Ebenezer Seaver by other means."[14]

Lowe was wary of the experiences that his other assistants had suffered when placed far into the field, and took pains to try to ensure a reasonably clear path for Seaver.

"I would very respectfully request that the aeronaut be furnished with such aid as may be required to manage the balloon to the best advantage,"

Lowe said in a letter to Gen. John W. Wool, the commander at Fortress Monroe.[15]

Whether Lowe fully realized the extent of the indifferent treatment that his former rival John La Mountain had suffered under Wool's command at Fortress Monroe is uncertain. As a relatively close confidant of John Starkweather and John Steiner, however, Seaver was undoubtedly well aware of how other aeronauts fared when they were stationed far from the Potomac. Nevertheless, Seaver remained duty bound and accepted the assignment to the fortress on Old Point Comfort.

On March 15, 1862, Seaver and the balloon *Constitution*, along with its support equipment, embarked on the journey to Fortress Monroe aboard the steam transport *Hugh Jenkins* and arrived the following day.

Seaver's arrival at the fort was greeted with somewhat more enthusiasm and support than had been extended to John La Mountain. Although Confederate army activity in the area had subsided to a great extent, a new threat was now presenting itself. It was the Rebel ironclad CSS *Virginia*.

Rumors and false sightings of the *Virginia*, the South's first seagoing ironclad vessel, were running rampant all over the eastern seaboard. Rebuilt from the scuttled Union frigate *Merrimack*, the ship was reputed to be indestructible. During the week prior to Seaver's arrival, the *Virginia* had engaged several Union vessels at Hampton Roads and the results were devastating. On March 8 it had rammed and sunk the USS *Cumberland* and forced the frigates USS *Minnesota* and *Congress* to run aground. The *Congress* later burst into flames and was completely lost.

The very next day, Sunday, March 9, the *Virginia* returned and moved in to finish off the *Minnesota*. But by this time the *Monitor*, the Union's first ironclad warship, had arrived. A four-hour gunbattle of shot and shell erupted between the two ships. The combat between the *Virginia* and the *Monitor*, though violent, proved inconclusive. The *Virginia* eventually withdrew to the Confederate-controlled shipyards at Norfolk, ceding control of Hampton Roads to the *Monitor*.

In spite of its withdrawal, the threat of the *Virginia* remained. The Rebel ironclad still protected the river approach leading to the Confederate capital at Richmond and had the potential to menace Union shipping lanes in Hampton Roads. On his arrival at Fortress Monroe, Seaver found himself pressed into constant duty monitoring Rebel naval activity in the Roads.

Meanwhile, Thaddeus Lowe also received new instructions. On March 23, Brig. Gen. Seth Williams, McClellan's adjutant general, forwarded orders to the aeronaut at his temporary residence in the National Hotel in Washington.

"The commanding general directs that you proceed with your balloons and apparatus to Fort Monroe, Va.," Williams wrote, adding that Lowe was to await further orders from McClellan pending his arrival in the area. Lowe would be contacted as soon as the general's floating headquarters, the *Commodore*, steamed into Hampton Roads.

Equally as important, Williams noted that he was also including a pay voucher so that Lowe could procure necessary supplies for the journey.[16]

Lowe wasted little time readying himself for action. Two of the corps' balloons were already en route to Virginia with the forces of Gens. Fitz-John Porter and James Samuel Wadsworth. With the help of Clovis Lowe and a newly enlisted maintenance assistant named John O'Donnell, the remaining balloons at the Columbia Armory were carefully packed aboard the *George Washington Parke-Custis* for transport. Food rations for the trip were also set aside—"three days' cooked provisions and three days' uncooked."[17]

In addition to the preparations for the Peninsular Campaign, Lowe also managed to employ other aeronauts to augment duties with the corps. Two of these new aeronauts, Ebenezer Locke Mason and Jacob C. Freno, were actually signed on in January, 1862.

Mason was something of an interesting character in his prewar career. Originally from Troy, New York, he was an associate of John La Mountain, but apparently the relationship was not deep enough to have prejudiced Lowe's decision to hire Mason following the bitter rivalry that erupted between the two men. Mason also traveled the carnival circuit as an agent for a magician known as "Wyman the Wizard," prior to becoming involved with Thaddeus Lowe in the autumn of 1861. Perhaps learning the skill of constructing balloon envelopes from La Mountain, Mason was hired by Lowe to oversee the construction of the last two balloons built for the Balloon Corps, the *Eagle* and *Excelsior*.[18]

Mason's first significant experience as an aeronaut with the Balloon Corps had its share of harrowing moments. He was placed in charge of one of the balloons assigned to surveillance along the Potomac and ordered to take the balloon aboard a small steamer to a position called Shipping Point. From there he ascended from the deck of the transport, but immediately fell under attack from a six-gun battery that had been established by the Rebels after Bull Run. Mason and the crew of the transport narrowly escaped capture or worse when they were rescued at the last moment by Union forces who moved in from the Maryland shore.[19]

Jacob C. Freno had an association with Lowe that went back as far as April, 1861, when he served as an assistant in the aeronaut's preparations for the Cincinnati to Unionville flight. Originally a resident of Philadelphia, Freno was an attorney and part-time balloon enthusiast. With his past association with Lowe, Freno seemed to be a perfect fit to work within the various egos that comprised the Balloon Corps. But Freno was a man with a checkered past.

Freno was mustered into the Union army in September, 1861, and was given a commission as first lieutenant with the 66th Pennsylvania Infantry. However, as a soldier Freno left much to be desired. He was an inveterate gambler and operated a notoriously crooked gaming operation within his regiment. His illicit operations were the source of a number of his problems with the 66th Pennsylvania but only served to indicate far worse derelictions lurking underneath the surface.

When the 66th Pennsylvania was ordered to take part in an engagement in the vicinity of Harpers Ferry, Virginia, Freno became completely unnerved. Displaying abject cowardice before his men in the face of the enemy, Freno was ordered to stand trial on court-martial charges regarding his conduct. He was saved from full military prosecution when the commanding officer of the 66th Pennsylvania allowed him to resign his commission in the aftermath of the incident. The officer wished to save his regiment any disgrace and embarrassment by calling attention to Freno's misconduct.[20]

Whether Thaddeus Lowe was aware of Freno's dubious military career—or just oblivious to it—is not known. What is known is that Lowe hired Jacob Freno as an aeronaut's assistant in January, 1862, where he was salaried at $3.75 a day, the same pay as allotted Ebenezer Mason. While Freno and Mason would join Lowe on the expedition to the Virginia Peninsula, the association between these men would eventually become estranged.

There was one more individual that Lowe added to the ranks of the Balloon Corps prior to his departure to Virginia. It was a name already well known to Union aeronautics—James Allen.

Although Allen had failed in his early attempts at demonstrating the military use of his balloon and gas-generating equipment at the time of the battle of Bull Run, he was nonetheless a valuable commodity as an experienced aeronaut. In February, 1862, Lowe wrote to Allen at his home in Providence, Rhode Island, asking him to join the Balloon Corps. Allen's acceptance would prove to be a boon to the Corps in a number of ways, especially since Allen was somewhat more adept at subordinating his own ego to Lowe's, despite having many more years of ballooning experience than that of the Corps's chief aeronaut.

Lowe and his crew arrived at Fortress Monroe during the last week of April, 1862. Seaver was already at work with daily observations around the fort and Lowe soon received orders to have himself ready to accompany General Porter on his advance towards Yorktown.

This was to be the first step in McClellan's attack on Richmond. Yorktown was only twenty miles northwest of Fortress Monroe and was considered the most strategic point along the peninsula of the York and James Rivers. But the siege of Yorktown was to be fraught with problems and delays.

McClellan privately seethed as he was forced to rearrange his battle plans because of Lincoln's insistence that General McDowell's corps be kept in reserve in defense of the capital. Logistical and supply problems also continued to plague McClellan as he assembled his forces at Fortress Monroe. By the first week of April most of the elements of the general's plan were in place.

Advanced ground scouts were sent up the peninsula to ascertain the strength of Rebel forces. These scouts were principally the agents of Allan Pinkerton, who was regarded by many as America's foremost detective. Prior to the war, Pinkerton had organized one of the first national detective agencies in the United States, and gained a strong, if not inflated, reputation for protecting U.S. mail shipments from highway robbers. In 1861, Pinkerton escorted president-elect Abraham Lincoln from Springfield, Illinois, to Washington, D.C., and was subsequently commissioned to organize the Federal secret service.

When war broke out Pinkerton was immediately called upon to render his services in the field of criminology to the defense of the Union. Just as McClellan relied on Thaddeus Lowe to provide the latest innovation in aerial surveillance, so he also availed himself of the trusted skills of America's top detective to provide accurate ground intelligence.

Unfortunately, the detective's vaunted reputation for apprehending criminals did not transfer well to the task of training and commanding field operatives to gather military information.

Thaddeus Lowe and one of his balloons in a photo probably taken during the Peninsular Campaign. Note the stars and strips adorning the balloon's control basket. LIGHTER-THAN-AIR-FLIGHT

With the unknown prospect of landing in the middle of the Confederacy's stronghold, McClellan's usual insecurities rose to a fever pitch. He dispatched Pinkerton and his men to work covertly in the Virginia countryside.

Pinkerton unequivocally relayed the dangers of working undercover in Confederate territories to his operatives. Detection by the enemy would mean certain death as a spy. As a result, Pinkerton's scouts took extraordinary measures to conceal their presence or national affiliation. Instead of directly observing Confederate positions, most of the operatives gathered information about troop strengths and locations from civilians and slaves.

Although Pinkerton never coordinated his intelligence operations with those of the Balloon Corps, he was not unaware of Lowe's airborne presence during the course of the Peninsula Campaign. When the Virginia invasion began, Pinkerton's teenage son, Willie, traveled from Chicago to the Army of the Potomac's headquarters near Fortress Monroe and reportedly accompanied Balloon Corps personnel on at least one occasion during the campaign.[21]

When Pinkerton presented his report on the strength of Confederate forces on the eve of the invasion, the results absolutely astounded McClellan. According to Pinkerton it was possible that more than 100,000 Confederates occupied the area across the peninsula between Yorktown and the Warwick River, sealing off the route to Richmond.

However, the reports were extraordinarily erroneous. Confederate strength was in fact surprisingly weak. Confederate major general John B. Magruder had been given orders to use his force of only 10,000 men to delay the Union approach for as long as possible. This was intended to buy time to muster the defense of the Confederate capital, which lay some fifty miles to the northwest.

Magruder fully realized that he was outnumbered ten to one by the Federals, and knew that a head-on confrontation with McClellan would result in the slaughter of his men. So, Magruder devised a clever ruse where he continuously moved his men between the Warwick River and Yorktown, giving the impression that his relatively small force was actually ten times larger than it was.

Had McClellan decided to dispatch the Balloon Corps to scout the area, an aerial observation would probably have revealed the deception. But as it remained, McClellan was thoroughly convinced that his army was looking at the prospect of a bloody and prolonged siege. An advance force commanded by Fitz-John Porter was therefore sent to establish a Union position along the peninsula to try to break through the Rebel lines.

On April 4, Porter's force, together with Lowe and elements of the Balloon Corps, left Hampton and proceeded toward the outskirts of Yorktown. Lowe was in charge of the aeronautic train consisting of four army wagons and two gas generators. James Allen also accompanied Lowe during the advance.

Some resistance along the way was encountered when Magruder's men opened fire on Porter's troops as they neared Yorktown. In addition to this, Porter's troops were also among the first to discover another new and deadly innovation to warfare—land mines that had been planted in the road by Rebels.

By the afternoon of April 5, camp was established and Lowe had succeeded in inflating the *Intrepid*. Early the next morning Lowe made his first ascent over the Virginian peninsula.

"I ascended and remained up until after daylight, observing the campfires and noting the movements of the enemy," Lowe recalled.

After he landed Lowe personally briefed Porter on his observations. It was obvious from what Lowe had seen that the number of Confederates in the area did not match the exaggerated reports taken by Pinkerton's ground scouts, and he strongly suggested that Porter accompany him on his next ascent in order to, "judge for himself the number of the enemy and strength of their works."[22] Porter agreed and accompanied Lowe on an ascent some 1,000 feet into the air, lasting more than an hour and forty-five minutes. Lowe noted that he and the general were probably less than a mile from the Confederate earthworks guarding Yorktown.[23]

After Lowe and Porter descended, a meeting of generals was held. In attendance was the French military observer Count de Paris, with whom Lowe was already acquainted. The count acted as an aide-de-camp on McClellan's staff and was given the honorary rank of captain, although he officially held no position within the Union army.

Lowe recalled that following the meeting, "several draughtsmen were sent up who sketched maps of the positions of the enemy," and that Porter and the Count de Paris also made an ascent late in the afternoon.

While Lowe made great note of the fact that all of these observations "were of the greatest importance, and readily enabled the commanding officer to decide what course he would pursue," the reality was that McClellan remained pat. Though aerial observations revealed that Magruder's troop strength was not as formidable as first thought, McClellan opted to remain cautious with his approach toward the capture of Yorktown.

Late in the evening of April 6, Lowe received a directive from McClellan's headquarters to report back to Fortress Monroe. Once there he was to have the *Constitution* ready to accompany Gen. Erasmus Keyes on his approach to Warwick Court House near Newport News. Lowe complied with the order and left James Allen in charge of the balloon in Porter's corps.

From the seat of one of the balloon's support wagons Lowe took charge of transporting the aeronautic equipment. The roads leading to Warwick Court House were heavily rutted and washed out in places due to recent storms and the journey proceeded at an excruciatingly slow rate. Lowe characterized the roads as "the worst I ever saw." For the next three days he was to establish balloon operations with Keyes's IV Corps.

On April 10, Lowe left Keyes's headquarters at the courthouse and began to make his way back to Porter's corps on horseback. However, during the time that Lowe had spent at the Warwick Court House, Porter had moved his base of operations from the position it had occupied on the outskirts of Yorktown three days before. By nine o'clock that evening, Lowe began to sense he was in deep trouble.

"I was not sensible of the danger I was in until I heard signals given by a low whistle, which I at once knew to be those of the rebels," Lowe said. "Accordingly I retraced my [horse's] steps and spent the night at the camp of one of our advanced regiments."[24]

The next morning, as Lowe made his way toward Porter's new headquarters, a curious sight suddenly met his eye. It was the *Intrepid*, and it was rapidly descending before him. Lowe immediately realized that something had gone wrong since James Allen had been left with explicit instructions to conduct tethered observations only.

Putting the spurs to his horse, Lowe swiftly galloped to the spot where the balloon had landed, its envelope now almost completely empty from rapid deflation. As Lowe reached the *Intrepid*, he was surprised to find Fitz-John Porter, the sole occupant, struggling to set himself free from the tangle of silk and cord netting.

Not long after Lowe's arrival on the scene, Union pickets from Porter's and McClellan's headquarters drew up on horses. Lowe quickly learned that the general had fallen victim to an accidental freeflight and had been aloft for several hours that morning.

Porter's adventure actually started around 5 A.M. He had told James Allen the previous day that he wished to make a pre-dawn reconnoiter to gauge Confederate activity in the area. Allen was aware that a greater observation point could be obtained by gaining more altitude with the *Intrepid*. Although Lowe always insisted that three, and sometimes four tethers be used on ascensions, Allen reasoned that by going with a single tether the weight of the additional ropes could be eliminated, thus allowing the balloon to achieve greater heights.

Unknown to Allen, however, was the fact that acid from one of the hydrogen generators was "accidentally" spilled on the single tether rope prior to the ascent that morning. The exact nature of the spillage was never determined, although Confederate sabotage was considered a strong possibility. Regardless, General Porter was already in the *Intrepid*'s control basket as Allen was making final preparations to join him. Suddenly, a loud crack—like the sound of a pistol shot—rang out as the single mooring rope snapped. The *Intrepid* was aloft and out of control.

Those on the ground were helpless to do anything as Porter and *Intrepid* rapidly rose into the air. But the general himself was hardly fazed. While he realized the predicament he was in, he had also ascended dozens of times with Lowe and his assistants and was familiar with the sensations and mechanics of a balloon. Even as the *Intrepid* began to drift over Confederate lines, Porter remained calm.

"I took good observations, some notes, but mainly instantaneous impressions like a photographic instrument," he said. "[I] had the enemy's position and defenses so grafted on my mind that when I descended I was able to give a good sketch of everything."[25]

The fact that Porter was able to remain so cool and collected was certainly a testament to his courage. As the balloon sailed over Confederate encampments, shot and shell erupted from down below. Fortunately for Porter, the *Intrepid* was out of range of Confederate fire.

Gradually the balloon began to drift over Union lines once again, where Porter was able to determine a safe spot to land. Although he had often witnessed Lowe and his assistants prepare for a landing, his lack of experience in aeronautics almost proved to be his undoing. Reaching for the rope that lead to the control valve, Porter started to bleed off hydrogen gas in order to make a landing. However, the general bled off too much gas all at once.

"The general in his eagerness to come to the ground had opened the valve until all the gas escaped," Lowe observed. "The balloon was constantly falling [but] the silk was kept extended, and presented so large a surface to the atmosphere that it served the purpose of a parachute, and consequently the descent was not rapid enough to be dangerous.[26]

Lowe went on to remark that, "a balloon suddenly relieved of its gas will always form a half sphere, provided it has a sufficient distance to fall in, to condense a column of air under it. A thousand feet, I presume, [would] be sufficiently high to effect this and to make the descent in safety."[27]

Porter was no worse for wear when Lowe and Union pickets caught up with him. The *Intrepid* was also fortunately spared any damage. Still, as Lowe was to learn, the main injury that had occurred was not physical in nature, but more psychological.

General McClellan, who was one of Lowe's most ardent supporters, summed up the feeling that many Union officers had in the aftermath of the accident, in a letter written to his wife that same day:

I am just recovering from a terrible scare. Early this morning I was awakened by a dispatch from Fitz Johns Hd Qtrs, stating that Fitz had made an ascension in the balloon & that the balloon had broken away & come to ground some 3 miles SW—which would be within the enemy's lines! You can imagine how I felt! I at once sent off to the various pickets to find out what they knew, & try to do something to save him—but the order had no sooner gone, than in walks Mr. Fitz just as cool as casual—he had luckily come down near my own camp after actually passing over that of the enemy!!

You may rest assured of one thing: you won't catch me in the confounded balloon nor will I allow any other Generals to go up in it![28]

Lowe immediately recognized the reluctance on the part of the officers to have anything more to do with ballooning.

"I found it difficult to restore confidence among the officers as to the safety of this means of observation on account on this accident," he said. "But the explanations and the personal ascensions I made, gradually secured a return of their favor."[29]

Probably the greatest asset that Lowe had in this regard was Fitz-John Porter himself, who remained undaunted and unafraid to continue aerial observations and reassured his fellow officers of this fact. No more than two days passed following the incident when Lowe received a note from Porter:

Professor,

General Barnard is General McClellan's chief engineer, and is located in his camp. General McClellan is anxious for him to have an ascension early in the morning, and General B. will be prepared to accompany your messenger, whom I beg of you to direct to wait to take General Barnard to the location of the balloon. I would ascend myself did not General B. wish and General McClellan wish him to go. . . . I beg of you to give him a good and safe ascension.[30]

Early the following morning Gen. John Gross Barnard arrived at Lowe's camp, where the *Intrepid* was waiting in readiness. At daybreak the balloon was launched and as soon as it rose into view, Confederate artillery from Yorktown opened up.

By this time Lowe was accustomed to enemy fire, but the heavy report of cannon fire prompted him to make note of it years later in his memoirs.

"Whenever the balloon ascended the enemy opened upon it with their heavy siege guns or rifled field pieces until it had attained an altitude to be out of reach," Lowe said. "[The enemy] repeated this fire when the balloon descended, until it was concealed by the woods."[31]

Lowe spent more than two hours aloft with General Barnard, who used all of his time in the air to carefully survey the terrain and plot the most effective locations for the use of siege guns to be aimed at Yorktown. After breakfast that morning, Lowe and the general ascended twice more.

"[He] expressed himself highly gratified from the information thus gained," said Lowe. "From this time . . . the balloons were kept in constant use, and reports were made by myself and many officers who ascended daily."[32]

In addition to Barnard, Lowe and his assistants were soon ferrying other members of McClellan's staff aloft, though several still had their reservations. One such individual was a cavalry lieutenant who was ordered to accompany James Allen on ascensions at Warwick Court House. Although the young lieutenant would go on to earn a reputation as a colorful and dedicated soldier—both for participating in nearly every battle the Army of the Potomac engaged in and for having eleven horses shot out from under him over the course of the war—he accepted his orders for balloon duty with "no little trepidation."[33]

The lieutenant was none other than George Armstrong Custer.

In the aftermath of General Porter's unintentional solo flight, Custer shared a rather dour opinion about the use of balloons.

"The large majority of the army, without giving [aeronautics] a personal test, condemned and ridiculed the system of balloon reconoissances," Custer said.[34]

From Custer's perspective, part of the reason for this condemnation was based simply on the idea of putting soldiers aloft. The theatrics of what was perceived as a "circus" act was anathema to many Union officers. Besides that, even more suspicion was squarely aimed at the civilian aeronauts themselves, who seemed to have far too much autonomy over the dissemination of intelligence gathered through aerial observations.

"Prof. Lowe and his assistants . . . frequently reported having seen 'clouds of dust,' 'a heavy column of troops moving,' 'a large encampment on the right,' 'great activity along the enemy's works,' all of which may have been true," said Custer. "But there were no means of verifying it or refuting it so long as only professional [aeronauts] made the ascensions."[35]

Although Custer was not certain that this mistrust of the Balloon Corps' observations was the motive behind his orders, he nonetheless complied. The young officer was to report to James Allen at the Warwick Court House, where the *Intrepid* once again stood ready.

As an officer, Custer had encountered balloons at various locations for months as Lowe and his assistants took part in military operations in and around Virginia. But now with the prospect of actually going up in a balloon for the first time, Custer began to see the craft in an entirely new light.

"The balloon was kept but a short distance from General Smith's headquarters, fastened to the earth by numerous ropes, like a wild and untamable animal," he recalled. "[As a cavalryman] I had a choice as to the character of the mount, but the proposed ride was far more elevated than I had ever desired or contemplated."[36]

At the aeronaut's camp, Custer cautiously looked over the balloon, attempting to ascertain its various functions and controls.

"Previous to this time I had never examined a balloon except from a distance. Being interested in their construction, I was about to institute a thorough examination when the aeronaut announced that all was ready."[37]

Allen, probably sensing the officer's reluctance to go aloft, casually inquired if Custer, "desired to go up alone."[38]

"My desire, if frankly expressed, would not have been to go up at all," Custer later wrote. "But if I was to go, company was certainly desirable. With an attempt at indifference, I intimated that he might go along."[39]

Custer in his later memoir went on to describe the balloon in detail.

"The basket in which we were to be transported was about two feet high, four feet long, and slightly over half as wide," Custer recalled. "[It] resembling in every respect an ordinary willow basket of the same dimensions, minus the handles."[40]

With his less than eager passenger aboard, Allen gave the word for the windlasses to be released. The sudden feeling of gravity giving way immediately disoriented Custer.

"We were leaving *terra firma*, and noiselessly, and imperceptibly, were ascending toward the clouds," Custer said, noting that Allen was standing upright in the basket.

"I was urged to stand up also. My confidence in balloons at that time was not sufficient, however, to justify such a course, so I remained in the bottom of the basket, with a firm hold on either side."

As the balloon ascended, Custer's thoughts once again turned toward the construction details of the balloon.

"To me [the basket] seemed fragile indeed, and not intended to support a tithe of the weight then imposed upon it," he observed. "The interstices [the gaps in the wickerwork] in the sides and bottom seemed immense, and the further we receded from the earth the larger they seemed to become, until I imagined one might tumble through.[41]

When Custer asked Allen just how safe the balloon's control basket was, the aeronaut responded by, "jumping up and down to prove its strength" to reassure his passenger.[42]

"My fears were redoubled," Custer said of the display. "I expected to see the bottom of the basket giving away, and one or both of us dashed to the earth."[43]

Later Custer was to learn that his fears were unfounded, as the control car was supported by a series of steel bands that kept it intact in addition to its wickerwork.

As the balloon reached its correct altitude, Custer gradually became more accustomed to his surroundings. Pulling out his field glasses, pencil, and notebook, he began to take notes of what he surveyed.

"I was able to cease estimating our altitude and turn to the contemplation of the magnificent scenery spread out beneath and around us as far as the eye could extend."[44]

From Custer's vantage point much of the peninsula could be taken in.

"To the right could be seen the York River, following which the eye could rest on Chesapeake Bay. On the left, and at about the same distance, flowed the James River . . . . Between these two rivers extended a most beautiful landscape, and no less interesting than beautiful."[45]

The natural beauty of the Virginia countryside and deep forest groves, however, concealed deadly intents.

"The point over which the balloon was held was probably one mile from the nearest point of the enemy's line. In an open country balloons would be invaluable in discovering the location of the enemy's camps and works. Unfortunately . . . the enemy's camps, like our own, were generally pitched in the woods . . .; his earthworks along the Warwick [river] were also concealed by growing timber. . . . With the assistance of good field glasses . . . I was able to catch glimpses of canvas through openings in the forest, while

Arthur Lumley's sketch of a Union army balloon overlooking the York River near Yorktown, Virginia, during the Peninsular Campaign. FRANK LESLIE'S ILLUSTRATED NEWSPAPER

camps located in the open space were as plainly visible as those of the Army of the Potomac.

"Here and there the dim outline of an earthwork could be seen more than half concealed by the trees which had been purposely left standing on their front. Guns could be seen mounted and peering sullenly through the embrasures, while men in considerable

numbers were standing in and around entrenchments, often collected in groups, intently observing the balloon, curious, no doubt,
to know the character or value of the information its occupants
could derive from their elevated post of observation."[46]

Gun emplacements were drawn around the approach to Yorktown.
Even the trained observations of officers such as Custer could not accurately
estimate the number of Rebels in the area. In the several flights that Custer
claimed to have undertaken, he could not substantiate the previous reports
of major Confederate activity in the area that had been made by Pinkerton's
ground scouts.

Nevertheless, confidence in the Balloon Corps gradually returned.
Soon Lowe and his assistants were able to put the incident regarding Fitz-
John Porter's accidental solo flight behind them.

The challenges of the Peninsular Campaign for the Army of the
Potomac were just beginning. While aerial reconnaissance of the area
around Yorktown provided an accurate summation of the battlefield that lay
ahead, General McClellan chose to proceed with extreme caution. Still
believing the ruse perpetuated by General Magruder and his small army,
McClellan expected a tough fight and was prepared for a long, drawn out
campaign.

By this time Southern strategists were growing weary of the daily spectacle of Union spy balloons floating overhead. While the aerial work of
Lowe and his assistants had gone unchallenged since the first balloon in
Union service emerged on the battlefield in the summer of 1861, this was
about to change. The South was poised to unveil the first Confederate air
force.

CHAPTER TEN

The First Confederate Air Force

The Balloon Corps's continuing operations began to have its affect on the morale and strategic planning of the Confederate army in Virginia by the beginning of 1862. The constant presence of the spy balloons forced Confederate troops to make considerable efforts to evade detection from the air.

The construction of so-called "quaker guns"—false gun batteries made of logs—was an early attempt by the Confederates to fool Union balloon observers that fortifications were stronger than they were. But the deception was usually detected from the air and proved to be of little success.

Confederate troops tried other means to evade detection from the air. Campfires were banned at night. Although this order was not well received by the troops, who had to suffer the bitter cold of winter nights in Virginia, at least the flickering flames could not be used to determine the strength and position of their forces in the field.

As Lowe and his assistants managed to normalize the operations of the Balloon Corps within the Union army in the early part of 1862, the appearance of the balloons became an almost daily occurrence on front lines throughout Virginia. The very sight of a balloon came to be a source of demoralization for Rebel troops, and soon ways were sought to counteract their presence in the sky.

It was no secret that the balloons used by the Union army contained highly flammable hydrogen or coal gas in order to achieve buoyancy. Yet, the Rebels never took advantage of this particular weakness. Invariably, Confederate artillery opened their barrages on Union aeronauts immediately as the balloons rose into view, but a number of elements prevented Southern firepower from inflicting any real damage.

First of all, Union balloonists were careful to conduct their operations well behind the front line. Consequently, when the Confederates opened fired on the appealing targets in the sky, their shot fell safely out of range. There was usually more danger to Union ground troops, who were positioned in advance of the balloons and had to bear the brunt of the mis-aimed Confederate artillery fire.

Still, there were those in Union ranks who doubted that the luck of the aeronauts would hold out against Southern marksmanship. At least one war correspondent took note of enemy artillery efforts to bring down Union balloons and made the following observations:

> It came at length to be our principal amusement in camp to watch the rebels fire at the balloon, as it sailed tranquilly above our picket line, and I have seen many a dollar staked by the 'boys in blue' on the skill of the gray-coated artillerists. It was laughable to watch these bets, and I think I shall not go so far astray from the truth when I say that some very good patriots would have been glad to see the balloon struck, since it would have enabled them to win their wagers.[1]

Another factor that contributed to the lack of effectiveness of Confederate guns against the balloons was the "cold shot" used as ammunition. There were rare instances when Confederate marksmen were within effective shooting range of a balloon as it was being launched or reeled in on its tethers for landing. In these instances a hail of bullets would shower the air and the aeronauts, along with any accompanying observers, would be forced to take cover in the balloon's armor-protected control basket. However, the enemy's lead minié balls would pass harmlessly through the silk fabric of the balloon's envelope without igniting the flammable gas inside. Fortunately for Union aeronauts, the use of "tracer ammunition"—shot that contained fragments of magnesium that burned super-hot when fired—was to be a development of a future generation of warfare.

The lack of success on the part of their artillery did not deter the Rebels from continuing their barrages whenever a Union balloon came into view, however. James Alexander Cooke, a war correspondent present at the battle of Yorktown, noted that every time the Confederates caught sight of Union balloons it, "gave them paroxysms of rage. They often brought their artillery to shell the balloon, or shot musketry at it, or cried at it in derision."[2]

In some instances, Rebel artillerymen were actually known to overwork their guns beyond safety in a vain attempt to bring one of the Union balloons down. A Union officer named Handy reported an interview he conducted with captured Confederates in which the men admitted that while firing on a balloon, "one of the big Armstrong guns had been elevated beyond safety, to get the range, and burst the gun" when it discharged.[3]

"A hawk hovering above a chicken yard could not have caused more commotion than did my balloons when they appeared," Lowe would proudly recollect.[4]

As their frustration mounted, more daring individuals within Confederate ranks began devising more elaborate methods of destroying Union balloons. The Savannah *Republican* reported a scheme later reprinted in several Northern newspapers by one Southern artilleryman who announced a plan to transport a small field gun into Union lines under the cover of darkness, and to open fire on one of the balloons as soon as it rose for its daily dawn patrol.[5] Although the plan never achieved its aims, the Richmond *Enquirer* later ran a purely fictitious account of how an artillery barrage lead by a Confederate captain by the name of Pegram struck one of the balloons, "tearing it to pieces." The headline for the article succinctly read, "Abe's Balloon Plugged."[6]

However, where firepower had failed, one direct act of sabotage almost succeeded.

"The Confederates adopted any device to destroy them," said Lowe. "Finding they could not hit me, they began to devise means to extinguish my entire corps."[7]

In the years following the war an unidentified former Confederate enlisted man told the Detroit *Free Press* about a plot he had been involved with to destroy Lowe's balloon during the siege of Yorktown in April, 1862. As the former soldier related:

A matter which greatly exercised the Confederates during the early part of the war was the use of balloons by the Federals to spy at our position. At Yorktown, where almost daily ascensions were made, our camp, batteries, field works and all defenses were plain to the vision of the occupants of the balloon, and it was also quite easy to form a reliable estimate of our numbers.

These balloon ascensions excited us more than all the outpost attacks, and it was officially determined to put a stop to them at whatever costs. The longest range rifles in the South were sent for, and they were put into the hands of Confederates noted for their marksmanship. But although the balloon seemed to be within easy range, it was too far away for any rifle to do execution from our outposts. Light artillery was then brought into play, using both shot and shell, but somehow the target could not be struck. We finally opened up with any and every piece of ordnance which could be brought to bear, but while we threw shot far beyond it, and apparently close to it, we could not frighten the men in the basket.

Between our outposts and those of the Federals was half a mile of neutral territory. One dark night thirty-five Confederate sharp shooters, each armed with the heaviest rifle known to our Southern hunters, were sent out to creep as far across the neutral ground as possible, find hiding places, and to open on the balloon in the morning.

The results were disastrous to us.

Ten of the men were captured before the balloon ascended, and the rest of us had hardly opened fire when a heavy force hunted us out and killed or captured all but six.

Rewards were then offered for the destruction of the balloon in the Federal camp, and I was one of five who undertook the task. I was promised $1,000 in gold and commission as second lieutenant if I succeeded, and I presume the same promise was made to the others. We left separately and by different routes, each one being told to make arrangements to suit himself.

I was nearly thirty-six hours getting in the rear of the Federal army, and when I entered the camp as a peddler of tobacco and notions, who would have been in the ranks, but for his lameness.

It was nearly a week after I left the Confederate camp before I reached the vicinity where Professor Lowe made his ascensions, and I was then to discover that the greatest precautions were taken to guard against what I had been sent to effect. Sentinels were stationed about the place in such numbers that it was useless to hope that I might pass them; and what made the matter worse was the fact that two of our spies had been captured and held on suspicion.

Nothing but fire would answer our purpose. Rents could be mended and holes patched, and while it was likely that a balloon could be made in a couple of weeks, the interval would permit the Confederates to make many changes.

On the day that [General] Fitz John Porter made his ascension and the rope broke and let the balloon float away, I was within rifle shot of the ascension. As he floated away over our position it seemed as if accident had sealed the fate of the balloon and given us a distinguished prisoner, but a change of wind occurred and back came the air ship to drop to the ground almost at my feet.

I was one of fifteen or twenty men who seized the basket and held it to the earth while Porter stepped out.

I had matches, and I had only to strike a light to destroy the balloon as a flame. I was about to take every risk, but as I drew a match from my pocket, having a filled pipe already in my mouth as an excuse, a big sergeant who stood beside me shouted:

'You infernal idiot! Do you want to fire the balloon?'

I did, but he had deprived me of the opportunity. Some of the men laughed. Some said I ought to be kicked out of camp, and prudence whispered to me to take myself off while I had the chance.

Only two of us out of five got back to our regiments. What became of the others was a mystery we were never able to clear up. Other plans to destroy the balloon were projected, but without success.[8]

Thaddeus Lowe, however, knew the true fate of the "Ex-Confederate's" fellow agents.

"I can clear up the mystery regarding the disappearances of his comrades," Lowe later wrote. "They were shot as spies."[9]

Faced with the prospect that neither sabotage or artillery fire would easily destroy the Union's balloons, Confederate military planners concluded that it was necessary to field a balloon of their own.

The first attempt at countering the Yankee balloons came in April, 1862. Although the Confederate army's resources were comparatively meager to those of the Union army, a small, one-man balloon somehow wound up in the possession of Gen. Joseph E. Johnston's Army of Northern Virginia.

The exact circumstances of how, or from whom, the balloon was acquired are unknown. There was the possibility, however, that the balloon may have made a brief appearance in northern Virginia in the autumn of 1861,[10] fueling the speculation that was rampant in newspapers at the time of a Confederate balloon countering Thaddeus Lowe's own craft.

What is known of the South's first balloon classified it as a decidedly inferior aerostat in comparison to any of its northern counterparts. The envelope was constructed of cotton fabric coated over with tar to make it airtight. Also, unlike the Union's gas-filled craft, the South's balloon was buoyed by hot air. The balloon did not even use an onboard hot-air generator, but was in fact filled while on the ground and then sealed off just prior to launching.

The first known pilot in the Confederate army was a twenty-one year old Virginian, Capt. John Randolph Bryan. Bryan was chief clerk in the adjutant general's office and acting as aide-de-camp on General Magruder's staff.

In mid-April, 1862, General Johnston wrote to Magruder requesting an individual who was "thoroughly acquainted" with the area surrounding the James River to perform reconnaissance duty. The request was intercepted by Bryan at the adjutant general's office. Perhaps in an attempt to keep the existence of the Confederate balloon a secret, Johnston's orders neglected to mention anything about the reconnaissance being performed above ground in a balloon. Nevertheless, Captain Bryan leapt at the opportunity to leave the confines of staff headquarters and to volunteer for duty as a scout.

"This order . . . passed through my hands, and being young, and, I fear, of a dare-devil spirit . . . I therefore at once asked that I might be detailed for this service," Bryan said, also adding, "I assumed that an assignment to this duty would bring me prominently into notice, and probably offer some opportunity for distinguishing myself."[11]

Bryan, however, was heavily discouraged by his superiors in his wish to quit a desk and undertake reconnaissance duties.

"My friends told me that it was more than likely that I would get myself into hot water, and very possibly (in case I should go over the enemy's lines) that I would get shot for my pains."[12]

Nevertheless, Captain Bryan "was so bent" on volunteering for the mission that he went to General Magruder personally about the matter. After "some little persuasion" on Bryan's part, Magruder granted him permission to report to General Johnston's headquarters.

"I joyfully received my orders, and mounting my horse, rode gaily over to Lee's farm, where General Johnston was, to report myself for special service," Bryan said. "There, I handed my orders in to the proper officer and reported for duty."[13]

After making his way to Johnston's tent Bryan was soon face to face with the general. Johnston, who was joined by his adjutant-general Colonel Rhett, looked the young officer over carefully. He was evidently not very enthused by the volunteer sent by Magruder.

"[The general] seemed surprised that I was only a boy (for I was just twenty-one years old)," said Bryan. "[He] began to question me quite closely as to what experience I had had in military affairs, how long I had been with the army, whether I could distinguish one branch of service from another, and the like."[14]

Bryan apparently answered Johnston's questions satisfactorily, because next Colonel Rhett laid out a map of the peninsula on a large table.

"[Colonel Rhett] began questioning me about the different roads and creeks and fording places, and other topographical matters on the Peninsula," Bryan said. "Having shown myself sufficiently familiar with these matters, the General then turned to Colonel Rhett and remarked, 'I think Mr. Bryan will do very well.'"[15]

Johnston then said to Rhett, "You will please assign Captain Bryan to the balloon service to make reconnaissances, and instruct him as to what information we want, and the kind of report we desire from him."

Bryan was immediately up on his feet. This was the first he had heard that flying in a balloon would be part of his new duty.

"On hearing this order . . . [I began] protesting that while I could ride a horse, and would gladly do anything in my power, that I had never even seen a balloon, and I knew absolutely nothing about the management of it."

Bryan tried to convince the general that if it was just a matter of determining the enemy's position that he would, "cheerfully go into the lines" on horseback and return as swiftly as possible with a full report. Johnston, however, was not disposed to listen to Bryan's protests.

"My words had . . . small effect upon the General," Bryan later said. "He told me very curtly and positively that I had been assigned to him for duty, and that he expected me to perform the duty to which I was assigned without any questions. He added that he had plenty of scouts already, and what he wanted was a man to go up in the balloon, and I could now go and prepare myself for readiness when called for."[16]

Bryan was left with no alternative but to, "bow and walk out with as brave an appearance as possible."[17]

The captain's next stop in Johnston's camp was the site where the balloon was being prepared. It was located about a half mile from Union pickets. Bryan's first impression of the balloon did little to instill confidence.

"It was nothing but a big cotton bag, coated over so to make it airtight," Bryan observed. "My ardor to go on special service had been much cooled at the bare thought of being suspended in mid air by what appeared to me as a mere thread under a hot-air balloon, with the chances pretty strong that it would be burst by the shrapnel or shells of the enemy, and would end up as down would come baby and all.'"[18]

The crew tending to the craft had only a rudimentary knowledge of balloons that was limited to procedures primarily involving its inflation and release on a single tether line. They quickly imparted all that they knew to Bryan.

"I was also instructed in the signals that I should make when up in the balloon, by means of a wig-wag flag" Bryan recalled. "[I was] to tell those below what was wanted, whether I wished to go fast or slow, up or down."[19]

Bryan was also briefed on the last known position and strength of Union forces in the area and given basic instructions on cartography, which would be of crucial importance when aloft.

On April 13, 1862, John Randolph Bryan was put to his first test as an aeronaut. Orders were sent by General Johnston for an early morning ascent.

The ground crew immediately went to work inflating the craft. A fire was built underneath a makeshift chimney flue, fueled with pine knots and turpentine. The balloon's valve was held open, allowing the heated air to rise up into the cotton envelope. The crew was careful to keep the balloon secured in its place as it was being inflated, and Bryan noted that it was anchored to a long rope, probably a half mile long, tied to a tree and then rolled into several coils, "sail fashion," which was then passed through a windlass and attached finally to the network connecting the control basket to the balloon's envelope.

"It did not take a very long time to fill the balloon with hot air," Bryan said. "In fact, it was accomplished much too quickly for my liking. Very soon I was told that my aerial horse was ready for me to mount and ride away.[20]

Taking nothing more with him than a pencil, a notebook, and a pair of field glasses, Bryan ambled into the control basket and the windlass was released. Slowly, the tether rope was paid out and the balloon was allowed to rise.

"At first the balloon was let off quite gradually, and I began to ascend slowly," said Bryan, recalling that his heart was also beating furiously during those first tense moments. "This is not so bad, I thought. But the worst was yet to come."[21]

Indeed, as the Confederate balloon rose above the surrounding tree-tops, the opposing Federals sprang into action. Bryan could plainly see the men scrambling to their artillery positions, and the officer in charge elevating a cannon to capture the balloon in its sights. When the order to fire was given, a torrent of shells and bullets, "whistled and sang . . . a most unpleasant music" around Bryan and his balloon.

"I was quite aware that after attaining a certain height the ordinary field cannon could not be trained to bear upon me," Bryan said. "So the danger zone was only between the time when I appeared above the top of the trees and the time when I should have reached such an elevation that their guns could no longer be trained upon me."[22]

Meanwhile, as the balloon climbed ever upward, Bryan suffered through several terrifying moments.

"As you may readily imagine, I did not feel very happy or comfortable," Bryan recalled. "On the contrary, I was scared nearly breathless, and was exceedingly nervous. I at once gave the signal, 'faster,' and the balloon went upward more rapidly. Before long I reached an elevation above the line of fire, when I again signaled them to stop."[23]

Above the battlefield, Bryan was presented with a vast panorama encompassing views of Chesapeake Bay, the York and James Rivers, Old Point Comfort, Fortress Monroe, and Hampton, and both the Confederate and Union fleets stationed in the surrounding waterways.

Bryan took out his pencil and notebook and began to sketch all that he saw of importance. The difficulty of the task was compounded by the fact that the balloon was attached by only a single tether. As the wind buffeted the aerostat, it began to spin and rotate "like a top," though as Bryan noted, "only very much slower."[24] Yet, Bryan persevered over this relatively minor tribulation and constructed a rough, but thorough diagram, showing the rivers, roads, and creeks, and "marking where the different bodies of the enemy's troops were . . . using the initial 'I' for infantry, 'C' for cavalry, 'A' for artillery, and 'W' for wagons." Bryan also recorded the number of men he could see in each location.

"I now began to recover my composure, when a most horrid thought intruded itself upon me," Bryan said. "'Whatever goes up is bound to come down,' is a trite, but a sad, true saying. I knew well I could not remain in this security forever; in fact, every moment that passed the hot air in my balloon became cooler."[25]

Satisfied that he had accomplished all that he was intended to accomplish, Bryan signaled his ground crew to begin cranking the windlass to lower the balloon. Again, as the balloon reached a lower elevation and came into range, Bryan was met with a fierce fusillade from Union artillery.

"I therefore gave the signal, 'faster—faster,' and the men at the windlass put forth their best efforts, working relays, and as fast as they could.

"However, it seemed too slow to me, for . . . the enemy's guns opened on me, firing this time by batteries, four and six at a time, and filling the air with shells and bullets, and how I escaped I do not know, for some of their shells passed very close to me."[26]

At long last the balloon touched earth once again, and Captain Bryan quickly mounted his horse waiting nearby and sped off to General Johnston's headquarters to make his report. As Bryan related the details of his ascent using the battle maps laid out over the large table in the general's tent, Johnston listened with intense interest. He questioned Bryan about the various divisions spread out beyond the York River, and directed the captain to "show him where the different bodies of troops, artillery, and so on, were posted."

Johnston was duly impressed with Bryan's work and complimented the captain on a job well done. Bryan, on the other hand, had hoped that that morning's aerial adventure would be his first and last experience with a balloon and he requested permission to transfer back to the adjutant general's office at Magruder's headquarters.

"My dear sir," replied the general. "I fear you forget that you are the only experienced aeronaut that I have with my army, and you will please hold yourself in readiness, as we may wish you to make another ascension at any time!"[27]

Bryan later recalled that he was complimented by Johnston's words, but wasn't elated.

Among the ranks in Johnston's camp, the captain also discovered that he had acquired a new nickname. He was now referred to as "Balloon Bryan."

Following Bryan's first ascent, Johnston passed on orders to the balloon crew to relocate their equipment closer to Yorktown. It was felt that it wasn't safe for Bryan to ascend from the same locale on successive occasions. Modifications were also made to the windlass arrangement, which now incorporated a team of six draught horses that could be used to haul the balloon down much more efficiently than was possible with the available manpower.

Two days later Bryan made his second ascent from the new location. As a "seasoned" aeronaut now, Bryan approached his duty, "with somewhat less trepidation." Still, he reported that some of his fellow soldiers began to suspect him, "of having a screw loose somewhere on account of his mad trips in the air."[28]

Despite having to subject himself to Union artillery target practice again, Bryan survived the flight and reported his findings to General Johnston afterwards. He repeated his plea for a transfer, but the general refused and ordered Bryan to remain in readiness for yet another mission.

The Confederate efforts at Yorktown were beginning to show signs of weakening by the end of April, 1862. While McClellan was still reluctant to commit the full resources of the Union army to the Peninsular Campaign, he had begun to transport men by boat from Washington, D.C., to assembly points in lower Virginia along Chesapeake Bay. By May there were more than 100,000 Union troops converging on Yorktown and Norfolk.

In the early morning of May 4, the day before Johnston's troops were forced to fall back from Yorktown to Williamsburg, Captain Bryan was ordered to take to the air.

"The balloon squad was woken up . . . with orders from General Johnston to fire up the balloon and make a reconnaissance as soon as possible," Bryan said. "The courier who brought the order informed me privately that information had been received at headquarters from some of the scouts that the enemy was in motion and that General Johnston was very anxious to ascertain in what direction the move was to be made, and whether their troops were advancing upon more than one point."[29]

The cool, morning darkness was illuminated by a full moon, as the balloon crew readied the aerostat for action.

"As soon . . . as the balloon was inflated I jumped into my basket, feeling quite at ease, as I had already made two ascensions, and as this was a night trip," said Bryan. "I had but little fear of discovery and of being fired upon, especially as the enemy was now in motion, and when marching could not so well arrange for this artillery service."[30]

But the danger would come from a different quarter that Bryan did not anticipate. Intense curiosity over the balloon gripped the men in Johnston's camp. Few of the men even knew such craft existed, and some gathered very close to the balloon's support gear as it rose up into the air.

An infantryman, with his eyes gazing upward, inadvertently stepped into one of the tether rope coils on the ground. As the balloon rose, the tether suddenly wound around the man's leg. Before anybody could react the hapless soldier found himself being dragged toward the wood and steel windlass, which would have surely severed his leg as the tether drew taut.

The man began to scream loudly, as pain and terror gripped his body. Before great bodily injury occurred, one of the man's comrades spied an axe that had been used to cut wood for the fire that fueled the balloon. With a swift stroke of the blade the rope was cut loose.

Up above, Bryan immediately felt something had gone wrong.

"The balloon jerked upward as if by some great force for about two miles, or so it seemed to me," he said. "I was breathless and gasping, and trembling like a leaf from fear without knowing what had happened beyond the surmise that the rope which held me to the earth had broken."[31]

As Bryan contemplated the potential fates that awaited him, the balloon continued to rise with abandon. Presently, however, it reached equilibrium and for a while suspended itself high above Confederate lines overlooking the York River country.

But much to Bryan's dismay the wind began to stir.

"I found myself being blown from Confederate lines over into those of the enemy. It is impossible to describe my feeling. I felt that I was not only leaving my home and friends forever, but was slowly drifting to certain capture."

Providence was in Bryan's favor, though. Soon the wind shifted direction again, and the aeronaut found himself over what he thought was friendly territory.

"I was blown from the enemy's lines over the Confederate army, but alas! in a far different locality from where I ascended."[32]

As it turned out, Bryan was drifting over the 2nd Florida Regiment. The men in camp scrambled out en masse, convinced that Bryan's aerostat was one of the Yankee spy balloons they had heard reports of operating in Virginia.

"In vain I cried to them that I was a good Confederate," Bryan said. "The only answer I received was from the whistling of their bullets. I was as a thing hunted, and knew not which way to turn."

Apparently the officers of the 2nd Florida were not briefed about Bryan's duties in General Johnston's camp. The hail of bullets continued until the wind shifted again, this time blowing the balloon over the wide waters of the York River, which was some three to four miles across at the point where Bryan was suspended.

"The balloon began to settle quite rapidly," said Bryan. "It was evident that I would be dumped in the middle of this broad expanse of water."[33]

Bryan prepared for the worst and began to strip off his clothing. When he got to his boots, he found them so tight to his feet that he was forced to take out his pocket knife and slice a long incision along the sides in order to remove them.

By this time the balloon was so close to the river that Bryan could hear the remainder of the tether line splashing over the surface. As the air in the balloon rapidly cooled it descended closer to the water, but at the last moment a gentle breeze took hold of the ship. Much to Bryan's surprise and relief the balloon landed ever so gently on the south bank of the York.

Grateful to reach the ground in one piece, Bryan quickly leapt from the control basket, grabbed the tether line, and secured the balloon to a tree in a nearby apple orchard. After dressing himself, he found a farmer and attempted to explain his predicament.

"After quite a hot discussion with the farmer, I succeeded in securing a horse and rode back to General Johnston's headquarters, a distance of about eight miles, and made my report as to what I had seen."[34]

Bryan went on to say that his report allowed Johnston to plan a counterattack on the Union forces the following day.

As for Bryan, his freeflight adventure proved to be his last aerial ascension of any kind. As Johnston's army began their retreat to Williamsburg, Bryan recalled how he threw his fortune in with the ground troops with a lot less trepidation compared to his duties as an aeronaut.

"I was among those who awaited the approach of the enemy, and you will pardon me if I say that it gave me no little satisfaction to aim my rifle at those who had so recently and so frequently taken a wing shot at me."[35]

Although John Randolph Bryan's experience with balloons was at an end, military planners within the Confederacy were not willing to abandon their use just yet. For the Confederacy's next attempt to create an effective air force one of the most enduring legends to emerge from the war would result in the legendary "Silk Dress Balloon."

CHAPTER ELEVEN

The Origins of the "Silk Dress Balloon"

W hen Joseph Johnston fell wounded at the battle of Seven Pines at the end of May, 1862, the next Southern commander to take up the cause of ballooning was James Longstreet.

"The Federals had been using balloons in examining our positions," recalled General Longstreet. "And we watched with anxious eyes their beautiful observations as they floated out of range of our guns."[1] It was determined that the antiquated cotton balloon that Bryan had operated near Yorktown would not be suitable for continued use. Longstreet's recollection of how the Army of Northern Virginia acquired its second balloon would go down as one of the most enduring and endearing legends of the Confederacy.

"While we were longing for the balloons that poverty denied us, a genius arose for the occasion and suggested that we send out and gather all the silk dresses in the Confederacy and make a balloon. It was done; and soon we had a great patchwork ship of many and varied hues which was ready for use in the Seven Days' campaign.[2]

As with most legends, the actual events that occurred diverged somewhat from the myths that came about in the years following the war.

While Longstreet was probably the most prominent Southern military leader to recognize the value of aerial reconnaissance, the task of actually procuring the next Confederate balloon fell to Gen. Thomas Fenwick Drayton.

Drayton was especially impressed with the potential a Confederate balloon could achieve. As district commander at Port Royal, South Carolina, during the time John Starkweather and the balloon *Washington* were operating in support of Gen. Thomas W. Sherman's Northern expeditionary force, Drayton witnessed a number of ascents made by the aeronaut there.[3] With the official blessing of the Confederate high command, Drayton assigned the project to Capt. Langdon Cheves.

Cheves (pronounced chi'-vis) was the son of a prominent South Carolina legislator, and a practicing lawyer and owner of a rice plantation near Charleston before the war. In December, 1860, Cheves was among the signatories of South Carolina's Ordinance of Secession[4] and subsequently volunteered his services to the Confederacy where he served as an engineer and aide-de-camp to General Drayton.[5]

Drayton charged Cheves with the full responsibility of finding a response to the Union's balloon, although resources for a Confederate aerostat would not be easy to come by. Cheves realized that the project required the ingenuity of an experienced balloon builder and aeronaut. So for the actual construction of the balloon, Cheves turned to Charles Cevor of Savannah, Georgia.

Cevor was an itinerant balloonist whose career stretched back nearly twenty years prior to the war. He was an early associate of John Wise and is believed to have purchased his first balloon from the veteran aeronaut in 1843.[6] As with many balloonists of the era, Cevor also had his share of misadventures.

While demonstrating his balloon *Montpelier* in Savannah in early March, 1860, Cevor and an associate known as Mr. Dalton ascended from the courtyard of Armory Hall. Within seconds the balloon climbed to more than 10,000 feet. At that altitude the balloon encountered the lower portion of the eastern jet stream, which swiftly took control of the balloon's course. The result was a fast and furious flight that took the aeronauts out over the fierce Atlantic past Calaboga Sound, where the balloonists were almost drowned.

The control car was dragged through the water as the balloon struggled to rise again. A Savannah newspaper later reported that Cevor, "would have discharged all of the gas and swamped the balloon, trusting his ability to swim ashore," but unfortunately Mr. Dalton, who couldn't swim, begged him to keep aloft.

"For God's sakes; don't go in the water," Dalton cried out. "I'd rather drop anywhere on land."[7]

For nearly an hour Cevor and his companion were waist deep in the cold ocean water as they struggled to lighten the ballast aboard and gain altitude once again.[8]

Cevor managed to safely guide the balloon toward the shore of Hilton Head, South Carolina, where the foundering balloon was spotted by George Savage, an overseer for a local plantation. With a number of slaves accompanying him, Savage set out in a boat in the choppy waters off Hilton Head to rescue Cevor and Dalton.

> Mr. Savage was enabled to reach the balloon some little time before its occupants had made the opposite shore, and with his negroes rendered every assistance in his power to extricate the aeronauts, and to make fast the balloon, which, however, defying all their power was driven across the marsh. After vainly endeavoring to recover control of it until they were all exhausted, Mr. Cevor gave the word to 'let her go,' and the *Montpelier*, perfect and uninjured by its rough contact with elements, shot up 'like a rocket,' and was soon out of sight in the distance.[9]

The *Montpelier* was never seen again.

Following the incident with the *Montpelier*, Cevor constructed a new balloon that was named *Forest City*. According to Cevor, the *Forest City* was the first gas balloon, "ever made south of the Mason-Dixon line." When war broke out between the North and South, Cevor also became the first Southern aeronaut to volunteer his services to the Confederacy.

"As early as April, 1861, the services of myself and balloon *Forest City*, . . . were offered to the Confederate government," Cevor later said. "But for reasons not known by me, not accepted."[10]

By the late spring of 1862, the reasons that the Confederate military had used to refuse Cevor's proposal were now reversed in light of the success of Professor Lowe's balloons on Union battlefields. Langdon Cheves contacted Cevor in May to build a balloon that would counter the Union's. It was a course of action heartily endorsed by General Drayton.

"I had an interview with General [John] Pemberton last night," Drayton wrote to Cheves. "He favors the balloon plan, particularly if Cevor has a balloon already made!"[11]

Cevor probably considered the *Forest City* to be too small and fragile for military service, but he was able to persuade Cheves to consider the construction of a new balloon. Cheves, who was under pressure to quickly procure a response to the Union army's Balloon Corps, agreed and was able to get the necessary authorization to begin the project.

The first item Cevor needed to start construction was a large supply of silk for the balloon's envelope. At the time, the Union navy was effectively blockading Southern ports and the silk required for the envelope was an item generally imported from the Orient through Britain. Given the state of affairs, a large quantity of new silk was an extremely scarce commodity to come by.

However, Cheves was fortunate to find a source of colored silk from the supply house of Kerrison & Leiding in Charleston. The material cost dearly, but Cheves bought all that he could. An invoice sent to Maj. Edwin Willis, the Confederate district quartermaster, revealed that Cheves purchased twenty bolts of silk on May 5, 1862. The costs totaled over $514.[12]

Concerned that his purchase from the Charleston supply house might not be enough material for the project, Cheves casually made the following remark to his daughters prior to leaving for Georgia:

"I'm buying up all the handsome silk dresses in Savannah, but not for you girls."[13]

The implication that the balloon was constructed from ladies' silk dresses would be a permanent part of Confederate lore from that point on.

The need for the "Silk Dress Balloon" was urgent, as revealed by a message from General Drayton to Cheves, dated May 9, 1862:

Captain,
    How soon will the Balloon be finished? Put night and day work upon it at your discretion.
                                        Yours Respectfully,
                                        Thom. F Drayton, Brig. Gen.[14]

Cheves traveled to Savannah not long after. There, along with Charles Cevor, he set up shop to construct the balloon inside the Chatham Armory. Cevor worked under circumstances of deprivation resulting from material shortages, and often made this fact known in his communications with Cheves.

In one letter Cevor wrote how he was trying to obtain the proper manila rope that would be used in the balloon's network from Confederate government storehouses, but "if not, the rope at Claghorn & Cunningham will do."[15] The record shows that an invoice for $8.20 was eventually paid out to the supply goods company.[16]

The construction of the balloon did proceed and was completed in a remarkable short period of time given the circumstances. It was composed of forty-foot strips of silk of various hues and patterns—yellow, green, black, and white. The envelope was finished with rubber dissolved from the coating on used wagon springs and vulcanized with heat to the silk. Also unique to its construction were two gas valves that were controlled by metal rods rather than rope.[17]

At over 7,500 cubic feet in capacity, it measured out to be significantly smaller than the smallest of the Union balloons. Still, it was a major achievement for the South. Cheves officially dubbed the Confederate balloon *Gazelle*.

On May 28, a letter was forwarded to Cheves from Lt. Ezra Young, assistant adjutant general at General Drayton's headquarters in South Carolina:

> Captain,
> I am instructed by Brig. Gen. Drayton to direct you to tender the use of the balloon to General Lawton, while we have to await the completion of the gas apparatus.
> Perhaps you had better offer it to General Lawton altogether, if he will pay the expenses, as he can make more use of it at present than we can.
>
> Yours respectfully,
> Lt. E. Young, A.A.G.[18]

As with its Union counterparts, it is interesting to note that a portable gas generator was also envisioned for use with the *Gazelle* so that it could be inflated far from city gas works. Unfortunately, Cevor was not quite ready with the apparatus when the balloon was called for in South Carolina.

"I have endeavored to experiment with the iron turnings," Cevor wrote to Cheves. "But have only partially succeeded in obtaining results of any certainty."[19]

By the time the new Confederate balloon was ready to enter service, the South's military priorities had shifted away from South Carolina. The Union army's expedition to Port Royal had neutralized the Confederate military's stronghold on the South Carolina coast.

"Fort Pulaski has fallen so suddenly and unexpectedly," Drayton wrote to Cheves on April 12. "The scheme for the Balloon must be abandoned for the present at least."[20]

Despite the fact that Fort Pulaski guarded the sea approach to Savannah, the Confederate army was now engaged in a bitter fight with Union forces on the Virginia peninsula. While late spring rains and logistics problems hampered Northern efforts, many Southerners feared that the Confederate capital at Richmond would fall if the Yankee onslaught continued unabated. In early June, Cheves and Cevor were ordered to bring the *Gazelle* directly to Richmond without delay.

The two men were to arrive just in time for the beginning of the bloody Seven Days' battles.

CHAPTER TWELVE

The Air War
over Virginia

As the South struggled to keeps its aeronauts aloft, Thaddeus Lowe and his assistants found themselves hard-pressed to keep up with the demands of the Union army. Firmly entrenched on the narrow peninsula leading from Fortress Monroe, McClellan became obsessed with gathering as much information about Confederate activity as possible. Although the Balloon Corps arguably had the best vantage point from which to accurately gauge Rebel activity in the surrounding area, McClellan could not allow himself to heed the observations of just one source. Indeed, as a result of the faulty intelligence received from Allan Pinkerton's scouts and captured Rebel soldiers—as well as the clever ruse perpetrated by General Magruder in constantly shuffling his small army of men—McClellan remained convinced that his forces were outnumbered by a margin of two to one.

Patience in McClellan's assessment of the situation in Virginia was beginning to grow thin in Washington. In a telegram to McClellan sent in early April, 1862, Lincoln wrote, "You now have over 100,000 troops with you. I think you better break the enemy's line from Yorktown to Warwick River at once."[1]

McClellan wrote to his wife afterwards, "The President . . . thought I had better break the enemy's line at once! I was very much tempted to reply that he had better come and do it himself."

In spite of the acrimony that was rapidly developing between the president and the Army of the Potomac's commander, McClellan ordered the bombardment of Yorktown to begin in late April. Gen. Fitz-John Porter was placed in charge of the assault.

McClellan's chief of engineers, Gen. John G. Barnard, was responsible for positioning over one hundred heavy Parrott guns, howitzers, and mortars aimed at the town based on observations he had made while accompanying Thaddeus Lowe mid-month.

While McClellan was able to set artillery in place, the land attack on Yorktown was an entirely different matter. The Warwick River, which rose about a mile and a half from Yorktown, was usually a small stream running diagonally across the peninsula and emptying into the James River. But heavy rains combined with deliberately built Confederate dams had managed to swell the river as much as a mile wide in places. Two crossings, one at Wynn's Mill and another at Lee's Mill, were heavily defended by Rebel earthworks.

Compounding all of this, Magruder was also successful in his request to Richmond to detach more men for the defense of Yorktown. By the time McClellan began his advance, Magruder's 12,000 or so men were joined by reinforcements under the commands of Jubal Early, Daniel H. Hill, and David R. Jones.

On May 1, Union gun batteries opened fire on Yorktown. For the next three days shells from both sides pounded away unmercifully.

"The whole atmosphere was filled with bursting shell and shot," Thaddeus Lowe later recalled. The intensity of the battle made balloon ascensions more dangerous than ever.

"On the 3d of May I made a reconnaissance . . . at sundown before Yorktown. . . . General Porter and myself ascended. No sooner had the balloon risen above the tops of the trees than the enemy opened all their batteries," said Lowe. The shelling was among the heaviest yet encountered by Lowe.

While Porter and Lowe remained unscathed by the heavy fire, the effect of the artillery directed at the balloon was devastating. With their field glasses, Porter and Lowe could see the overextended Confederate shot exacting a heavy toll on Union ground forces below.

"[One shot] struck near to the place where General McClellan stood," Lowe observed while in the air. "Another 64-pounder struck between two soldiers lying in a tent, but without injury.

Portrait of Thaddeus Lowe during the early months of the Peninsular Campaign. Although Lowe dressed as a Union army officer and held the honorary rank of "colonel," he never received a military commission. LIBRARY OF CONGRESS

"Fearing that by keeping the balloon up the enemy's shots would do injury to the troops that were thickly camped there, General Porter ordered the balloon down."[2]

The shelling directed at the balloon not only brought danger to Union infantry troops. Gen. George Stoneman, of the cavalry, voiced his criticism that the excessive Rebel fire was affecting his operations.

"[Stoneman] complained that I drew the enemy's fire over his great pack of horses," Lowe said. "When I called his attention to the fact that all of the shot fell at least one mile beyond his camp he replied that while so, it did not prevent every horse from humping up his back every time those large siege guns were fired. It must have been annoying to the General, who prided himself on his ten-thousand fine cavalry horses."[3]

Not long after Lowe's ascent with General Porter, the tempo of the battle began to change. During the early morning of May 4, Lowe received word from General Heintzelman, who was commanding the Union III Corps, that there was a strong possibility that the Rebels were pulling out of Yorktown and setting fire to the town as they left. In the pitch darkness of night, Lowe went aloft.

"I immediately ascended and saw the fire was confined to one building or vessel near the wharf," said Lowe. "I did not consider it a sufficient indication that they were evacuating, for if destruction of property was intended, they would burn their barracks, tents, wharves, store-houses, &c. I therefore considered the fire to be accidental."[4]

Lowe was later to learn that a Confederate munitions dump was the source of the blaze.[5]

After making his report, Lowe was told by Heintzelman to ascend again. His next ascension came just before dawn.

"At this time in the morning, I could see no campfires. As soon as it became a little lighter I discovered that the enemy had gone."

Lowe immediately relayed his observations to Heintzelman, who insisted on going up with Lowe to confirm the information.

From above, Lowe and Heintzelman saw the rear guard of Magruder's army at a position one mile distant of Yorktown. The Rebels were falling back in anticipation of an attack on Richmond.

"At first the general was puzzled on seeing more wagons entering the forts than were going out," Lowe observed. "But when I called his attention to the fact that the ingoing wagons were light and moved rapidly, while the outgoing wagons were heavily loaded and moved slowly, there was no longer any doubt as to the object of the Confederates."[6]

"It [was] fair to presume that the first reliable information given on the evacuation of Yorktown was that transmitted from the balloon to General McClellan by General Heintzelman and myself," Lowe said.[7]

General Heintzelman seconded Lowe's assessment.

"We could not distinguish any guns or men in or around the fortifications of Yorktown," Heintzelman reported. "The smoke of [the Rebel] camps was very much diminished."[8]

Lowe noted the Army of the Potomac's advance as word spread of the Rebel evacuation.

"We . . . saw our troops advance upon the empty works, throwing out their skirmishers, and feeling their way as if expecting to meet an enemy," said Lowe.

There was good reason for the Federals to "feel their way" as they advanced. The Confederate army had seen to it that every foot of Virginia soil would be hard won by the Yankees and the placement of land mines and booby traps was widespread in the Virginia peninsula in the wake of the Rebel withdrawal. The land mines were simply eight- or ten-inch Columbiad cannon shells, buried a few inches below ground, using a friction primer that exploded the device when stepped on. Thaddeus Lowe witnessed the deadly results first hand on May 4.

"[I] found a telegraph operator climbing poles and repairing wires towards the Yorktown fortifications," Lowe recalled. "He was an expert not only in operating but in climbing and repairing and as he came down from one of the poles he stepped upon a torpedo [mine] intended to blow up any one who made such repairs and was instantly killed before my eyes."[9]

The fate of the telegrapher was repeated all too often as McClellan's men made their way up the peninsula. The problem with land mines became so acute that McClellan ordered captured Confederate prisoners to clear the roads in advance of Union soldiers and horses.

While Lowe and his assistants continued to deal with the dangers and adversities of the Virginia invasion, Charles Cevor was struggling in a race against time to complete the new Confederate balloon for service. With expectations of a massive military assault by McClellan's Army of the Potomac, many feared that the Confederate capital at Richmond would fall. All resources available for its defense were deemed of vital importance, and Cevor's balloon was no exception.

In addition to the element of time, other factors took their toll on Cevor. His personal expenses on the *Gazelle* were mounting as Confederate paymasters took their time issuing reimbursements. Some idea of the costs that the aeronaut incurred can be gathered from an invoice that Cevor later submitted to the Confederate States War Department:

Network attached to balloon "Gazelle"	$ 110.00
Car	$ 25.00
Concentrating hoop	$ 150.00
300 feet of leading hose (for gas inflation)	$ 150.00
1 anchor	$ 3.00
75 yards of canvas	$ 336.00[10]

Compared to the costs involved with the Union's Balloon Corps, it was obvious that Cevor did his level best to contain costs. Despite the problems that confronted him, Cevor was able to report by May 22 that all was in readiness.

"I fear that you may have come to the conclusion that I have not displayed proper energy in the construction of the balloon," Cevor wrote Captain Cheves. "But I can only say that I have met many unexpected obstacles which has caused delays. However, I am happy to be able to report myself for duty and subject to your orders."[11]

Though Cevor had managed to complete the *Gazelle* in an astonishingly rapid fashion, an important element to the total package was still missing—a portable gas generator. Though Cevor toiled endlessly with experiments based on the generator that John Wise had developed for his own balloons twenty years before, the apparatus was never capable of generating sufficient amounts of hydrogen to fill even the relatively small 7,500, cubic-foot envelope of the *Gazelle*.

With Union forces driving up the Virginia peninsula and less than fifty miles from Richmond, further experiments were no longer possible. Not long after Cevor's last letter to Cheves, orders came for the aeronaut to accompany the balloon to Richmond, where it would be inflated from the city's gas works.

It was fortunate that Cevor's *Gazelle* and its supporting paraphernalia comprised far less equipment than a typical outfit in the Union's Balloon Corps. Cevor was forced to endure over 500 miles and over two weeks of travel mostly by backtracking on Confederate rail and dirt roads in order to evade Yankees in South Carolina and Virginia before reaching Richmond.

Meanwhile, the Army of the Potomac was beginning to suffer its own share of problems on Rebel soil. While the Union's campaign had effectively captured Yorktown, it was something of a Pyrrhic victory. Magruder had outmaneuvered the Yankees to gain time for the defense of Richmond. General Stoneman's cavalry was in full pursuit of Magruder's men as they fell back to join up with the rest of the Army of Northern Virginia. But Stoneman's troopers found the advance to be a hard slog. Heavy spring rains turned roads into thick mud. In addition to the mud, Union cavalry charges were effectively repulsed by the presence of newly freed-up Confederate forces led by Generals Stuart and Longstreet. In the no man's land that developed before Williamsburg near Halfway House, Magruder was able to stabilize his line, which further delayed McClellan's advance.

In retrospect, McClellan could have probably pushed his superior forces to break through the Rebel defenses. However, cautious now to a fault, the general found himself forced to rethink his strategy. He feared a bloodbath would be awaiting his forces the closer they approached to Richmond. These fears were further compounded by continuing intelligence reports fed to him by Allan Pinkerton and his agents, who had managed to convince the general that the Confederate army was now more than 120,000-men strong in Virginia—a figure inflated by at least double the actual number.

The unusually heavy spring rains that hampered the Federals were having surprisingly little effect on the Balloon Corps. Thaddeus Lowe was able to hone the field procedures for his balloons to the point where inclement weather was more of a nuisance than a total impediment. The danger of keeping balloons aloft was great, with many of the storms often brooding with lightning strikes that could have easily ignited the hydrogen-filled balloons. But the worst of the storms passed without incident.

Poor weather was not the only concern that preoccupied Lowe or the men of the Army of the Potomac that spring. By the beginning of May there was a definite sense that the advance on Richmond was not progressing well.

"On the afternoon of [May] 4th I received orders to move everything pertaining to my department by water, with General Franklin's command," said Lowe. "Judging from my orders, it would seem the battle of Williamsburg was not expected."[12]

Williamsburg was the next objective on the road to Richmond. The Confederates intended the fight to be another delaying tactic to buy time for Richmond. Magruder had ordered the construction of crude earthworks about two miles east of the colonial town. The battle would prove to be a costly one for both sides.

The engagement began early on the morning of May 5 and lasted little more than a day. Lowe was present with one of his balloons as the battle commenced.

"Every gun in the fortification [was] turned on the balloon . . . they were pointing upward in the hope of preventing us in some form from further annoying the Confederates by watching their movements."[13]

Although the battle from the air was treacherous—with the whistling of Confederate artillery coming dangerously close particularly during ascents and landings—the threat was equally high on the ground as Lowe always camped near one his balloons.

"[One] shot, fired after dark, came into General Heintzelman's camp and completely destroyed his telegraph tent and instruments, the operator having just gone to deliver a despatch," Lowe recalled. "The general and I were sitting together, discussing the probable reasons for the unusual effort to destroy the balloon, when we were both covered with what appeared to be tons of earth, which a great 12 inch shell had thrown up. Fortunately it did not explode."[14]

In the aftermath of that evening's close encounter with the enemy's artillery, Lowe suggested to Heintzelman that the balloon should be moved so as to draw the enemy's fire in another direction.

"But the general said that he could stand [the fire] if I could," Lowe said. "Besides, he would like to have me near by, as he enjoyed going up occasionally himself. He told me that, while I saw a grand spectacle by watching the discharge of all those great guns that were paying their compliments to a single man, it was nothing as compared with the sight I would look down upon the next day when our great mortar batteries would open their siege-guns on the fortifications, which General McClellan expected to do."[15]

While Lowe was no doubt impressed with Heintzelman's glorified vision of the Williamsburg battlefield, the aeronaut was given new orders to proceed to nearby West Point.

"I could see readily that I could be of no service at Williamsburg, both armies being hidden in a great forest," Lowe said. "Therefore, General McClellan at the close of battle sent orders to me to proceed with my outfit, including all the balloons, gas-generators, the balloon-inflating boat, gun boat, and tug up the Pamunkey River, until I reached White House and the bridge crossing the historic river, and join the army which would be there as soon as myself."[16]

It may have been just as well that Lowe departed before the battle of Williamsburg was finally over. Over 1,700 Southerners were lost on the battlefield by the dawn of the next day. The Union casualty list was even greater, with over 2,200 men lost.

The battle of May 5 shocked McClellan, who immediately telegraphed Washington to dispatch General McDowell and his Army of the Rappahannock to reinforce the Army of the Potomac against the Confederates. McClellan had hoped to land McDowell's men by boat, but the plan was modified to allow for an overland march, where they would meet with William B. Franklin's division at West Point.

By the time McDowell's men were ready to move a new wrinkle in the war was beginning to play out. A small Confederate army under the command of Thomas "Stonewall" Jackson cut a wide swath through the Shenandoah Valley. Union forces under Gen. Nathaniel Banks were engaged by Jackson's men at Front Royal, about forty miles east of Washington. The fears of a Confederate attack on the capital suddenly became very real.

On May 24, Lincoln broke the news to McClellan that McDowell's troops were to remain in Washington, where they were needed for the defense of the Union.

"In consequence of General Banks' position, I have been compelled to suspend McDowell's movement to join you."[17]

Following the battle of Williamsburg, Lowe was ordered to take his balloons up the York River to West Point. West Point was located on the outlet of the Pamunkey River and was about twenty miles east of the Confederate capital and twenty miles north of Williamsburg. A Union supply base was to be established there.

On May 6, Lowe made the precarious journey aboard the balloon barge *George Washington Parke-Custis* to his new outpost. According to Lowe, his unit was to be the advanced guard for the Union's new position, where he was to be headquartered on the grounds of White House several miles upriver.

White House was a large plantation house that had belonged to Robert E. Lee's son, William. It had also once been the residence of George and Martha Washington in the years before the Revolutionary War.[18]

"We arrived at the Lee mansion and found the bridge crossing the Pamunkey on fire, which fully convinced me that I was well within the enemy's country," Lowe said.[19]

"The balloon boat was the first to reach the White House Landing and was even some distance ahead of the gunboats," Lowe said of his arrival. "On the first night the balloon guard was the advance picket on the river bottom. I instantly realized my precarious situation."[20]

According to Lowe there was no indication of Confederate troops in the area, but the atmosphere was eerily quiet in the grounds of the plantation. With roughly 150 infantrymen comprising the West Point landing party, Lowe knew that an enemy ambush would be disastrous. The situation was made even more perilous because the gunboat that had accompanied the Balloon Corps to West Point was under orders to continue up the James River to take part in the bombardment of Fort Darling. Faced with a potentially dangerous situation, Lowe took it upon himself to flesh out the relative strength of the unit attach to him.

"To carry out a bluff I immediately rushed a long line of tents along the edge of the locust grove in which the house stood, reaching down the river a quarter mile and built as many fires as my men could get material for," Lowe later said. "The purpose, making it appear as though we were strong, not only in numbers, but in equipment."[21]

Lowe also carried out one other deception. By this time the Union's first ironclad warship, the *Monitor*, had entered service and its destructive power was well known to the Confederates. Although Lowe, of course, did not have the legendary warship with him at White House, he reckoned that the flat top *George Washington Parke-Custis* was a passable substitute, at least in appearance.

"My balloon-boat was almost a facsimile of our little *Monitor* and about its size," Lowe recalled. "With the flag which I kept at the stern it had the appearance of an armed craft, which I think is all that saved me and my command, for the *Monitor* was what the Confederates dreaded at that time more than anything else."[22]

As the men constructed their camp, Lowe ventured to the White House mansion. Upon entering the house he quickly learned just how precarious the situation had been for the plantation's previous occupants.

"We found the overseer and two house servants," said Lowe of what he discovered inside. "The family had left a few minutes before [our arrival] on a special [rail] car that took them to Richmond. On entering the house I found that dinner was being served when my boats made their appearance, and that coffee was still warm in the cups [and] an inviting, friendly looking fire blazed in the great fireplace."[23]

Lowe was still apprehensive of a Rebel attack and turned to question the plantation's overseer.

"[He] was a man of about fifty years, was exceedingly bright and evaded all my questions with unusual tact," Lowe said. "He then stated that if I had got through with him he would like to go home. I stated that his home for the present would be with us and we would take good care of him. I then questioned the negroes separately and got a large amount of valuable information."[24]

Lowe may have felt his position lacked sufficient strength in numbers, but he was determined to carry out flight operations nonetheless. The portable hydrogen generators were put to work all through the night and by the following morning one of the three balloons in Lowe's charge was inflated. Ascending at dawn, the aeronaut scoured the surrounding countryside.

"[I] could see scouts on the ridge two miles beyond, but no apparent movement to disturb us," Lowe observed. "A small force could have captured us in a few minutes if they had known my situation."[25]

From his aerial vantage point Lowe desperately searched for signs of Union reinforcements. What he saw was not very encouraging.

"I let the balloon up to view the surrounding country and over the ridge beyond the Pamunkey River valley," Lowe recalled. "I saw the rest of the retreating Confederates, which showed me that our army had not gotten along as fast as was expected."[26]

However, as the morning wore on, Lowe finally caught sight of what he was hoping to see. A column of mounted soldiers emerged from the woods around 8 A.M.

"With my glasses I assured myself that they were our troops headed by General Stoneman's cavalry," Lowe said, in obvious relief. "I immediately started out with my favorite orderly to meet them and soon outriders from the head of the column came out. In a few minutes a second rider and orderlies left the head of the column and galloped towards me and soon General Stoneman and myself met again."[27]

Lowe reported that the general was extremely pleased to see him but was somewhat surprised that the aeronaut had managed to get to White House before his own troops.

"He said . . . he thought he was in the lead to Richmond, but found himself mistaken," Lowe remarked. "I told him that I was there to report to him, and I should be glad to be of service in his command."[28]

Stoneman gladly accepted the aeronaut's offer and Lowe soon found himself a part of the general's command. For the next two weeks Lowe made a number of observations in the vicinity of White House and tended to the repairs of the balloons and gas generators.

On the morning of May 20, Stoneman ordered his troops and Lowe's Balloon Corps to converge on the banks of the Chickahominy River, less than fifteen miles east of the outskirts of Richmond.

"Accompanied by General Stoneman I ascended and there had a distinct view of Richmond, the general being the first to point out the city as we were rising," Lowe said. "As we gained altitude we saw that the Confederates, who had made their way from Yorktown, were camped about Richmond."

But the aerial view of Richmond was not the only sight Lowe and Stoneman took in that morning. A Confederate force stood between Stoneman's men and the high ridge on the banks of the Chickahominy River. The force seemed rather insignificant from the air and Stoneman wanted to find a place to regroup his troops. A large wheat field, complete with an adjacent mill, was spotted from above and seemed to offer a safe location. It was a farm that belonged to Dr. William Fleming Gaines.

Following his ascent with Stoneman, Lowe later claimed that he also acted as an advance scout and was among the first in the Union vanguard to arrive at the site of the Gaines farm.

"I took one orderly and rode towards a great open field, with extensive buildings on the main promenade" Lowe said. "It proved to be a 1,000 acre wheat field nearly ready for harvest.

"As our horses jumped over the fence and we approached the house through this wheat field, a tall commanding looking gentleman stood at his gate with a dark expression on his face.

"When saluted he replied, 'Gentlemen, why could you have not taken the road to reach the house instead of riding through and tramping down so fine a field of grain.'

"Said I, 'This is Dr. Gaines, is it not?'

"He said, 'Yes.'

"'Well Doctor, I am sorry to see such a fine field of grain such as this trampled down, but it is inevitable. Our army is just behind us and will soon occupy its most commanding position which, unfortunately, at this time is where we are standing. But I assure you that your horse and gardens will be properly guarded.'"[29]

The Constitution *encamped at the farm of Dr. William Gaines, near Gaines's Mill. The balloon was equipped with an aerial telegraph device and observation made from above helped the Union army to secure the area.*
PHOTOGRAPHIC HISTORY OF THE CIVIL WAR

Despite the fact that Lowe was a civilian and that Dr. Gaines was considered a Confederate, the assurance of protection was carried out. Lowe was able to assign several of the men detailed to the Balloon Corps to act as sentries around the doctor's home. Not long after the guard was established the rest of Stoneman's force approached.

"The lead of the army had arrived in sight, which made the Doctor turn pale indeed," Lowe said. "He soon saw the force of my argument and my desire to protect him and his family."[30]

Fannie Gaines, Dr. Gaines's daughter, vividly recalled the details of the Union army's occupation of her family's home:

When the Yankee army came up from White House, we were in a great state of excitement. The morning after they came up, the officer for the day came to the house and put a guard of thirty men around it for our protection. The schoolhouse was taken for the surgeons, they stayed there. The carriage house was taken for the Yankee hospital, and the sick and wounded were carried there.[31]

Lowe later reported that the doctor and his family repaid him for the respect that he accorded to the sanctity of their home by sending the aeronaut a basket of fresh vegetables at his campsite.

"I knew what was short with the Confederates and selecting such things as I knew they could not get, I sent my cook over to the house to return the compliment," Lowe said.[32]

Although some units of the Confederate army remained in the vicinity of the Gaines's farm, Stoneman was determined to use the farm as a resting place for his men and horses. Once again, Lowe proved to be invaluable in ridding the area of an enemy presence by having the balloon *Constitution* ready to ascend with its airborne telegraph apparatus.

"General Stoneman ascended with me to an elevation of a thousand feet," Lowe later recalled. "[We] had a splendid view of the enemy's country [and] discovered a force of the enemy near New Bridge, concealed to watch our movements.

"The general then took two batteries and placed them to the right and left of Doctor Gaines' house, and caused the enemy to retreat for at least a mile and a half, while he remained in the balloon with me, directing the commanders of the batteries where to fire, as they could not see the objects fired at."[33]

During the time that Lowe was quartered on the Gaines's farm, Dr. Gaines's daughter regularly observed the Balloon Corps' operations:

Every day the Yankees sent up a balloon in front of our house to see what was going on in Richmond. General Low[e] was the man who ascended in the balloon, and he told many wonderful things that he saw going on in Richmond—such as people going to church, the evacuation of Richmond, wagon trains crossing Mayo's bridge, etc.[34]

The Gaines family was undoubtedly overwhelmed by the aeronaut's exploits and Lowe probably did little to correct Fannie Gaines's mistake regarding his military position.

While members of the Gaines family may have been impressed by the Union army's display of high technology at their front doorstep, others in the vicinity were somewhat more nonchalant. Fannie also recalled an incident involving an elderly widow who lived nearby and her reaction to the balloon flights near her home:

> There was an old lady, Mrs. Woody . . . and a balloon was sent up from her house too. When they were telling her what they had seen, she replied, 'Yes, Moses also viewed the promised land, but he never entered.'[35]

Lowe took great pride in the work that his balloon was able to accomplish at the Gaines's farm.

"The enemy was so concealed behind woods and hills, that it was impossible to ascertain their positions in any other way than by ascending to a great elevation," Lowe said afterward. "The artillery might have fired a whole day without doing any injury, unless the proper range had been obtained."[36]

According to Lowe, Stoneman then ordered the balloon to land, and went on to prepare his troops to ride to nearby Mechanicsville. Lowe was to return to the air and report any signs of a larger Confederate force marching in Stoneman's direction.

Stoneman's march on Mechanicsville proceeded with relatively few problems on May 21. All that seemingly stood between his forces and Richmond was the Chickahominy River.

On the 25th Lowe received orders to join up with Stoneman at Mechanicsville. The *Constitution* remained inflated and in use at the Gaines farm, where James Allen was left in charge. Allen's younger brother, Ezra, was also present, having made the journey from Providence, Rhode Island, to assist in balloon handling. Combined with their duties to attend to the *Constitution*, the Allen brothers were also in charge of caring for the uninflated *Intrepid*.

At Mechanicsville, Lowe made a number of ascents in the *Washington* that scarcely went unnoticed by the residents of Richmond. As the May 26 edition of the Richmond *Examiner* reported:

> The enemy are fast making their appearance at the banks of the Chickahominy. Yesterday they had a balloon in the air the whole

day, it being witnessed by many of our citizens from the streets and house-tops. They evidently discovered something of importance to them, for at about four o'clock A.M. a brisk cannonading was heard at Mechanicsville, and the Yankees now occupy that place.[37]

Farther up the Chickahominy, Union engineers were at work building a pontoon bridge. While McClellan's army had Richmond within their sights, Lowe's observations revealed that the situation was far from secure.

"The Confederate camp in Richmond grew larger every day," said Lowe. "My night-and-day observations convinced me that with the great army then assembled in and about Richmond we were too late to gain a victory, which a short time before was within our grasp."[38]

As the Federals approached Richmond, the Confederate army grew stronger in its resistance. Even Lowe's daily ascents now came under greater fire from Rebels who were determined to bring one of the giant balloons down.

"At one point they masked several of their best rifle-cannon," Lowe said. "While taking an early morning observation, all the twelve guns were simultaneously discharged at short range, some of the shells passing though the rigging of the balloon and nearly all bursting not more than two hundred feet beyond me, showing that through spies they had gotten my base of operations and range perfectly."

The close contact with the enemy's artillery forced Lowe to descend, narrowly averting disaster as the windlasses wound the cables in. Afterwards he immediately changed the location of his balloon before it ascended again. This attack was the closest in the aeronaut's experience.[39]

The following day Lowe ascended near the construction site of the Union army's bridge over the Chickahominy. From an altitude of over 800 feet Lowe could see Rebel soldiers over a mile away on the opposite side of the river, lying in the shade of the woods. A gun battery consisting of several field pieces was also observed.

"I . . . find the enemy quite strong opposite Mechanicsville," Lowe wrote in his report to one of McClellan's staff officers.[40]

Heavy rains drenched the region on May 30, swelling the banks of the Chickahominy. Through it all, however, Lowe remained undaunted and later that evening he was again in the air.

"The great camps around Richmond were ablaze with fires," Lowe observed that evening. "I had then experience enough to know what this meant, that they were cooking rations preparatory to moving."[41]

Lowe's assumption proved correct. McClellan had once again fallen under the handicap of self doubt, believing that his Army of the Potomac was undermatched for the Confederate forces defending Richmond. In addition, McClellan had split his forces, with part of his army guarding the Union's supply lines at White House while several divisions were positioned on the Richmond side of the Chickahominy.

McClellan could have dealt the Confederacy a death blow with the forces he had on hand. But he delayed giving the order to launch an assault. Even as late as May 30, McClellan still held out hope that McDowell's Army of the Rappahannock would be allowed to join the Army of the Potomac from the north. The delay allowed the Confederate army under Joseph E. Johnston to strike back at the Union's weak points at Fair Oaks and Seven Pines Roads.

Erasmus Keyes's IV Corps had advanced to the south bank of the Chickahominy and farther south was General Heintzelman's III Corps. While both corps were only a few miles from Richmond, they were also quite isolated from the main body of the army.

Johnston planned to capitalize on this weakness.

From his vantage point above Mechanicsville, Lowe was able to ascertain the movements of the Confederate army early on the morning of May 31.

"At daylight . . . I took another observation, continuing the same until the sun lighted up the roads," Lowe said. "The atmosphere was perfectly clear. I knew exactly where to look for their line of march, and soon discovered one, then two, and then three columns of troops with artillery and ammunition wagons toward the position occupied by General Heintzelman's command."[42]

Lowe quickly relayed his observations to General McClellan. According to Lowe, McClellan was unable to send reinforcements across to bolster the positions of Keyes and Heintzelman. The torrential rains were incessant and work on the bridge across the Chickahominy was wasted when flood waters swelled the river. McClellan sent orders to Gen. Edwin Sumner, commander of II Corps, to redouble the efforts of his men to rebuild the river crossing at New Bridge as quickly as possible.

Back in the air with the *Washington* later that day, Lowe continued with his observations of Rebel movements.

"I ascended at Mechanicsville and discovered bodies [units] of the enemy and trains coming from Richmond toward Fair Oaks," Lowe said. From his position on the opposite shore of the Chickahominy, the Confederates were only four miles from Lowe's position. "I remained in the air watching their movements until nearly two o'clock when I saw the enemy form in line of battle, and cannonading immediately commenced."[43]

The confusion created by Johnston's bold move prompted Lowe to expand his aerial observations. He realized that rapid communication of his observations was necessary, but the relatively weak lifting ability of the *Washington* and the *Constitution* negated the use of telegraph equipment. When Lowe returned to earth he had a message dispatched to James Allen at the Gaines farm to prepare the *Intrepid* for inflation.

The *Intrepid* was considerably larger than the *Constitution*, which was already on duty there, and Lowe planned to use its greater lifting ability to obtain an even more commanding view of the battlefield.

"I then took a six-mile ride on horseback to my camp on Gaines' Hill, and made another observation from the balloon *Constitution*," said Lowe. "[However], to carry my telegraph apparatus, wires and cables to this higher elevation, the lifting force of the *Constitution* proved to be too weak."

It would also be necessary for the balloon to carry not only an aeronaut but also a telegraph operator, since Lowe was not proficient in maintaining the delicate connection between the air and the ground.

With Heintzelman's and Keyes's corps under heavy Confederate fire and the remainder of the Army of the Potomac suddenly placed in a state of confusion, Lowe realized that pinpoint accuracy with his aerial observations was critical.

"As I saw the two armies coming nearer and nearer together, there was no time to be lost," Lowe recalled of that desperate hour. "It was then that I was put to my wits' end as to how I could best save an hour's time, which was the most precious hour of all my experience in the army."

The Allen brothers were struggling with the two portable gas generators, but the *Intrepid* was still only partially filled. There was at least another hour to go before the aerostat would be sufficiently inflated for liftoff when Lowe was suddenly struck by a spark of inspiration.

"It flashed through my mind that if I could only get the gas that was in the smaller balloon, *Constitution*, into the *Intrepid*, which was then half-filled,

In order to carry an aeronaut and telegrapher aloft during the battle of Fair Oaks, the greater lifting capacity of the Intrepid *was required. In a moment of inspiration, Lowe devised a way to help speed along the inflation of the* Intrepid *by transferring the gas from the* Constitution. *Lowe believed that his actions and the intelligence gained from the subsequent observation of the enemy saved the Union army "a million dollars a minute" during the battle.* PHOTOGRAPHIC HISTORY OF THE CIVIL WAR

I would save an hour's time, and to us that hour's time would be worth a million dollars a minute."[44]

But transferring the highly flammable hydrogen from the *Constitution* to the *Intrepid* presented its own share of problems. It had never been accomplished before, nor even contemplated.

"How was I to rig up the proper connection between the balloons?" Lowe asked himself. "To do this within the space of time necessary puzzled me until I glanced down and saw a 10-inch camp kettle, which instantly gave me the key to the situation.

"I ordered the bottom cut out of the kettle. The *Intrepid* was disconnected with the gas-generating equipment, and the *Constitution* brought down the hill.[45]

The kettle was used as a coupling between the two balloons and the ground crew worked furiously to force the gas from the *Constitution* into the *Intrepid*. According to Lowe, the process took only five to six minutes.

Before giving the word to release the balloon for launch, Lowe ordered James Allen to ride back to Mechanicsville to oversee operations with the *Washington*. When everything was ready Lowe clambered aboard the *Intrepid* accompanied by Parker Spring, the telegraph operator.

"I ascended to a height of a thousand feet and there witnessed the Titanic struggle," said Lowe. "The whole sequence of action was plainly visible and reports were constantly sent till darkness fell upon the grand but terrifying spectacle."

Lowe made sure that Spring kept "the wires hot with information" throughout the entire day of observations. Orders came from McClellan's general staff that telegraph messages were to be sent, "at least every 15 minutes."[46]

Early the next morning Lowe and Spring were once again in the air. As daylight approached, Lowe could distinguish that all of the roads on the Richmond side of the Chickahominy were clogged "with [Rebel] Infantry and Cavalry moving toward Fair Oaks." Although he could detect no weapons fire, there was "nothing but pickets visible."[47] Lowe later expressed his amazement that his reports provided the first actual grasp of the developing battle at McClellan's headquarters.

"I [was] fascinated from what I heard . . . that an attack by the enemy was not expected," Lowe said, adding that his reports provided, "timely notice that the enemy did really intend making a more severe attack than even of the previous day. [The reports] must certainly have been of the

A depiction of Thaddeus Lowe piloting the Intrepid *during the battle of Fair Oaks. Note the soldiers acting as ground handlers for the balloon.*
PHOTOGRAPHIC HISTORY OF THE CIVIL WAR

greatest importance and gave our forces an opportunity of preparing for a vigorous defense."[48]

Although Lowe's recollection of the battle of Seven Pines and Fair Oaks was fraught with his usual flair for the dramatic, the battle itself began to lose its momentum on the Confederate side. General Longstreet failed to move his division along the route that Johnston had originally prescribed in the battle plan the previous day. The mistake created problems with the advance of Rebel troops assigned to Generals Hill and Huger. Hill's four brigades made a hard charge against Erasmus Keyes's IV Corps, but they lacked reinforcements to continue the fight. Consequently, Heintzelman was able to send men to bolster Keyes's position.

By late in the afternoon of May 31, General Sumner's engineers were finally able to complete construction of the bridge across the Chickahominy, allowing II Corps to take part in the battle across the river. An intense battle ensued on Fair Oaks road as dusk approached. One of the casualties was General Johnston, who was severely wounded as he rode along Confederate lines, putting him out of the fight.

On June 1, Longstreet again proved to be the weak link in the Confederacy's counterattack when he half-heartedly sent in two brigades against Keyes's positions believing that the Yankee was outnumbered. From the air, however, the situation appeared to be entirely different.

"About two miles still further to the road of White Oak Station, and on the Williamsburg Stage Road, Charles City road and Central road are also large bodies of troops," Lowe reported. "In fact I am astonished at their numbers, compared to ours, altho' they are more concentrated than we are, their whole force seems to be paying their attention to their right.

"A regiment has just marched to the front where we are preparing a crossing. Their large barracks to the left of Richmond is entirely free of smoke, . . . which enables me to see . . . the enemy's earthworks."[49]

At Mechanicsville, James Allen was also very active. Lacking telegraph equipment aboard the *Washington*, Allen was forced to ascend and land numerous times throughout the day in order to pass along his observations. From up above, the aeronaut had a distinct view of Richmond.

"10:45 A.M.—The rebels are moving a brigade out of Richmond in the direction of New Bridge," read one of Allen's dispatches.

"11:10 A.M.—The brigade that I saw moving out of Richmond at 10:45 A.M. seems to be a very large one. They are followed by a train, consisting of twenty-four wagons and have just entered the woods, which carries them out of my sight. Think they are going in the direction of New Bridge."[50]

James Allen's report, as well as the reports of scouts and field commanders, contributed to a rumor that circulated on the afternoon of June 1 that Rebel artillery had been drawn up on the opposite side of the Chickahominy and aimed at New Bridge. Destruction of the crossing would be a disaster for the Federals. Lowe was telegraphed with orders to investigate.

"About one hour ago a full regiment moved up into the woods toward where our left crossing is being made," Lowe observed. "I have seen no artillery moved up, nor could I see any from here. I think, however, there is artillery in the woods."[51]

At around 1 P.M. Johnston's successor, Gen. Robert E. Lee, issued orders for his men to withdraw to their defensive line at Richmond. Not long after, there were signs that the worst of the fighting was subsiding. In a telegraph dispatch to Lowe, Fitz-John Porter sought confirmation of this.

"The enemy remains quiet opposite New Bridge," Lowe stated in response. "By the appearance of the smoke when up I would say that we can hold our ground and more too."[52]

A few hours later, Lowe had an even more intense report to make.

"Last [cannon] firing is two miles nearer Richmond than this morning. Camp-fires around Richmond as usual, showing that the enemy are back [at the city]."

In the evening Lowe was joined by General Humphreys and his officers of McClellan's staff, who made several ascents. While the Rebel army was plainly visible along the Williamsburg and New Bridge roads toward Richmond, there was no evidence of heavy troop or wagon movement. The battle was over for the moment.

By the time the battle reached its crescendo more than 42,000 troops on both Confederate and Union sides were drawn into the carnage. When the smoke finally cleared, the Union was able to claim a tactical victory by the grace of being able to hold their position on the banks of the Chickahominy opposite Richmond. But the victory came at a high price with over 5,000 Union soldiers counted on the casualty list. Confederate losses were even greater, with over 6,000 men listed as casualties.

"I would . . . remark that of all the battles I have witnessed, that of Fair Oaks was the most closely contested and most severe," Lowe said afterwards.[53]

In the view of many observers the Army of the Potomac's close brush with disaster completely unnerved McClellan. Even after the battles of Fair Oaks and Seven Pines, McClellan's force was still numerically and materially superior to Robert E. Lee's army. But McClellan, who was still mindful of the inflated reports of Confederates defending Richmond, was kept in stasis by his own inertia. He bitterly and openly complained that he could not accomplish the destruction of the Confederate army without the addition of more troops. Mentally unable to commit his troops to a decisive blow against Richmond, McClellan chose to dither after Fair Oaks and Seven Pines, allowing Lee to regroup and plan new counteroffensives.

Meanwhile, aeronautic activity within the Confederacy gathered pace. The *Gazelle* finally arrived in Richmond on June 24, where Capt. Langdon

Lt. Col. Edward Porter Alexander piloted the Confederate army's "Silk Dress Balloon" Gazelle *during the Seven Days battles. Porter, who was later promoted to the rank of general, was also the Confederate army's chief of artillery during the battle of Gettysburg in July, 1863.* PHOTOGRAPHIC HISTORY OF THE CIVIL WAR

Cheves and Charles Cevor readied it for service. At Richmond, Cheves and Cevor found a staunch ally in a lieutenant colonel named Edward Porter Alexander.

Shortly after Cheves and Cevor arrived in Richmond, Robert E. Lee ordered Alexander to take charge of the Confederacy's new aeronautic corps. Alexander accepted responsibility for the new balloon with some trepidation.

"I was not at all enamored of my prospective assignment," Alexander recalled years later. "When a boy I had no fear of high places at all, but at West Point as a cadet I had had a serious fall on [the] left bank of 'Indian Falls' . . . one winter afternoon. . . . Ever after that fall high places gave me an almost irresistible impulse to jump."[54]

But in many ways Alexander was an appropriate choice for the assignment. Before the war Alexander had helped Albert Myer devise a signal flag communication system known as "wigwag." While the system was considered slow—only three words per minute could be transmitted —on a clear day messages could be sent as far as twenty miles. In the first months of the war Alexander was credited with helping to thwart Union victory at Manassas by using the wigwag system to warn General Beauregard of a Union movement against his flank.

Though Alexander may have been uneasy about ascending for balloon observations, the *Gazelle*'s builder was elated at the prospect of proving his

creation's viability to the Southern cause. Cevor, unlike his Union counterparts, had received his full commission as a captain in the Confederate
army by the time he reached Richmond. The first launch of the Confederacy's "Silk Dress Balloon" came on June 24, with gas supplied to the balloon by the Richmond city gas works.

"I am happy to be able to report very favorably the flight commenced
at day break yesterday morning," Cevor said in a letter to Captain Cheves.
"I was on the field at that hour with [the] Balloon and kept her suspended
the greater portion of the day. [I] was able to render invaluable servis [sic].
We could see all that was done and was in signal of Gen. Lee. I was highly
complimented for my success. It is no longer a question of experiment in
the minds of leading men."[55]

Success with the trials of the *Gazelle* came at a most opportune time for
the Confederacy. While McClellan still fumed that there weren't enough
men with the Army of the Potomac to capture the Confederate capital,
Robert E. Lee was about to seize the initiative. On June 12, several days
before the "Silk Dress Balloon" was proven ready for deployment, Lee
ordered Brig. Gen. J. E. B. Stuart's cavalry to reconnoiter the entire perime-
ter of the Federal army to pinpoint its exact location and strength on the
peninsula. The result was a three-day mad dash that became known as,
"Stuart's Ride Around McClellan." Stuart and his men captured hundreds
of prisoners and destroyed vital Union supplies whenever possible. But more
importantly, Lee learned from Stuart that the northern flank of McClellan's
army was extremely vulnerable to an attack.

Lee came up with a plan that was bold in concept. Leaving 25,000 men
south of the Chickahominy in the defense of Richmond, Lee sent his
remaining 47,000 troops up against McClellan's 70,000 then deployed in
the area around the Confederate capital. Realizing that he was leaving
Richmond open to attack, the mission of the *Gazelle* took on even greater
significance.

"General Lee ordered me to take charge of [the balloon and] . . . to go
up in it, to observe, specially, any transfers or crossing of the Chickahominy—from one side to the other," said Alexander. "[I was also to
observe] any indications of any disposition of the enemy to assume the
aggressive on the south side. And I was ordered to provide signals to be displayed to indicate whatever I might see."[56]

Working with Cevor—who had not yet finished his device to produce
the balloon's hydrogen—Alexander discovered that the *Gazelle* could only

lift 1,000 pounds using the coal gas provided by the Richmond gas works. Early operations forced the aeronauts to have the balloon tethered to a flat-car and then transported by locomotive via the Richmond & York River Railroad where the battlefield could be observed.[57] Combined with the weight of the tethers and other necessary equipment only one observer at a time could be accommodated. For signaling purposes, Alexander took, "four big, black-cambric balls" with him that were to be suspended under-neath the balloon's control basket.

"I devised a little signal code of one or more of these balls, hung out below the balloon," Alexander said. "[These codes] were given to all the principal officers along our lines."[58]

Alexander's preparations were extremely timely as General Lee was planning to begin his counteroffensive at any moment. On June 25—the day before Lee was ready to strike—McClellan ordered General Heintzel-man's III Corps to occupy a position at White Oak Swamp, a boggy, forested area about six miles east of Richmond. After Stuart's three-day ride around his army, McClellan was now completely convinced that the Rebels were about to attack, and he wanted the swampy ground seized, thus secur-ing it on his front lines in anticipation of a general advance on Richmond. This tentative movement by III Corps signaled the opening maneuvers in what would become known as the blood-drenched Seven Days' battles.

By early morning on the 25th, Northern and Southern troops came together in combat. Union general "Fighting Joe" Hooker's men encoun-tered Rebel troops commanded by Gen. Benjamin Huger. An intense fire-fight ensued, which degenerated further as reinforcements from both sides were sent in. The Confederates showed their resolve and gave ground only at a high price for the advancing Union army. At the end of the day, Union casualties totaled more than 500 men, while Confederate losses numbered slightly more than 300.[59]

Though Lee was somewhat concerned that the usually cautious McClellan had finally revealed that he actually had some fight in him, Lee also realized that the relatively minor assault would do little to alter his plans to launch a full-scale counteroffensive the next day. The Southern com-mander was intent on ridding the Virginia peninsula of Yankees and would not be as easily intimidated as his Northern counterpart.

Back in Richmond, Lieutenant Colonel Alexander prepared for his ini-tiation into his role as an aeronaut. Just before his first ascent, Alexander was given a full briefing by Cevor on what to expect during a balloon flight.

Alexander's uneasy feelings did not subside as the moment for his launch approached.

"As I was about to step into the basket, . . . a sort of dismal joke to keep my courage up [came to me]," Alexander recalled. "I said to [Cevor] . . ., 'I'd advise you not to stand immediately beneath this basket, for the chances are that at 500 feet I'll jump out. And if I fell on you I doubt it would help me any to speak of, and yet might be a little rough on you."[60]

With his response Cevor tried to ease Alexander's anxiety.

"Oh, you're afraid of what people have on steeples and precipices, but you needn't be. You never have that with a balloon," Cevor told Alexander. "The reason is this—when on a steeple or a precipice one feels that the centre of gravity is below him and that if once started from the perpendicular the tendency is to go further and the whole will pitch over. It is a feeling of unstable equilibrium.

"But [in a balloon] one has the instinctive feeling that the centre of gravity is up above, in that big swelling globe. If one started to swing out, the tendency is to come back, and that makes stable equilibrium."[61]

Alexander listened intently to Cevor, but was not sure of the aeronaut's assurance until the windlass tethers securing the *Gazelle* to the ground were released. As the "Silk Dress Balloon" rose, Alexander quickly came to terms with his fears.

"The balloon had not risen 50 feet before I felt as safe and as much at home as if I had lived in one for years," Alexander said, personally marveling at the change in his own disposition. "I had thought before hand that I could only hope not to jump by avoiding looking directly downward. Now it was most fascinating to do it and watch how small the people seemed to grow. If balloons were plenty I could imagine one's acquiring the 'balloon habit,' and going up every day just to gaze."[62]

Alexander's abrupt change in attitude toward ballooning was fortunate, for he held a deep-rooted opinion that only trained military men were capable of providing useful intelligence information.

"I am sure that on certain occasions *skilled observers* in balloons could give information of priceless value," Alexander said. "But the observers in the balloon should be *trained staff officers*, not the ignorant class of ordinary balloonists, which I think were generally in charge of the Federal balloons.[63]

Although Cevor's balloon was as good as the meager resources of the Confederacy could provide, Alexander soon discovered some of the *Gazelle's* deficiencies. Despite the work that Cevor put into sealing the balloon's envelope, the silk dress cloth that Captain Cheves procured was far from the ideal material for aerostat use.

"The balloon would leak so fast that it would not keep up at the full height more than three or four hours," said Alexander. "After 6 or 7 hours it had to be emptied and refilled, which took some hours."[64]

But Alexander accustomed himself to the balloon's inadequacies with a resolve to accomplish the assignment given to him. And the assignment was a vitally important one. On June 26, Robert E. Lee took the biggest gamble yet in the war by launching an offensive on the Union's stronghold at Mechanicsville. Lee sent more than 47,000 Confederates up against Fitz-John Porter's V Corps on the north side of the Chickahominy. Porter's men were well-trained and put up a fierce resistance, while Lee was hampered by his junior officers' poor execution of his battle plan. Rebel troops managed to sweep through Mechanicsville at one point in the battle, but were forced to fall back in the face of heavy Union artillery fire. This time the battle came at a high price for the Confederacy. Nearly 1,500 Rebels were lost compared with only 361 Union casualties.

Although Southern losses were high, McClellan opted to take a defensive posture when fighting resumed the next day. He ordered the supply base at White House to be abandoned and began circling his troops in anticipation of another assault. In hindsight, McClellan was severely criticized for not seizing the offensive on the 27th. Union divisions under the commands of Heintzelman, Keyes, Sumner, and Franklin still remained on the Richmond side of the Chickahominy, but inexplicably were not ordered into action. The brunt of the fighting fell upon the men of Porter's V Corps, who had moved into the vicinity of the grain mill on Dr. Gaines's farm.

Remembered now as the battle of Gaines's Mill, the carnage that took place on June 27 was even more brutal than that on the previous day at Mechanicsville. Edward Porter Alexander observed much of the battle from across the Chickahominy in the control basket of the *Gazelle:*

> I ascended from a point about 2 miles out on the Williamsburg Road and, while I could seldom see the troops, the smoke of the firings gave a very fair idea of the action. . . . I saw and signaled the crossing of [Union general] Slocum's division to reinforce Porter during the action. The troops of the enemy on our side of the river made no move.[65]

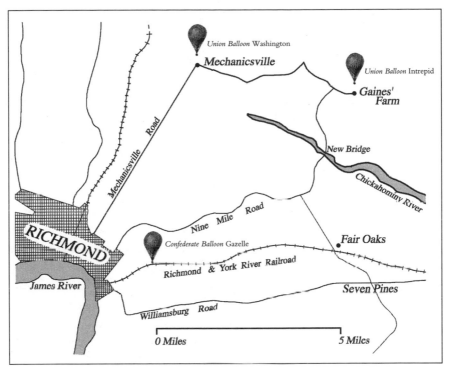

Relative positions of Union and Confederate balloons on June 27, 1862, during the Seven Days' battles.

Porter was not the only aeronaut surveying the battlefield. From Gaines's farm Thaddeus Lowe was also in the air in the *Intrepid*, though in a somewhat diminished condition. Lowe was among the many in McClellan's command who had fallen victim to malaria, one of the most common afflictions in the Chesapeake region.

"Although I reported myself ill on this occasion I will remain constantly in the balloon," Lowe reported to McClellan's staff. "If you will send me two orderlies I will keep headquarters constantly informed of what can be seen from the balloon."[66]

In the weeks prior to the start of the Seven Days' battles, Lowe had witnessed the buildup of Confederate strength and the gradual degeneration of the Union army's momentum. Severe rainstorms throughout the month of June continued to bog down Union operations, and the heavy rains and warm weather combined to provide the perfect breeding ground for disease-carrying mosquitoes.

"The unhealthy swampy bottom lands of the Chickahominy were full of malaria, striking down large numbers of the troops," Lowe observed. "At one time two thousand men were invalided home because of this pestilential fever."[67]

According to Lowe, McClellan planned to attack Richmond in the early part of June. But the incessant rains kept his corps of engineers from completing the bridges over the Chickahominy that would unite the separated parts of his army into one attack force. As the Union army grew more enfeebled before Lowe's eyes, the Rebels were busy fortifying themselves in anticipation of a breakout against their invaders.

". . . from my perch in the balloon two-thousand feet in the air, I watched all that was going on about the Confederate capital," Lowe said. "[I] reported the great activity of the enemy in fortifying himself and the increase in the number of troops. Beauregard with his fine army had come up from the south and Jackson, having accomplished his purpose of frightening Washington into withholding the support McClellan needed so badly, was now rapidly marching to attack the Federal troops on the north of the Chickahominy before the bridges could be complete that would enable them to join McClellan."[68]

When Lee's army began to make its move in late June, Lowe was among the first to witness it.

"On the 26th I reported verbally to General Humphreys that the enemy had crossed the Chickahominy in large force," Lowe said. "[And it] was engaging our right wing at Mechanicsville."[69]

In response to the Rebel movement, Humphreys ordered Lowe to remain airborne and to report everything he could see. But Lowe was beginning to succumb to the worst symptoms of malaria.

"The heaviest cannonading at this time is near where the last Headquarters were, between Dr. Gaines' House and Mechanicsville," he reported. "We have large reserves across the river; . . . the enemy appears to be a large force in and about their entrenchments on this side of the river.

"The dense smoke prevents me from seeing to Richmond. I am very unwell and think it advisable for some good person to be constantly up."[70]

Lowe was not the only Union aeronaut suffering from the Union army's reversal of fortune. When the Confederates stormed the village of Mechanicsville the men of the Balloon Corps were barely able to flee the battlefield with the *Washington*, and all of its attendant supplies.

"My assistants . . . are trying to save the property in their charge," Lowe reported to General Humphreys. "In an exact north direction from here, and about two miles and a half from the river . . . there are a large bodies of troops . . . On a hill this side of Dr. Gaines' house there is a long line of skirmishers stationary."

But that wasn't all that Lowe observed from the air that day. "About four miles to the west from here the enemy have a balloon about 300 feet in the air."[71]

Lowe's sighting of Alexander aloft in the multihued *Gazelle* marked the first time that a Northern aeronaut and a Southern aeronaut met in line of sight during the war. An hour later Lowe reported that, "the rebel balloon suddenly disappeared."[72] Alexander was probably forced to land because of the *Gazelle*'s chronic leakage.

The battle at Gaines's Mill only served to escalate the death tolls on both sides. Wave after wave of Confederate troops under the command of Gen. A. P. Hill threw themselves against Maj. John Porter's V Corps, which was deeply entrenched on Dr. Gaines's farm. Yet as the day wore on the battle only grew worse. Just before twilight General Lee ordered a three-mile phalanx of men to make one final push forward against Porter's position. From his vantage point on the far end of the Gaines's farm Thaddeus Lowe could see the coming slaughter.

"At 6 o'clock I reported that the enemy on Gaines' Hill were making a desperate advance," said Lowe. "A large column was moving to outflank our forces on the extreme right, and evidently intended to intercept our crossing at Woodbury's bridge.[73] Soon after this report was made our reserves were sent to protect the crossing and to relieve troops that had been engaged for two days.[74]

Lowe later stated that he believed that his report from the battlefield late that day saved a large number of Union soldiers from being killed or taken prisoner.[75]

Although Union cavalry tried to repulse the onslaught, in the end it was to no avail. The Confederate Texas Brigade was the first to break the Union's position, forcing V Corps to withdraw.

Charles Cevor, who was aiding Alexander around the clock, was up in the *Gazelle* at the time the Confederate charge finally broke through Porter's line. Aloft above Richmond, Cevor's account was most vivid:

The fight for miles was desperate, but our gallant army drove them back steadily with immense slaughter. Stonewall [Jackson]'s attack was sublime. I could see him and his brave band when they struck the enemy's lines, and dreadful was the shock produced. Lawton's brigade gallantly charged a battery, but failed to carry it. The Texas brigade . . . succeeded in taking it—since which the enemy has been kept in motion towards Washington. . . . The Yankee prisoners are coming in continually. Over three thousand have arrived and more are expected to come in to-morrow. I am happy to say that I received the compliments of the Generals and their staff for my successful operations. It was of material aid to them.[76]

Though the battle may have seemed glorious from up above, the losses were staggeringly high. While Lee's army controlled the plateau above Dr. Gaines's farm by the end of the day, the victory cost the South over 8,700 lives. Porter's V Corps suffered more than 6,800 casualties. Fannie Gaines, whose family fled their home on the farm the night before, later recalled the human toll that littered the road leading back to the house:

The dead were strewed [sic] on every side. I had to keep my eyes shut all the way to keep from seeing the horrible sights. We left Mother and Father at Mr. Johnson's, but they went home that day.

When Mother got to the front door there was a dead Yankee there. When we left home an officer had given this man orders that he was never to leave his post. And he did stay, and was shot while performing his duty.

Mother tried to have him buried, but she had nobody to do it. She offered to pay one of our soldiers to do it, and he consented to bury him right at the door, but said he would not take him any further. Later she succeeded in getting him buried in the orchard.[77]

The battle, however, was a turning point for Lee as it forced McClellan to begin an organized retreat towards the James River. The following day Lowe and the rest of the men of the Balloon Corps were ordered to pack up everything. The cumbersome iron shavings used to manufacture hydrogen were left behind because of a scarcity of transport. For this reason Union balloon operations were suspended until new supplies were obtained at Harrison's Landing.

As for Lowe, not long after the battle of Gaines's Mill he became totally incapacitated by a high fever resulting from the malaria infection, and would not return to duty until August. This left Clovis Lowe in charge of maintaining the balloons, and James Allen in charge of Balloons Corps operations. A few weeks later John Steiner, whose services with the Army of the Mississippi were now complete, also joined Allen, although his issues over back pay were not yet resolved.[78]

For the remaining engagements fought during the Seven Days' battles the only active aeronauts left in Virginia were Charles Cevor and Edward Porter Alexander in the "Silk Dress Balloon." The leaky *Gazelle* was hindered in its operations by the fact that it needed to remain in the vicinity of Richmond in order to draw its gas supply from city pipelines. But Alexander hit upon a plan to work around the balloon's shortcomings.

"When the enemy got away from his original lines and we could not follow with the balloon by land, I had it filled and towed down the James River by a little armed tug, the *Teaser*," Alexander recalled. The *Teaser* was a steam paddle wheeler that had served as a consort to the Rebel ironclad *Virginia* during its famous engagements at Hampton Roads back in April.

While Lieutenant Colonel Alexander became more accustomed to his newfound role as aeronaut, a number of major battles still raged on. On the same day that bloody battles took place on the Gaines farm, a minor skirmish erupted on the Richmond side of the Chickahominy. Rebels led by Gen. John Magruder tried to dislodge Samuel Heintzelman's III Corps, which was occupying a position at Garnett's Farm. Casualties were comparatively few in comparison to those lost in battle across the river—368 Union casualties against 461 Confederates—but the assault heightened McClellan's fears that his forces south of the Chickahominy were vulnerable to a full-scale attack by Lee's army.

By now the main Union battle tactic became one of withdrawal, allowing Lee and his generals to assume the offensive. At Savage's Station on June 29, Magruder struck once again, this time attacking the retreating rear guard of McClellan's army commanded by General Sumner.

A series of miscues left Sumner's men vulnerable to attack, although Magruder suspected the same for his men and delayed his assault until late in the afternoon. Still, the action exacted a toll on Union forces when they were forced to abandon a field hospital with over 2,500 men left behind, along with a large quantity of supplies. Additionally, battle action that day cost McClellan nearly 1,600 lives. Worse damage may have been inflicted by the Rebels but for a severe thunderstorm that curtailed any further fighting that evening.

Although McClellan's army was on the defensive, Lee made the assumption that it was now completely demoralized and ripe for a decisive and permanent blow. This assessment turned out to be far too optimistic, but Lee chose to unleash the bulk of his army against the Federals in their stronghold at Malvern Hill. The battle, fought on July 1, 1862, turned out to be one of Lee's worst strategic decisions. Union artillery firing from a nearly impregnable position gave McClellan the upper hand. Magruder's men made a suicidal charge up toward the Federal position with 15,000 men, but they were no match for heavy cannon. When the day was over, Lee had lost over 5,300 men, though the Union losses were nearly as grave with over 3,200 dead.

Even three days later, General Lee still harbored hopes that a weakness could be found in McClellan's defenses. Stealthy reconnaissance of the area was ordered and Lieutenant Colonel Alexander and the *Gazelle* were to play an integral role.

Late in the evening of July 3, the *Gazelle* was inflated in Richmond and towed by train to a wharf on the James River and placed on board the CSS *Teaser*. Though Charles Cevor had attempted to correct the chronic leakage that limited the amount of time the *Gazelle* could remain aloft, Alexander was acutely aware that time was of the essence. With the balloon tethered to its deck the *Teaser* steamed down the James River near to Malvern Hill.

Just before sunrise on the morning of July 4, Alexander ascended, but his time in the air did not last very long.

"After sunrise when the balloon began to get very weak we emptied and folded her," said Alexander. "The [*Teaser's*]captain, [Hunter] Davidson offered to run down a little further and land me where I could get out and probably make my way to Gen. Lee to report."[79]

Davidson started to do so, but as the *Teaser* made its way down the James, it ran aground on a mud bank in the middle of the river.

"The tide was falling, and it would be three hours before it would release us," remarked Alexander. The crew and aeronauts aboard the *Teaser* had no choice but to wait it out.

At 3 P.M. fate chose a new heading for the *Teaser*—a Union gunboat, the *Maratanza*, steamed into view. The *Maratanza* was on a reconnaissance mission when her crew spotted the stricken tug. The *Teaser* was armed with only one thirty-pound cannon. She was no match for the Union gunboat.

"She took one shot at the *Maratanza*," Alexander recalled. "But I don't think she hit her."

The *Maratanza* returned the fire. The captain of the *Maratanza*, Commander Stevens, described the brief battle:

> We trained our 100-pounder on her. . . . Bang went our gun, making a beautiful shot, and knocking over several loose articles from the enemy's deck. Bang went our second shot, and never did the fatal messenger take a truer course, tearing straight through the enemy's vessel, and blowing her half to pieces.[80]

The *Teaser's* crew realized that putting up a fight would be useless. The decision was made to abandon ship.

"Davidson kindled a fire on the *Teaser*, and lashed down his safety valve so as to try and explode her boiler, and he and his men jumped overboard and swam and waded to shore, while the *Maratanza* showered grape and canister after them and after us in the woods indiscriminately . . . we took to the shelter of the woods and trees, and all escaped damage."[81]

But Captain Davidson's attempt to scuttle the *Teaser* failed as her boiler did not explode. The *Maratanza* sent a boarding party over to the tug, where they secured a tow line to pull the boat off the mud bank.

"The *Maratanza* pulled her out of the mud and carried her off, balloon and all," Alexander said, somewhat wistfully. "So, I left the sailors . . . [and] I struck out for the army, which I soon found, and Gen. Lee also, and made my final balloon report."[82]

Once on board the *Teaser* the *Maratanza's* commander listed a number of the seized items of interest:

> The officers and crew . . . [left] everything behind. We got the officers' uniforms, swords, belts, pistols, muskets, silver chains, bedding clothes, letters and papers; among the latter a full description of the submarine batteries at Drury's Bluff, and a diagram of all the fortifications.
>
> We also found a balloon made of silk dresses."[83]

Following the capture of the Confederate riverboat and its contents, the legend of the balloon made of silk dresses began to take root in Confederate history. Gen. William Booth Taliaferro wrote that after the contents of the boat were seized, the captured *Gazelle* represented "the last silk dress in the Confederacy. This capture was the meanest trick of the war and one I have never forgiven."[84]

With the capture of the *Gazelle*, balloon operations for the South were over. For all that it mattered, the Confederate air force and the future of any balloon activities for the remainder of the war were now in the hands of the Yankees.

CHAPTER THIRTEEN

The Winter of Disappointment

In the aftermath of the Seven Days' battles the potential of success for General McClellan's once grand scheme to destroy the heart of the Confederacy was seriously in question. Even though the last engagement at Malvern Hill had resulted in significantly more Confederate casualties than Union, from June 26, McClellan had begun to withdraw to Harrison's Landing, which would become the Union army's new supply base. The base of operations was now the ancestral home of former U.S. president William Henry Harrison and was situated on the James River, where the army could continue to be supplied and still be protected by Union gunboats.

While McClellan's "strategic withdrawal" was soundly criticized in the North, in Virginia the action signified a temporary respite from war. Both Union and Confederate forces had suffered considerable losses, but the psychological damage inflicted by General Lee's fierce counterattack was a shock to the system as far as the Army of the Potomac was concerned. Moreover, the unseasoned Yankees proved to be even more vulnerable to the native maladies of the Virginia peninsula, such as salmonella from contaminated food and water, dysentery, typhoid fever, and malaria.[1]

As a casualty of this latter group, Thaddeus Lowe returned to the National Hotel in Washington, D.C., to recover from the malarial fever he contracted in the weeks prior to the Seven Days' battles. While in Washington Lowe was presented with the remnants of the *Gazelle*, the Confederacy's

245

Thaddeus Lowe in a portrait taken after the Peninsular Campaign. Malaria combined with the arduous duty of serving on the battlefield had visibly taken its toll on the aeronaut.

U.S. ARMY SIGNAL CORPS PHOTO

"Silk Dress Balloon" that had been captured by the crew of the Union gunboat *Maratanza*.

"[It was] a veritable Joseph's coat of many colors," Lowe said of Charles Cevor's creation. "The fashions in silks at that period were ornate, large flowery patterns, squares and plaids in blues, greens, crimsons, ebony and rich heavy watered silks. . . . The silk dress balloon was a very brilliant and handsome object."[2]

Despite the Confederate balloon's unique appearance, Lowe judged its construction to be inferior in comparison to the balloons already in service with the Union and of no practical use. The balloon was subsequently sliced into many different pieces and given to various members of Congress and others as mementos of the failed Confederate experiment. Lowe himself kept one of the larger pieces as a personal souvenir.

Lowe also helped to perpetuate the legend of Southern belles donating their dresses to the Confederate balloon effort in an interview given years after the war.

"Their aeronaut evidently thought nothing but silk would answer his purpose [in the balloon's construction]. But good cotton would have been much better than the silk they used," Lowe reminisced. "Having none of the requisite quality, a convention of ladies was held in Petersburg, of whom 200 each gave a silk dress toward building the balloon."[3]

Flying Artillery—A hint to General McClellan's "Onward to Richmond."

In the aftermath of the Army of the Potomac's defeat during the Peninsular Campaign, General McClellan shouldered much of the blame for his troop's poor performance. In this Northern political cartoon even the use of military balloons during the campaign is subject to ridicule. FRANK LESLIE'S ILLUSTRATED NEWSPAPER

Meanwhile, back in Virginia, Lowe's assistants, James Allen, Jacob Freno, Ebenezer Mason, John Steiner, and Clovis Lowe, continued to operate balloons with the Army of the Potomac. But without the enthusiastic leadership of the Balloon Corps's chief aeronaut, their efforts did not have quite the same impact as they had prior to the Seven Days'. For some of the aeronauts, the deprivations of field service and the ongoing hassles with Union army paymasters strained the limits of their patriotism. John Starkweather had already returned to Boston. And not long after Starkweather's resignation, the long-suffering John Steiner also departed and went back to his prewar occupation as an itinerant balloonist.

In the grander scheme of things, however, the Army of the Potomac was in the middle of a major reorganization and employment of the Balloon Corps's men, and materiel was not considered high priority. General McClellan shouldered the brunt of the blame for the army's reversal after coming so close to Richmond. As a result he was relieved as commander of Union forces in Virginia, although he retained command of the Army of the Potomac for the time being.

McClellan's successor in Virginia was Gen. John Pope, the former commander of the Army of the Mississippi. On June 26, Pope was given the authority to reorganize the military forces in Virginia and he proceeded to incorporate the army's Mountain Department, the Department of the Shenandoah, and General McDowell's Department of the Rappahannock into a newly formed group known as the Army of Virginia.

While the Army of the Potomac did not fall under Pope's initial reorganization, the announcement that Pope was replacing McClellan was not received as particularly good news by members of the Balloon Corps, especially John Steiner, who had complained bitterly of the general's inattention to his plight while he served as an (unpaid) aeronaut in the West during early 1862.

Members of McClellan's senior staff did not accord Pope an altogether enthusiastic welcome either. Many of McClellan's technical staff and some corps commanders were brought into the new Army of Virginia to serve under Pope, whose abrasive personality rankled more than a few. Most officers remained loyal to McClellan, despite his inability to capture the Rebel capital during the Peninsular Campaign.

The changes also caused some to reevaluate the future of military aeronautics. With the army in transition and Lowe on sick leave in Washington, there were many who believed that the Balloon Corps's days were over. Even without Lowe's leadership, however, James Allen managed to continue observations at Harrison's Landing. In the latter part of July, 1862, Allen was ordered by Commodore Charles Wilkes to head up a reconnaissance expedition of the James River.

For this mission Allen was accompanied by John Steiner in his last assignment with the Balloon Corps. Allen also chose the *Intrepid*, the largest aerostat in the Balloon Corps's inventory on the peninsula, with which to make the reconnoiter. Having the greatest capacity, the *Intrepid* could ascend to more than 2,000 feet with both an aeronaut and military observer on board.

Employing the balloon barge *George Washington Parke-Custis* towed behind the steam tug *Stepping Stones*, Allen and his crew left Harrison's Landing on the afternoon of July 29. Commodore Wilkes also ordered the warship *Wachusset* to act as escort. Wilkes hoped to ascertain the strength of the Confederate navy and gun batteries along the banks of the James, and the unique aerial platform that the *Intrepid* offered could provide the commodore with a distinct advantage.

No limits to precautions of safety were spared, as Wilkes also ordered the gunboats *Delaware* and *Port Royal* to rendezvous with the balloon squadron.

Despite high winds that kicked up along the James, Allen and Steiner managed several ascents at various points on July 30. Extreme secrecy was exercised, as one correspondent for the Philadelphia *Inquirer* reported:

> The nature and extent of these observations we were not informed, as the parties giving us our information were not among those who made the ascensions. . . . While the reconnoissance [*sic*] was in progress, the little steamer that runs about . . . carrying despatches . . . came down with all steam on, having on board Commodore Wilkes.
>
> He at once ordered the balloon operations to cease, and that all . . . gunboats thereabouts must make all haste up the river to City Point . . . and await further orders. The extent of the observations are unknown to us, but all and every one with who we have spoken . . . are unanimous in the assertion that . . . it was among the most successful balloon ascensions ever made.[4]

There seemed to be more than just a little hyperbole in the *Inquirer* correspondent's record of events that day. Certainly with members of the press aboard the *Wachusset*, Wilkes may have just been grandstanding and showing off his navy's dominance of the river in light of the ineffective performance by the Army of the Potomac. The addition of an observation balloon certainly provided an interesting angle to a more or less routine river patrol. At any rate, Wilkes made sure that the newspapermen were given a rather dramatic presentation.

Aside from this demonstration the Balloon Corps remained mostly dormant for the remainder of the summer in Virginia. But sweeping changes were under way that would profoundly affect the future of aeronautics in the Union army. By early August, 1862, President Lincoln ordered the Army of the Potomac to return by ship to Washington, D.C., where it would await new orders. McClellan personally seethed at this reversal, especially given the fact that he was now subordinated as chief strategist to Gen. Henry Halleck, an officer he characterized as one, "whom I know to be my inferior."[5]

As for the Balloon Corps, it too returned to its adopted headquarters at the Columbia Armory, where much needed repairs on equipment were carried out, supervised by Clovis Lowe.

The withdrawal of the Army of the Potomac from the Virginia peninsula was a long, drawn-out affair. Pope hoped that McClellan's army would join up with his force of 55,000 men comprising the Army of Virginia, but the transfer of men and equipment by water back to Washington took weeks to accomplish.

During this period General Lee took advantage of the North's disorganization and in the latter part of July and August sent "Stonewall" Jackson to counter Pope's movements in northern Virginia. Lee gambled that the Federals would not make a major move against Jackson's troops, despite the fact that initially Jackson's army numbered only 12,000.

As both Union and Confederate armies jockeyed their positions in northern Virginia, actual fighting between both sides was occasionally very heavy. At Cedar Mountain, Gen. Nathaniel P. Banks, who had lost a pivotal battle with "Stonewall" Jackson in the Shenandoah Valley back in the spring, attempted to avenge himself when the opportunity to attack the Southern general presented itself again. By early August, Jackson was reinforced by three divisions totaling 24,000 men and was additionally assisted by a division led by Ambrose P. Hill. With less than 9,000 men under his command, Banks found himself overwhelmed. The results of the battle on

August 9 were predictably bloody, with Union forces suffering losses of over 2,400 men while Jackson lost less than 1,400.

Jackson followed up his tactical victory against Banks on August 26 by setting his men out on a fifty mile march of destruction over the course of two days. Hungry, threadbare, but with a fighting spirit that made the impossible achievable, Jackson's corps descended upon the Union supply depot at Manassas Junction with a ravenous fervor. The small garrison guarding the depot was taken by surprise and the Confederates took everything they could carry with them and destroyed what remained by fire. It was both a crippling and embarrassing blow to the Union army.

With the Rebels on a rampage, General Pope's response was hardly tepid, but his efforts did little to consolidate his new position as commander of the Army of Virginia. Pope sought to take revenge against the vandalism inflicted by Jackson's men at Manassas Junction by massing his troops at the old Bull Run battlefield, the site of the Union army's defeat the previous year. Pope hoped that units of McClellan's Army of the Potomac would join up with his force of 55,000 men, but only the corps commanded by Fitz-John Porter and Samuel Heintzelman were ready by the time the battle commenced on August 29.

Pope attacked Jackson at Groveton, but the battle turned out to be a trap for the Union army when it was discovered that Jackson's men were firmly entrenched. Lee then launched a counterattack on the flank with General Longstreet's corps of 30,000 men. With the piercing sound of the Rebel yell, Lee's Army of Northern Virginia delivered a resounding defeat to Pope's men on August 30.

Again, the toll was heavy for both sides. The Union wound up with more than 10,000 casualties, with nearly 6,000 men missing in action. While over 1,400 Rebels were killed and 7,600 more were wounded, the second battle of Bull Run was a victory for the South.

Pope attempted to lay blame for his defeat at the hands of senior officers who still remained loyal to McClellan. Fitz-John Porter, who was outspokenly critical of Pope, was particularly singled out by the general as being disloyal and disobedient in the aftermath of the battle. But the truth was that Pope seriously misjudged the situation at Bull Run and wasted a substantial portion of his army as a result. For his ineptitude Pope was relieved as commander of the Army of Virginia on September 2 and sent west to Minnesota to campaign against Indians in the frontier lands.

Following the second battle of Bull Run the dispirited Union army retreated to the defense of Washington, D.C. Pope's reassignment prompted

Lincoln to merge the Army of Virginia into the Army of the Potomac in order to form one cohesive unit. The morale of the army was at its lowest point, however, and choices for its new leader were slim. Despite the fact that George McClellan actively promoted the rancor that developed among senior officers following Pope's appointment as leader of the Army of Virginia, he was still considered an individual who commanded the respect and admiration of his men. It was a reluctant decision, but Lincoln authorized McClellan to resume command of the Union army's main fighting force.

No one received the news of McClellan's reinstatement with more jubilation than Thaddeus Lowe.

"When the troops learned that [McClellan] had been recalled to command, they indulged in the most extravagant expressions of joy," Lowe recalled. "When [McClellan] appeared among [them], they cheered and cheered and threw their caps in the air, and crowded about him, and needless to say the retreat came to a halt. Soon he had the army in fighting trim and turning on the Confederate forces, he swept on to victory. It was at this time I rejoined him."[6]

Lowe may have been slightly generous in his assessment of McClellan's onward victory over the Rebels, but there was a reason behind his enthusiasm. It was no secret that McClellan was one of Lowe's most ardent supporters when it came to employing aeronautics in the military. Yet, even after more than one year of service with the Union army the Balloon Corps remained a civilian unit. But Lowe was given hope that this was about to change.

Lowe met with McClellan in September and informed the general that the Balloon Corps had been idle since the end of July. In the interim period Lowe learned that the Balloon Corps's transport wagons had been seized by the Quartermaster's Corps. Lowe bitterly complained that the Balloon Corps was still treated as a second-class adjunct to the army in spite of the fact that aeronautics had proved its merit on the battlefield many times over.

"[McClellan] replied that he was fully aware of the opinion that I could not operate my department to its greatest efficiency unless its full command was vested in me," said Lowe. "He would recommend it be made a distinct branch of the army and that I be given a commission."[7]

Lowe was elated. Finally, aeronautics would be given full respect and recognition from one of the highest sources in the land. Unfortunately, Lowe's most fervent hope would never be truly realized.

At best, McClellan held only a tenuous grasp on his command. Lincoln already suspected that McClellan might revert to his former tendency of overestimating the strength of the enemy and shy away from taking the offensive in battle. As a result McClellan was given only a very short time to prove himself worthy once again in the eyes of his commander in chief.

The next major engagement in the war came on September 9, when Robert E. Lee moved his army into Maryland. While it may have been more prudent to rest following the victory at Bull Run, Lee felt that the momentum to push onward was with his men. Again, Lee split his forces with "Stonewall" Jackson and six divisions converging on Harpers Ferry, and Gen. James Longstreet and three divisions moving on Hagerstown. The invasion of Maryland nearly proved to be a fatal decision for Lee, when a copy of his orders accidentally fell into Union hands.

McClellan was given the opportunity to take a decisive and potentially fatal blow to the Confederate army, but once again moved the Army of the Potomac sluggishly. In McClellan's defense some of his cautiousness was due to the fact that he believed the discovered orders might have been bait for a trap. Regardless, the delay resulted in yet another lost opportunity for the Union.

Lee soon discovered that McClellan was aware of his army's next move and quickly issued new orders that consolidated Jackson's and Longstreet's forces at Sharpsburg, Maryland—a move that probably saved the Rebel army from complete destruction. On September 17, North and South came to bloody blows at a small creek known as Antietam. It was a battle that would be forever remembered as the bloodiest single day of the entire Civil War. The Army of the Potomac lost 12,410 men (2,108 killed, 9,549 wounded, and 753 missing), while the casualties for Lee's army totaled over 13,724 (2,700 killed, 9,024 wounded, and more than 2,000 missing).

Though Confederate casualties were greater, the battle shook McClellan's last reserve of confidence. When Lee withdrew from the battlefield the following day, the Army of the Potomac did not pursue, allowing the Rebels to retreat safely back into Virginia.

Back in Washington, Thaddeus Lowe was ready to join up with the rest of the army at Antietam.

"I received no orders until the morning after the battle of Antietam," Lowe said. "I started immediately, and on the third day from Washington I arrived with the train at Sharpsburg. The delay was occasioned by Gen.

A. A. Humphreys being ordered to take command of a division, and the aeronautic department having been left, without proper authority being vested in me to act independently, I was unable to accompany the army as formally."[8]

Lowe later said that at the battle of Antietam McClellan remarked on several occasions that a balloon would have been invaluable to him.

"He repeated this when I arrived," Lowe recalled. "It was evident that he was extremely anxious to obtain information of movements which could only be obtained by the aeronaut, which if he had obtained might have resulted in the complete defeat and utter rout of the enemy while trying to effect his escape [back to Virginia]."[9]

In the aftermath of Antietam it is likely that McClellan seized on the Balloon Corps's absence as part of the excuse for his dismal performance. It certainly would have fit the general's long-standing pattern of complaining that he lacked both the men and the materiel to defeat Confederate forces— forces he consistently overestimated during the course of the war. But in the end, Lincoln and his war cabinet were finished with the general's litany of excuses. McClellan remained as commander of the Army of the Potomac until early November, 1862, when he was replaced by Gen. Ambrose Burnside. McClellan returned to his home in Trenton, New Jersey, not long after, although he retained his commission in the army until 1864.

With McClellan's departure from the Army of the Potomac, Thaddeus Lowe's hopes of finally gaining formal recognition for the Balloon Corps were dashed. Lowe remained at the Antietam battlefield near Bolivar Heights, Maryland, until orders were issued for him to return to the Columbia Armory in Washington. From this point onward the fate of aeronautics would be subject to the whims and prejudices of whatever officer was given its charge. In his later years, Lowe was extremely critical of the cavalier manner in which the Balloon Corps was employed by the army:

> And right here I would like to say that what delays, annoyances etc., fell to my lot while connected with the army came through being a civil employee. From the first I had hoped to organize the balloon corps as a military branch and applied for a commission to command it. But all that 'the powers that be' could do was to grant me the courtesy title of Colonel and accord me the privileges of that rank but not the authority.

Consequently I was subject to every young and inexperienced lieutenant or captain, who for the time being was put in charge of the Aeronautics Corps. These young fellows had no knowledge whatsoever of aeronautics and were often a hindrance to me rather than a help.[10]

Things hardly improved for Lowe and the Balloon Corps when Burnside took over the reins. Lowe's opinion of the new army commander was not altogether enthusiastic.

"General Burnside, . . . was well liked but was by no means a military genius," Lowe lamented. "The depression of the troops over the loss of [McClellan] . . . must have been keenly felt by his successor."[11]

By the latter part of November, 1862, the Balloon Corps had been idle for more than two months since its missed opportunity at Antietam. Despite the fact that the Corps's personnel continued to receive their daily pay allowances—even while not performing any aerial observations—Lowe grew increasingly restless from the lack of activity.

Lowe drafted a letter to Burnside's chief of staff, Maj. Gen. John Grubb Parke, in which he took great pains to point out the work of the Balloon Corps during the course of over a year of service to the army. He enumerated the various technological achievements that his, "six superior silk balloons" had accomplished and summarized his statement by saying that, "having reduced all of these [achievements] to a practical everyday working, I can be called upon for any or all of them at any time.[12]

"[I do] not consider it necessary to give a detailed account of what may be done," Lowe said in conclusion. "But I am hoping soon to be called into active service again."[13]

It was not long before Lowe received a response from Burnside through Major General Parke.

"The commanding Gen'l desires that you proceed to Washington, and bring up the apparatus and materiel, so that an ascension can be made as early as possible," Parke wrote. "[General Burnside] desires that the Quartermaster's Dept. furnish you such aid and assistance in Washington and en route, that you may require."[14]

Parke's letter came from the Army of the Potomac's new headquarters just opposite of the town of Fredericksburg, Virginia, about sixty miles southwest of Washington, D.C. For over a week Burnside had been maneu-

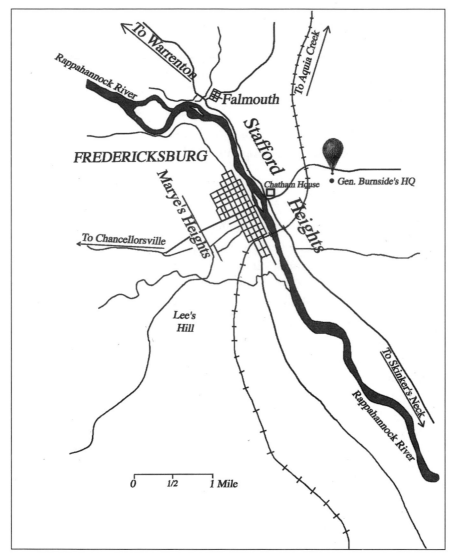

Lowe's position during the battle of Fredericksburg, December 12, 1862.

vering Federal troops into the vicinity to prepare for a new drive on Richmond. Burnside himself was aware that he lacked the total confidence of his army following the dismissal of McClellan, and he personally believed he was not right for the job of army commander. But he doggedly took on the task of reorganizing the Army of the Potomac yet again.

The decision to invade the South through Fredericksburg, however, proved to be a daunting one. Burnside had hoped for a rapid campaign through Virginia. Initially, the plan was to take a force of 122,000 troops—considerably more men than McClellan had used in the Peninsular Campaign—and cross the Rappahannock River to provoke Robert E. Lee's army into fighting a massive battle somewhere between Fredericksburg and Richmond.

But the invasion was fraught with problems almost from the beginning. Nature played a contributing role, with relentless rains inundating northern Virginia in the week proceeding Burnside's arrival opposite Fredericksburg on November 19. As a result, the banks of the Rappahannock were swollen beyond normal capacity and in places it was more than 400 feet from shore to shore.

The flooded conditions of the river prompted Burnside to order the use of prefabricated pontoon bridges. Unfortunately the pontoons didn't completely arrive until November 25, allowing Lee time to place his opposing force of 78,500 men on heights dominating the town and Burnside's line of advance. By the time winter set in the stage was set for a battle of epic proportions.

For his part Lowe was chomping at the bit to return to active duty, but the difficulties that Burnside's army experienced during the early part of the campaign delayed the redeployment of the balloons.

"Gen. Burnside . . . desired the balloons should not be shown to the enemy until he was ready to cross the river," said Lowe. The implication was that since the balloons had not seen service since their brief appearance in the aftermath of Antietam, it was assumed by many that their use had been discontinued. Lowe hoped that when his balloons received their callback into action with Burnside's advancing army their reemergence would be viewed as a renewed endorsement of military aeronautics.[15]

However, it may have been unfortunate that Burnside opted not to use Lowe's balloons sooner. While his army stalled at the Rappahannock, even after the arrival of the pontoon bridges, Lee's Army of Northern Virginia steadily fortified their defenses in and around Fredericksburg. As a result, Burnside did not completely comprehend the strength of Confederate forces under the commands of "Stonewall" Jackson and General Longstreet, who were anxiously awaiting the Yankee invaders. With his army divided into three "Grand Divisions," Burnside hoped that the superior numbers of his force would simply overwhelm the Confederates. But the ground-based intelligence reports that Burnside relied upon in forming his attack strategy failed to inform the general of the nearly impregnable position the Confederates had taken up on a ridge known as Marye's Heights.

Thaddeus Lowe learned that Burnside was finally ready to move against the Rebels on December 12, when he received orders to prepare one of the observation balloons for ascent. The craft chosen for the mission was the *Eagle*, the smallest of the aerostats in the Balloon Corps's inventory. Lowe worked with his assistants throughout the night and early morning to inflate it. As dawn broke the battle of Fredericksburg was under way.

In the first phase of the battle, Burnside ordered two of his Grand Divisions into a full frontal assault of the enemy position. Once again, Lowe found himself thick in the midst of a horrific struggle.

"During the day many Staff Officers ascended, and much valuable information was furnished to the Commanding General [Burnside] whose headquarters [was] . . . directly under the balloon. . . .," Lowe observed. "Several shots were fired at the balloon during the day, one passing close to it, [but] striking about two miles beyond the balloon."[16]

One of these staff officers was Lt. Col. William W. Teall, who served under General Sumner. Teall was stationed on the east side of the Rappahannock at the Chatham plantation, where he was also assigned to transmit intelligence data to one of the army's telegraph signal stations. On the morning of December 12, Teall was ordered to report to Burnside's headquarters. The young officer recorded his impressions of that day in a letter home to his wife, Harriet:

> At 8 minutes past 11 the balloon "Eagle" was brought in front of our HdQrs. It was a beautiful sight & at 11:12 it went up with 2 men in it. It was up for 3 minutes. At ½ past 11 it ascended again, carrying this time Professor Low's [*sic*] assistant & [your] loving husband who for the first time in his life assumed a hazard [your] father declared was greater than marching in front of the cannon's mouth. The atmosphere was somewhat smoky but the view was beautiful . . .[17]

Teall neglected to mention any significant observations during his first flight. Like most officers who were presented with balloon duty for the first time, Teall was undoubtedly preoccupied with the rare experience of witnessing the battlefield from a seemingly omnipotent viewpoint. After spending several minutes aloft Teall returned to earth to gather his wits. An hour later Teall attempted another ascent, "but it was too windy either to be entirely safe or to make good observations."

While waiting for the winds to die down, Teall returned to the signal station on the bluff near Chatham House. There, with the use of a powerful spyglass, he witnessed the horrible tableau of the battle taking place below.

> I observed the Infantry fight for the crest of the hill directly in front of . . . [the] Right Grand Division. The wounded & killed were as plainly visible as if I stood on the field itself. I saw one poor fellow badly wounded limping from the field accompanied by some friend, toward the gorge on the left through which the Rail-Road passes & as they reached the brink how quickly they slid down the bank. I could not but rejoice to see them sink suddenly from the murderous fire of the rebel sharpshooters. . . .[18]

But Teall's day as an aerial observer was not over quite yet. Around 4 P.M. he received orders to return to Burnside's headquarters. The high winds had subsided and Lowe was preparing the *Eagle* for its next ascent.

> Professor Low [sic] called on me & said it was so clear & still that I had better make another reconnoisance, which I immediately did. I remained up this time for 20 or 30 minutes & at an altitude of from 800 to 900 feet. A view of the entire line of battle from the extreme right to the extreme left, say from 6 to 8 miles was spread out before me. The scene from this height & at this moment of the battle was magnificent beyond description.
>
> Language could not do it justice & any attempt to describe it would be useless & impotent in the extreme. It was a scene I never expect to live to see again. Surely no mortal ever witnessed one so fearfully sublime.[19]

In spite of the carnage that was taking place on the ground, Teall waxed eloquently about his observations, much like a casual passenger might have in a peacetime excursion ride. But the danger of the young officer's mission was ever present, as he learned suddenly when the balloon was reeled back to the ground.

> Several shots were fired at the balloon & one from a battery undisclosed before. But on the instant several of our own [batteries] poured into it & no further demonstration from that quarter was known.[20]

Throughout the day Lowe made numerous ascents and landings such as the missions at which Lieutenant Colonel Teall was present. While Lowe had regained command over his balloons he didn't have the use of the telegraph train that supported air-to-ground communications. As a result, only verbal dispatches were passed from the balloon to Burnside's headquarters, forcing Lowe to make several relatively dangerous ascents and landings under heavy fire throughout the day. But given the fact that Burnside and his staff were operating directly underneath, Lowe's balloon was considerably farther away from the front line than was the case in earlier battles.

In at least one brief instance during the battle of Fredericksburg, Gen. Daniel Butterfield, commander of V Corps, ascended with Lowe.

"My short ascent in the balloon had given me a view of the topography, ravines, streams, roads, etc.," Butterfield later said. "That was of great value in making dispositions and movements of troops."[21]

Even with the return of aerial reconnaissance to his intelligence resources, Burnside and the Army of the Potomac fared dismally at Fredericksburg. Two of the general's Grand Divisions commanded by Joseph Hooker and Edwin Sumner were thrown in against the Confederate army's well-reinforced positions in the town. Despite heavy support from artillery that managed to reduce much of Fredericksburg to rubble, the Rebels held their line—and then some.

In an all too familiar scene, waves of Union infantrymen hurled themselves suicidally against the position that General Longstreet's men had taken up high above the town on Marye's Heights. Before the battle, Longstreet was asked about prospects of holding the line from that position. The general answered in return by stating, "If you put every man now on the other side of the Potomac in the field to approach me over the same line, and give me enough ammunition, I will kill them all before they reach me."

Those words were to unfortunately ring true for the Army of the Potomac. When the battle commenced the number of the dead and the wounded multiplied quickly, literally piling up at the base of the nearly impregnable Confederate position. In the end the Federals suffered over 12,700 casualties, compared with only 5,300 casualties from the ranks of the considerably smaller force of Rebel defenders. It was yet another devastating blow to the beleaguered Union army.

The following day Burnside wished to renew the assault on Marye's Heights, but was talked out of it after casualty reports revealed the severe damage that his army had suffered. On December 15, Burnside ordered his army to withdraw back to a safe zone on the north bank of the Rappahannock. Lee, who did not want to repeat the bloody losses the South had suffered at Antietam, opted not to pursue.

Lowe remained with the army as Burnside attempted to plot his next move. On December 22, Lowe made an ascent at Burnside's headquarters several miles from Fredericksburg. His observation that day did little to provide much in the way of optimism.

"[The Confederates'] main camps are opposite to our left and extend down the river from four to six miles back," Lowe reported. "Earthworks appear to be thrown up on the next range of hills, beyond the first line of woods, but nothing definite could be ascertained concerning them, owing to the heavy smokes."[22]

Lowe concluded his report by stating that it did not appear as if any of the Rebels in the area had withdrawn.

In the days following the bleak Christmas of 1862, Burnside still entertained ideas of ordering the Army of the Potomac back into Fredericksburg. The plan that Burnside formulated was a vain attempt to regain his reputation as a commander and more importantly restore the morale of his battered army. But circumstances and just plain bad luck both conspired to work against the Federals once again.

On January 19, 1863, Burnside ordered the lead elements of the Army of the Potomac to start moving several miles upriver of Fredericksburg at a point where the portable pontoon bridges could be used to ford the Rappahannock. Several of the general's senior officers cautioned that the poor state of mind infecting the army in Virginia truly dictated yet another retrenchment that would hopefully restore confidence to the men. However, Burnside was determined to turn the tables on Lee. For Burnside, if the plan proved successful the Rebels would have to abandon their fortified positions along the ridges of Fredericksburg and be forced to come out into the open in a face-to-face confrontation.

Yet as soon as Burnside's army began its move, the unusually dry weather that had held during the entire month of January to this point suddenly turned to unrelenting rain and extremely high winds. Despite the fact that Thaddeus Lowe managed to overcome many weather obstacles in Balloon Corps's operations, the miserable conditions that set in made ascents in support of the advance impossible.

Ascents by balloon were the furthest thing from General Burnside's mind as the heavy downpours continued into the second and third day of the advance. Wagon roads became deep, slimy bogs and once again the banks of the Rappahannock disappeared under a rapidly swelling current. Rampant disorganization and chaos ensued, which was only relieved, in part, by the lack of action taken by the Confederates during the course of the ill-fated maneuver. On January 23, Burnside finally realized the futility of going on with his plans and recalled the army back to its temporary headquarters at Stafford Heights, opposite Fredericksburg.

Once again in the aftermath of a major campaign, the commanding general of the Army of the Potomac was completely discredited. Following Burnside's infamous January "Mud March," President Lincoln was faced with the prospect of finding a new commander. While there were those in the Union army who fervently favored the return of George McClellan, Lincoln was not swayed by such sentiment. However, the man who Lincoln did select would have a profound change upon the future fortunes of the Union army Balloon Corps.

CHAPTER FOURTEEN

Thaddeus Lowe's
Last Battle

On January 26, 1863, Abraham Lincoln appointed Gen. Joseph Hooker to lead the Army of the Potomac. Hooker was a controversial choice for a number of reasons. As far back as the Seven Days' battles he openly criticized George McClellan's uninspired leadership and was even more vociferously disparaging of Burnside's clumsy performance at Fredericksburg.

Hooker was also somewhat vainglorious and not one to mince his words. Before his appointment he gained some degree of notoriety by telling a newspaper reporter that what the country needed was a dictator in order to lead the Union onward to victory and put the nation back together. This was a point of contention that had hardly gone unnoticed by the president. But Lincoln was looking for a fighter and Hooker had distinguished himself on a number of occasions, including Antietam, where he sustained a wound to the foot that sidelined him for several weeks. By the time he returned to active duty the nickname "Fighting Joe" had become a permanent attachment to the legend surrounding Hooker.

When Hooker took command of the Army of the Potomac the immediate result was yet another reorganization. After two unsuccessful bids to cross the Rappahannock the decision was made to make a winter camp at Falmouth, some twenty miles northeast of Fredericksburg. Hooker attacked the army's low morale by improving food, cleaning up camps and hospitals, and granting furloughs during the lull to stem the tide of rising desertions from the ranks. At his headquarters though, Hooker fought a different kind of war than his predecessors. Described as "a place which no self-respecting man liked to go, and no decent woman could go,"[1] the army headquarters could best be characterized as a combination of mobile saloon and bordello. In an incidental note, the Hooker legend took on an everlasting notoriety when the general's name was applied to a certain variety of camp-following females.

With the Army of the Potomac in winter hibernation at Falmouth, what all of this meant to Thaddeus Lowe and the Balloon Corps was weeks of inactivity as the new powers-that-be figured out a way to employ a group of civilian balloonists. As Lowe noted during previous shakeups of the army's organization, each leadership change seemed to diminish his influence on how the Balloon Corps was managed, and Hooker's assumption of command proved no different. While Lowe and his crew tended to the balloons back at the Columbia Armory in Washington, major changes were afoot that would drastically affect the Corps's future. The first of these came in the form of a new military overseer for the Balloon Corps.

Capt. Cyrus Ballou Comstock was a career military engineer who had taught at West Point prior to the war. Comstock was General Sumner's chief engineer during the Peninsular Campaign and had later commanded his own battalion of engineers. The earliest known contact that Comstock had with the Balloon Corps came during Burnside's attempted assault on Fredericksburg, as noted by Capt. W. A. Glassford:

> . . . Comstock . . . made many ascensions, sometimes going to a height of 2,000 feet and frequently remaining up for an hour or more. His experience resulted in a favorable impression of the value of the balloon for the observation of the topography and the disposition and movement of troops. But it must be remembered that this officer had received a training so thorough and so specialized that, as soon as experience had endowed him with confidence in the balloon, he became such an observer as could scarcely be found outside a corps of true military balloonists.[2]

There were some in the army who saw Comstock as the answer to the problem of having military aeronautics in the hands of civilians. Even during the Peninsular Campaign a number of individuals, such as Lt. George Custer, voiced their opinion that only trained officers should be in control of aerial observations. Comstock's appointment was indicative of this senti-

Capt. Cyrus Ballou Comstock took over as military overseer of the Union army Balloon Corps in February, 1863. The appointment marked the beginning of the end for Thaddeus Lowe's role as chief aeronaut.

U.S. ARMY SIGNAL CORPS PHOTO

ment and the thirty-two-year-old officer began to promote this new change in attitude.

As behind-the-scenes maneuvering began to substantially change the way the Balloon Corps operated, Lowe not only began to lose control over his balloons, but he was also called upon to justify the very existence of military aeronautics. In the aftermath of several battles and campaigns that revealed a definite weakness in the Union army's fighting ability, members of Congress began to openly criticize the enormous expenditures going toward the war effort. In February, 1863, Thaddeus Lowe was summoned before a House committee on the conduct of the war to testify on the Corp's contribution to the war effort.

Part of the reason that Lowe had to defend his department's operations was that outside critics of the Balloon Corps were also finding a voice within the War Department. In March, 1863, an inventor by the name of England, from 1724 Rittenhouse Street, Philadelphia, wrote to Gen. Rufus Ingalls, the chief quartermaster of the Army of the Potomac, claiming to have devised a more efficient way of generating hydrogen gas for military balloons.

In a lengthy letter to Ingalls, England claimed to have learned, "that the expense of [the] Balloon corps was about $200 per day," during the period in which the army was engaged in the Peninsular Campaign.[3] Furthermore, England broke down these expenses along with "the vast amount of material" used to support the Balloon Corps:

> I was informed that a steamboat, costing $85 per day, was constantly employed for transportation and storage; also some 40 horses, and 10 wagons, and 30 men were employed in that department.[4]

Exactly from what source England obtained his information was never mentioned. However, the inventor went on to state that he had a proposal that would reduce the Corps's expenses, "to about one half or less."[5]

"By the present crude method now used to generate gas, it cannot cost them less than $4.50 for 1000 cubic feet, and, a full 15 hours is required to generate a sufficient amount to inflate one of their balloons," England stated, profusely underlining the various claims in his letter to emphasize his points. "I propose to furnish quite a good gas, for, from 20 cents to 40 cents per 1000 cubic feet, and, will generate enough to inflate one of the balloons in about 3 hours."[6]

England continued his letter by claiming that he had developed a new type of hydrogen generator that would "dispense entirely [with] the vast amount of valuable material, and cumbersome apparatus" that was used by the corps and that his process would provide a total savings of "$300 to $400 per day."[7]

Although England did not reveal any significant details of his new invention he emphatically exclaimed that "the overwhelming advantages gained over the present method of inflation . . . [will] certainly add to the efficiency" of military aeronautics.

From what England did reveal of his invention, however, this new process of generating gas only required two men, "at most," to operate the apparatus and only one wagon to contain all requisite supplies. Providing further endorsement of his proposal, England also mentioned that he was assisted in developing his gas generator by fellow Philadelphian William Paullin, and that his process was given a "thorough examination" by John Steiner.[8] By referring to both of the former Balloon Corps aeronauts, England's letter was given serious consideration by those in the army who wished to cut costs from the war effort.

As a final part of his proposal, England supplied a comparison of his method of generating gas in relation to the Balloon Corps's current process, with data presumably supplied by Paullin and Steiner:

COMPARISON OF TWO METHODS

By Present Mode	By New Plan
Time required for a single inflation—15 hours	Time. One hour or less
Cost of single inflation $400	Cost—Less than $25
12,000 lbs acid & iron used for a single inflation	Materials used, 100 pounds
Wagons required = 12 or 14 Horses [required] about 50 Teamsters [required] 12 or 14	Wagons required = 2 Horses [required] 8 or 10 Teamsters [required] 2 or 3
Renewal of apparatus, and Frequent repairs required	Apparatus will last in good order for two or three years
Some 40 men are detailed as assistants	20 men will be sufficient

The cost of materials is from 4 cts to 8 cts. per pound. 100 pounds inflates a balloon of 50 feet diameter or 68,000 feet capacity, which will lift 1000 pounds; Weight of car 75 lbs; Apparatus 110 lbs.; Materials, 90 lbs; rope nettings, 175 lbs.; Two men, 300 lbs., Total, 750 lbs giving margin of 250 lbs.[9]

Ingalls forwarded England's proposal to Brig. Gen. Seth Williams, who served as assistant adjutant general to Hooker. Thaddeus Lowe was livid when he received word of England's proposal. In a lengthy response to Williams, Lowe refuted every one of England's claims.

"In examining the papers I find many misstatements concerning the present balloon operations," Lowe wrote. "In justice to myself and those connected with the balloon department, I feel in duty bound to set right.

First, . . . in comparing the two methods [England] states that the 'time required to inflate a balloon . . . [at] present . . . is fifteen hours' when in fact it never required over three hours and fifteen

minutes. . . . Since adding improvements [to the present gas gener-
ator] . . . the gas now makes in two hours and thirty minutes.

Second. [England] states that the cost . . . of a simple inflation is
$400, when the actual cost is only about $60 now. When the iron
(which we now obtain free of charge from the Washington Navy-
Yard) had to be purchased, the cost was then in the neighborhood
of $75, which, when divided by fourteen (the number of days the
balloons will retain their power, on the average), the cost per day
for gas will be about $5.30. Of course this does not include con-
tingent expenses.

Third. Mr. Englend [sic] stated that it now requires 12,000
pounds of acid and iron for a single inflation, when, in fact, that
amount will keep two balloons inflated from three to four weeks.

Fourth. [England] states that it now requires twelve or fourteen
wagons, when the facts are that it never did require over seven
wagons to haul four balloons and appendages and material to keep
them inflated, and all camp and garrison equippage for the whole
aeronautics corps.[10]

After defending the record of the Balloon Corps, Lowe shifted his
argument to attack England's proposal in general.

"First. According to the statement of Mr. Englend [sic], it requires a
bulk of 68,000 cubic feet [for a balloon envelope] to lift the same weight
that now requires 15,000 cubic feet, much less than a quarter of the capacity of the balloon which he proposes," stated Lowe, who also noted that the
two biggest balloons in the Corps's inventory—the Union and Intrepid—
were already nearly 32,000 feet in capacity. The Union and the Intrepid, as
well as several of the Corps's smaller balloons, were already capable of sus-
taining a lifting force equal to England's proposed behemoth. Additionally,
Lowe pointed out that the enormous balloon that England proposed was
not only inefficient by the inventor's own admission, but would be nearly
impossible to handle by a ground crew.

"[A] balloon of 68,000 feet capacity and weighing 750 pounds, with a
lifting force of a 1,000, could not be held by fifty men against the wind, and
would be blown to the earth."[11]

Lowe did not let up on his critique. Realizing that mobility played a
major role in providing successful reconnaissance, Lowe also noted that a
68,000 cubic foot aerostat could not be easily transported from place to place.

"Should two ascensions be required at different points in one day (as is often the case in order to make a full and correct report), [England's proposed] balloon would have to be inflated at each point," said Lowe. "[This] would be another impossibility and would involve the expense of $250, according to the cost set down for each inflation. Besides, the constant handling of the machinery must necessarily soon wear it out."[12]

Lowe could hardly temper his annoyance over the serious consideration with which England's plan was given. The aeronaut emphasized that the Corps's current complement of balloons and equipment had served for nearly two years, withstood the storms of two winters, and had achieved altitudes hitherto unreached by tethered ascents. Some of the balloons were often kept inflated and ready for service for months at a time without completely changing out the gas. With his usual flair for defending his efforts without equivocation, Lowe averred that his accomplishments amounted to, "circumstances which history affords no parallel in any country."[13]

But Lowe was willing to acknowledge that there was at least the possibility that England's claim of an improved gas generator existed and he set forth the following challenge:

> I would respectfully recommend that Mr. Englend [sic] be permitted to try his experiments in the field beside the present balloon operations in order to compare fairly the relative advantages of the two upon precisely the same grounds that I was allowed to try my first experiments, namely, with his own balloon and apparatus and at his own expense.[14]

Also, to counter England's endorsements from Steiner and Paullin, Lowe enlisted testimony from the Allen brothers in support of his own method of aeronautics. As James Allen wrote in a letter to Lowe that April:

> In accordance with your request that I should furnish you with a report of my operations previous to my employment under your direction and opinion of your system of aeronautic . . . I would most respectfully submit the following.
>
> For a number of years previous to the breaking out of this war I followed the profession of an aeronaut. . . . At the commencement of the rebellion I was induced by friends to offer my services to the Government. I did so, and for the purpose of demonstrating what

I could do I brought two balloons in July, 1861. Some experiments were made before an officer of the Topographical Engineers appointed for the purpose. After witnessing my operations he pronounced them unsatisfactory.

. . . I returned to my home in Providence and subsequently watched with much interest in the reports of your progress, until in the spring of 1862 you invited me to join your corps, since which time I have received much valuable information from you in the use of your inventions.

. . . In conclusion, I can conscientiously say that the Government is indebted to you alone for the introduction of this useful branch of the public service, and were it not for your improvements in the construction of balloons and invention of portable gas generators, your untiring perseverance, hard labor and exposure against great obstacles, aeronauts could never have been of service to our Army.

Balloons, as usually constructed, could not be kept inflated in heavy winds, and at best could not hold their power but a few hours, whereas now the balloons are kept constantly ready to go up, day or night. From this manner of construction and great strength they are able to withstand any storm, and enables the aeronaut to ascend in nearly all weathers, and are so impervious that they can be kept inflated for months with but little replenishing, and consequently trifling expense. These are qualities heretofore unknown in the history of aeronautics, and are merits that deserve the highest commendation.[15]

Ezra Allen heartily seconded his brother's assessment.

"I cordially concur in the foregoing as regards the superiority of Professor Lowe's system of aeronautics over former attempts," Ezra wrote. "I have been engaged in ballooning for a number of years past and have been employed under the direction of Professor Lowe for the past five months. I have received much valuable instruction from him in the use of his new system of aeronautics for army purposes, without which balloons could not be used to any advantage in the field.[16]

Despite the endorsements and Lowe's objections to England's proposal, orders were apparently handed down directing the chief aeronaut to travel to Philadelphia to ascertain any merits of the new gas-generating process.

Although records of Lowe's assessment have not be found, England indignantly wrote to General Ingalls, strenuously objecting to Lowe's visit.

"Mr. Lowe has been here with an order from Gen. Hooker to investigate my new method of ballooning," England wrote. "I have, for obvious reasons . . . declined to go into such an investigation with him. I stated, however, all I could consistently without betraying any secrets."[17]

While England continued to correspond with various Union army officials over his gas-generating invention, the entire matter seemed to quietly fade away following Lowe's trip to Philadelphia. Lowe undoubtedly viewed England as a self-serving interloper trying to gain favor in a practice in which he (Lowe) had placed a considerable amount of his effort and reputation. England's attempt to assert himself as an aeronautical expert, however, paled in comparison to other factors that contributed toward undermining Lowe's position as chief aeronaut of the Union army Balloon Corps.

From within Lowe's own ranks came one individual whose act of betrayal was a source of serious damage to the Corps's reputation. Jacob C. Freno, who had served reasonably well with Lowe during most of the Peninsular Campaign, began to fall back into the old criminal habits that had prompted his dismissal from the 66th Pennsylvania Infantry the previous year. When the Balloon Corps returned to Washington following the army's withdrawal from Virginia, Freno began operating an illegal faro bank operation that efficiently fleeced enlisted men.

Gambling was nothing new in the ranks of the army. Illegal gambling halls sprang up in various camps as a way to relieve the monotony of army life. More often than not, these gambling operations were rigged in favor of whoever represented the house and Freno's faro bank was no exception. It wasn't long before Freno's card game was exposed as a money pit for unsuspecting enlisted men to part with their money.

Lowe—who abhorred anything that might taint the Balloon Corps's reputation—moved quickly to dismiss Freno in December, 1862. But the trouble with Freno had only just begun. He began to circulate a number of serious and unsubstantiated charges against Lowe. Freno alleged that Lowe's father, Clovis, was ill and convalescing in Philadelphia, although the Corps's chief aeronaut kept him on the government payroll.

Freno also alleged that Lowe had stolen government property, including an entire balloon outfit for his own commercial purposes. He also maintained that Lowe stole scarce military food rations and lavished them on influential news reporters in the field in order to curry favorable publicity for himself. And perhaps one of the most outlandish charges of all came when Freno accused Lowe of misappropriating military carriages and drivers for pleasure excursions around Washington, D.C., with his wife, Leontine.[18]

Lowe was forced to answer each of the allegations. The charge that he had stolen a balloon was simply not true. The craft in question was a small, experimental aerostat intended as an unmanned signaling device that had been taken from the Columbia Armory to Philadelphia for repairs. As for Lowe's father, the old man was far from being a convalescent, having served nearly nonstop since Lowe's appointment as chief aeronaut. And as for carriage rides around the capital with Leontine, Mrs. Lowe had remained in Philadelphia since October, 1861.[19]

Even when his charges were proved unfounded, Freno did not refrain from continuing his spiteful campaign. While the balloon *Constitution* was undergoing repairs in the Columbia Armory, Freno gained access to it and maliciously slashed out a large portion of its silken envelope. In the aftermath of the incident Lowe pressed charges against his former assistant, but the Washington provost marshal's office failed to bring the elusive Freno to justice.[20]

Meanwhile, as the outside distractions to Lowe's efforts mounted, Captain Comstock began to assert his control over the Balloon Corps's future course of action. Lowe was already notified that no, "issues or expenditures" were to be made without direct authorization from Comstock,[21] but the captain was looking to further rein in what remained of the chief aeronaut's autonomy.

On April 11, 1863, Comstock met with Lowe to discuss the new direction that aeronautics would take under his command. The following day, Comstock followed up his conversation with the aeronaut with a written communiqué that formally outlined this plan. The new directives had the effect of completely alienating Lowe's continued efforts with the army.

"I do not think the interests of the public service require the employment of C[lovis] Lowe, your father, or of John O'Donnell," Comstock wrote to Lowe. "Please inform me whether you have, as desired, notified them of the fact."[22]

The order to cut the services of his father may have been a result of the stigma left by Freno's unsubstantiated charges, but Comstock did not limit his cutback to just personnel.

"I also stated that it might be necessary for the public interest to reduce your pay from $10 to $6," Comstock continued, again probably remedying

Thaddeus Lowe (right) with his father, Clovis Lowe, during the Peninsular Campaign. Thaddeus Lowe is shown demonstrating aerial signals. The elder Lowe proved to be an invaluable asset in keeping the inventory of the Balloon Corps in working order, despite charges to the contrary. PHOTOGRAPHIC HISTORY OF THE CIVIL WAR

the common complaint from some army officers that the civilian balloonist was earning as much as a full colonel.

Comstock also stated that Lowe and his aeronauts would be subject to
a new series of rules and codes of conduct, including the demand that in
future no absences would be permitted without Comstock's express permission, and that all wages would be stopped during these periods.

"In camp, when the wind is still, ascensions should be made at morning, noon, and night, the labor being equally divided among the aeronauts,
and reports made to me in writing of all that is observed during the day,"
said Comstock. "You [Lowe], as having larger experience, are expected to
make these ascensions frequently . . . You will also be held responsible that
the apparatus is kept in good order that the aeronauts attend to their duty;
that the necessary requisitions are sent in for supplies, and generally for the
efficiency and usefulness of the establishment, as well as its economical
management."[23]

Comstock ended with the addendum that Lowe was also to provide
"an inventory of all public property under" his control—another apparent
allusion to the charge that Lowe was using government balloons for his own
private purposes.

Comstock's draconian measures were probably motivated by a genuine
desire to protect the considerable amount of government resources that
were being poured into the war effort. After the number of severe setbacks
the Union army had suffered, loud and powerful cries were being heeded
to put the war effort into some sort of economic order lest the entire country collapse from the burden of funding rampant and uncontrolled military
spending.

Lowe, however, was taken aback and grossly insulted by Comstock's new
directives. The aeronaut felt that he was already lending his efforts at a rate of
compensation that was eminently fair to the government. In many ways,
Lowe's service to the government came at a cost that was partially contributing to his own economic detriment, which not only affected him but also his
family. A note sent from Leontine at the time Comstock's orders were issued,
closed with a plea to her husband to, "send money immediately."[24]

Lowe's first reaction to Comstock's orders was to attempt to circumvent
them. On the same day that he received Comstock's directive Lowe wrote
to Gen. Daniel Butterfield, General Hooker's chief of staff. Butterfield had
been one of the Balloon Corps's staunchest supporters during the Peninsular Campaign and Lowe hoped to appeal to the general's sentiment to find

some way to neutralize Comstock's authority.

"From a copy of Special Orders, No. 95 . . . I am informed that the balloon establishment is placed in charge of Capt. C. B. Comstock," wrote Lowe. "In conversation with him yesterday I learned that different arrangements were to be made, and, among other things he informed me that my compensation for services were reduced from $10 per day to $6. This Captain Comstock does, I have no doubt, in good faith, and from the point of view which he takes of this department as it now stands.

"Now, in justice to myself and the service in which I am engaged, I beg to submit the following succinct statement:

"At the breaking out of the rebellion I was urged to offer my services to the Government as an aeronaut. I did so, at the sacrifice of my long-cherished enterprise in which I had expended large sums of money and many years of hard labor and which, if successful, would compensate me for my expenditure and place aeronautics among the first branches of useful science."[25]

Lowe went on to restate his position that at the beginning of the war he had several competitors attempting to prove the value of military aeronautics, most notably John Wise, John La Mountain, and James Allen. Each of these men tried and eventually failed to make ballooning a viable resource in military reconnaissance. Only Lowe, through his own efforts with the balloon *Enterprise*, successfully proved that aeronautics could be used with a modern field army.

"I used my own machinery and expended considerable private means, and two months' labor, for all of which I have never received pay," Lowe reminded Butterfield.[26]

"My system of aeronautics was selected, and I was offered $30 per day for each day I would keep one balloon inflated in the field ready for officers to ascend. (This was when it was supposed that balloons could not be kept constantly inflated, as is now the case.)

"I declined this offer and offered my services for $10 per day, as I desired to continue during the war and add to my reputation; besides, that amount would be sufficient to support my family. Ever since I have labored incessantly for the interest of the Government, and I have never shrunk from duty or danger whenever it was necessary to gain information for the commanding general."[27]

In addressing the actions taken by Comstock, Lowe unsparingly described the extensive damage that the orders had inflicted upon his personal pride.

"General, I feel aggrieved that my services should not have been better appreciated. As it is, I cannot honorably serve for the sum named by Captain Comstock without first refunding to the Government the excess of that amount which I have been receiving ever since I have been in the service," he stated. "This my very limited means will not allow, for it requires full the salary I have received to support myself in the field and my family at home.[28]

Concluding his letter Lowe expressed his terms for continuing in service with the army, notwithstanding the withdrawal of Comstock's directives. As can be readily observed, Lowe's sentiments revealed a man whose morale had almost entirely evaporated.

"I have promised the commanding general [Hooker] that nothing should be lacking on my part to render the greatest possible service during the next battle and as I consider that all should be done that genius can devise to make the first move successful, I will offer my services until that time free of charge to the Gov't."[29]

Lowe hoped by appealing to Butterfield that he would rid himself and the Balloon Corps of Captain Comstock's overbearing presence. But the aeronaut's effort actually produced the opposite affect. It is not known whether Butterfield even received the letter from Lowe. Brig. Gen. Simon Barstow, assistant adjutant general to General Hooker, responded to Lowe on April 13, informing the chief aeronaut that all communications were "to be forwarded through the proper channel to Captain Comstock."[30]

From Barstow, Lowe's letter was forwarded on to Brig. Gen. Seth Williams, who "respectfully returned" the letter back to Lowe, adding that Lowe should refer to "an indorsement of Captain Comstock, Engineer Department, in charge of balloons."[31]

Comstock was completely aware of Lowe's end run around him and began to lobby his own allies among the army's senior officers. The captain remained firm on his position, particularly on the question of pay.

"Relative to the reduction of pay from $10 to $6 per day . . . and [Lowe's] offer of his services during the coming engagements free," Comstock reiterated. "It is believed that during the two years Mr. Lowe has been receiving $10 per day for his services, he has been compensated for the sacrifices made, and that $6 per day is ample payment for the duties he has to perform at present."[32]

The die was cast with Comstock's decision to stand pat on the pay issue. Lowe would remain as chief aeronaut—*sans* salary—only until the Army of the Potomac completed its preparations for its next major battle.

By this time, Lowe was completely demoralized. Only one more significant clash between Lowe and Comstock took place, when in mid-April assistant secretary of war P. H. Watson wrote to Lowe requesting confirmation on whether a complete balloon apparatus and aeronaut could be sent to the vicinity of Charleston, South Carolina, or Baton Rouge, Louisiana, "at short notice."[33]

Lowe, in his "zeal to render service to the Government,"[34] personally responded to Watson, stating that James Allen, "would be best suited for the assignment."[35]

For the simple action of responding to the assistant secretary's request for information, Lowe was thoroughly rebuked for attempting to subordinate Comstock's authority.

"The accompanying communication is respectfully returned to Professor Lowe, to be forwarded through Captain Comstock, who has returned it with the accompanying note," wrote Seth Williams. "The commanding general desires to be informed why the letter to the Secretary of War, to which the answer is in reply, was not transmitted through headquarters."[36]

Lowe subsequently apologized profusely for his action that, "overstepped the bounds prescribed by military law," adding that the transgression "was unintentional."[37] Comstock further hammered the point in by writing to Hooker's headquarters, informing staff there that Lowe had been informed that orders pertaining to the Balloon Corps came through Comstock first. Lowe, ". . . not being in charge of the balloon establishment had not the power to change" the chain of command when it involved military decisions involving aeronautics.[38]

This last incident marked the final time that Thaddeus Lowe would try to demonstrate leadership as chief aeronaut. From this point on Lowe would not seize the initiative within the Balloon Corps ever again.

Despite the frustration that Lowe undoubtedly experienced over losing administrative control over his beloved Balloon Corps, the aeronaut still managed to serve out the remainder of his tenure with more than just perfunctory attention to duty. While Comstock had responded to the Secretary of War that James Allen would be available to serve the army in the southern theater of operations, no action was taken.

For some time after this Lowe found that there was very little to do with regards to gathering intelligence for the army. The Army of the Potomac maintained its dormancy at Falmouth until late April. Hooker was buried deep in conferring with his senior officers over new plans to attack Lee's Army of Northern Virginia. During these planning sessions Hooker completed his own reorganization of the Army of the Potomac. Burnside's Grand Divisions were completely eliminated, while the commanding general made sweeping changes regarding who was to command the various corps that were reinstated as separate units within the army. It was not until April 15 that President Lincoln finally gave his approval to Hooker's final reorganization.

The next phase in the general's plan soon started to come into focus. Hooker envisioned a maneuver that would attempt to envelope Lee's army—still in position above Fredericksburg—by marching a significant portion of the Army of the Potomac from Falmouth up the Rappahannock River. From there they would cross over the Rappahannock and then the Rapidan River. At that point the advance guard of Hooker's army would approach the Confederates from their rear and left flank, where they would be most vulnerable. To accomplish this feat Maj. Gen. John Sedgwick was to take a corps of some 40,000 men and create a diversionary attack on Fredericksburg, keeping the bulk of Lee's army at bay.

Once again, Thaddeus Lowe found himself in the midst of great activity as Hooker demanded up-to-the-minute reports on enemy strength in the area. During his ascents Lowe was ordered to provide his written observations to Comstock only, contrary to the previous practice of reporting directly to the various Union officers who requested his services. All that Lowe observed in the days before the great battle proved exceedingly useful, particularly to General Sedgwick.

"I examined the enemy's position more closely this P.M., between 4 and 6 o'clock, than I have had an opportunity for a number of days past," Lowe stated in his report of April 22, 1863. "If I might be permitted to venture an opinion as to the relative strength of the enemy, I should say that they are about three to our four. I should estimate their supports to the batteries immediately back of the city of Fredericksburg to be about 10,000."[39]

Lowe went on to say that he could also see a very dense concentration of men along the railroad station approximately three miles to the south of the Rappahannock.

"I should say that there were 25,000 troops camped," said Lowe.[40]

"Still farther to the left and south of the railroad there are also several large camps. During the time I was up I noticed many regiments on parade, near the various camps," Lowe continued. ". . . I am inclined to believe that the enemy are either strengthening their army or bringing up their troops from, Bowling Green and the Junction. The latter is the most probable, as there is not as much smoke visible in that direction as heretofore."[41]

On the eve of battle Hooker's position appeared remarkably solid. The scouting reports from beyond enemy lines reinforced his feeling that now was the optimum time for an attack against the Rebels, and with the addition of Lowe's reconnaissance Hooker was characterized as "the best informed Union general who had ever taken the field.[42]

On April 27, Hooker ordered his army to begin its initial advance. Seventy thousand infantrymen were ordered to march upstream of the Rappahannock. Heavy rain once again made the Rappahannock difficult to ford, particularly by Stoneman's cavalry. Still, the onset of the maneuver was nothing like Ambrose Burnside's ill-fated "Mud March."

But the journey was still arduous. After crossing the Rappahannock Hooker's men were required to swiftly cross over the smaller Rapidan River, a feat in itself considering the vast number of men and the logistics involved. By April 30 this much of the plan was accomplished, but after that the men encountered a thick, tangled mass of untamed woods that was ominously known locally as, "the Wilderness." When Hooker's men finally emerged from the woods they arrived at the site of the Chancellor's House plantation at a crossroads hamlet known as Chancellorsville.

Although Hooker's move was bold in its initial execution, Robert E. Lee was not a general to be underestimated. Lee quickly assessed the potential dangers. Earlier encounters with McClellan and Burnside, while successful, had seriously depleted his army of men and materiel. Lee realized the necessity of seizing the initiative or face total annihilation.

Once again Lee turned to the strategy that had served him well thus far. He split his force of approximately 60,000 men into two parts. A smaller force of 10,000 under the command of Jubal Early were to be left at Fredericksburg. The nearly impregnable position at Marye's Heights still remained and Lee gambled that Early's men could hold off Sedgwick's VI Corps. The remaining force was to attack the bulk of Hooker's men at Chancellorsville in an attempt to short circuit the Union army's momentum. On his way to meet Hooker, Lee was joined once again by "Stonewall" Jackson and the Confederate II Corps.

Lee knew that he faced a dire situation with Hooker's rejuvenated and resupplied Army of the Potomac ready and waiting to do battle with his own ragged army. He had already called on his men to do the impossible more than once already and the results had been successful, though mostly at a high cost of life and resources. Now Lee gambled with his army once again, anticipating that the impending clash with Hooker would bring another victory.

On the evening of May 1, Lee and Jackson conferred, seeking a way to check Hooker's next move. In a setting that has since taken on mythic proportions, the two Confederate generals sat on overturned cracker boxes, backlit by the flame of a burning campfire. It was decided that Jackson would take 26,000 men on a hazardous daylight movement across the front of Hooker's advance guard scarcely two miles away. The idea was that Jackson's men would be in a position to attack Hooker's army from its right flank, while the remaining divisions under Lee would strike the Yankees head on.

On the morning of May 2, Jackson and his troops began their long march. Although the maneuver was detected late in the day by elements of the Union XI Corps, under the command of Oliver O. Howard, Hooker did nothing to prepare for the coming onslaught.

Meanwhile, Thaddeus Lowe was assigned to monitor the Rebels on Marye's Heights as General Sedgwick prepared his assault on Jubal Early's position. The bloody lessons learned during the battle of Fredericksburg were foremost in the minds of Union soldiers as their eyes focused on the Confederate line.

Lowe and the Allen brothers were constantly in action just prior to the commencement of the battle. On the evening of April 30, Lowe made the following report:

> After my report at 4:45 this P.M. I came down to General Sedgwick's headquarters and ascended at 7 o'clock, remaining up until after dark in order to see the location of the enemy's camp-fires. I find them most numerous in a ravine about one mile beyond the heights opposite General Sedgwick's forces. . . . From appearances I should judge that full three-fourths of the enemy's force is immediately back and below Fredericksburg.[43]

Lowe considered this last observation to be of great significance to Sedgwick and Hooker as they prepared their respective attacks.

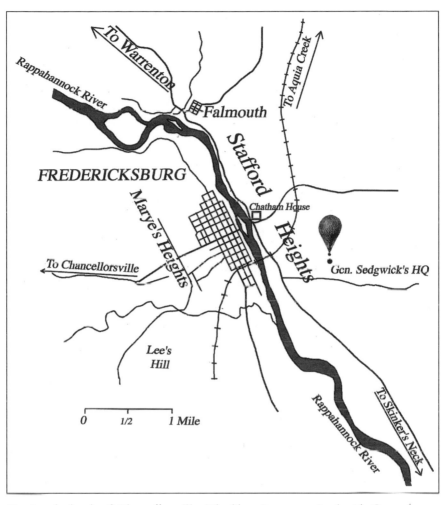

During the battle of Chancellorsville, Thaddeus Lowe remained with General Sedgwick's troops at Fredericksburg. Lowe provided much of the reconnaissance that Sedgwick used in planning the assault on the Confederate stronghold at Marye's Heights.

"It gave the commanding general correct information as to the position of the enemy, and he was enabled to regulate his operations . . . accordingly," Lowe said. "I was confident that the enemy had brought up reserves. . . . I also concluded from General Hooker's movements that the enemy would learn them, and probably move up the river the next morning."[44]

Lowe immediately sent word to Ezra Allen to have a balloon ready to ascend at Banks' Ford, a river crossing between Fredericksburg and Chancellorsville.

"Commence observations at daylight to-morrow, and look out for the enemy moving on the roads, either up or down," Lowe said. "Report by telegraph, having your dispatch sent to General Hooker at United States Ford, and to General Sedgwick, Franklin's Crossing. Be sure of the correctness of your reports, and report promptly."[45]

It is interesting to note that Lee's army was already en route to meet Hooker by the time that Lowe made his observations and dispatched Ezra Allen to investigate further. Yet no preparatory action seemed to come from Hooker at Chancellor's House, if indeed Lowe's intelligence reports actually reached him. Moreover, on the morning of May 2, Lee was reduced to a force of only 16,000 men, as Jackson worked furiously to move his troops around the Union flank. Jackson's men were, for the most part, barefooted and ill-equipped and the progress they made was nothing short of miraculous. Had Hooker chosen to make a frontal assault his army could have potentially devastated Lee's vastly outnumbered force. But Hooker hesitated, in what was probably the first sign that his nerve was rapidly failing.

When the Confederates finally struck, they hit hard at the Army of the Potomac's position at Chancellorsville. Jackson had succeeded in flanking the Union army, emerging at its rear from out of the Wilderness by day's end on May 2. Chaos ensued as Hooker's army was taken by surprise by Rebel forces attacking from what seemed like every direction. Oliver O. Howard's men, who first alerted Hooker to the possibility of a surprise attack the previous day, bore the brunt of the casualties. As darkness began to fall, the firefight descended further into confusion and madness. Union soldiers, completely unnerved, fired blindly not knowing whether their guns were aimed at friend or foe.

But the Rebel loss would be even greater, with the casualty of a single man. Thomas "Stonewall" Jackson, who had acted so successfully as the executor of Lee's masterful plans, was accidentally shot by Confederate sentries as he and his staff were returning from a scouting mission. Jackson's arm was severely wounded and required amputation. At first it seemed that Jackson would recover but infection set in shortly after. He died eight days later of complications from pneumonia.

Hooker didn't learn of Jackson's wounding for several days, but the news would have mattered little. The Army of the Potomac's commanding general was seriously shaken by the Rebel's bold move. As dawn broke on the morning of May 3, Hooker was in a state of mental confusion and self-doubt. All through the night, the wounded from the previous day's fight streamed into Chancellor's House, where surgeons worked feverishly to save those they could, while orderlies piled the corpses of the dead outside. Amputated limbs were haphazardly strewn around parts of the mansion in a ghastly array.

With the rays of the morning's first light, Hooker desperately hoped that Sedgwick would be able to subdue the Confederates entrenched at Marye's Heights and to come to squeeze Lee's force between them.

But Sedgwick's progress was none too rapid. Lowe's dispatches during Sedgwick's siege of Marye's Heights were indicative of the great amount of activity taking place. As one contemporary historian noted, Lowe and the Allen brothers, "were up and down like jumping jacks" during the battle.[46] Lowe was ordered by Sedgwick to make a close examination of the enemy's position in order to point out the strongest and weakest points along their lines. In his reports Lowe noted that the earthworks on the ridge was gradually becoming abandoned.

"The enemy's infantry is very light along the whole line opposite here, and especially immediately in the rear of Fredericksburg," Lowe reported in one of his dispatches. "Heavy cannonading has just commenced on the right toward Chancellorsville."[47]

Even from his aerial vantage point and with the aid of a strong spyglass, Lowe could not see the carnage that was taking place at Chancellorsville. The heavy smoke in the distance bore witness to the destruction. Yet, Lowe was more concerned with matters aimed at Fredericksburg as Sedgwick began his next assault.

"Our troops were immediately concentrated in front [of Marye's Heights], and at 11 o'clock the point reported by me to be the weakest was charged and very handsomely taken," said Lowe. "I do not believe that any other point could have been taken by the same number of men."[48]

"Handsomely taken" was something of a misleading statement by Lowe. With the remainder of the Army of the Potomac in a state of confusion at Chancellorsville, Sedgwick had received the following orders from Hooker's staff on May 2:

The major general commanding directs that General Sedgwick cross [the Rappahannock] as soon as indications will permit; capture Fredericksburg with everything in it, and vigorously pursue the enemy.[49]

However, taking Marye's Heights was easier said than done. Sedgwick staged several charges on the Heights, each time being repulsed. But with word coming back that Hooker was in need of assistance at Chancellorsville, Sedgwick gambled the lives of his men in one final, daring push.

Relying on Lowe's intelligence reports that parts of Marye's Heights were weakly manned, Sedgwick ordered his men to storm the hill with unloaded weapons. The implication was immediately clear. The men would not be delayed by reloading their weapons as in previous charges, but would rely solely on their bayonets. It was to be a savage bloodbath, without even the impersonal swish of minié balls cutting the air to render the final moment in another man's life.

Sedgwick was successful in taking Fredericksburg this time. Jubal Early ordered his men to withdraw back to the outskirts of the town. But his retreat was orderly and by no means a rout, as Sedgwick would soon learn.

Back at Hooker's headquarters, the Rebel attack on the night of May 2 had caused a stultifying paralysis in the Army of the Potomac. The chaotic scene at Chancellor's House was compounded when a Confederate shell struck a pillar on the front porch of the mansion near where Hooker happened to be standing. The shell came close to killing the general and knocked him senseless for a while. Hooker soon recovered well enough to remain in command, but the shock to his system further reinforced his reluctance to move decisively.

In the meantime, General Sedgwick was finding Confederate resistance to be very strong as he attempted to move his force toward Chancellorsville. His advance effectively came to a halt at Salem's Church, two miles away from Fredericksburg, where heavy fighting was encountered. With the threat from Hooker greatly reduced, Lee split off part of his army to reinforce Early. Lowe continued to make observations throughout the course of the battle on May 4.

"The enemy that entered the earth-works in the rear of Fredericksburg still remains," Lowe stated. "They also have considerable infantry and some wagons with their artillery on the heights to the left of Hazel Run. A portion of General Sedgwick's command occupies a position to the right commanding the enemy. I should estimate the enemy to be in sight at least 15,000 strong."[50]

Sedgwick's VI Corps put up a valiant fight against Jubal Early's men, but the Southerners were able to turn the tide and hold their own toward the latter part of the afternoon. This was reflected in Lowe's other dispatches during the day.

"The enemy are advancing in large force to attack our forces on the right of Fredericksburg," Lowe warned at 6:15 P.M. A half hour later the aeronaut followed up by reporting that, "The enemy are engaged in full force and driving our forces badly."[51]

VI Corps's efforts on the field concluded by the end of May 4. Word eventually reached Sedgwick that Hooker had decided to break off any further engagement with Lee at Chancellorsville and withdraw back beyond the Rappahannock River. Without any reason to continue the battle, Sedgwick recalled his men and fell back to a safe position across the west bank of the Rappahannock.

It was another ignominious defeat for the Union, but the Rebels suffered heavily as well. The numbers spoke of both the horror and the sheer waste of human lives. More than 17,000 Union soldiers were dead, wounded, or missing. The Confederacy lost nearly 13,000. Some of the dead would not be removed from the battlefield for many months to come.

The Balloon Corps returned to Falmouth along with the rest of the Army of the Potomac. Hooker remained in command, but the position was temporary as Lincoln searched for yet another general to replace him. The mood was fittingly somber at the Union army's camp. Heavy rains fell on May 5 and 6. The storms were as relentless as Lee's army had proven to be thus far.

"The heavy storm . . . caused the loss of the entire gas from one balloon," Lowe reported in a letter to Captain Comstock. "[The storm] also destroyed ten carboys of acid and four barrels of iron trimmings."[52]

Not long after this Lowe met with Comstock to find out if there was to be any change in his status. Lowe quickly found out that the captain was adamant that the changes he ordered to be instituted back in early April were still standing.

"I called on [Comstock] personally . . . to learn what decision had been made relative to my communication of April 12, 1863," Lowe recalled, adding that there was also an issue involving further maintenance of the balloons. "Capt. Comstock informed me that he would select the person to superintend the delicate business of putting balloons in order. He also informed me that the terms were indicated in his endorsement on my communication. I informed that this was not satisfactory, and inasmuch as I had

Despite his success in demonstrating the usefullness of observation balloons on the battlefield, the constant battles with military skeptics and the loss of his control over the Balloon Corps contributed to Thaddeus Lowe's decision to resign his position as chief aeronaut with the Union army in May, 1863. LIBRARY OF CONGRESS

given notice on the 12th of April that I could not serve on the terms he named."[53]

If Lowe was attempting to put a bluff past Comstock in the hope that the captain would reconsider his previous decision to cut Lowe's pay and certain key personnel, Comstock didn't rise to the bait. The aeronaut told Comstock at this point, with the last major battle concluded, he wished to be relieved.

"Captain Comstock replied that if I was going I could probably be spared better than any other time," Lowe said. "I received pay up to April 7 inclusive, and then came to Washington."[54]

The entire affair was a bitter pill to swallow for Lowe. His enthusiasm to prove the Balloon Corps's military worth had evaporated from him almost entirely. He wouldn't miss the constant battle to obtain supplies or the sharp rebuke of criticism and suspicion he sustained from officers who still regarded military aeronautics as little more than a circus novelty. Comstock was just the straw that finally broke the camel's back.

On the day after Lowe's resignation he received a dispatch from General Hooker's headquarters. Hooker, who was dealing with a number of issues following the rout at Chancellorsville, had not been informed of Lowe's resignation.

"General Hooker sent one of his aides over at 10 A.M. to tell you to have two balloons up, and to keep them up all the time," read the dispatch from J. F. Gibbons, an aide-de-camp at army headquarters. "I informed the aide that you had left the Army of the Potomac. Will you not write to Hooker?"[55]

At a different point in time, when a different attitudes prevailed, Lowe would have probably jumped at the opportunity to command his beloved balloons in the service of the Union army once again. But for all intents and purpose, the era of Thaddeus Sobieski Constantine Lowe's reign as chief aeronaut of the Union army Balloon Corps had drawn to an end.

CHAPTER FIFTEEN

The Last Days of the Corps

Following Thaddeus Lowe's departure from the Balloon Corps, the mantle of chief aeronaut leadership fell to James Allen. But Allen's tenure as head of the Corps proved short-lived.

With the defeat at Chancellorsville—the latest in a series of Union army setbacks and defeats—there was no patience left for conducting the war in the manner that it had been. The perception of many in the North was that since the ill-fated Peninsular Campaign in the spring of 1862 the best efforts of the Army of the Potomac had been thrown at Lee's army all to no avail. Indeed, a good measure of panic began to set in with many Northerners genuinely fearing that Rebel forces would soon overrun Northern cities.

As a result, preparations to counter a Confederate invasion were immediately ordered. These preparations had an immediate affect on the Balloon Corps when Cyrus Comstock was reassigned to oversee defense plans in Pittsburgh, Pennsylvania.[1] Though Comstock was seen as more of an impediment than an asset to Balloon Corps operations, he was still a vital liaison between the corps and army headquarters, securing both necessary supplies and reconnaissance assignments. Unfortunately, when Comstock left he made no arrangements to transfer his authority over the corps to another officer.

Without an officer to oversee the corps, James Allen soon discovered that continuing balloon observations was a nearly impossible task. However, with Allen's personal perseverance, along with the inestimable assistance provided by his younger brother, Ezra, the Balloon Corps managed to soldier on for at least a while after Lowe left. But Allen found his situation tenuous at best. Without Lowe's zeal and fanatical devotion to maintaining the Corps's equipment to its optimum capabilities the balloons quickly fell into a state of deterioration.

In a letter to Lowe in June, 1863, shortly after the aeronaut's departure from the Corps, James Allen described the *Washington* as being "in very bad order," replete with a series of small holes in its envelope ranging from $1/64$ to $1/8$ of an inch in diameter.[2] Attempts to repair the balloon were hindered by the fact that the seams of the balloon had become "very rotten."[3]

While Allen made obligatory protests to every officer he hoped could alter his situation, assistance was not forthcoming. Despite the poor condition of the *Washington*, Allen was ordered to have the balloon inflated and ready for an observation party. James's brother, Ezra, made an ascent with a Lieutenant Williams on the Rappahannock River on May 28, followed by another series of ascents later in the day with a Captain Paine of the Topographical Engineers. After this, the Allen brothers and the remaining balloon apparatus were ordered to return to Falmouth.

Back at Falmouth circumstances deteriorated from bad to abysmal. Early on the morning of May 30, James Allen received orders to ascend and take observations. Allen continued to voice his concerns over the flightworthiness of the *Washington* but the directive to be "in the air" remained, "without regard to consequences."[4]

As the day wore on, heavy winds developed, battering the fragile balloon relentlessly. Allen ground his nerves raw with each gust that blew against the balloon's weakened seams, preparing for a disaster at any moment. Miraculously the balloon held together. The next morning, Allen again took to the air, "although the wind was almost blowing to a gale" by that time.[5]

"I at first attained to an altitude of about three hundred feet with five hundred feet of rope, but I was soon blown down one third of that distance making me about two hundred feet high," said Allen. "The balloon exploded upon the side exposed to the wind, causing a rent—in a seam I ascertained of thirty-six feet in length. The escape of the gas was instantaneous, but with the help of men familiar with the Balloon and their strict attention to my orders, it was brought safely to the Earth."[6]

Amazingly, in almost two years of operations with the army this incident was the closest thing to a disaster that any military aeronaut had encountered.

However, coming this close to tragedy prompted the Allen brothers to take their case for improvements to the balloon equipment to a higher authority. The brothers first contacted Gen. Gouverneur Kemble Warren, chief topographical engineer of the Army of the Potomac. Warren was no help in the cause, primarily because there wasn't a military liaison assigned to the Balloon Corps to act as a go-between.

The Allens even tried to enlist Thaddeus Lowe's help, optimistically hoping that the deposed chief aeronaut might still have some influence inside military channels.

"We are satisfied that if General Hooker had personally known the cause by which you left the Army he would have soon removed it," James Allen said in his letter to Lowe. "It was certainly very presumptuous for men without knowledge of the art to dictate to you, who have spent a lifetime in the study of Aeronautics."[7]

Unfortunately for James and Ezra Allen, Lowe could not provide any assistance for their plight, although their letter expressing how much the Corps missed his presence undoubtedly touched him deeply.

By this time the end was rapidly approaching for the Balloon Corps. Several ascents took place at Falmouth through early June, presumably with a more reliable balloon. But problems still persisted, as one of the last letters written by James Allen to army headquarters revealed.

"I made an attempt to get up early this morning," Allen said in a letter to General Warren. "But found my [gas control] valve . . . broken."[8]

If the Allen brothers had been allowed to continue their efforts with the Army of the Potomac, the timing may have proved propitious. A new battlefront was forming to the north, as Robert E. Lee pulled his men from the vicinity of Fredericksburg and began a long march toward Pennsylvania. The Army of the Potomac, now under the command of Gen. George Meade, began its maneuver to counter the Southern invasion threat. The two great armies would eventually meet in a battle that would prove to be the turning point for the Union army in the east—Gettysburg.

Unfortunately, the Balloon Corps was not present when the momentous turn of events took place. Interest in continuing further aeronautical reconnaissance had evaporated among those in command. Without financial and material support to maintain and construct new balloons and equipment, James and Ezra Allen were left with little choice but to end their work with the army and return to their homes in Rhode Island.

Without much in the way of ceremony or circumstance, the United States's first organized air force was allowed to fade into the annals of history.

There were a few who took notice of the loss to the Union army, however. One of the first public announcements regarding the Balloon Corps's demise was found in the New York *Times*. A war correspondent wrote an extensive epitaph for the Balloon Corps declaring that, ". . . the 'Aeronautic Corps' of the Army of the Potomac had been dispensed with, and the balloons and inflating apparatus have been sent back to [Washington]."[9]

The correspondent went on to say that the end of aeronautic reconnaissance "implied" that ". . . balloons have been found of no value in the conduct of military operations. This will excite some surprise, for the public had been led to put considerable confidence in balloon reconnaissances from facts heretofore given."

But the writer was not altogether correct in the "implication" that aeronautics in the Union army was considered to have "no value"—at least not as far as Thaddeus Lowe was concerned.

Never one to shirk from aggrandizing the Balloon Corps's legacy, Lowe later collected endorsements from a number of prominent army officers who heaped great praise on the role that aeronautics played in military operations. Lowe openly hoped that by garnering the support of key generals, the Balloon Corps would be restored as a recognized branch of the army with himself commissioned as its official leader.

"Many of the generals in the field expressed deep regret at my departure," Lowe remarked. "And [they] predicted the Balloon Corps would not hold together after I resigned from the service. I fondly hoped that the War Department would consider the value of balloon observations of sufficient importance to accede to my suggestions and in furtherance of this I asked several of the generals for an expressing of their opinion as far as their experiences were concerned."[10]

The endorsements generally sung high praise of both the Corps and, not surprisingly, its chief aeronaut. Gen. Samuel Heintzelman, who commanded the Army of the Potomac's III Corps during the Peninsular Campaign, expressed a common sentiment over the usefulness of balloon reconnaissance.

"It affords me much pleasure to be able to give my feeble testimony in relation to the value of the balloon service, whilst under your direction with the Army of the Potomac," Heintzelman eloquently wrote. "The first time

I had an opportunity to observe its value . . . in the spring of 1862, when I ascended with you and observed the position and extent of the Rebel camps and a few days later, when the most of them had disappeared. This was the first indication we had of the evacuation of Manassas. I again had the benefit of your services when on the morning of the 4th of May we discovered that the enemy had evacuated Yorktown."[11]

Heintzelman also offered his estimation of how well Lowe's system of aeronautics performed in the field, far from the supply centers of major cities.

"From my observations and experience with the portable gas generating apparatus and others of your inventions, I would consider your balloon indispensable to an army in the field," Heintzelman said. "Should I ever be entrusted with such a command I would consider my preparations incomplete without one or more balloons."[12]

John Sedgwick, the general who led the force that finally broke the Confederate resistance at Marye's Heights in Fredericksburg during the battle of Chancellorsville, also weighed in with a personal round of accolades.

"I take pleasure in certifying to the important service rendered by the balloon under your charge during the operations near Fredericksburg," said Sedgwick. "Full and frequent reports were furnished of the movements of the enemy, and a vigilant watch kept on all the operations by the officer in charge of the balloon. Staff officers detailed for that purpose made frequent ascensions to reconnoiter the position of the troops on the other side of the Rappahannock and obtained valuable information which could not have been obtained by any other measures then at my command.

"In a situation such as that then existing the importance of careful balloon reconnoissances [sic] and accurate reports therefore cannot be over estimated."[13]

Gen. George Stoneman, the Army of the Potomac's cavalry commander, also echoed the sentiments of his colleagues, adding:

I trust you will not be discouraged but still persevere in your laudable endeavors to serve the Gov't and the cause, feeling assured that in the end you will be able to do away with the prejudices with which you have had to contend, and prove to the world the great ability of Balloons and balloon signals in the conduct of a war.[14]

Even though the letters from Heintzelman, Sedgwick, and Stoneman carried some influence, Lowe's efforts to procure reinstatement were to no avail. In the fall of 1863, the War Department refused Lowe's request to reinstate the Balloon Corps as part of a regular reconnaissance unit with the Union army.

The "prejudice" of many officers that General Stoneman touched on in his letter to Lowe undoubtedly contributed to the War Department's decision. The idea of former *carnival* and *circus* performers running intelligence-gathering operations was an anathema to many of the academy-trained and war-hardened army officers.

Typical of the attitudes held by many officers were those recorded by George Armstrong Custer, the young lieutenant who accompanied James Allen on an ascent from the grounds of the Warwick Courthouse during the Peninsular Campaign:

> . . . it was a common remark in the army, when referring to any report made as the result of a balloon reconnoissance [sic], that 'it was to the interest of the aeronauts to magnify their statements and render their own importance greater, thereby insuring themselves what might be profitable employment; and they could report whatever their imagination prompted them to, with no fear of contradiction.[15]

Even in light of personal prejudices against the idea of civilians and their flying machines meshing with the ranks of a highly compartmentalized army, there was an even more grim reality that needed to be faced. The slaughter of men and the destruction of property were continuing at an alarming rate at the time balloon operations were suspended. The nation, as a whole, had no more time to waste on novel ideas concerning the war effort. The time for experimenting with fanciful contraptions of war was over. Proven concepts of technology, such as ironclad ships, the telegraph, the railroad, and the Gatling gun would remain, because their effectiveness was categorically tested on the field of battle.

The Union army Balloon Corps, in comparison, suffered the ignominious fate of being consigned to the scrap heap of military invention. It didn't matter that Thaddeus Lowe had accomplished more with his balloons in a few short years, under the most arduous of conditions, than others had in over eighty years of ballooning history. Perhaps the final reasons that aeronautics ultimately failed in the army was that Lowe's balloons were always associated with losing battles during the early years of the war, and that a device associated only with defeat was forced to bear that stigma. If

Lowe and his balloons could have only participated at the Union's watershed victory at Gettysburg, fate may have been kinder to the legacy of the Balloon Corps.

Yet, even after the war, the debate continued over whether the Union army discontinued the Balloon Corps prematurely. George McClellan, the deposed general in chief, also threw in a fond recollection of Lowe and his accomplishments, recorded in the *Official Records of the Union and Confederate Armies*, published postwar.

"To Professor Lowe, the intelligent and enterprising aeronaut, who had the management of the balloons," McClellan wrote in his acknowledgments to his staff. "I was greatly indebted for the valuable information obtained during his ascensions.[16]

Another tribute came from Gen. Adolphus W. Greely in 1900. Greely, who served with the Union army during the Civil War, was the chief officer of the U.S. Army Signal Corps who oversaw a brief revival of military aeronautics in the 1890s. Writing in the pages of *Harper's Magazine*, Greely said:

> It is surprising that such a hybrid organization as the Balloon Corps did such excellent work and held together two years. With no titular military head, it fell under the incidental care of this and that officer of engineers who chanced to serve for the time being with the commanding general of the army.[17]

However, it is possible that the greatest words of praise lauded upon the work of the Balloon Corps did not emanate from a Union officer, but from the Confederate Edwin Porter Alexander. The erstwhile balloonist, who piloted the "Silk Dress Balloon" *Gazelle* over Richmond during the peninsular campaign was promoted to ordnance chief in 1863.

From his actual, yet brief, experience as an aeronaut, Alexander probably had a deeper understanding of balloons than anyone in the Confederate army. And as an artillery chief he knew that balloons were capable of carrying observers who could survey a battlefield for miles around. Even though Union balloons were not present at Gettysburg, Alexander noted that he was careful to keep the artillery, "out of sight" near Round Top in the event that an elevated observer was in the area.[18]

Interviewed for a magazine article in 1891, Alexander gave what might have been the greatest compliment bestowed upon the Corps and an insight into the true significance that the Union army's balloons may have had upon the Confederacy's war effort.

"I have never understood why the enemy abandoned the use of military balloons early in 1863 after using them extensively up to that time," said Alexander. "Even if the observers never saw anything they would have been worth all they cost for the annoyance and delays they caused us in trying to keep our movements out of their sight."[19]

If only this fact had been understood by the Union army's decision makers, the fate of the Balloon Corps may have ended on an entirely different note.

CHAPTER SIXTEEN

After the Balloon Corps

When the Union army Balloon Corps ceased operations in the summer of 1863, military aeronautics effectively came to an end for both the Union and Confederacy. After Thaddeus Lowe's attempt to lobby a number of influential generals to reinstate his position as chief aeronaut with a full military commission, there was some movement toward reviving a revamped Balloon Corps. But nothing came of the effort other than some brief optimism on Lowe's part.

While balloon reconnaissance may have been dead as far as American military forces were concerned, the novel experiment had attracted widespread attention around the world. One foreign government even directly approached Thaddeus Lowe himself, shortly after the aeronaut's resignation from the corps.

"I was surprised to receive a letter from the Government of Brasil asking if I would form an aeronautic corps for the Brasilian army," Lowe recalled.[1] Brazil, along with Uruguay and Argentina, was then engaged in a war against Paraguay, the War of the Triple Alliance. Brazil's king, Dom Pedro II, had read reports of Lowe's Balloon Corps and was keen on adding aeronautics to his army's capabilities.

But as flattered as Lowe was to receive what he characterized as "a very handsome offer," the aeronaut reluctantly declined.

"I replied that I was not longer engaged in aeronautics but that I would be pleased to prepare a complete outfit and recommend capable army aeronauts trained by myself," Lowe said. "[I] asked if this would be acceptable to the Emperor."[2]

Not long after this, Lowe received word from Dom Pedro's government to make all of the necessary arrangements to secure military aeronauts. Lowe immediately contacted James and Ezra Allen.

The two brothers had returned to Providence, Rhode Island, after balloon operations came to an end. With Lowe's encouragement, the two men took the Brazilian government's offer.

"To do [the Allen brothers] justice I do not think that the pecuniary inducement played nearly as great a part in their decision to accept, as the novelty of the expedition," Lowe noted. "They were young, and still thrilled to the spirit of adventure. They did splendid work. . . ."[3]

Lowe occasionally received reports from the Allen brothers about their further aeronautic exploits. In one lengthy letter, Ezra Allen provided details of the duo's Brazilian adventures:

> You are no doubt feeling desirous to hear what the Allens and the balloons are doing in South America and we are at this time very happy to report to have accomplished the thing we came to do not withstanding we have had very many serious obstacles to contend with.
>
> In the first place the iron and acid that we ordered at Rio [de Janeiro] did not and has not up to this time arrived. We both thought we had taken every precaution to have everything on board of the ship that we came down in and upon the deck of the ship was assured that everything was on board, the acid iron being particularly mentioned. But upon arrival, [we] found the most important item had not been shipped upon that ship. We learned, however, that it had been put on board of another ship that sailed the same day. But be that as it may, we have not seen it yet.
>
> We, however, set to work to do something and found that a Frenchman . . . here had iron and acid at Correntios. A ship was immediately dispatched for it . . ., but upon opening the barrels found it to be wrought iron of enormous sizes from 10 penny nails up to 5, 10, and 15 pounds junk. But nothing daunted, [we] went to work to do what we could. We took the nails and the smallest iron and got the balloon inflated.

In the meantime, the General [in charge] was busy trying to get us everything we wanted and did procure at Montevideo some very nice zinc,—so far so good. We in the time of waiting, were busy making everything secure; varnished both balloons, over-hauled the nets etc., etc. James went to work and wove a nice manila rope through the large basket in place of the iron rods. We gave the balloon two coats of varnish as also we did the small one.

We have not as yet been able to get the large balloon up for the reason stated—want of material, but have been more than success-ful with the small one. We have made some ten or a dozen of the finest ascensions that we ever made.

And what we cannot say of the United States Army, it is appre-ciated by all concerned. They think it strange that an army can do without balloons for by their use we have been able to give them some very valuable information. We have kept the balloon up in front of the enemy all the time possible and the General in Com-mand, Marquis de Caxies, is more than pleased. James is now at work preparing the basket and everything to take him—General Marquis de Caxies—up.

Being in a great hurry at this time, I will close by saying that we have been successful beyond all our expectations.[4]

However, there were others who were more inclined to disagree with Ezra Allen's assessment of the success that military aeronautics enjoyed dur-ing the course of the War of the Triple Alliance. Latin American historian Harris Gaylord Warren summed up the venture by saying that the Allen brothers, "directed fourteen or more ascents to an altitude of about 50 feet. When pot shots failed to destroy this aerial reconnaissance, the Paraguayans used a crude smoke screen with good effect."[5]

Nevertheless, for the part they played in aiding the Brazilian Army to defeat Paraguay and its dictator, Solano Lopez, James and Ezra Allen were hailed as heroes. And their efforts were handsomely rewarded. The Allens reportedly received a salary of $150 a week from the government of Brazil, plus an extraordinary bonus of $10,000 at the war's end.[6]

The Allen brothers were also successful in reviving their domestic bal-looning career in the late 1860s. Although James and Ezra parted company professionally, each of them managed to independently tour the United States for many years, bringing other family members into their aerial acts.

James Allen, along with his sons James Jr. and Malvern, and eventually even his grandchildren, were active in ballooning into the 1890s. The Allen family was probably responsible for introducing ballooning to more people than any other balloonists in the late nineteenth century, taking thousands aloft.

While James and Ezra Allen were able to resume a successful and prosperous continuation of their prewar aerial work, other veterans of Civil War aeronautics faired less well. John La Mountain, Thaddeus Lowe's chief rival in the early days of balloon service in the Union army, flew sporadically after the war. La Mountain's last ascent took place in October, 1869, in Bay City, Michigan. Equipped with only a dilapidated and fragile balloon, La Mountain struggled to ascend that day. While up in the air the balloon suddenly burst. Fortunately, the remnants gathered into a parachute, which slowed La Mountain's descent. Upon impact with the ground, however, the aeronaut lost consciousness. La Mountain miraculously escaped other injury and eventually recovered. He died in Lansingburg, New York, in 1878 at the age of 48.

John Wise also faced similar problems making a go of his profession in the years following the Civil War. As a postscript to his failed attempt to secure a position as an aeronaut with the Union army, Wise attempted to collect monetary damages incurred for the loss of the balloon he demonstrated in August, 1861. Working with attorney J. B. Livingston of Lancaster, Pennsylvania, a letter detailing Wise's losses was submitted to Maj. Hartman Bache in May, 1863.

"John Wise . . . has a claim against the government for services as Aeronaut, or Balloonist, under employment of Secretary of War, Simon Cameron, and under the immediate direction of Major Bache, & Captain (now) Major Woodruff of the Topographical Engineers department, as follows," Livingston's letter read. The attorney summarized the claim in the following manner:

SERVICE FROM JULY 19, 1861 TO AUGUST 13, 1861,

with War Balloon @ $5 per day	$ 125.00
For assistants service 25 days @ $2 per day	$ 50.00
For 29 yards oiled linen & work repairing Balloon from damage sustained in crossing Aquaduct Bridge	$ 45.00
Amount in all to the sum of	$ 220.00[7]

It's not known whether Wise's claim was ever acted upon, but the aeronaut did manage to gather the means to construct additional balloons in the late 1860s and 1870s. But advanced age began to take its toll on an individual who was once hailed as America's foremost aeronaut. In 1873, Wise made one last stab at conquering the Atlantic by balloon. Working with Washington Harrison Donaldson, and briefly John Steiner, the veteran aeronaut was involved in the ill-fated balloon venture sponsored by the New York *Daily Graphic*. Unfortunately, Wise, as well as Steiner, pulled out of the project when it was discovered that the *Daily Graphic* balloon was of shoddy construction and unsafe for such an ambitious flight.

In 1879, while touring with his grandson, Wise ascended from Sterling, Illinois. The ascent involved a relatively untried balloon, and the seventy-one-year-old aeronaut was accompanied by one passenger.

Once aloft, Wise and his passenger were seen floating over remote parts of Illinois before disappearing over Lake Michigan. When sightings of the balloon ceased and there were no reports of a landing, Wise's grandson organized a search party fearing that the worst had happened. Weeks went by with no news until the body of Wise's passenger washed up on the shores of the Great Lake near Tolseston, Indiana.

John Wise's remains were never found.

As for other Union army aeronauts who flew under the auspices of Thaddeus Lowe's Balloon Corps, the postwar fortunes of these individuals was a decidedly mixed lot. Ebenezer Locke Mason, Ebenezer Seaver, and John Starkweather all faded into the ether of past glories when their terms of service with the Balloon Corps came to an end. And the scandalous Jacob Freno was also heard from no more.

John Steiner, however, continued his life in aeronautics and played a pivotal role in the next major advancement to take place in the annals of aviation. After Steiner left the Balloon Corps in the summer of 1862, he took up exhibition ballooning in earnest once again, traveling extensively in Northern states. In August, 1863, Steiner found himself in St. Paul, Minnesota, where he was making ends meet by taking paying passengers up for excursions in his balloon. During the course of his stay in St. Paul, Steiner encountered a twenty-five-year-old German count, who had recently spent several months as a foreign military observer with the Union army in northern Virginia.

The young count's name was Ferdinand von Zeppelin.

German count Ferdinand von Zeppelin (center, seated) was among the many foreign military observers attached to the Union army during the Civil War. In 1863 Zeppelin met former Balloon Corps aeronaut John Steiner in St. Paul, Minnesota, and became fascinated with lighter-than-air flight. Zeppelin's interest in flight continued even after his return to Germany and resulted in the count forming a company that created mammoth dirigible airships bearing his name in the early twentieth century. PHOTOGRAPHIC HISTORY OF THE CIVIL WAR

The exact reasons for Zeppelin's visit to Minnesota have been lost to history, but most of his biographers conclude that the count was merely touring the country following his stint as an observer for the German military. Zeppelin's trip to Minnesota would fundamentally change his life.

The young Zeppelin heard of Steiner's presence in St. Paul and eagerly sought out the aeronaut. Sharing a common bond in the German language, Zeppelin undoubtedly questioned Steiner extensively about his experiences as a civilian aeronaut. But of even more importance to the young count, the nature of military aeronautics, balloon construction, and flight characteristics were foremost topics of inquiry.

In a letter sent to his father, Zeppelin mentioned his first encounter with Steiner.

"I have made the acquaintance of the famous aeronaut Prof. Steiner, who invented a new kind of balloon suitable for military reconnaissance," Zeppelin wrote.[8]

Not long afterward, Zeppelin followed up this letter with news to his father of his first aerial adventure. During the flight, Steiner obviously revealed most of the military advantages of aeronautics as developed by Thaddeus Lowe:

> Just now I ascended with Prof. Steiner, the famous aeronaut, to an altitude of six or seven hundred feet. The ground is exceptionally fitted for demonstrating the importance of the balloon in military reconnaissance. . . . There is no tower, no elevation high enough to study the distribution of the defender's troops on the gentle, open slope behind his battle line.
>
> From the high position of the balloon these could be completely surveyed. Should one want to harass with artillery fire the troops deployed in reserve on the other slope, the battery could be informed by telegraphic signals where their projectiles hit. The above technique has at times been used with great success by this country's armies. No method is better suited to viewing quickly the terrain of an unknown, enemy-occupied region.[9]

For years after, thoughts of improving lighter-than-air craft filled Zeppelin's head. In 1891, Zeppelin retired from the German military and turned his attention toward advancing airship design. He intended to combine the envelope of a balloon, covered over a rigid airframe, filled with hydrogen. The craft would also be powered by internal combustion engines and fully navigable. The technology involved was leaps and bounds ahead of the simple balloons that had flown during the Civil War.

Years of experiment and failure went on until 1906, when Zeppelin was finally able to keep one of his airships safely aloft. Through government and public support, Zeppelin continued his experiments and the airship design was perfected to the extent that a passenger service was begun. From 1909 to 1914, Zeppelin ships made about 1,600 flights in Europe, carrying over 37,000 passengers without accident.

But with the outbreak of the First World War, Zeppelin's airships came into great demand with the German military for a far more sinister purpose. Unlike the observation balloons of the Civil War, Zeppelin airships were used not only for reconnaissance but also to carry out the first aerial bombing raids of civilian targets when squadrons of Zeppelin airships dropped incendiary bombs on London.

In the post–World War I period, Zeppelin's airship company eventually resumed passenger service, traversing thousands of miles around the world until the infamous Hindenburg disaster in 1937 effectively ended commercial lighter-than-air travel.

Zeppelin was not the only foreign military observer who was duly impressed by reconnaissance balloons. A British captain with the Royal Engineers, F. Beaumont, traveled extensively with the Union army Balloon Corps during the Peninsular Campaign. Upon his return to England in late 1862, Beaumont reported his findings in a paper presented at Chatham, Kent.

"I have been asked to give some account of my ballooning experiences in the States of America, and I do so the more readily," Beaumont said. ". . . I believe that the art, even as it at present stands, is capable of being turned to practical account."[10]

Beaumont's presentation must have had some effect. Ten years later, the Royal Balloon Detachment was formed and their balloons saw diverse reconnaissance duties over a number of British colonies in Africa.

After the loss of the "Silk Dress Balloon" *Gazelle*, the Confederate army never launched a balloon on the battlefield again. Capt. John Randolph Bryan, the hapless young officer who flew the first Confederate balloon under Joseph E. Johnston's command, returned to service on the staff of General Magruder. After the war he returned to Virginia, where he and his family maintained a dairy and fruit farm. He died in Richmond, Virginia, in 1917.[11]

Capt. Langdon Cheves, the young Confederate who told his daughters that he, "was buying up all the handsome silk dresses in Savannah," hence starting the legend of the "Silk Dress Balloon," was promoted to the rank of captain of engineers shortly after his involvement with the *Gazelle*. Cheves was in charge of the construction of Battery Wagner and other defenses on Morris Island near Charleston, South Carolina. He was killed at Battery Wagner by a shell on July 10, 1863, when the Union fleet attempted to attack Charleston Harbor.

After the capture of the *Gazelle*, Capt. Charles Cevor returned to Savannah, Georgia, where he was authorized to begin construction of a new balloon and continue work on his portable gas generator. By September, 1862,

Cevor was ready to proceed to Richmond with his new balloon, but the threat to the Confederate capital had subsided for the time being.

Unfortunately, Cevor had failed in his mission to build a workable gas generator that would have made his new balloon useful for the Confederate army in the field. Without any way to operate the balloon outside of cities with metropolitan gas supplies, Cevor's newest creation was extremely limited in its use. On October 21, 1862, Col. Francis Gilmer, chief engineer of the Department of North Virginia, ordered Cevor to report for duty with the balloon to General Beauregard's command in Charleston, South Carolina.

Cevor conducted a number of experimental ascents with his balloon in Charleston, but the new balloon never saw active service with the Confederacy. In February, 1863, Cevor's balloon was lost in a storm.[12]

Edwin Porter Alexander, the pilot of Cevor's *Gazelle*, went on to greater things following his stint as an aeronaut. In 1864, Alexander was promoted to the rank of brigadier general, and was in charge of Confederate artillery at Chancellorsville and Gettysburg. Following the war Alexander was a professor of engineering at South Carolina University, and was also employed in the oil and railroad business. He shot to fame once again in 1907 when he published his autobiography, *Memoirs of a Confederate*.

While there would be no more Confederate balloons, there was at least one report of a far-fetched aeronautical experiment. According to an article published in the *Southern Historical Society Papers* in 1900, when Robert E. Lee's army was defending Petersburg, Virginia, in 1864, the men of a Colonel McGowan's brigade were paid a curious visit by an itinerant "professor." He was known only as "Professor Blank" and he unfolded a plan to drive away the invading Yankee army:

> He had just invented an airship. In shape it was something like a bird, and for that reason he had called it 'Artis Avis,' or 'The Bird of Art.' . . .
>
> The frame was made of hoop-iron and wire. It was covered with white-oak splints. It was to be run by a one-horsepower engine, and one man to each bird was sufficient. The engine was to be in the body of the bird and to furnish power for keeping the wings in motion.
>
> A small door at the shoulder was opened or closed to control the direction of the Bird of Art. A door under the throat was

opened when it was desirable to descend and a door on top of the neck when the operator wished to go higher.[13]

The article went on to say that "in the body of the bird there was room for a number of shells, and the operator, by touching a spring with his foot, could drop them upon the enemy from a safe distance."[14]

Despite the marvelous description of Professor Blank's flying machine, the entire scheme came to naught. The professor reportedly asked the soldiers of McGowan's brigade to donate a dollar apiece to bring the flying machine to fruition. However, after collecting the donation, "the 'Professor' moved on and disappeared."[15]

With the last gasp of aeronautics aired during the war, the one man responsible for taking aerial observations from fantasy to reality retired to a postwar life as fantastic as any of his wartime exploits. In spite of all the bureaucratic travail that Thaddeus Lowe experienced, the aeronaut briefly entertained the notion of taking to the air again for the Union army. He hoped to establish a new aeronautics wing under the command of Maj. Albert Myer of the Signal Corps, and even offered his services to Maj. Gen. Quincy A. Gilmore, the commander of X Corps and, later, the Department of the South. Neither of these proposals, however, was seriously considered.[16]

Lowe also attempted to recoup some of his expenses and the wages he had agreed to waive during his final conflict with Captain Comstock, but unfortunately this also turned out to be a lost cause. Lowe estimated that he was owed $4,030.97, which included $830 in wages from April 8 to June 31, 1863. The remainder of Lowe's claim also included $1,500 for the cost of his first military balloon, *Enterprise*, $1,558.17 in travel expenses, and $142.50 for secretarial services paid to W. J. Rhees at the Smithsonian for organizing his official papers.[17]

Maj. Gen. Edward Canby reviewed Lowe's request and only allowed $280 from Lowe's total claims. Part of the problem in granting Lowe his due stemmed from the scurrilous charges that Jacob Freno had leveled at the aeronaut back in late 1862. Although Freno's charges were never substantiated, the damage caused by these allegations influenced Canby's decision to deny the bulk of Lowe's claims. The unfounded charges even worked to delay the portion of Lowe's claim that Canby was willing to allow.

"Neither should the amount be paid until Mr. Lowe can satisfactorily account for a government saddle, . . . two silk balloons . . . , and a lot of new Government tents, poles, and pins, together with a new silk balloon belonging to the Government that was conveyed by the steamer *Rotary* from the [Virginia] peninsula to Philadelphia on account of Mr. Lowe," Canby said in his conclusions.[18]

Lowe eventually appealed to his old friend Professor Joseph Henry at the Smithsonian to intervene on his behalf. After a considerable amount of time passed by, the army finally made a partial settlement with Lowe.

With service to the military now firmly in the past, Lowe turned his attentions to newer and bolder ventures. For a while the aeronaut returned to ballooning after he arranged to formally purchase the balloon *Washington* as war surplus. Lowe spent several months in Philadelphia in 1864 providing daily ascents with his tethered balloon from the corner of Coates and Fifteenth Avenue. Lowe reportedly had over 15,000 passengers during the course of his stay in the City of Brotherly Love.[19]

But the Philadelphia performances paled in comparison to the aeronautic extravaganza that Lowe later staged in New York City during the following year. On the corner of 59th Street and Sixth Avenue, Lowe presented the "Aeronautic Amphitheatre," a spectacular arena that featured freeflight balloon ascents, tethered balloon rides, large novelty balloons formed in the shapes of various animals and human figures, which were not unlike the balloons displayed at the annual Macy's Thanksgiving Day parade of a future generation.

But the spectacle hardly ended there. The Aeronautic Amphitheatre also featured a large pond with scale model warships acting out historic battle scenes and trapeze artists performing acts of derring-do from beneath Lowe's balloons. Lowe, ever the sensation monger, even managed to create more popular interest in his endeavors when he hosted an aerial honeymoon.

On November 8, 1865, Dr. John Boynton of New York wed his fiancée at the Fifth Avenue Hotel. Afterwards, the newlyweds celebrated their nuptials by ascending with Thaddeus Lowe to view the city, "from the clouds."

"I was delighted and immediately set to work to provide a suitable setting for the happy event," Lowe later recalled. "I enclosed the car of the balloon with curtains in a way to afford protection and yet not obscure the view, and the interior, capable of holding several persons, was fitted with comfortable chairs."[20]

Lowe relished the idea of providing the happy couple with a seat among the heavens to begin married life. He had originally hoped that the

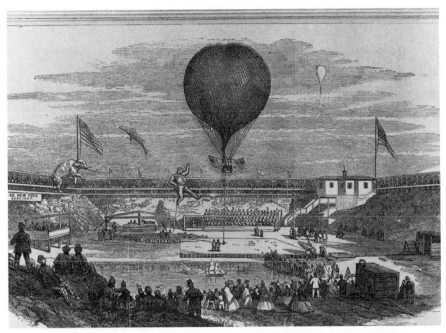

After resigning as chief aeronaut of the Union army Balloon Corps, Thaddeus Lowe continued to work in aeronautics for a while. As this illustration depicts, Lowe produced an aerial extravaganza known as the "Aeronautic Amphitheatre" on the corner of 59th Street and 6th Avenue in New York City. HARPER'S WEEKLY

marriage itself might be performed in the air, but the minister, Reverend Henry Ward Beecher, refused to leave the ground.

"Mr. Beecher, who had often sang vociferously, 'Shall I be carried to the skies on flowery beds of ease,' did not wish to be carried there by my means," Lowe noted. "[He] preferred to keep his feet firmly planted on Terra Firma."[21]

The Aeronautic Amphitheatre was simply the greatest air show of the era, presented by the country's foremost air showman. But it was also Thaddeus Lowe's last true venture in aerial adventure. In 1866, the Aeronautic Amphitheatre came to an end and Lowe returned to Pennsylvania. In Norristown, the former aeronaut established Lowe Manufacturing. There, he concentrated his efforts on building elaborate heating and refrigeration machines.

With his wife, Leontine, faithfully at his side, the early postwar years were contented ones for Thaddeus Lowe. The first of the Lowe's ten children was born, a baby daughter named Louise.[22] In April, 1867, Lowe was granted a patent for an ice-making machine that he had high hopes of obtaining success in commercial application. Lowe even outfitted a steam cargo ship with his ice-making machinery. Working with a group of investors, Lowe was able to raise the enormous sum of $87,000 for the venture. In the spring of 1869, the *William Tabor* sailed from San Francisco around Cape Horn to New York, carrying perishable California produce. Lowe's refrigeration machinery performed flawlessly and the *William Tabor's* cargo arrived safely.[23]

Unfortunately, the scheme to refrigerate shipboard cargo was an idea too far ahead of its time. Operational costs proved to be too high to justify the cost of further installations. But Lowe was as undaunted as ever. Working off smaller versions of his patented invention, Lowe was able to sell his refrigeration devices to small companies selling artificial ice.[24]

For a time Lowe was also involved with developing a more economical source of heating and illumination gas. Using the waste coke that was left over from the production of coal gas, Lowe was to extract water gas from what had previously been considered worthless slag. Eventually Lowe was able to profitably market this process to a number of communities in the eastern United States and also Europe, enabling the construction of city gas works outside major metropolitan areas. For his advancement in the production of gas, Lowe was awarded the Franklin Institute's highly coveted "Grand Medal of Honor" in 1887. In 1891, Lowe was internationally recognized by the Paris Academy of Industry and Science for his scientific achievements.[25]

In 1886, at the age of 54, Thaddeus Lowe decided to reinvent his life one more time. With a small fortune amassed, Thaddeus, Leontine, and the younger members of the Lowe clan pulled up stakes in Norristown and moved to the sunny climate of southern California. The Lowes settled in Pasadena at the foot of the San Gabriel mountains. Although Lowe was at an age when most men of his era were close to retirement, the ever restless inventor took on one final challenge.

From Pasadena looking out toward the San Gabriels, Lowe envisioned a "White City of the Clouds." The "City" was to consist of a lavish tavern, hotel, and even an astronomical observatory. To establish his vision Lowe first needed to build a complex, cable-driven, narrow-gauge railroad that would snake its way up the steep mountain pass. Once again, Lowe went to work courting investors for his ambitious plan. When he was finally able to seal a deal for financing, the 6,100 foot peak atop Echo Mountain was dubbed Mount Lowe.

In 1891, construction on the Great Cable Incline—alternatively known as the Mount Lowe Railway—began. Despite the intense engineering challenges involved with its construction the incline railway opened on July 4, 1893.

Lowe's astronomical observatory opened in 1894 and became an international attraction. Typically, Lowe spared no expense in the observatory and hired world-renowned astronomers such as Lewis Swift and Edgar Lucien Larkin as directors of the facility.[26]

By 1894, Lowe's "City in the Clouds" included the Ye Alpine Tavern and the lavish Echo Mountain House, a forty-room, three-story hotel built at the summit of Mount Lowe. It was the inventor's crowning achievement, but unfortunately "The City in the Clouds" also proved to be Lowe's ultimate financial undoing. Although Lowe's various operations in the San Gabriel mountains were extremely popular tourist destinations in the early 1890s, the financial panic of 1893 along with mounting operational costs of the incline railroad and hotels exceeded Lowe's financial resources. In 1898 Lowe was forced to sell his interest in the "City in the Clouds" for $175,000, a small fraction of the total amount of money invested in the venture.[27]

Despite the financial setback, Thaddeus Lowe was not defeated. Indefatigable as ever, Lowe returned to marketing his patents for gas production and refrigeration and founded a number of profitable enterprises in southern California. In the early twentieth century—with Count Zeppelin's dirigibles making aviation news—Lowe even briefly entertained the idea of returning to aeronautics once again. He went as far as organizing the Lowe Airship Construction Corporation with the idea of attracting investors to his plans, but the effort came to naught.

On May 16, 1912, Leontine Lowe passed away. With Leontine's death Lowe's zest for life quickly left him. Partially paralyzed by a fractured hip he suffered during a trip to Norristown in 1911, Lowe's health declined rapidly. On January 16, 1913, Thaddeus Sobieski Constantine Lowe died at his home in Pasadena at the age of 81.

If anything, the legacy of Lowe's vision of aeronautics during the Civil War clearly pointed the way to the future. While the Union army never again ventured into ballooning during the Civil War, the concept of military aeronautics was not altogether a dead issue. In 1891, the United States

Army once again delved into ballooning when Gen. Adolphus W. Greely was given the duty of organizing a new balloon unit under the auspices of the Signal Corps. Funding was limited for the balloon's new military role, but the unit still managed to carry out experiments in aerial photography and telephone communications during the 1890s.

During the early part of the twentieth century Wilbur and Orville Wright brought aeronautics to the forefront again when they were successful in demonstrating their airplane at Kitty Hawk, North Carolina, in 1903. By the early 1910s the airplane had supplanted the balloon in military aviation, and some of the early accomplishments of the Union Army Balloon Corps were hailed as remarkable achievements by a completely new generation of pilots.

In 1911, Eugene Ely performed the first takeoff and landing of an airplane from the deck of a warship in San Francisco Bay, mirroring the idea that Lowe pioneered with his balloon support barge, the *George Washington Parke-Custis*. Lt. Thomas Selfridge, at the controls of a Wright Model B biplane, sent the first air-to-ground wireless communication during the San Francisco Air Show in 1912, scarcely more than fifty years after Lowe sent his first telegraph message from the balloon *Enterprise* to Abraham Lincoln in Washington, D.C.

If Thaddeus Lowe and the other aeronauts who served for both the Union and Confederate armies had been allowed to continue their efforts and aerial exploits they may have been able to make a more significant contribution toward hastening rapid closure to one of the most horrific conflicts in the history of mankind. But the discussion of what could have been is a topic that can only be left to speculation.

Taken at their own record, however, the aeronauts of the Civil War proved themselves to be genuine pioneers of the air in the truest sense.

NOTES

CHAPTER ONE: A YANKEE AERONAUT BEHIND CONFEDERATE LINES

1. T.S.C. Lowe, *My Balloons In Peace and War*, 35 (unpublished manuscript). Transcribed by Augustine Lowe Brownbeck, 1931, National Air & Space Museum, Washington, D.C.
2. Lowe, *My Balloons in Peace and War*, 33.
3. Ibid., 34.
4. Cincinnati *Daily Commercial*, "A Night Balloon Ascension!" April 20, 1861, 1.
5. Ibid.
6. Lowe, *My Balloons in Peace and War*, 10.
7. Ibid., 35.
8. Ibid., 36.
9. Ibid.
10. T.S.C. Lowe, "Professor Lowe's Experience With Balloons," *Scientific American*, February 2, 1895, 71.
11. Ibid., 37–38.
12. F. Stansbury Hayden, *Aeronautics in the Union and Confederate Armies* (Baltimore: The Johns Hopkins Press, 1941), 163.
13. Lowe, *My Balloons in Peace and War*, 40.
14. Ibid.
15. The city's name was shortened to Union after the Civil War to avoid confusion with Unionville, North Carolina.
16. Lowe, *My Balloons in Peace and War*, 43.
17. Ibid., 41.
18. Ibid., 42.
19. Ibid.
20. Ibid., 46.

21. Ibid., 46, 47.
22. Ibid., 48.
23. Ibid.
24. Ibid., 49.
25. Ibid.
26. Ibid., 51–52.
27. Ibid., 52.
28. Ibid., 53.
29. Ibid., 54.
30. Ibid.
31. Cincinnati *Daily Commercial*, "Return of Professor Lowe," April 27, 1861, 1.

CHAPTER TWO: A BRIEF HISTORY OF EARLY BALLOONING

1. Eric Hodgins and F. Alexander Magoun, *Sky High, The Story of Aviation* (Boston: Little, Brown, and Company, 1935), 20.
2. Ibid., 21–22.
3. Ibid., 22.
4. Carl van Doren, *Benjamin Franklin* (New York: Viking Press, 1938), 700.
5. Although all non-powered lighter-than-air vehicles are generically classified as balloons, for many years there was a distinct difference in nomenclature between hot-air and gas-filled balloons. Hot-air balloons were often referred to as "montgolfiers" in honor of their original creators, while the terms "balloons" and, for a short period "charliéres," in honor of Jacques Charles, were applied to gas-filled conveyances. Further compounding the confusion was the term "aerostat," a corruption of the phrase "aerial station," which was also commonly applied to both gas-filled and hot-air vehicles. Additionally, the entire science relating to ballooning became known as "aerostatics." Eventually the distinctions blurred as non-powered, lighter-than-air vehicles were simply referred to as balloons. However, the aforementioned terms were frequently and often interchangeably used throughout the eighteenth and nineteenth centuries.
6. Although the use of a wicker basket to contain these first aeronauts came about by happenstance, wicker also proved to be one of the lightest materials that could be use for a control basket and also provide the greatest shock absorption upon landing. Even today virtually all freeflight balloons use wicker in the construction of control baskets.

7. Don Dwiggins, *The Complete Book of Airships Dirigibles, Blimps & Hot Air Balloons* (Blue Ridge Summit, Pennsylvania: TAB Books, 1980), 15.

8. Alvin M. Josephy, Editor, *The American Heritage History of Flight* (New York: American Heritage Publishing Company, 1962), 41.

9. Tom D. Crouch, *The Eagle Aloft* (Washington, D.C.: Smithsonian Institution Press, 1983), 31.

10. Ibid., 37.

11. Benjamin Franklin to John Ingenhauz, January 16, 1784, John Bigelow, Editor, *The Complete Works of Benjamin Franklin*, Volume VIII, (New York: G.P. Putnam's sons, 1888), 432–33.

12. Josephy, ed., *The American Heritage History of Flight*, 44.

13. Thomas Martyn's military applications for balloons appeared in a work entitled *Hints of Important Uses To Be Derived From Aerostatic Globes* published in 1784. The author described how lanterns and pyrotechnics could be used to signal ground forces from tethered balloons regarding enemy troop movements.

14. Dwiggins, *The Complete Book of Airships. . .*, 16.

15. Edita Lausanne, *The Romance of Ballooning—The Story of the Early Aeronauts* (New York: A Studio Book, 1971), 41.

16. L.T.C. Rolt, *The Aeronauts—A History of Ballooning 1783–1903* (New York: Walker and Company, 1966), 123.

17. John Wise, *Through The Air* (Philadelphia: To-Day Publishing Company, 1873), 249.

18. Ibid., 249.

19. Ibid., 258.

20. Ibid., 281–82.

21. Crouch, *The Eagle Aloft*, 187.

22. Ibid.

23. L.T.C. Rolt, *The Aeronauts*, 116.

24. Crouch, *The Eagle Aloft*, 190.

25. Ibid., 197.

CHAPTER THREE: THE GREAT TRANSATLANTIC QUEST

1. John Wise, *Through The Air*, 600.

2. Crouch, *The Eagle Aloft*, 197.

3. Wise, *Through The Air*, 375.

4. Ibid., 427.

5. Ibid.

6. Ibid., 430.

7. John Steiner, "Crossing The Ocean In A Balloon," *Harper's Weekly*, July 10, 1858, 438.

8. During his early career as a balloonist and scientific lecturer, Lowe adopted the name Calincourt, which he believed to be more theatrical than Thaddeus.

9. Lowe, *My Balloons in Peace and War*, 1.

10. Ibid., 1–2.

11. Eugene Block, *Above The Civil War—The Story of Thaddeus Lowe* (Berkeley, California: Howell-North Books, 1966), p. 15. This is the only reference to the professor's name.

12. Lowe, *My Balloons in Peace and War*, 2.

13. Ibid., 3.

14. Ibid., 5.

15. Ibid., 4.

16. Block, *Above The Civil War*, 21, 23.

17. John Wise, "To All Publishers Of Newspapers On The Globe," *Lancaster Intelligencer*, Lancaster, Pennsylvania, June 1843. Also, Kurt R. Stehliung and William Beller, *Skyhooks* (New York: Doubleday & Company, 1962), 64–65.

18. *Skyhooks*, Ibid., 65.

19. Crouch, *The Eagle Aloft*, 246.

20. Ibid., 248.

21. Ibid.

22. Ibid.

23. Munson Baldwin, *With Brass and Gas: An Illustrated and Embellished Chronicle of Ballooning in Mid-Nineteenth Century America*, Boston: Beacon Press, 1967, 65, quoting the Troy *Times*, June 14, 1859, 1.

24. Ibid., 85.

25. Ibid., 88, quoting William Hyde, St. Louis *Republican*, July 8, 1859.

26. Ibid., 91.

27. Ibid., 93.

28. Ibid., 94.

29. Ibid., 95–96.

30. Ibid., 100.

31. Ibid., 103.

32. George Demers quoting John La Mountain, Troy *Times*, July, 1859, from Baldwin, *With Brass and Gas*, 140–1.

33. *Harper's Weekly*, September 24, 1859, 1.

34. Baldwin, *With Brass and Gas*, 153.

35. Ibid., 160.

36. Lowe, *My Balloons in Peace and War*, 15.

37. Ibid., 17.

38. Blondin was a popular nineteenth-century circus performer renowned for tightrope walking on ice skates.

39. From *City Items*, "Jonathon to Lowe," by Jacques Maurice, also from Baldwin, *With Brass and Gas*, 236.

40. John Wise to the editors of the New York *Express*, October 29, 1859, also in Baldwin, *With Brass and Gas*, 230.

41. John La Mountain to Mary La Mountain, September 1, 1859, also in Baldwin, *With Brass and Gas*, 154.

42. John A. Haddock, *Mr. Haddock's Account Of His Hazardous And Exciting Voyage In The Balloon "Atlantic" With Professor John La Mountain* (Philadelphia: Press of Haddock and Son, 1872), 12–13.

43. Lowe, *My Balloons in Peace and War*, 18.

44. Ibid., 20.

45. Garrick Mallory, "A Ride In The Mammoth Of The Air," Philadelphia *Inquirer*, June 30, 1860, 1.

46. John Wise to T.S.C. Lowe, September 9, 1860, from Crouch, *The Eagle Aloft*, 275.

47. Lowe, *My Balloons in Peace and War*, John C. Cresson, *et al* to Joseph Henry, December, 1860, 32.

48. Lowe, *My Balloons in Peace and War*, Joseph Henry to T.S.C. Lowe, January, 1861, 33.

49. Following the Civil War there was only one attempt in the immediate postwar years to cross the Atlantic Ocean by balloon. Sponsored by the New York *Daily Graphic*, the balloon was piloted by Washington Harrison Donaldson, Alfred Ford, and George Lunt. The flight, however, was not successful and the aeronauts were forced to land before embarking on the open sea. It wasn't until 1978, when Larry Anderson, Ben Abruzzo, and Maxie Anderson finally conquered the goal that had eluded balloonists for over a hundred years, when the *Double Eagle II* made the journey from Presque, Maine, to Miserey, France.

CHAPTER FOUR: CREATING AN ARMY IN THE AIR

1. Lowe, *My Balloons in Peace and War*, 56.

2. Hayden, *Aeronautics in the Union* . . ., 25–27.

3. John Wise, "Easy Method of Capturing the Castle of Vera Cruz," Philadelphia *Ledger*, October 26, 1846.

4. Lowe, *My Balloons in Peace and War*, Salmon Chase to Murat Halstead, May 20, 1861, 56–57.

5. Ibid., Murat Halstead to T.S.C. Lowe, May 23, 1861, 57.

6. Ibid.

7. *Providence Post*, April 19, 1861. James Allen Scrapbooks, vol. 1, 45, box 228, *Archives of the Institute of Aerospace Sciences, 1783–1962,* History Collection, Library of Congress. (Cited hereafter as *AIAA*, LC)

8. Unidentified clipping in James Allen scrapbook, *AIAA*, LC.

9. Brig. Gen. Henry L. Abbot, U.S. Army, Retired, "Early Experience With Balloons In War," *Professional Memoirs, Corps of Engineers* (Washington, D.C.: U.S. Army and Engineer Department at Large, September/October, 1912), p. 681.

10. Ibid.

11. Ibid.

12. Lt. Henry L. Abbot to Capt. Amiel Whipple, July 9, 1861, *AIAA*, LC.

13. Ibid.

14. *War Of The Rebellion: A Compilation of the Official Records of the Union and Confederate Armies*, (128 vols., Washington, D.C.: Government Printing Office, 1899–1901, vol. 3, ser. 3, 301 (hereafter referred to as *OR*).

15. Lowe, *My Balloons in Peace and War*, 57.

16. *OR*, vol. 3, ser. 3, 254.

17. William Jones Rhees, "Reminiscences Of Ballooning In The Civil War," *The Chautauquan*, June 1898, 260.

18. Lowe, *My Balloons in Peace and War*, 60. Also found in Frank Moore, *Rebellion Record I* [Diary], (New York: G.P. Putnam, 1861), 108.

19. Lowe, *My Balloons in Peace and War*, 61.

20. Washington *Evening Star*, June 19, 1861.

21. Editorial, New York *Herald*, June 20, 1861.

22. *OR*, vol. 3, ser. 3, 254–55.

23. *OR*, vol. 3, ser. 3, 255, and Lowe, *My Balloons in Peace and War*, 63.

24. Ibid.

25. Frank Moore, ed., *The Rebellion Record: A Diary of American Events*, second volume. (New York: G.P. Putnam, 1862), Diary 6. Also New York *Herald*, June 26, 1861.

26. Report, Brig. Gen. Daniel Tyler to Gen. Edwin McDowell, June 24, 1861. Letters Received, Department of Northern Virginia.

27. *OR*, vol.3, ser. 3, 255, and Lowe, *My Balloons in Peace and War*, 63.

28. John Wise to Simon Cameron, May 3, 1861, MS W72 Letters Received, Secretary of War, War Department Division, National Archives, College Park, Md. (cited hereafter as NA).

29. John Wise, *Through The Air: A Narrative of Forty Years' Experience As An Aeronaut* (New York: To-Day Printing and Publishing, 1873), 554.

30. F. Stansbury Hayden, *Aeronautics . . .*, 61.

31. Ibid., 61–62.

32. *OR*, vol. 3, ser. 3, 256.

33. Lowe, *My Balloons in Peace and War*, 63.

34. Ibid., 63.

35. Ibid., 64.

36. John La Mountain to Secretary of War Simon Cameron, May 7, 1861. National Archives, War Department Division.

37. Ibid.

38. Petition, Citizens of Troy, New York, to Secretary of War Simon Cameron, May 1, 1861, NA.

39. *Op cit.* La Mountain to Cameron.

40. Benjamin Butler, *Private and Official Correspondence of General Benjamin F. Butler During The Period Of The Civil War* (Norwood, Massachusetts, 1917), 132.

41. John La Mountain to Maj. Gen. Benjamin F. Butler, June 10, 1861, from *Private and Official Correspondence of General Benjamin F. Butler*, (Plimpton, Massachusetts: Privately Issued, 1917), 132.

42. Lowe, *My Balloons in Peace and War*, 64.

43. John Wise, *Through The Air*, 554.

44. Ibid.

45. Lowe, *My Balloons in Peace and War*, 63, and *OR*, vol. 3, ser. 3, 256.

46. Ibid.

47. F. Stansbury Hayden, *Aeronautics . . .*, 66.

48. John Wise, *Through The Air*, 554.

49. Ibid., 554.

50. Capt. Daniel T. Davis, "The Air Role in the War Between the States." *Air University Review*, July–August, 1976, 13.

51. John Wise, *Through The Air*, 554.

52. *OR*, vol. 3, ser. 3, 257, Thaddeus Lowe to Maj. Hartman Bache, July 29, 1861.

53. Lowe, *My Balloons in Peace and War*, 64.

54. Ibid., 65.

55. Ibid., 65.

56. Abraham Lincoln to Gen. Winfield Scott, July 25, 1861. Original note in Lowe Collection, National Air & Space Museum, Washington, D.C.
57. Lowe, *My Balloons in Peace and War*, 65.
58. Ibid., 65.
59. Ibid., 66.
60. Ibid.
61. Ibid.

CHAPTER FIVE: EARLY OPERATIONS

1. Arlington House was the home of Confederate general Robert E. Lee in the years leading up to the Civil War. It was here, in 1861, that Lee wrote the letter resigning his commission from the U.S. Army to fight for his native Virginia. After leaving for Richmond, he never returned to the house. A wartime law required that property owners in areas occupied by Federal troops appear in person to pay their taxes. Unable to comply with this rule, the Lees saw the estate confiscated in 1864. The land was subsequently set aside for Arlington National Cemetery.
2. Lowe, *My Balloons in Peace and War*, 70.
3. Ibid., 71.
4. Thaddeus Lowe to War Department, July 28, 1861, Lowe papers, *AIAA*, LC.
5. Lowe, *My Balloons in Peace and War*, Capt. Amiel Whipple to Thaddeus Lowe, July 29, 1861, 71. Also, *OR*, vol. 3, ser. 3, 258.
6. Lowe, *My Balloons in Peace and War*, 72.
7. Ibid.
8. Hayden, *Aeronautics . . .*, 197. Also Capt. Amiel Whipple to Capt. Israel Woodruff, August 1, 1861, MS W 912, Letter Received, Bureau of Topographical Engineers.
9. Lowe, *My Balloons in Peace and War*, 77, and *OR*, vol. 3, ser. 3, 258–59. Joseph Henry to Capt. Amiel Whipple, August 2, 1861.
10. Wise, *Through The Air*, 555.
11. Lowe, *My Balloons in Peace and War*, 69.
12. *OR*, vol. 3, ser. 3, Capt. Amiel Whipple to T.S.C. Lowe, August 2, 1861.
13. Ibid.
14. Although the outpost on Old Point Comfort is now officially referred to as Fort Monroe, it was alternately referred to by both military officials and the press as Fortress Monroe during the Civil War period. For

purposes of consistency, it will be referred to as Fortress Monroe in this work.

15. Alfred H. Guernsey and Henry M. Alden, *Harper's Pictorial History Of The Great Rebellion, Part First* (Chicago: McDonnel Brothers, 1866), 186.

16. OR, vol. 3, ser. 3, Report, Gen. Benjamin F. Butler to Col. Thomas Scott, assistant secretary of war, August 8, 1861, 600.

17. OR, vol. 3, ser. 3, 572, Gen. J. Bankhead Magruder to Headquarters, Bethel, Virginia, August 9, 1861.

18. John Wise, *A System Of Aeronautics* (Philadelphia: Joseph A. Speel, 1850), 266.

19. OR, vol. 3, ser. 3, 600–01, Report, John La Mountain to Gen. Benjamin F. Butler, August 10, 1861.

20. Benjamin F. Butler, *Private and Official Correspondence of General Benjamin F. Butler*, vol. 1, April, 1860 to June, 1861 (Plimpton, Massachusetts: Privately Issued, 1917), 183.

21. OR, vol. 3, ser. 3, 568, Report, Gen. Benjamin F. Butler to Headquarters Department of Virginia, August 8, 1861.

22. OR, vol. 3, ser. 3, 572, Report, Gen. J. Bankhead Magruder to Headquarters, Bethel, Virginia, August 9, 1861.

23. *Scientific American*, "Balloon Reconnaissance," August 17, 1861, 104.

24. Frank Moore, ed., *The Rebellion Record: A Diary of American Events*, Second Volume. (New York: G.P. Putnam, 1862), Diary, 63. Also New York *Times*, August 13, 1861.

25. OR, vol. 3, ser. 3, 600, Report, Maj. Gen. Benjamin F. Butler to Lt. Gen. Winfield Scott, August 10, 1861.

26. Benjamin F. Butler, *Private and Official Correspondence of Gen. Benjamin F. Butler*, vol. 1, April, 1860 to June, 1861, (Plimpton, Massachusetts: Privately Issued, 1917), 206.

27. Ibid, 210–11.

28. Ibid., 211.

29. New York *Times*, "From Fortress Monroe," August 17, 1861, 1.

30. Lowe, *My Balloons in Peace and War*, 62.

31. Report, Maj. Gen. John Ellis Wool to Secretary of War Simon Cameron, September 18, 1861, NA.

32. Frank Leslie to T.S.C. Lowe, June 20, 1861.

33. Lowe, *My Balloons in Peace and War*, 77.

34. Washington *Star*, June 26, 1861.

35. Cincinnati *Commercial*, June 28, 1861.

CHAPTER SIX: THE UNION ARMY BALLOON CORPS

1. Philadelphia *Inquirer*, "Professor Lowe to Build a Mammoth Balloon for the Government," August 6, 1861, 1.
2. Patricia Faust, ed., *Historical Times Illustrated Encyclopedia of the Civil War*, (New York: Harper & Row, Publishers, 1986), 36.
3. Maj. Hartman Bache to Gen. Irvin McDowell, August 17, 1861, *AIAA*, LC.
4. Edward Hagerman, *The American Civil War and the Origins of Modern Warfare* (Indianapolis: Indiana University Press, 1988), 36.
5. *OR*, vol. 3, ser. 3, 260, Maj. I.C. Woodruff to T.S.C. Lowe, August 28, 1861.
6. *OR*, vol. 3, ser. 3, 260, letter from Capt. A.W. Whipple to T.S.C. Lowe, August, 29, 1861.
7. Ibid., Lowe narrative.
8. Ibid.
9. Lowe, *My Balloons in Peace and War*, 79.
10. *OR*, vol. 3, ser. 3, 260.
11. T.S.C. Lowe to Brig. Gen. Fitz-John Porter, September 7, 1861, NA.
12. T.S.C. Lowe to Brig. Gen. Fitz-John Porter, September 9, 1861, NA.
13. Lowe, *My Balloons in Peace and War*, Gen. Fitz-John Porter to T.S.C. Lowe, September 10, 1861, 79.
14. Francis Trevelyan Miler, editor in chief, *The Photographic History of the Civil War, Volume V* (New York: The Review of Reviews Co., 1911), 96.
15. Lowe, *My Balloons in Peace and War*, Gen. Fitz-John Porter to T.S.C. Lowe, September 11, 1861, 80.
16. Ibid., Gen. Fitz-John Porter to T.S.C. Lowe, September 18, 1861, 80.
17. Ibid., 81.
18. Ibid.
19. Ibid.
20. Gen. William Smith to Gen. George B. McClellan, September 20, 1861, NA.
21. *OR*, vol. 3, ser. 3, 262, Gen. W.F. Smith to T.S.C. Lowe, September 23, 1861.
22. Francis Trevelyan Miler, editor in chief, *The Photographic History of the Civil War, Volume V* (New York: The Review of Reviews Co., 1911), 76.

23. Lowe, *My Balloons in Peace and War*, 82, and *OR*, vol. 3, ser. 3, 263, Lt. James F. McQuesten, aide-de-camp, to T.S.C. Lowe, September 24, 1861.

24. Lowe, *My Balloons in Peace and War*, 82, and *OR*, vol. 3, ser. 3, 263, Brig. Gen. William Farrar Smith to T.S.C. Lowe, September 24, 1861.

25. Lowe, *My Balloons in Peace and War*, 82.

26. Pierre Toutant Gustave Beauregard to Col. G.B. Anderson, October 15, 1861.

27. Lowe, *My Balloons in Peace and War*, 83.

28. Ibid., 83.

29. Lowe, *My Balloons in Peace and War*, 83, and also Robert Underwood Johnson and Clarence Lough Buell, *Battles and Leaders of the Civil War, Volume III* (New York: Thomas Yoseloff Inc. (reprint), 1956, 400–01. The incident to which Longstreet referred occurred during the battle of Seven Pines, May 31, 1862.

30. Lowe, *My Balloons in Peace and War*, 83

31. Lowe, *My Balloons in Peace and War*, 83, and *OR*, vol. 3, ser. 3, 264, Brig. Gen. Montgomery C. Meigs, quartermaster general, to T.S.C. Lowe, September 25, 1861.

32. *OR*, vol. 3, ser. 3, 264.

33. Lowe, *My Balloons in Peace and War*, 84–85, and *OR*, vol 3, scr. 3, 265.

34. Ibid.

35. Philadelphia *Inquirer*, "Professor Lowe's Truant Balloon," October 19, 1861, 4.

36. Ibid.

37. Capt. Frederick E. Beaumont, Royal Engineers, "On Balloon Reconnaissance As Practised By The American Army," paper read at Chatham, November 14, 1862. Reprinted in *Military Ballooning 1862* (Middlesex, England: Aviation Press, 1967), 29.

38. Ibid.

39. Ibid.

40. Ibid., 29–30.

41. T.S.C Lowe to John Starkweather, January 26, 1862.

42. Based on a photo of Lowe's generators being tested in front of the unfinished capitol building in Washington, late 1861. As published in Ronald H. Bailey, *Forward to Richmond* (Alexandria, Virginia: Time-Life Books, 1983), 146–47.

43. The *Enterprise* was permanently retired from service shortly after the *Union* entered into service in the summer of 1861.

44. Philadelphia *Inquirer*, "Government Balloons," October 22, 1861, 8.
45. Ebenezer Seaver to T.S.C. Lowe, December 17, 1861, Lowe Papers, *AIAA*, LC.
46. Col. John N. Macomb to Maj. S. Williams, assistant adjutant general, Army of the Potomac, August 24, 1861, NA.
47. Col. John N. Macomb to Maj. Hartman Bache, October 23, 1861.

CHAPTER SEVEN: THE BATTLE OF EGOS
1. John La Mountain to Gen. John E. Wool, Fortress Monroe, September 2, 1861, NA.
2. A.B. Lockstader, Secretary of Citizen's Committee of Lansingsburg, New York, to Gen. Benjamin Butler, July 31, 1861. From Benjamin Butler, *Private and Official Correspondence of General Benjamin F. Butler During the Period of the Civil War* (Norwood, Massachusetts, 1917), 132.
3. Ibid.
4. John La Mountain to General Wool, September 6, 1861, NA.
5. Gen. William Smith to Col. Robert B. Marcy, September 20, 1861, NA.
6. Gen. Fitz-John Porter to Col. R.B. Marcy, September 21, 1861, NA.
7. Ibid.
8. Ibid.
9. Ibid.
10. Ibid.
11. Timothy J. Dennée, "John La Mountain and the Alexandria Balloon Ascensions," *Historic Alexandria Quarterly*, Fall 1997, vol. 2, no. 3, 5.
12. New York *Herald*, October 6, 1861.
13. *OR*, vol. 5, ser. 1, p. 490, Gen. William Buell Franklin to Maj. Gen. George B. McClellan, October 3, 1861.
14. Maj. A.W. Whipple to Lt. Col. John N. Macomb, October 16, 1861, NA.
15. Gen. William Buell Franklin to Maj. Gen. George McClellan, October 19, 1861, *AIAA*, LC.
16. Jefferson Davis, *The Rise and Fall of the Confederate Government, Volume I* (New York: D. Appleton & Company, 1881), 452.
17. *Scientific American*, November 2, 1861, 284.
18. John La Mountain to Gen. William Buell Franklin, October 21, 1861, NA.
19. Ibid.

20. Report, Col. John N. Macomb to Headquarters, Army of the Potomac, October 26, 1861, NA.

21. Frank Moore, ed., *The Rebellion Record—A Diary Of American Events—Third Volume* (New York: G.P. Putnam, 1862). Citing an article that appeared in the Cincinnati *Gazette*, October 22, 1861.

22. "Frank" [War Correspondent], Boston *Journal*, November 22, 1861, 3.

23. John La Mountain to Gen. William Buell Franklin, December 21, 1861, NA.

24. Ibid.

25. Ibid.

26. Gen. William Buell Franklin to Col. John N. Macomb, December 21, 1861, NA.

27. Lowe, *My Balloons in Peace and War*, 87–88.

28. Ibid., T.S.C. Lowe to Lt. Col. A.V. Colburn, December 3, 1861, 91–92.

29. Ibid.

30. Clovis Lowe to T.S.C. Lowe, December 15, 1861, NA.

31. Clovis Lowe to T.S.C. Lowe, December 19, 1861, NA.

32. Special Requisition For Two Balloons, Nets, and Valves, signed John La Mountain, aeronaut, Brig. Gen. W.B. Franklin, undated (probably late December, 1861), NA.

33. T.S.C. Lowe to Gen. George B. McClellan, December 18, 1861.

34. Ibid.

35. T.S.C. Lowe to Col. A.V. Colburn, December 18, 1861, Library of Congress.

36. Col. John N. Macomb to T.S.C. Lowe, February 15, 1862, NA.

37. Ibid., note attached.

38. Col. John N. Macomb to T.S.C. Lowe, February 17, 1862, NA.

39. Ibid., note attached.

40. John Steiner to T.S.C. Lowe, February 15, 1862.

41. T.S.C. Lowe to Gen. Seth Williams, February 19, 1862.

42. Ibid.

43. Col. John N. Macomb to Gen. Seth Williams, February 24, 1862, NA.

44. John La Mountain to Gen. William F. Franklin, March 8, 1862, NA.

45. Gen. William B. Franklin to Col. Robert Barnes Marcy, March 8, 1862, NA.

46. Philadelphia *Inquirer*, March 19, 1862, 1.

CHAPTER EIGHT: DISILLUSIONED AERONAUTS

1. Lowe, *My Balloons in Peace and War*, 86.
2. Ibid., 97, T.S.C. Lowe to Lieutenant Colonel Colburn, November 12, 1861.
3. Ibid.
4. *OR*, vol. 3, ser. 3, 266, T.S.C Lowe to Lt. Col. Colburn, November 21, 1861.
5. Don Dwiggins, *The Air Devils* (New York: J.B. Lippincott, 1966), 42.
6. Lowe, *My Balloons in Peace and War*, Lt. Col. A.V. Colburn to T.S.C. Lowe, November 22, 1861, 88.
7. Special Correspondent, New York *Herald*, November 13, 1861, 1.
8. Ibid.
9. Lowe, *My Balloons in Peace and War*, 89, Gen. Joseph Hooker to T.S.C. Lowe, November 24, 1861.
10. Col. William F. Small to Gen. Joseph Hooker, December 9, 1861, *AIAA*, LC.
11. F. Stansbury Hayden, *Aeronautics in the Union . . .*, 261.
12. Lowe, *My Balloons in Peace and War*, 89, T.S.C. Lowe to Brig. Gen. Thomas W. Sherman.
13. Dumas Malone, ed., *Dictionary of American Biography* vol. XVII (New York: Charles Scribner's Sons, 1933), 33.
14. John Starkweather to T.S.C. Lowe, March 10, 1862, *AIAA*, LC.
15. John B. Starkweather to T.S.C. Lowe, April 15, 1862, *AIAA*, LC.
16. John B. Starkweather to T.S.C. Lowe, January 7, 1862, *AIAA*, LC.
17. John Starkweather to T.S.C. Lowe, June 13, 1862, *AIAA*, LC.
18. John Starkweather to T.S.C. Lowe, September 14, 1862, *AIAA*, LC.
19. John H. Steiner to T.S.C. Lowe, January 20, 1862, *AIAA*, LC.
20. James McPherson, *The Battle Cry of Freedom* (New York: Oxford University Press, 1988), 313.
21. Don Dwiggins, *The Air Devils* (New York: J.B. Lippincott Company, 1966), 42.
22. Gen. Lorenzo Thomas, adjutant general, March 18, 1862, NA.
23. St. Louis *Daily Missouri Democrat*, March 28, 1862. Also, footnote, F. Stansbury Hayden, *Aeronautics In The Union . . . ,* 395.
24. Philadelphia *Inquirer*, "Skirmish At Pittsburgh Landing," March 24, 1861, 1.
25. John L. Steiner to T.S.C. Lowe, March 26, 1862, *AIAA*, LC.
26. John H. Steiner to T.S.C. Lowe, April 15, 1862, *AIAA*, LC.
27. John H. Steiner to T.S.C. Lowe, June 9, 1862, *AIAA*, LC.

28. Philadelphia *Inquirer*, March 14, 1862, 8.

29. Ibid.

30. John H. Steiner to Gen. John Pope, June 16, 1862, NA.

31. John H. Steiner to T.S.C. Lowe, March 8, 1862, *AIAA*, LC.

32. John H. Steiner to T.S.C. Lowe, April 15, 1862, *AIAA*, LC.

CHAPTER NINE: THE BALLOON CORPS AND THE PENINSULAR CAMPAIGN

1. Lowe, *My Balloons in Peace and War*, 140.

2. Ibid., 141.

3. Ibid.

4. Ibid., 93.

5. Brig. Gen. Charles Pomeroy Stone to T.S.C. Lowe, January 20 and 25, 1862, *AIAA*, LC.

6. Lowe, *My Balloons in Peace and War*, 95.

7. *OR*, vol. 3, ser. 3, 271.

8. George Alfred Townsend [attributed], "A Balloon Ascension At Night With Prof. Lowe," Philadelphia *Inquirer*, March 8, 1862, 1.

9. Lowe, *My Balloons in Peace and War*, 95.

10. Ibid., 96.

11. The reference is to Brig. Gen. Daniel E. Sickles. A somewhat vainglorious and controversial Union general who rose to notoriety in the prewar period when in 1859 he killed Phillip Barton Key, his wife's lover and the son of "Star Spangled Banner" author Frances Scott Key. He was acquitted of the crime by pleading "temporary insanity" (a first in the U.S. legal annals) and was later appointed to the rank of brigadier general by Lincoln after supporting the president's war policy in New York.

12. Letter, Clovis Lowe to T.S.C. Lowe, January 25, 1862, *AIAA*, LC.

13. F. Stansbury Haydon, *Aeronautics in the Union and Confederate Armies*, 277.

14. Lowe, *My Balloons in Peace and War*, T.S.C Lowe to Lt. Col. John N. Macomb, March 15, 95–96.

15. Letter, T.S.C. Lowe to Maj. Gen. John W. Wool, March 10, 1862.

16. Lowe, *My Balloons in Peace and War*, Brig. Gen. Seth Williams to T.S.C. Lowe, March 23, 1862, 99.

17. Ibid., Capt. Frederick Thomas Locke, assistant adjutant general, to T.S.C. Lowe, March 21, 1862, 98.

18. F. Stansbury Haydon, *Aeronautics in the Union . . .*, 264.

19. Capt. W.W. Glassford, Signal Corps, U.S.A. "Prolegomenon With Historic Sketch of the Balloon During the Civil War," Reprinted from *Journal Military Service Institution*, 1896, 261.
20. F. Stansbury Hayden, *Aeronautics in the Union . . .* , 266.
21. James A. Mackay, *Allan Pinkerton—The First Private Eye* (New York: J. Wiley & Sons, 1997), 181.
22. *OR*, vol 3, ser. 3, 273.
23. Ibid.
24. Lowe, *My Balloons in Peace and War*, 102, and *OR*, vol. 3, ser. 3, 274.
25. Crouch, *The Eagle Aloft*, 376.
26. Lowe, *My Balloons in Peace and War*, 102, and *OR*, vol. 3, ser. 3, 275.
27. Ibid.
28. From: Stephen Sears, ed., *The Civil War Papers of George Brinton McClellan, Selected Correspondence* (New York: Ticknor & Fields, 1989), 235. Letter, Gen. George B. McClellan to Mary Ellen McClellan, April 11, 1862.
29. Lowe, *My Balloons in Peace and War*, 102.
30. Ibid., Maj. Gen. Fitz-John Porter to T.S.C. Lowe, April 13, 1862, 108.
31. Ibid., 109.
32. Ibid.
33. George Armstrong Custer, "War Memoirs," *The Galaxy—A Magazine of Entertaining Reading*, Volume XXII, November, 1876, 686.
34. Ibid., 685.
35. Ibid.
36. Ibid., 686, 685.
37. Ibid., 686.
38. Ibid.
39. Ibid.
40. Ibid.
41. Ibid., 686–87.
42. Ibid., 686.
43. Ibid.
44. Ibid.
45. Ibid.
46. Ibid., 687.

CHAPTER TEN: THE FIRST CONFEDERATE AIR FORCE

1. From "A Balloon Adventure on the Potomac," 151, as cited in F. Stansbury Hayden, *Aeronautics in the Union and Confederate Armies*, 340.

2. From James Alexander Cooke, "The Siege of Richmond," 32, as cited in Hayden, *Aeronautics in the Union and Confederate Armies*.
3. Lt. Col. (Brevet) W.J. Handy, to T.S.C. Lowe, December 1, 1909, *AIAA*, LC.
4. Lowe, *My Balloons in Peace and War*, 103.
5. Savannah *Republican*, May 28, 1861; Philadelphia *Inquirer*, June 17, 1862.
6. Richmond *Enquirer*, "Abe's Balloon Plugged," June 17, 1862, 1.
7. Lowe, *My Balloons in Peace and War*, 103.
8. Detroit *Free Press*, "The Yankee Balloon—An Attempt to Destroy The One Used At Yorktown," 1896, also reprinted in Lowe, *My Balloons in Peace and War*, 163–65.
9. Lowe, *My Balloons in Peace and War*, 165.
10. Crouch, *The Eagle Aloft*, 381–82.
11. John Randolph Bryan, "Balloon Used For Scout Duty in C.S.A., *Southern Historical Society Papers*, volume XXXIII (Richmond, Virginia: Southern Historical Society, 1905), 33.
12. Ibid., 34.
13. Ibid.
14. Ibid.
15. Ibid.
16. Ibid., 34–35.
17. Ibid., 35.
18. Ibid., 33, 35.
19. Ibid., 35.
20. Ibid., 36.
21. Ibid.
22. Ibid.
23. Ibid.
24. Ibid., 37.
25. Ibid., 36–37.
26. Ibid.
27. Ibid., 38.
28. Ibid.
29. Ibid., 38–39.
30. Ibid., 39.
31. Ibid.
32. Ibid., 40.
33. Ibid., 41.

34. Ibid.
35. Ibid., 42.

**CHAPTER ELEVEN: THE ORIGINS OF THE
"SILK DRESS BALLOON"**

1. Capt. A.W. Glassford, "Prolegomenon With Historic Sketch of the Balloon During The Civil War," *Journal Military Service Institution*, March, 1896, 259.
2. Ibid.
3. Gen. Thomas F. Drayton to Capt. Langdon Cheves, aide-de-camp, May 28, 1862. From the Langdon Cheves collection of the South Carolina Historical Society (cited hereafter as the Cheves collection).
4. Ralph A. Wooster, *The Secession Conventions of the South* (Princeton, New Jersey: Princeton University Press, 1962), 16.
5. Langdon Cheves, III to Mr. Duane Squires, August 12, 1935. From the Cheves collection.
6. John Wise, *A System Of Aeronautics*, 376.
7. "Balloon," Savannah *Daily Morning News*, March 12, 1860, 2.
8. William H. Whitten, "Daring Balloon Trip in 1860 Thrilled Crowd," Savannah *Morning News*, January 9, 1977.
9. "Balloon, Savannah *Daily Morning News*, March 12, 1860, 2.
10. Charles Cevor, Savannah *Daily Morning News*, July 17, 1862, 2.
11. Gen. Thomas F. Drayton to Capt. Langdon Cheves, April 9, 1862. From the Cheves collection.
12. Invoice, Kerrison & Leiding, May 5, 1862. From the Cheves collection.
13. Langdon Cheves, III to Gen. James Longstreet, C.S.A., ret., May 6, 1896. From the Cheves collection.
14. Brig. Gen. Thomas Fenwick Drayton to Capt. Langdon Cheves, May 9, 1862. From the Cheves collection.
15. Letter, Charles Cevor to Capt. Langhorn Cheves, May 30, 1862. From the Cheves collection.
16. Receipt, Confederate States of America to Claghorn & Cunningham, May 31, 1862. From the Cheves collection.
17. Langdon Cheves II to Mr. Duane Squires, Colby Junior College, New Hampshire, August 12, 1935. From the Cheves collection.
18. Lt. E. Young, assistant adjutant general, to Capt. Langdon Cheves, May 26, 1862. From the Cheves collection.

19. Charles Cevor to Capt. Langdon Cheves, July 29, 1862. From the Cheves collection.

20. Gen. Thomas F. Drayton to Capt. Langdon Cheves, April 12, 1862. From the Cheves collection.

CHAPTER TWELVE: THE AIR WAR OVER VIRGINIA

1. President Abraham Lincoln to Gen. George B. McClellan, April 7, 1862, as quoted in Warren W. Hassler, Jr., *General George B. McClellan—Shield of the Union* (Baton Rouge: Louisiana State University Press, 1957), 90.

2. Lowe, *My Balloons in Peace and War*, 109.

3. Ibid., 110.

4. Ibid.

5. *OR*, vol. 11, ser. 1 456, Gen. S.P. Heintzelman to Gen. George B. McClellan, May 7, 1862.

6. T.S.C. Lowe, "The Balloons With the Army of the Potomac," from *The Photographic History of the Civil War in Ten Volumes*, volume VIII, "Soldier Life, Secret Service" (New York: The Review of Reviews Co., 1911), 370.

7. Lowe, *My Balloons in Peace and War*, 111.

8. *OR*, vol. 11, ser. 1, 456, Gen. S.P. Heintzelman to Gen. George B. McClellan, May 7, 1862.

9. Lowe, *My Balloons in Peace and War*, 111.

10. Charles Cevor to Confederate States of America War Department, September, 1862. From the Cheves collection.

11. Charles Cevor to Capt. Langdon Cheves, May 22, 1862. From the Cheves collection.

12. *OR*, vol. 3, ser. 3, 277.

13. T.S.C. Lowe, "The Balloons With the Army of the Potomac," from *The Photographic History of the Civil War in Ten Volumes*, Volume VIII, "Soldier Life, Secret Service" (New York: The Review of Reviews Co., 1911), 372.

14. Ibid.

15. Ibid.

16. Ibid.

17. President Abraham Lincoln to Gen. George B. McClellan, May 24, 1862, as quoted from Warren W. Hassler, *General George B. McClellan—Shield of the Union* (Baton Rouge: Louisiana State University Press, Baton Rouge, 1958), 109.

18. Lowe, *My Balloons in Peace and War*, 112.

19. Ibid.

20. Ibid.

21. Ibid., 113.

22. T.S.C. Lowe, "The Balloons With the Army of the Potomac," from *The Photographic History of the Civil War in Ten Volumes*, Volume VIII, "Soldier Life, Secret Service," (New York: The Review of Reviews Co., 1911), 374.

23. Lowe, *My Balloons in Peace and War*, 112–13.

24. Ibid., 113.

25. Ibid.

26. Ibid., 112.

27. Ibid., 113.

28. Ibid.

29. Ibid., 114.

30. Ibid.

31. Fannie Gaines Tinsley, "Mrs. Tinsley's War Recollections, 1862–1865," *The Virginia Magazine Of History And Biography*, October 1927, Volume XXV, No. 4, 394.

32. Lowe, *My Balloons in Peace and War*, 114.

33. Ibid., 114–15.

34. Fannie Gaines Tinsley, "Mrs. Tinsley's War Recollections, 1862–1865," *The Virginia Magazine Of History And Biography*, October 1927, Volume XXV, No. 4, 394.

35. Ibid., 395.

36. Lowe, *My Balloons in Peace and War*, 115.

37. Richmond *Examiner*, May 26, 1862.

38. T.S.C. Lowe, "The Balloons With the Army of the Potomac," from *The Photographic History of the Civil War in Ten Volumes*, Volume VIII, "Soldier Life, Secret Service" (New York: The Review of Reviews Co., 1911), 376.

39. Ibid.

40. Lowe, *My Balloons in Peace and War*, T.S.C. Lowe to Brig. Gen. Andrew Atkinson Humphreys, May 29, 1862, 120.

41. Ibid.

42. Ibid.

43. Ibid., 122.

44. T.S.C. Lowe, "The Balloons With the Army of the Potomac," from *The Photographic History of the Civil War in Ten Volumes*, Volume VIII,

"Soldier Life, Secret Service" (New York: The Review of Reviews Co., 1911), 380.

45. Ibid.
46. Lowe, *My Balloons in Peace and War*, Brig. Gen. Andrew Atkinson Humphreys to T.S.C. Lowe, June 1, 1862, 125.
47. Lowe, *My Balloons in Peace and War*, T.S.C. Lowe to Brig. Gen. Andrew Atkinson Humphreys, (or Gen. Randolph Barnes Marcy), June 1, 1862, 124.
48. Ibid.
49. Ibid., 126.
50. Dispatch from James Allen, June 1, 1862, from *OR*, vol. 3, ser. 3, 283.
51. Lowe, *My Balloons in Peace and War*, T.S.C. Lowe to Gen. John Henry Martindale, June 1, 1862, 127.
52. Lowe, *My Balloons in Peace and War*, T.S.C. Lowe to Brig. Gen. Fitz-John Porter, June 1, 1862, 126.
53. Ibid., 125.
54. Gary W. Gallagher, ed., *Fighting For The Confederacy—The Personal Recollections of General Edward Porter Alexander* (Chapel Hill: The University of North Carolina Press, 1989), 116.
55. Capt. Charles Cevor to Capt. Langdon Cheves, June 28, 1862. From the Cheves collection.
56. Alexander, *Fighting For The Confederacy*, 116.
57. From "Charles Cevor of Savannah, Georgia" an unpublished article provided by the Georgia State Historical Society, 4.
58. Ibid.
59. Union losses at Oak Grove were estimated to be 51 killed, 401 wounded, 64 missing. Confederate losses were 40 killed, 263 wounded, 13 missing. From Patricia Faust, ed., *Historical Times Illustrated Encyclopedia of the Civil War* (New York: Harper & Row, Publishers, 1986), 541.
60. Alexander, *Fighting For The Confederacy*, 116.
61. Ibid.
62. Ibid., 117.
63. Ibid., 115.
64. Ibid., 116.
65. Alexander, *Fighting For The Confederacy*, 117.
66. Lowe, *My Balloons in Peace and War*, T.S.C. Lowe to Brig. Gen. A.A. Humphreys, June 27, 1861, 11 A.M., 132–33.
67. Ibid., 131.
68. Ibid.

69. Ibid.

70. Lowe, *My Balloons in Peace and War*, T.S.C. Lowe to Brig. Gen. A.A. Humphreys (or Gen. Randolph Barnes Marcy), June 27, 1861, 8:15 A.M., 132.

71. Ibid., T.S.C. Lowe to Brig. Gen. A.A. Humphreys (or Gen. Randolph Barnes Marcy), June 27, 1862, 9:20 A.M., 132–133.

72. Ibid., T.S.C. Lowe to Brig. Gen. A.A. Humphreys (or Gen. Randolph Barnes Marcy), June 27, 1862, 11 A.M., 133.

73. Woodbury's Bridge was named after Gen. Daniel Woodbury, whose engineers constructed a pontoon bridge over the Rappahannock River at Fredericksburg.

74. Lowe, *My Balloons in Peace and War*, 134.

75. Ibid.

76. Charles Cevor, Savannah *Republican*, "The Battle Field Viewed from a Balloon," July 4, 1862, 1.

77. Fannie Gaines Tinsley, "Mrs. Tinsley's War Recollections, 1862–1865," *The Virginia Magazine Of History And Biography*, October 1927, Volume XXV, No. 4, 403–04.

78. Philadelphia *Inquirer*, "Acquisition to the Balloon Corps," July 29, 1862, 1.

79. Alexander, *Fighting For The Confederacy*, 117.

80. Philadelphia *Inquirer*, "Capture of the 'Teaser,'" July 11, 1862, 2.

81. Alexander, *Fighting For The Confederacy*, 117.

82. Ibid.

83. Philadelphia *Inquirer*, "Capture of the 'Teaser,'" July 11, 1862, 2.

84. *Battles and Leaders of the Civil War, Volume III.* (New York: Thomas Yoseloff Inc. (reprint), 1956.

CHAPTER THIRTEEN: THE WINTER OF DISAPPOINTMENT

1. Maladies associated with the environment surrounding the Chesapeake Bay region were not only limited to humans. The Union army's cavalry and draft horses also suffered mightily. Virginia farmers were often quoted as saying they would never work a Northern horse during its first summer in the region, for they invariably died before they could be acclimated.

2. Lowe, *My Balloons in Peace and War*, 135.

3. Thaddeus S. C. Lowe, "Balloon Army Service." *Scientific American*, February 2, 1895, 71.

4. Philadelphia *Inquirer*, "Balloon Reconnaissance," August 2, 1862, 1.

5. James McPherson, *Battle Cry of Freedom* (New York: Oxford University Press, 1988), 525.

6. Lowe, *My Balloons in Peace and War*, 138.

7. Ibid., 137.

8. *OR*, vol. 3, ser. 3, 292.

9. Ibid.

10. Lowe, *My Balloons in Peace and War*, 137.

11. Ibid., 139.

12. Letter, T.S.C. Lowe to Maj. Gen. John Grubb Parke, November 20, 1862, *AIAA*, LC.

13. Ibid.

14. Letter, Maj. Gen. John Grubb Parke to T.S.C. Lowe, November 24, 1862, *AIAA*, LC.

15. Lowe, *My Balloons in Peace and War*, p.142.

16. Ibid.

17. Editors of Time-Life Books, *Voices of the Civil War—Fredericksburg* (Alexandria, Virginia: Time-Life Books, 1997), 120.

18. Ibid.

19. Ibid.

20. Ibid.

21. Capt. W. A. Glassford, "Prolegomenon With Historic Sketch of the Balloon During the Civil War," *Journal Military Service Institution*, 1896, 265.

22. *OR*, vol. 3, ser. 3, 294, T.S.C. Lowe to Maj. Gen. John Grubb Parke, December 22, 1862.

CHAPTER FOURTEEN: THADDEUS LOWE'S LAST BATTLE

1. Charles Francis Adams, Jr., as quoted by Shelby Foote, *The Civil War: A Narrative, Fredericksburg to Meridian* (New York: Random House, 1963), 233–34.

2. Capt. W.A. Glassford, "Prolegomenon With Historic Sketch of the Balloon During the Civil War," *Journal Military Service Institution*, 1896, 265.

3. B. England to Gen. Rufus Ingalls, March 18, 1863, NA.

4. Ibid.

5. Ibid.

6. Ibid.

7. Ibid.

8. A letter from John Steiner, dated March 9, 1863, exists in the file at the National Archives containing England's proposal. However, as previously noted, the German-born Steiner was nearly illiterate. Comparing the letter with other examples written in Steiner's own hand, the letter was obviously written in another individual's handwriting and with a far greater command of the English language than Steiner possessed. Therefore, it is not known whether the Steiner letter of endorsement represents an accurate view of the aeronaut's assessment of England's machine or not.

9. "Comparison of Two Methods" supplied by B. England, Philadelphia, undated, NA.

10. Lowe, *My Balloons in Peace and War*, T.S.C. Lowe to Brig. Gen. Seth William, assistant adjutant general, March 30, 1863, 149.

11. Ibid., 150.

12. Ibid.

13. Ibid.

14. Ibid.

15. *OR*, vol. 3, ser. 3, 301, James Allen to T.S.C. Lowe, April 1, 1863.

16. Ibid., Ezra Allen to T.S.C. Lowe, April 1, 1863.

17. B. England to Brig. Gen. Rufus Ingalls, March 25, 1863, NA.

18. Letter, Jacob C. Freno, December 22, 1863, NA.

19. T.S.C Lowe to O. Howard, January 31, 1863, and T.S.C. Lowe to Brig. Gen. Edward M. Canby, January 22, 1863, NA.

20. Tom Crouch, *The Eagle Aloft*, 406.

21. *OR*, vol. 3, ser. 3, 302, Special Orders No. 95, dated April 7, 1863.

22. *OR*, vol. 3, ser. 3, 303, Capt. Cyrus B. Comstock to T.S.C. Lowe, April 12, 1863.

23. Ibid.

24. Mrs. T.S.C. (Leontine) Lowe to T.S.C. Lowe, undated, 1863, NA.

25. Lowe, *My Balloons in Peace and War*, T.S.C. Lowe to Gen. Daniel Butterfield, April 12, 1863, 156.

26. Ibid., 157.

27. Ibid.

28. Ibid., 158.

29. Ibid.

30. *OR*, vol. 3, ser. 3, 304, Brig. Gen. Simon Forrester Barstow, assistant adjutant general, to T.S.C. Lowe, April 13, 1863.

31. Ibid., Brig. Gen. Seth Williams, assistant adjutant general, to T.S.C. Lowe, April 15, 1863.

32. Lowe, *My Balloons in Peace and War*, Capt. Cyrus B. Comstock to T.S.C. Lowe, April 13, 1863, 159.

33. Ibid., P. H. Watson, assistant secretary of war, to T.S.C. Lowe, April 13, 1863, 159–60.

34. Ibid., T.S.C. Lowe to Capt. Cyrus B. Comstock, April 20, 1863, 161.

35. Ibid., T.S.C. Lowe to P.H. Watson, assistant secretary of war, April 19, 1863, 160.

36. Ibid., Brig. Gen. Seth Williams to T.S.C. Lowe, April 19, 1863, 160–61.

37. Ibid., T.S.C. Lowe to Capt. Cyrus B. Comstock, April 20, 1863, 161.

38. Ibid., Capt. Cyrus B. Comstock to Headquarters Army of the Potomac, April 20, 1863, 162.

39. *OR*, vol. 3, ser. 3, 309, T.S.C. Lowe to Capt. Cyrus B. Comstock, April 22, 1863.

40. Ibid.

41. Ibid.

42. Ernest B. Furguson, *Chancellorsville 1863—The Souls of the Brave* (New York: Alfred A. Knopf, 1992), 34.

43. *OR*, vol. 3, series 3, 312, T.S.C. Lowe to Gen. Daniel Butterfield, April 30, 1863.

44. Ibid.

45. Ibid., T.S.C. Lowe to Ezra S. Allen, April 30, 1863.

46. Gen. Edward J. Stackpole, *Chancellorsville.* (Harrisburg, Pennsylvania: Stackpole Press, 1958), 162.

47. Lowe, *My Balloons in Peace and War*, 184–85.

48. Ibid., 185.

49. Stackpole, *Chancellorsville*, 217.

50. Lowe, *My Balloons in Peace and War*, T.S.C. Lowe to Gen. John Sedgwick and Gen. Daniel Butterfield, May 4, 1863, 12 P.M., 186.

51. Ibid., T.S.C. Lowe to Gen. Sedgwick and Butterfield, May 4, 1863, 186.

52. Ibid., T.S.C. Lowe to Capt. Cyrus Comstock, May 7, 1863, 188.

53. Ibid., 188.

54. Ibid.

55. Ibid., J.F. Gibbons to T.S.C. Lowe, May 8, 1863, 189.

CHAPTER FIFTEEN: THE LAST DAYS OF THE CORPS

1. Walter H. Hebert, *Fighting Joe Hooker* (Lincoln, Nebraska: University of Nebraska Press, 1999), 235.

2. James Allen to T.S.C. Lowe, June 6, 1863, LC, AIAA Collection.

3. Ibid.

4. Ibid.

5. Ibid.

6. Ibid.

7. Ibid.

8. Letter, James Allen to Brig. Gen. Gouverneur Kemble Warren, June 12, 1863, NA.

9. New York *Times*, "Use of Balloons in War," July 12, 1863, 8.

10. Lowe, *My Balloons in Peace and War*, 193.

11. Ibid., 194, Maj. Gen. Samuel Heintzelman to T.S.C. Lowe, July 1, 1863.

12. Ibid., 195.

13. Ibid., Maj. Gen. John Sedgwick to T.S.C. Lowe, September 3, 1863.

14. Ibid., 193, Maj. Gen. George Stoneman to T.S.C. Lowe, July 19, 1863.

15. George Armstrong Custer, "War Memoirs," *The Galaxy—A Magazine of Entertaining Reading*, November, 1876, 685.

16. *OR*, vol. 5, ser. 1, 32.

17. Gen. Adolphus W. Greely, Chief Signal Corps, U.S.A., "Balloons in War," *Harper's Monthly Magazine*, June, 1900, 43–44.

18. Ibid., 44.

19. William Jones Rhees, "Reminiscences of Ballooning in the Civil War," *Chautauquan*, June, 1898, 261.

CHAPTER SIXTEEN: AFTER THE BALLOON CORPS

1. Lowe, *My Balloons . . .*, 197.

2. Ibid.

3. Ibid.

4. Lowe, *My Ballons*, Ezra Allen to T.S.C. Lowe, July 14, 1867, 197–98.

5. Harris Gaylord Warren, *Paraguay An Informal History* (Norman, Oklahoma: Univeristy of Oklahoma Press, 1949), 23.

6. Tom Crouch, *The Eagle Aloft*, 423.

7. J. B. Livingston to Maj. Hartman Bache, May 23, 1863, NA.

8. Rhoda D. Gilman, 'Zeppelin in Minnesota: The Count's Own Story.' Minnesota History, Volume XL, No. 6, Summer 1967.

9. Ibid., 276.

10. Captain F. Beaumont, Royal Enginners, "On Balloon Reconnaissance As Practised By The American Army," *Military Ballooning, 1862*. Three papers reprinted from the professional papers of the Corps of Royal Engineers, 1863. (Middlesex, England: Aviation Press, 1967), 27.

11. Confederate Veteran, "Capt. John Randolph Bryan," April 1918, Volume XXVI, No. 4, 168.

12. 'Charles Cevor of Savannah, Georgia.' Unattributed manuscript in the collection of Georgia Historical Society, Savannah, Georgia.

13. 'A Confederate Airship: The Artis Avis Which was to Destroy Grant's Army,' Southern Historical Society Papers. Volume XXVII, 1900, 304.

14. Ibid.

15. Ibid., 305.

16. T.S.C. Lowe to Maj. Albert J. Myer, July 13, 1863, Library of Congress, AIAA Collection.

17. Maj. Gen. Edward B. Canby to T.S.C. Lowe, December 3, 1863, Library of Congress, AIAA Collection.

18. Ibid.

19. Tom Crouch, *The Eagle Aloft*, 419.

20. Lowe, *My Balloons . . .*, 199.

21. Ibid., 200.

22. The complete list of Thaddeus and Leontine Lowe's children is as follows: Louise E Lowe, Ida Alpha Lowe, Leon Percival Lowe, Ava Eugenia Lowe, Augustine Marguerite Lowe, Blanche Lowe, Thaddeus Lowe Jr., Edna Lowe, Zoe Lowe, and Sobieski Constantine Lowe. Also of special note: Thaddeus Lowe Jr.'s daughter, Florence, also rose to some degree of fame in aviation circles during the twentieth century. Better known by her nickname and married name, 'Pancho' Lowe Barnes was one of the most famous aviatrixes of the late 1920s and 1930s. She later operated the notorious 'Happy Bottom Riding Club' near Edwards Air Force Base in Southern California in the 1940s.

23. Eugene R. Block, *Above the Civl War . . .*, 125.

24. Ibid.

25. Ibid., 127.

26. Eugene R. Block, *Above the Civl War . . .*, 138.

27. Ibid., 157. As a side note, the "City of the Clouds" did not enjoy much success after Lowe was forced out in 1898. The Echo Mountain House was destroyed by fire in 1905. A windstorm in 1928 caused the Lowe Observatory to collapse. The Mount Lowe Railway fell rapidly into disrepair in the 1930s and was rendered unsalvagable in 1938 when a cloudburst washed out large portions of track. The final blow came in 1936 when a fire broke out and consumed Ye Apline Tavern.

BIBLIOGRAPHY

UNPUBLISHED MANUSCRIPTS AND SPECIAL COLLECTIONS

American Institute of Aeronautics and Astronautics (AIAA). *Archives of the Institute of Aerospace Sciences, 1783–1962*. History Collection, Library of Congress. Library of Congress, Manuscript Reading Room, Biographical file boxes, 80–84.

Georgia Historical Society, *Charles Cevor Collection*. Savannah, Georgia.

Lowe, Thaddeus Sobieski Constantine. *My Balloons In Peace and War*, (unpublished memoirs). Transcribed by Augustine Lowe Brownbeck. National Air & Space Museum, Washington, D.C. TL 620 L6A1 RB NASM, 1931.

National Archives. *Records Relating to Pilots, Balloon and Construction Corps, and Sutlers* (Balloons Folder). Records Group Number 94.

South Carolina Historical Society. *Langdon Cheves Collection*. Charleston, South Carolina.

BOOKS

Bailey, Ronald H. ed. *Forward to Richmond*. Alexandria, Virginia: Time-Life Books, 1983.

Baldwin, Munson. *With Brass and Gas: An Illustrated and Embellished Chronicle of Ballooning in Mid-Nineteenth Century America*. Boston: Beacon Press, 1967.

Beaumont, Capt. Frederick E. Royal Engineers. "On Balloon Reconnaissance As Practised By The American Army," paper read at Chatham, November 14, 1862. Reprinted in *Military Ballooning 1862*. Middlesex, England: Aviation Press, 1967.

Bigelow, John ed. *The Complete Works of Benjamin Franklin*, (Vol. VIII). New York: G.P. Putnam's sons, 1888.

Block, Eugene. *Above The Civil War—The Story of Thaddeus Lowe*. Berkeley, California: Howell-North Books, 1966.

Butler Benjamin. *Private and Official Correspondence of General Benjamin F. Butler During the Period of the Civil War*. Plimpton, Massachusetts: Privately Issued, 1917.

Crouch, Tom D. *The Eagle Aloft*. Washington, D.C.: Smithsonian Institution Press, 1983.

Crozier, Emmet. *Yankee Reporters, 1861–1865*. New York: Oxford Press, 1956.

Davis, Jefferson. *Rise and Fall of the Confederate Government*, Volume I. New York: D. Appleton & Company, 1881.

Dwiggins, Don. *The Air Devils*. New York: J.B. Lippincott, 1966.

———. *The Complete Book of Airships—Dirigibles, Blimps & Hot Air Balloons*. Blue Ridge Summit, Pennsylvania: TAB Books, 1980.

Faust, Patricia, ed. *Historical Times Illustrated Encyclopedia of the Civil War*. New York: Harper & Row, Publishers, 1986.

Foote, Shelby. *The Civil War: A Narrative, Fredericksburg to Meridian*. New York: Random House, 1963.

Furguson, Ernest B. *Chancellorsville 1863—The Souls of the Brave*. New York: Alfred A. Knopf, 1992.

Gallagher, Gary W. ed. *Fighting For The Confederacy—The Personal Recollections of General Edward Porter Alexander*. Chapel Hill: The University of North Carolina Press, 1989.

Guernsey, Alfred H. and Alden, Henry M. *Harper's Pictorial History Of The Great Rebellion, Part First*. Chicago: McDonnel Brothers, 1866.

Haddock, John A. *Mr. Haddock's Account Of His Hazardous And Exciting Voyage In The Balloon "Atlantic" With Professor John La Mountain*. Philadelphia: Press of Haddock and Son, 1872.

Hagerman, Edward. *The American Civil War And The Origins Of Modern Warfare*. Indianapolis: Indiana University Press, 1988.

Hassler, Warren W. Jr. *General George B. McClellan—Shield of the Union*. Louisiana State University Press, Baton Rouge, 1957.

Haydon, F. Stansbury. *Aeronautics in the Union and Confederate Armies, Volume I*. Baltimore: The Johns Hopkins Press, 1941.

Hebert, Walter H. *Fighting Joe Hooker*. Lincoln, Nebraska: University of Nebraska Press, 1999.

Hodgins, Eric, and Magoun, F. Alexander. *Sky High, The Story of Aviation.* Little, Brown, and Company, Boston, 1935.

Johnson, Robert Underwood and Buell, Clarence Clough, eds. *Battles and Leaders of the Civil War, Volumes II and III.* New York: Thomas Yoseloff, Inc., 1956 (reprint).

Josephy, Alvin M. ed. *The American Heritage History of Flight.* New York: American Heritage Publishing Company, 1962.

Lausanne, Edita. *The Romance of Ballooning—The Story of the Early Aeronauts.* New York: A Studio Book, 1971.

Mackay, James A. *Allan Pinkerton—The First Private Eye.* New York: J. Wiley & Sons, 1997.

Malone, Dumas, ed. *Dictionary of American Biography,* New York: Charles Scribner's Sons, 1933.

McPherson, James. *The Battle Cry of Freedom.* New York: Oxford University Press, 1988.

Miller, Francis Trevelyan ed. *The Photographic History Of The Civil War, Volume V.* New York: The Review of Reviews Co., 1911.

Moore, Frank ed. *The Rebellion Record: A Diary of American Events, Second Volume.* New York: G.P. Putnam, 1862.

Rolt, L.T. C. *The Aeronauts—A History of Ballooning 1783–1903.* New York: Walker and Company, 1966.

Sears, Stephen ed. *The Civil War Papers of George Brinton McClellan, Selected Correspondence.* New York: Ticknor & Fields, 1989.

Stackpole, (General) Edward J. *Chancellorsville.* Harrisburg, Pennsylvania: Stackpole Press, 1958.

Stehliung, Kurt R. and Beller, William. *Skyhooks.* New York: Doubleday & Company, 1962

Time-Life Books eds. *Voices of the Civil War—Fredericksburg.* Time-Life Books, Alexandria, Virginia, 1997.

Turnor, Hatton. *Astra Castra, Experiments and Adventures in the Atmosphere.* London, 1865.

Van Doren, Carl. *Benjamin Franklin.* Princeton, New Jersey: Princeton University Press, 1950.

———. *War Of The Rebellion: A Compilation of the Official Records of the Union and Confederate Armies,* Volume 3, Series 3. Washington, D.C.: Government Printing Office, 1899.

Warren, Harris Gaylord. *Paraguay—An Informal History.* Norman, Oklahoma: University of Oklahoma Press, 1949.

Wise, John. *A System Of Aeronautics*. Philadelphia: Joseph A. Speel, 1850.
———. *Through The Air: A Narrative of Forty Years' Experience As An Aeronaut*. New York: To-Day Printing and Publishing, 1873.
Wooster, Ralph A. *The Secession Conventions of the South*. Princeton, New Jersey: Princeton University Press, 1962.

JOURNALS, NEWSPAPERS ARTICLES
Abbot, Brig. General Henry L., "Early Experience With Balloons In War," *Professional Memoirs, Corps of Engineers*, U.S. Army and Engineer Department at Large, September/October, 1912
———. "Abe's Balloon Plugged," Richmond *Enquirer*, June 17, 1862, 1.
———. "Acquisition to the Balloon Corps," Philadelphia *Inquirer*, July 29, 1862, 1.
———. "Balloon," Savannah *Daily Morning News*, March 12, 1860, 2.
———. "Balloon Reconnaissance," Philadelphia *Inquirer*, August 2, 1862, 1.
Bryan, Captain John Randolph. "Balloon Used For Scout Duty in C.S.A," *Southern Historical Society Papers*, Volume XXXIII, Richmond, Virginia: Southern Historical Society, 1905, 32–42.
———. "Capt. John Randolph Bryan," *Confederate Veteran*, April, 1918. Volume XXVI, No. 4, 168.
———. "Capture of the 'Teaser,'" Philadelphia *Inquirer*, July 11, 1862, 2.
Cevor, Charles, "The Battle Field Viewed from a Balloon," Savannah *Republican*, July 4, 1862, 1.
———. Savannah *Daily Morning News*, July 17, 1862, 2.
Cincinnati *Commercial*, June 28, 1861, 2.
———. "A Confederate Airship—The Artis Avis Which was to Destroy Grant's Army," *Southern Historical Society Papers*. Volume XXVII, 1900, 304.
Custer, General George Armstrong. "War Memoirs," *The Galaxy A Magazine of Entertaining Reading*, Volume XXII, November 1876, 684–94.
Davis, Captain Daniel T. "The Air Role in the War Between the States." *Air University Review*, July–August, 1976.
Dennée, Timothy J. "John La Mountain and the Alexandria Balloon Ascensions," *Historic Alexandria Quarterly*, Fall 1997, Volume II, No. 3, 5.
Evans, Charles M., "Air War Over Virginia," *Civil War Times Illustrated*, October 1996, 36.
Gilman, Rhoda D. "Zeppelin in Minnesota: The Count's Own Story," *Minnesota History*, Volume XL, Number 6, Summer 1967, 265–78.

Glassford, Capt. W. A. "Prolegomenon With Historic Sketch of the Balloon During the Civil War," *Journal Military Service Institution*, 1896, 255–66.

———. "Government Balloons," Philadelphia *Inquirer*, October 22, 1861, 8.

Greely, Gen. Adolphus W., Chief Signal Corps, U.S.A. "Balloons in War," *Harper's Monthly Magazine*, June 1900, 43–44.

———. *Harper's Weekly*, September 24, 1859, 1.

Lowe, Thaddeus S. C. "Balloon Army Service." *Scientific American*, February 2, 1895, 71.

Mallory, Garrick, "A Ride In The Mammoth Of The Air," Philadelphia *Inquirer*, June 30, 1860, 1.

New York *Herald*, October 6, 1861, 6.

———. "A Night Balloon Ascension!" *Daily Commercial* (Cincinnati), April 20, 1861, 1.

Philadelphia *Inquirer*, February 19, 1862, 1.

———. March 14, 1862, 8.

———. June 17, 1862.

Philadelphia *Ledger*, October 26, 1846, 3.

———. "Professor Lowe to Build a Mammoth Balloon for the Government," Philadelphia *Inquirer*, August 6, 1861, 1.

———. "Professor Lowe's Truant Balloon," Philadelphia *Inquirer*, October 19, 1861, 4.

Providence *Post*, April 19, 1861, 4.

———. "Return of Professor Lowe," Cincinnati *Daily Commercial*, April 27, 1861, 1.

Rhees, William Jones. "Reminiscences of Ballooning in the Civil War, *Chautauquan*, June 1898, 257–62.

Scientific American, "Balloon Reconnaissance," August 17, 1861, 104.

———. November 2, 1861, 284.

———. "Skirmish At Pittsburgh Landing," Philadelphia *Inquirer*, March 24, 1861, 1.

———. "Special Correspondent," New York *Herald*, November 13, 1861, 1.

Tinsley, Fannie Gaines. "Mrs. Tinsley's War Recollections, 1862–1865," *The Virginia Magazine Of History And Biography*, October 1927, Volume XXV, No. 4, 394.

Townsend, George Alfred [attributed], "A Balloon Ascension At Night With Prof. Lowe," Philadelphia *Inquirer*, March 8, 1862.

———. [War Correspondent], Boston *Journal*, November 22, 1861, 3.

Washington *Evening Star*, June 19, 1861, 3.

Whitten, William H., "Daring Balloon Trip in 1860 Thrilled Crowd," Savannah *Morning News*, January 9, 1977.

Wise, John, "Easy Method of Capturing the Castle of Vera Cruz," Philadelphia *Ledger*, October 26, 1846, 5.

Wise, John, "To All Publishers Of Newspapers On The Globe," Lancaster *Intelligencer*, Lancaster, Pennsylvania, June 1843, 2.

INDEX

Abbot, Lt. Henry L.,
  Evaluation of James Allen's bal-
    loon, 65–68
Aeronautic Amphitheatre, 306–307,
    307
Aeronautics Department,
    171–172
Aérostatiers, Les
  World's first military balloon
    unit, 24–25
  Disbanded by Napoleon Bona-
    parte, 25
Alexander, Lt. Col. Edward
    Porter,
  Ordered to take charge of Con-
    federate balloon, 232
  Helped devise "wigwag" signal-
    ing system, 232
  Career as Confederate aeronaut,
    233–237
  Devises aerial signaling system,
    234
  Observations during Battle of
    Gaines's Mill, 236–237
  Observations from James River,
    241–242
  Evades capture from crew of
    Maratanza, 243
  Opinion regarding Balloon
    Corps, 295
  Commander of artillery at
    Chancellorsville and Gettys-
    burg, 304
  Postwar career, 304

Allen, Ezra,
  Assistant aeronaut in the Bal-
    loon Corps, 223
  Supports Lowe's methods, 270
  Observations of Battle of Chan-
    cellorsville, 280–283
  Assistant to James Allen after
    Chancellorsville, 288–290
  As aeronaut in Brazil during
    War of Triple Alliance,
    297–298
  Postwar career, 299
Allen, James, *64, 275*
  Arrives in Washington. D.C., 62
  Early career, 62–63
  Demonstrates military balloon,
    63–68
  Difficulties with portable
    hydrogen generator, 65–66
  Assistant aeronaut in the Bal-
    loon Corps, 176
  Balloon flight with George
    Armstrong Custer, 184–188
  In charge of *Constitution* at
    Gaines's's farm, 223
  Readies *Intrepid* for inflation at
    Gaines's's farm, 226–228, *227*
  Observations at Mechanicsville,
    228, 230
  Observations of Battle of
    Gaines's Mill, 236
  In charge of Balloon Corps
    while Lowe recovers, 241

Reconnaissance near Harrison's
landing, 249–250
Supports Lowe's methods,
269–270
Observations of Battle of Chan-
cellorsville, 280–283
Brief tenure as chief aeronaut,
288–290
As aeronaut in Brazil during
War of Triple Alliance,
297–298
Postwar career, 299
Annonay, France, 20
Antietam, Battle of, 253–254
Antoinette, Marie,
Witness to early Montgolfier
balloon ascent at Versailles, 23
Armistead, General W. K., 61
Army of the Potomac,
Peninsular Campaign, 167–168,
170, 177
Reorganized, 248
Burnside appointed as com-
mander, 254–255
Hooker appointed as comman-
der, 263–264
Artillery,
Directed from air by balloon,
112–114
Danger to aeronauts from, 184
Confederate attempts to bring
down balloons, 189–191, 224
Atlantic (balloon),
Construction of, 41–42, 135
Flight from St. Louis to Hen-
derson, N.Y., 42–48, *49, 46
(map)*
Used as a military balloon at
Fortress Monroe, 96–101,
128, 134
Retired from service, 138

Bache, Maj. Hartman, 83, 106
Evaluates John Wise's military
balloon proposal, 76–77

Authorizes Lowe to build addi-
tional military balloons,
93–94
Balloon Corps (*see also* Union
Army Aeronautical Corps),
Name adopted by journalists,
88, 173
Addition of new balloons,
121–123
Spare balloon parts, 122–123
Hydrogen generators, 118–121,
119, 120
George Washington Parke-Custis
(balloon barge), 147–150,
148, 150
Cap insignia, 173
Assistants' salaries, 176
Danger to aeronauts from
artillery, 184
Confederate attempts to bring
down balloons, 189–191,
216, 224
Attempted sabotage of balloons
by Rebels, 191–193
Damage from storms to equip-
ment, 215, 285
Changes initiated by Comstock,
272–274
Disbanded, 291
Banks, Gen. Nathaniel,
Defeated by Jackson at Front
Royal, 217
Barnard, Gen. John Gross,
Surveys approach to Yorktown
from balloon, 183–184
Siege of Yorktown, 210
Barry, General, 168
Barstow, Gen. Simon, 276
Beaumont, Capt. F, Royal Engi-
neers,
Observes Balloon Corps, 303
Organizes Royal Balloon
Detachment, 303
Beauregard, Pierre Gustave
Toutant, 82, 103

Attack on Fort Sumter, 8
Orders camouflage of Confed-
    erate camps, 113
Benham, Brig. Gen. Henry
    Washington, 155
Big Bethel, Battle of, 95, 99
Black's Inn, Unionville, South
    Carolina, 12–13
Blair, Montgomery, 100
Blanchard, Jean-Pierre Francois,
    First aeronaut to cross English
    Channel with Jeffries, 25
Demonstrates balloon in
    Philadelphia, 27
Blank, "Professor,"
    And "Artis Avis," 304–305
Blenker, Gen. Louis, 132
Boatwright, W. H.
    Mayor of Columbia, South
    Carolina, 15
    Presents T. S. C. Lowe with
    Confederate "passport," 16
Bonaparte, Napoleon,
    Disbands French Aerostatiers in
    1803, 25
Brooks, Silas
    Pilot of the Comet, 43–44
Butterfield, Gen. Daniel,
    Ascends with Lowe at Freder-
    icksburg, 260
    Lowe attempts to seek support
    from, 274
Bryan, Captain John Randolph,
    On General Magruder's staff,
    194
    As first Confederate aeronaut,
    195–201
    Given nickname, "Balloon
    Bryan," 199
    Aerial observations of, 197–198
    Accidental freeflight, 199–201
    Postwar career, 303
Budd's Ferry,
    Balloon barge arrives at,
    151–153
Buell, Don Carlos, 161

Burnside, Gen. Ambrose, 63
    Appointed commander of
    Army of the Potomac,
    254–255
    At Battle of Fredericksburg,
    255–262
Butler, Gen. Benjamin,
    Employs John La Mountain at
    Fortress Monroe, 78–79
    Contraband order, 98
    Relieved of command at
    Fortress Monroe, 99–100
Butt, Capt. Richard, 106

Cameron, Simon, Secretary of
    War, 69
    Receives report from Joseph
    Henry regarding military bal-
    loons, 72–74
    Engages John Wise for military
    balloons, 76
Canby, Maj. Gen. Edward,
    305–306
Carnes, Peter,
    Exhibitor of first balloon in the
    United States, 26
Cavallo, Tiberius, 38
Cavendish, Henry,
    Early experiments with hydro-
    gen, 21
Cevor, Charles,
    Career as aeronaut, 204–205
    Constructs "Silk Dress Balloon"
    for Confederacy, 205–207
    Costs in constructing balloon,
    213–214
    Difficulties with hydrogen gen-
    erator, 214
    Arrives at Richmond, 231
    Commissioned as captain, 233
    Observes Battle of Gaines's
    Mill, 239–240
    Attempt to construct another
    Confederate balloon,
    303–304
Chain Bridge, 117

Charles, Jacques Alexander Cesar,
  Inventor of gas-filled balloon,
    21–24
  Exhibits first gas-filled balloon
    at Champ de Mars, 22
Chancellorsville, Va.,
  Battle of, 278–285, *281*
Chase, Salmon P., 62, 68
Cheves, Captain Langdon,
  Ordered to procure Confeder-
    ate balloon, 204
  and Charles Cevor, 205, 214
  Purchases dress silk for balloon,
    206–207
  Arrives at Richmond, 231
  Death of, 303
City of New York (balloon, later
  renamed *Great Western*),
  Construction of, 50–52, *51*
"clay-eaters,"
  T. S. C. Lowe's encounter with,
    11, 12
Coal gas,
  Use in balloons, 30
Colburn, Maj. Ledyard, 75, 137,
    149, 150
College of William and Mary,
  "Balloon Club," 27
Columbia Armory, 80
  Headquarters of Union Army
    Aeronautical Corps, 108
Columbia, South Carolina,
  T. S. C. Lowe taken to, 15–17
Columbus, Christopher, 1
Commodore (McClellan's head-
  quarters), 175
Comstock, Capt. Cyrus Ballou,
  Appointed to oversee Balloon
    Corps, 264–265, *265*
  Initiates changes to Balloon
    Corps, 272–274
  Accepts Lowe's resignation, 277,
    285–287
  Assigned to defense of Pitts-
    burgh, 288

Confederate balloons, 193–202
  Description of balloon in Gen-
    eral Johnston's camp, 194
  John Randolph Bryan as first
    Confederate aeronauts,
    195–201
  See also "Silk Dress Balloon"
Congress, (frigate),
  Sunk by *Virginia*, 174
Constitution (balloon),
  Description, 121, 122
  At Budd's Ferry, 137
  Ordered to accompany Seaver
    at Fortress Monroe, 174
  Observations on the Virginia
    Peninsula, 180
  Observations at Gaines's Farm,
    221, 222–223
  Used in emergency inflation of
    Intrepid, 226–228, *227*
  Vandalized by Freno, 272
Count de Paris, 116
Coeur de Lion (balloon tugboat),
    149, 151
  Arrives at Budd's Ferry, 152
Cresson, John C., 54, 58
Cullum, Brig. Gen. George
    Washington, 157
Cumberland (frigate),
  Sunk by *Virginia*, 174
Custer, Lt. George Armstrong,
  Balloon flight with James Allen,
    184–188
  Opinion concerning civilian
    aeronauts, 293

Daedulus, 20
Dahlgren, Capt. Adolph Bernard,
    115, 149
Davidson, Capt. Hunter, 242–243
D'Arlandes, Marquis,
  First balloon passenger, 23
Darwin, Charles, 1
Davis, Jefferson, 103
  Nearly killed by balloon-
    directed artillery, 114

De Rozier, Jean Francois Pilatre,
First balloon aeronaut, 23
First untethered flight, 23
Attempted English Channel
crossing by balloon, 24
First balloon related fatality, 24
Demers, George, 48, 50
Dickinson, George R.,
Assistant aeronaut in the Bal-
loon Corps, 116
Dinkelhoff, Professor, 38
Dom Pedro II, Brazilian Emperor,
Requests military balloon, 296
Donaldson, Washington Harrison,
300
Douglas, Stephen, United States
Senator, 35
Drayton, Gen. Thomas Fenwick,
Orders procurement of Confed-
erate balloon, 203–204
Dupont, Admiral Samuel, 150
Du Porotail, Louis Le Béque, 25
Durant, Charles Ferson, 61

Elsworth, Elmer, 67
Eagle (balloon), 121
Description, 122
Used by Steiner at Cairo, Illi-
nois, 158–160
Used by Lowe at Fredericks-
burg 258–260
Early, Gen. Jubal,
Defense of Yorktown, 210
Defense at Marye's Heights, 279
Ely, Eugene, 310
Empire (transport ship), 154
England, B.,
Proposes new hydrogen genera-
tor, 265–271
Enterprise (balloon), 105, 275
T. S. C. Lowe's balloon for
Cincinnati to South Carolina
journey, 2, 3–19
Description of, 3
Used in first telegraph message
sent from the air, 69

Military flights of, 74–75,
89–90
Retired from use (note), 121
Entrepenant (*Enterprise*, balloon),
25
Ericsson, John, 50
Excelsior (balloon), 121
Description, 122

Fair Oaks, Va.,
Battle of, 226–230
Falls Church, 74–75
Fanny (tugboat),
Used by La Mountain as bal-
loon boat, 98–99
Farragut, Admiral David, 3
First Rhode Island Regiment, 63
Foote, Adm. Andrew H.,
Used balloon to reconnoiter
Island No. 10, 159–160
Forest City (balloon), 205
Fort Beauregard, 150
Fort Corcorran, 83, 112
Fortress Monroe, 78, 94–95
Balloon view, *95*
Fears of Rebel takeover, 96
Balloon operations at, 78–79,
94, 96–102, 125–126, 171,
175, 177
Fort Pulaski, 156
Fort Sumter,
Attack upon, 8
Fort Walker, 150
Fourteenth New York Regiment,
Personnel used as balloon
ground handlers, 106
Fourth Michigan Regiment, 152
Frank Leslie's Illustrated News, 102
Franklin, Benjamin, 1, 76
Witness to J. A. C. Charles's
first balloon flight in France,
23
Comments regarding applica-
tions of balloon, 23
Description of one of De
Rozier's untethered flights, 23

Predicts military applications of balloons, 24

Franklin, Gen. William B.,
La Mountain assigned to, 129–132
Endorses La Mountain's request for new balloons, 136

Fredericksburg, Va.,
Battle of, 255–262, *256*
Second Battle of, see Chancellorsville

Freno, Jacob C.,
Assistant aeronaut in the Balloon Corps, 175
Background, 176
Troubled military career, 176
Salary, 176
Dismissed from Balloon Corps, 271
Charges Lowe with misappropriating resources, 271–272
Vandalizes *Constitution*, 272

Front Royal,
Battle of, 217

Fry, Gen. James Barnett, 105

Fullerton, William J., 167

Gager, Oscar A.,
Underwrites Wise's proposed transatlantic voyage, 40–41
As "scientific landsman," 41
First flight of the *Atlantic*, 42–48

Gaines (Tinsley), Fannie,
Witnesses Lowe's balloon at Gaines's farm, 221
Mistakes Lowe for general, 222
Mrs. Woody's remarks, 223
Witnesses aftermath of Battle of Gaines's Mill, 240

Gaines, Dr. William Fleming,
Encounters T. S. C. Lowe, 220–222

Gaines's Mill,
Battle of, 236, 239–241

Gazelle, (Confederate balloon),
See "Silk Dress Balloon"

George Washington Parke-Custis, (balloon barge), *148*, *150*
Construction of, 147
Assigned to patrol Potomac River, 149–151
Damaged, 173
Prepared for Fortress Monroe deployment, 175
Transports Lowe to West Point, Va., 217
Mistaken for Union ironclad, 218

Gilmore, Maj. Gen. Quincy, 305

Globe (balloon),
First gas-filled balloon, 22
Construction of, 22
First flight at Champ de Mars, Paris, 22–23

Gonesse, France,
Terrified villagers encounter early balloon, 22

Goodyear's Rubber, Belting, and Packing Company, 119

Grant, Gen. Ulysses, 161

Great Western (balloon, formerly *The City of New York*),
Test flown in Philadelphia by T. S. C. Lowe, 56–57
Remnants used as inflation pad, 123

Green, Charles, aeronaut,
Inventor of guide of rope, 27
Balloon voyage from England to Holland, 27–28

Haddock, John
Accompanies La Mountain on flight, 55

Halleck, Gen. Henry,
Commander of the Department of the Mississippi, 157

Halstead, Murat,
Editor of *Daily Commercial*, 2, 3–4
Letter to Salmon P. Chase on Lowe's behalf, 62

Harpers Ferry, 8, 64–65, 176
Heintzleman, Maj. Gen. Samuel
    Peter, 168, 225, 229, 234
    Discovers Confederate with-
        drawal from Yorktown from
        balloon, 212–213
    Balloon attracts artillery fire
        into headquarters of, 216
    Letter in support of Lowe, 292
Henry, Joseph, 84
    Advice to Lowe regarding air
        current theories, 2, 58–59
    Role in adapting telegraph for
        use with balloons, 68
    Arranges balloon tests at Smith-
        sonian Institution, 69
    Report endorsing military bal-
        loons, 72–74
    Letter to Amiel Whipple sup-
        porting Lowe, 92
Hill, Gen. Daniel H.,
    Defense of Yorktown, 210
Hooker, Brig. Gen. Joseph, 150,
    260
    At Budd's Ferry, 152–153
    Appointed commander of
        Army of the Potomac,
        263–264
    Battle of Chancellorsville,
        278–285
    Unaware of Lowe's resignation,
        287
Huger, Gen. Benjamin, 234
Hugh Jenkins (transport), 174
Humphries, Joshua,
    Involved in attempt to construct
        first balloon in United States,
        26
Hyde, William
    Report of the Atlantic's first
        flight, 43–47
Hydrogen,
    Early experiments with, 21
    Use in balloons, 21

Hydrogen Generator,
    Use in inflating balloons, 22
    T. S. C. Lowe's. 93, 108, 111,
        115, 118–121, 119, 120
    La Mountain's, 78, 96, 124
    Cevor's, 214
    England's, 265–271

Intrepid (balloon), 121, 137
    Description, 122
    Assigned to duty at Edward's
        Ferry, 157
    Damage sustained at Pooleville,
        167
    And Fitz-John Porter's acciden-
        tal freeflight, 181–183
    At Gaines's farm, 223
    Emergency inflation of,
        226–228, 227
    Used in observations during
        Battle of Fair Oaks, 228–231,
        229
Island No. 10, 159–160

Jackson, Gen. Thomas Jonathon
    "Stonewall,"
    Forces threaten Washington,
        D.C., 170
    Death of, 282
Jefferson, Thomas, 27
Jackson, Gen. Thomas
    "Stonewall," 82
    Battle of Front Royal, 217
Jeffries, John,
    First aeronaut to cross English
        Channel with Blanchard, 25
Jet stream, 34
Johnson, Mademoiselle, aeronaut,
    27
Johnston, Gen. Joseph E., 82, 225
    Use of balloon in Army of
        Northern Virginia, 193–196
    Wounded at Fair Oaks, 230
Johnston, Gen. Albert Sydney,
    161

Keyes, Gen. Erasmus, 106, 180, 225, 229

King, Samuel
Association with James Allen, 63
Experiments with aerial photography, 166

Kinney's Mammoth Pavillian, 34

La Mountain, John, *41*, 175, 275
Association with John Wise, 40–41
First flight of the *Atlantic*, 42–48
Rivalry with John Wise, 48–50
Resumes transatlantic quest, 54
Flight of reconfigured *Atlantic*, 54
Petitions to become military aeronaut, 77–78
Portable gas generator, 78, 96
Balloon operations at Fortress Monroe, 78–79, 94, 96–102, 125–126
Map sketched by, *97*
Uses *USS Fanny* as balloon boat, 98–99
Proposal to arm military balloons, 100
Expenses at Fortress Monroe, 101, 125
Difficulties with Gen. Wool, 102, 124, 125–126
Suffers severe burns, 124
Rivalry with Lowe, 126–129, 138–146
Salary established, 129
Assigned to Gen. Franklin, 129–132
Freeflight reconnaissance of, 130–134
Nearly killed by Blenker's German Brigade, 132
Compensated for equipment, 133
Loss of the *Saratoga*, 134

Requests new military balloons, 135–136
Attempts to use *Union* and *Washington* balloons, 138–146
Dismissed from military service, 145
Postwar career, 299

Land Mines, 179
Lowe witnessed telegrapher's death from, 213

Lee, Robert E., 103
Nearly killed by balloon-directed artillery, 114
Succeeds Johnston, 231
Orders Alexander to take charge of Confederate balloon, 232
At Fredericksburg, 261
At Chancellorsville, 279–285

Leslie, Frank, 102

Lincoln, Abraham, *72*
Election of, 8
Recipient of first telegraph sent from a balloon, *70*, 71
Invites Lowe to White House, 71
Intervenes on Lowe's behalf, 84–87, *84*
Difficulty with McClellan, 209–210

Longstreet, Gen. James,
Relates balloon-directed artillery incident, 114
Responsible for "Silk Dress Balloon" legend, 203
At Fredericksburg, 260

Louis XVI,
Witness to early Montgolfier balloon ascent at Versailles, 23

Lowe, Clovis, *273*
Balloon Corps equipment maintenance, 137, 138–139, 167, 175, 241
Dismissed by Comstock, 272

Lowe, Leontine Gauchon, 272
  Meets and marries T. S. C.
    Lowe, 38–39
  Rescues T. S. C. Lowe, 90
  Life after the Civil War,
    306–309
Lowe, Thaddeus Sobieski Con-
  stantine, *5, 178*
  Journey from Cincinnati to
    South Carolina, 1–17, (Map)
    9
  Theories regarding air currents,
    1–2, 39
  Provisions for Cincinnati to
    South Carolina journey, 4
  Return to Cincinnati following
    journey to South Carolina,
    17–19
  Early life and experiments,
    36–39
  Plan to cross Atlantic Ocean by
    balloon, 39, 50–54
  Construction of the *City of New
    York* (later renamed *Great
    Western*), 50–52, *51*
  Fails at attempt to launch
    transatlantic flight from New
    York, 52–54
  Resumes transatlantic quest in
    Philadelphia, 54, 56–58
  First flight of *The Great Western*
    (formerly *The City of New
    York*), 56–57
  Arrives in Washington, D.C., 62
  Devises plan to used telegraph
    with balloons, 68, 69–71
  Invited to White House by Lin-
    coln, 71
  Ordered to Falls Church for
    aerial observations, 74–75
  Resentment of John Wise, 77,
    83–84
  Rivalry with John La Moun-
    tain, 79, 83–84, 126–129,
    136, 138–146

  Observations in the aftermath
    of First Bull Run defeat, 83
  Lincoln's intervention on
    behalf, 84–87
  Appointment as chief aeronaut,
    87
  Military free-flights of, 88–90
  Rescued by Leontine Lowe, 90
  Negotiates salary as military
    aeronaut, 90–91, 94
  Portable hydrogen generator of,
    93, 108, 111, 115, 118–121,
    119, 120
  Proposal and construction of
    military balloons, 93,
    104–105
  Devises ground handling tech-
    niques, 107, 123
  Construction of additional bal-
    loons, 111, 115, 121–123
  Directs Union artillery fire from
    balloon, 112–114
  Introduces balloon barge,
    147–150
  At Budd's Ferry, 151–153
  Expands use of aerial telegraph,
    165–166
  Considers aerial photography,
    166–167
  Prepares Seaver for duty at
    Fortress Monroe, 173
  Lowe ordered to Fortress Mon-
    roe, 175
  Peninsular Campaign, *178,*
    179–180, *211*
  Responds to reaction over
    Porter's accidental freeflight,
    182–183
  Ascends with McClellan during
    siege of Yorktown, 210
  Discovers Confederate with-
    drawal from Yorktown from
    balloon, 212–213
  Witnesses telegrapher's death
    from land mine, 213

Observations during Battle of
Williamsburg, 215–216
At White House mansion,
217–219
Observations of Richmond,
Va., 220–225
Observations at Gaines's farm,
220–222
Observations at Mechanicsville,
223–226
Emergency inflation of *Intrepid*,
226–227
Observations during Battle of
Fair Oaks, 228–231, *229*
Contracts malaria, 238, 241,
245–246, *245*
Observes "Silk Dress Balloon"
over Richmond, 239
Assessment of Confederate
"Silk Dress Balloon,"
245–246
Unable to participate at Anti-
etam, 253–254
Petitions Burnside to restore
Balloon Corps to active duty,
255–256
Reconnoiters Fredericksburg,
258–260
Ascends with Gen. Butterfield,
260
Answers charges of misuse of
expenditures, 265–266,
271–272
Responds to B. England's
hydrogen generator, 267–271
Responds to Comstock's
changes, 275–277
Chastised for bypassing Com-
stock's authority, 277
Tenders resignation, 277,
285–287, *286*
Observations during Battle of
Chancellorsville, 278–285
Attempts to revive Balloon
Corps, 291–293, 305

Contacted by Dom Pedro II,
296
Attempts to collect expenses
and salary, 305–306
Postwar career and family life,
306–310
Lumley, Arthur, 102–103

Macomb, Col. John N.,
Replaces Whipple as Balloon
Corps supervisor, 123
Intervenes in rivalry between
Lowe and La Mountain,
138–139, 141–142, 144
Relays orders to send balloon to
Fortress Monroe, 171, 173
Magruder, Gen. John Bankhead,
96, 98
Deceives McClellan, 179, 188,
209
Defense of Yorktown, 210
Withdrawal from Yorktown,
212
Malaria, 238, 241, 245–246
Mallory, Garrick, 56–57
Malvern Hill,
Battle of, 242
Manassas,
First Battle of, 65, 80, 104
Second Battle of, 250–251
Maratanza (gunboat),
Captures *CSS Teaser*, 242–244
Marcy, Col. Robert Barnes, 127
Martyn, Thomas
Early proponent of military bal-
loons, 24–25
Marye's Heights,
Siege during Battle of Freder-
icksburg, 260–261
Siege during Battle of Chancel-
lorsville, 279–283, *281*
Mason, Ebenezer Locke, 300
Assistant aeronaut in the Bal-
loon Corps, 175
Early career, 175
Salary, 176

Mayflower (steamship),
  Used to transport *Washington*
  balloon, 156
McClellan, Maj. Gen. George
  Brinton, 117, 137
  Appreciation for new military
  technology, 107
  First balloon ascent of, 108
  Recommends construction of
  additional balloons, 115
  Orders Fitz-John Porter to set-
  tle Lowe and La Mountain
  rivalry, 127–129
  Orders balloon to Port Royal
  expedition, 151
  Plans to launch Peninsular
  Campaign, 167–168, 170,
  177
  Reliance on Allan Pinkerton,
  177, 179–180, 209, 215
  Deceived by Magruder's move-
  ments, 179, 188, 209
  Reaction to Porter's accidental
  freeflight, 182–183
  Clashes with Lincoln, 209–210
  Ascends with Lowe during siege
  of Yorktown, 210
  Delays action after Battles of
  Fair Oaks and Seven Pines,
  231
  Criticized for Peninsular Cam-
  paign failure, 245, *247*
  Reaffirmed by Lincoln after
  Pope's failure, 252
  Relieved after Anitietam,
  253–254, 262
  Letter in support of Lowe, 292
McDowall, Gen. Irvin, 65, 80.
  131
  Ordered by McClellan to
  defend Washington, D.C.,
  170
  Ordered to reinforce McClel-
  lan, 217, 225
McDowall, George, 69

Mechanicsville,
  Battle of, 236
Meigs, Montgomery, Quarter-
  master General,
  Approves Lowe's request for
  additional balloons and gas
  generators, 115
Meteor (balloon), 29
Minnesota (frigate),
  Sunk by *Virginia*, 174
Monitor (ironclad),
  Battle with *Virginia*, 174
Montgolfier Brothers (Joseph and
  Ettienne),
  Inventors of hot-air balloon,
  20–21
  Early balloon flights with ani-
  mal passengers, 23
Montpelier (balloon), 205
Morse, Samuel, 1
Myer, Maj. Albert, 305
  Supervises James Allen's balloon
  demonstration, 64
  Escorts John Wise's balloon to
  Battle of First Bull Run,
  81–82
  Devises "wigwag" signaling sys-
  tem, 232

O'Donnell, John,
  Balloon Corps maintenance
  assistant, 175
  Dismissed by Comstock, 272
O'Rorke, Lt. P. H., 156

Paracelcus, Theophrastus,
  Experiments with hydrogen, 21
Paris, Count de,
  Aide-de-camp in McClellan's
  camp, 180
Parke, Maj. Gen. John Grubb,
  255
Patterson, Maj. Gen. Robert, 64
Paullin, William,
  Early career as an aeronaut, 30

"Aerial duel" with John Wise, 31

Tours South America, 33

Witnesses Lowe's test flight of *The Great Western*, 57

Assistant aeronaut in the Balloon Corps, 116, 137

Accompanies Lowe and Stark-weather to Budd's Ferry, 151

Left in charge of balloon river patrol, 153

Dismissed, 153

Associated with B. England, 266

Pea Ridge, South Carolina,
Lowe's landing after journey from Cincinnati, 7–11

Peale, Charles Wilson,
Involved in attempt to construct first balloon in United States, 26

Peninsular Campaign,
Early planning stage, 167–168, 170, 177

McClellan overestimates Confederate strength, 179, 209, 215

Siege of Yorktown, 210–212, 215

Delays from spring storms, 215

Photography, aerial, 166–167

Pinkerton, Allan,
Employed by McClellan to gather intelligence, 177–178

Inaccurate estimate of Confederate troop strength, 179, 180, 209, 215

Pinkerton, William (Willie),
Accompanies Balloon Corps, 178

Poe, Edgar Allen, 35

Poinsett, Joel, 61

Pope, General John, 160, 162, 248
Failure at Battle of Second Manassas, 252

Porter, Brig. Gen. Fitz-John, 109, *128*, 170, 175

Praises Lowe, 110, 111

Attempts to resolve rivalry between Lowe and La Mountain, 127–129

Accidental freeflight, 181–183, 193

Port Royal, S.C., Battle of, 150–151

"Quaker guns," 114, 189

Raveneth, Francis,
Accusations of disloyalty, 125

Rhees, William Jones, 69

Rhett, Colonel, 195

Richmond, Va.,
Attempt to capture during Peninsular Campaign, 215, 224

Roberts Brothers (Jean and Noel),
Association with J. A. C.
Charles in the construction of gas-filled balloon, 21–22

Robertson, Eugene, 27

Saratoga (balloon), 101, 135
Arrives at Fortress Monroe, 125

La Mountain's freeflight ascents with, 130–134

Lost at Cloud's Mill, 134

Scott, Thomas, 100

Scott, Gen. Winfield, *86*, 99
Reluctance to accept military balloons, 84–87

Seaver, Ebenezer, *172*, 300
Assistant aeronaut in the Balloon Corps, 171

Ordered to Fortress Monroe, 171, 173–174

Designs "Aeronautical Department" uniform, 171

Secession of Southern States, 8

Sedgwick, Maj. Gen. John,
  Diversionary attack on Freder-
    icksburg, 278, 280–285
  Letter in support of Lowe, 292
Selfridge, Lt. Thomas, 310
Seminole Wars, 61
Seven Days' Battle, 237–244, *237*
Sheburne, Col. John C.,
  Suggest use of military balloons
    during Seminole Wars, 61
Sherman, Gen. Thomas W.,
  Expedition to Port Royal, S.C.,
    150
  Presented balloon for Port
    Royal expedition, 153
  Career background, 154, 155
Shiloh, Battle of, 161
Sickles, Gen. Daniel, 150
  Questions Seaver's uniform, 171
"Silk Dress Balloon," 203–208
  Dress silk purchased for by
    Cheves, 206–207
  Balloon named *Gazelle*, 207
  Description and costs, 206–207,
    213–214
  Ordered to Richmond, 208,
    213–214
  Arrives at Richmond, 231
  Observations at Richmond,
    233–236
  Chronic leakage, 235–236, 239
  Used in observations on James
    River, 241–242
  Captured by the crew of
    Maratanza, 243–244
  Cut up for souvenirs, 245–246
Sixty-sixth Pennsylvania Infantry,
  176
Small, Colonel William F.,
  Sketches map from balloon at
    Budd's Ferry, *152*, 153
Smithsonian Institution, 69
Smith, Brig. Gen. William
  "Baldy," 110, 116, 126
  Uses balloon to direct artillery,
    112

South Carolina College,
  Faculty vouches for T. S. C.
    Lowe's character, 16
Sprague, William, 63
Spring, Parker, Western Union
  telegrapher,
  Assigned to Balloon Corps, 166
Starkweather, John B., 139, *172*,
  300
  Assistant aeronaut in the Bal-
    loon Corps, 137
  Accompanies balloon expedi-
    tion on river, 149–150
  Assigned to Port Royal expedi-
    tion, 151, 153–154
  Difficulties at Port Royal,
    154–156
  Resigns from Balloon Corps,
    248
Steiner, John
  Declares intent to cross Atlantic
    by balloon, 36
  Assistant aeronaut in the Bal-
    loon Corps, 137
  Support of Lowe, 142
  Accompanies balloon expedi-
    tion on river, 149–151
  Assigned to Gen. Stone, 157
  Assigned to Cairo, Illinois, 157
  Difficulties under Halleck's
    command, 158, 162–163
  Assistance provided to Admiral
    Foote, 159–160
  Frustration at Battle of Shiloh,
    161–162
  Assists Allen at Harrison's Land-
    ing, 249–250
  Resigns from Balloon Corps,
    248
  Associated with B. England,
    266
  Postwar career, 300–303
  Association with Count von
    Zeppelin, 300–303
Stepping Stones (tugboat), 249

Stone, Gen. Charles Pomeroy,
  167, 170–171
  Used balloon at Edward's Ferry,
  157
Stoneman, Gen. George, 219
  Hazard to cavalry from artillery
  directed at balloon, 212
  Observations from balloon, 220
  Observations at Gaines's Farm,
  222
  Advance on Mechanicsville,
  223
  Difficulties at Chancellorsville,
  279
  Letter in support of Lowe, 292
Sumner, Gen. Edwin, 225, 260

Teal, Lt. Col. William W.,
  Reconnoiters Fredericksburg
  with Lowe, 258–260
Teaser (tugboat),
  Used to transport *Gazelle*,
  241–244
  Captured by the *Maratanza*,
  243–244
Telegraph,
  As used in military balloons, 68,
  69, 70, 71, 73, 166
Texas Brigade, 239
Thirty-first New York Regiment,
  90
Thomas, Gen. Lorenzo, 158
Townsend, George Alfred,
  Relates a balloon ascension
  with Lowe, 168–169
Tyler, Gen. Daniel, 75

Union (balloon), 116, 117, 137
  Construction details, 104–105
  Used to direct Union artillery
  fire, 112–113
  Escapes from ground handlers,
  117–118
  Rebuilt, 122

Kept in reserve at Columbia
  Armory, 138
Union Army Bureau of Topo-
  graphical Engineers, 105, 118
  Accepts Lowe's balloon for mili-
  tary use, 75
  Manages Union Army Aero-
  nautical Corps, 88
Union Army Aeronautical Corps
  (*see also* Balloon Corps)
  Created, 87
  Comprised of civilian aeronauts,
  88
Union naval blockade of South-
  ern Ports, 8
Unionville, South Carolina,
  T. S. C. Lowe taken to, 11,
  12–15
United States (balloon), 121
  Description, 122

Virginia (ironclad, former *Merri-
  mack*),
  Threat to Union ships, 174
  Battle with *Virginia*, 174

Wachusset, (gunboat) , 249
Wadsworth, James Samuel, 175
War of the Triple Alliance,
  Balloon used during, 296–298
Warren, Edward,
  First United States aeronaut, 26
Watson, P. H., assistant Secretary
  of War,
  Requests balloon to be sent to
  south, 277
Washington (balloon), 137
  Description, 121, 122
  Kept in reserve at Columbia
  Armory, 138
  Sent to Port Royal, S.C., 153
  Damaged during river patrol,
  156
  Used by Lowe at Mechan-
  icsville, 223–226

Damaged by deterioration at
  Falmouth, 289
Purchased by Lowe as war sur-
  plus, 306
Washington, George,
  Comments regarding French
    military balloons, 25
  Attends Philadelphia balloon
    demonstration, 27
Welles, Gideon, Secretary of the
  Navy, 149
Whipple, Capt. Amiel, 76, 80,
  91, 94
  Supervises Lowe's early balloon
    experiments, 74, 104
  Contacts John Wise to build
    military balloon, 77
  Negotiates salary with T. S. C.
    Lowe, 90–91, 94
  Frustrations with military bal-
    loon operations, 91–92
  Organizes ground handlers for
    balloons, 105–107
  Promoted to general, 123
Wilkes, Com. Charles, 249
Williams, Gen. Seth, 143–144,
  274
  Relays order for Lowe to report
    to Fortress Monroe, 175
Williamsburg, Va.,
  Battle of, 215–217
Wise, John, 28, 93, 137, 275
  Early career as an aeronaut,
    28–29
  Explosion of the Meteor, 29–30
  Resumes career as aeronaut,
    30–31
  Invents rip-panel, 31
  Theories regarding air currents,
    32, 34
  "Aerial duel" with William
    Paullin, 31
  Plan to cross Atlantic Ocean by
    balloon, 33–35, 39–50
  Petitions U.S. Congress for
    financial aid, 34, 35

Tours with Kinney's Mammoth
  Pavillion, 34
Publishes A System of
  Aeronautics, 35
First flight of the Atlantic, 42–48
Rivalry with La Mountain,
  48–50
Criticizes T. S. C. Lowe's
  transatlantic flight plans, 54,
  57–58
Suggests use of military balloons
  during Mexican War, 61
Proposal to provide military
  balloons, 76–77
At the Battle of First Bull Run,
  80–81
Construction of Wise's military
  balloon, 81
Balloon destroyed en route to
  First Battle of Bull Run, 82
Postwar career, 299–300
Woodruff, Maj. Israel, 106, 107
Wool, Maj. Gen. John Ellis, 124,
  174
  Takes over command at Fortress
    Monroe, 99, 101–102
  Lack of instructions for La
    Mountain, 125–126
Wright, Wilbur and Orville, 310
"Wyman the Wizard,"
  Associate of Ebenezer Locke
    Mason, 175

Yorktown, Va.,
  Siege of, 210–212
  Confederate withdrawal from,
    212–213
Young, Lt. Ezra, 207

Zeppelin, Count Ferdinand von,
  301
  Influenced by John Steiner's
    balloon, 299–303
Zouaves,
  Detailed to transport James
    Allen's balloon, 67–68